MW00570357

Kinesis

For Harry,

with very best regards,

Edith

Kinesis

THE ANCIENT DEPICTION OF GESTURE, MOTION, AND EMOTION

ESSAYS FOR DONALD LATEINER

Christina A. Clark, Edith Foster, and Judith P. Hallett, editors

UNIVERSITY OF MICHIGAN PRESS

ANN ARBOR

Copyright © Christina A. Clark, Edith Foster, and Judith P. Hallett 2015
All rights reserved

This book may not be reproduced, in whole or in part, including illustrations,
in any form (beyond that copying permitted by Sections 107 and 108 of
the U.S. Copyright Law and except by reviewers for the public press),
without written permission from the publisher.

Published in the United States of America by the
University of Michigan Press
Manufactured in the United States of America
♾ Printed on acid-free paper

2018   2017   2016   2015   4   3   2   1

A CIP catalog record for this book is available from the British Library.

Library of Congress Cataloging-in-Publication Data

Kinesis : the ancient depiction of gesture, motion, and emotion : essays for Donald
    Lateiner / Christina A. Clark, Edith Foster, and Judith P. Hallett, editors.
      pages   cm
    Includes bibliographical references and index.
      ISBN 978-0-472-11959-2 (hardcover : alk. paper) — ISBN 978-0-472-12116-8
    (ebook)
      1. Greek literature—History and criticism.   2. Latin literature—History and
    criticism.   3. Motion in literature.   4. Gesture in literature.   I. Lateiner, Donald.
    II. Clark, Christina A.   III. Foster, Edith (Edith Marie)   IV. Hallett, Judith P.,
    1944–
    PA3014.G47K56   2015
    880.9′001—dc23

                                                          2015013337

Acknowledgments

The editors would like to thank Donald Lateiner, first and foremost, for his inspiring scholarship and generous friendship. We would also like to thank the contributors for their excellent essays and unstinting support of this volume. Finally, the anonymous referees commissioned by the University of Michigan Press and the editorial staff of the University of Michigan Press, especially Ellen Bauerle, Alexa Ducsay, Susan Cronin, and Mary Hashman have been most helpful; together they have improved the volume and guided it through to publication.

Contents

περὶ τῆς σχόλης τοῦ Λατείνου

MICHAEL MCOSKER

ῥᾳστώνην κἄμπαυμα πόνων ἤκουσα σ᾽ ἑλέσθαι
    ἀντὶ διδασκαλίης καὶ μεγάλων καμάτων
τοῦ πρήσσειν τά τε τῆς πόλιος καὶ ἔργα μαθητέων,
    ἐσθλὲ Λατεῖν᾽ ἥρως—τεσσεράκις δέκ᾽ ἐτέων.
ἐς Κίνησιν πρῶτ᾽ ἀπὸ Λυσίεω ἡγεμονεύσας
    (καὶ μάλα δὴ πλεῖον!) τρηχέαν ἦλθες ὁδόν,
ἡμέας ὅς γ᾽ ἐδίδαξας ἅπαντας βῆτα καὶ ἄλφα,
    καὶ τὴν γενναίην ὕβριν Ἀριστοφάνους,
δαιμονίους τε λόγους καὶ ἔπη τοῦ θείου Ὁμήρου
    δημοσίους τε νόμους Κεκροπίης πόλιος-
συλλήβδην σύνεσιν τὴν σὴν ἔνεμες φιλόμουσον
    καὶ χρηστὰς πυρσῆς νουθεσίας γραφίδος
τοὔνεκ᾽ ἔφηβος ἐὼν πέμπω δόσιν, ὥστ᾽ ἐπιδοῦναι
    μνημόσυνον μικρὸν, φίλτατε, τῆς σοφίης.

(Courtesy of John Holliger.)

Donald Lateiner

A Sketch

Judith P. Hallett

In attributing the Egyptian queen Cleopatra with "infinite variety" that "age could not wither, nor custom stale," William Shakespeare does not appear to be translating, verbatim, from his ancient Greek source for his ancient Roman tragedy of *Antony and Cleopatra*. Nevertheless, for plot and detail, Avon's Bard could and did draw abundantly from Plutarch's *Life of Mark Antony*, as Englished by Sir Thomas North. To be sure, the headstrong, irresolute military and political colossus Marcus Antonius, whom Shakespeare renders heroic as well as tragic in this play, bears scant resemblance to the distinguished and influential scholar and teacher Donald G. Lateiner, whose contributions to the field of classics we honor in this volume. But I, fortunately, share a key literary advantage with Shakespeare: that of having in hand a comparable source, a "Life of Donald Lateiner" by Donald Lateiner—that is, an unpublished memoir that I summarize, paraphrase, or even quote directly in the narrative to follow. My words draw heavily on Don's own, *pedemtemptim et ordinatim*, if not exactly verbatim.

Hail the Kalends of June

Donald Lateiner was born to Alfred and Mary Klein Lateiner in New Rochelle, New York, just after midnight on the first of June 1944, the date originally planned for the Allied invasion of Europe and remembered by his family thereafter, by Donald's first initial, as "D-day." Don's paternal grandparents had emigrated from Vienna to the United States on the *SS*

Ulysses S. Grant, landing in New York City on the first of June in 1910. Karl Lateiner (1880–1968) was a nonobservant Jew, an atheist. His first career in the United States was making and repairing watches in his own store, at one time in Grand Central Station. Later he became a house-building contractor in the developing suburban areas of New Rochelle and Larchmont in West-chester County, New York, until the Great Depression bankrupted him.

Don's maternal grandparents remain unknown to him. His mother's mother died in Philadelphia during the 1918 influenza epidemic. After plac-ing Mary Elizabeth Klein in the Philadelphia Hebrew Orphans' Home, his mother's father, a housepainter, returned to Poland to marry his late wife's sister (reversing the Jewish custom called the levirate, in which a widow is obligated to wed a brother of her late husband). Years later, as a young teen-ager, Mary Klein ran away to join her sister and two brothers in New York. The Klein siblings refused to speak about their family upbringing. When Lateiner asked them about his grandparents, his caustic, chain-smoking aunt Doris Heyn replied, "Donnie, all you need to know about your family is that you're not a Hapsburg." In the 1930s, Mary's brother Albert left a note saying that he was emigrating to Palestine. He has not been located since.

Lateiner was a poor student at his grade school—Chatsworth Avenue School in Larchmont. Even in junior high school, he was known to put his head in his desk to avoid learning English grammar. He enjoyed painting, despite his lack of talent. His paternal uncle Bob Lateiner, an ophthalmolo-gist, scoffed at Donald's earnest effort to paint the Eiffel Tower on poster scale upon returning from time spent in Paris (discussed shortly); in response to his nephew's clumsily formed capital letters, Uncle Bob asked Don, "PARTS, where is PARTS?" Lateiner loved reading, however, and his mother often took him to the Larchmont Public Library. Once he started French in the eighth grade, he had a philological conversion experience and began to pay attention. When he achieved his first perfect score on an eighth-grade English grammar exam, his teacher wrote two comments, "100" and "Too bad," the latter apparently a sarcastic reference to his change of heart. He long treasured that candid pedagogical document.

At the age of ten, Lateiner sailed to Paris in first class on a steamship, the *SS United States,* with his mother and his sister Bonnie, five years his junior. In Paris, they joined his father, who was employed as a safety consultant and trainer for heavy industries in eleven European nations (from Norway to Tur-key) for the U.S. government's Marshall Plan after World War II. Their parents dispatched Donald and Bonnie to L'Institut Ascher in Bex Les Bains, near Geneva, Switzerland, to study French and Hebrew, briefly and simultaneously, when Donald was starting fifth grade.[1] The two American children proved a poor fit for these educational surroundings and were brought back to an apartment in Courbevoie, just outside Paris. Donald learned little French and no German at the American School of Paris. Aboard the school bus, he slapped a teacher (who had slapped him first) and was expelled for two weeks from the school's transport. He consequently had to take two metros alone from Courbevoie to school, although his father Alfred shadowed his urban underground voyage the first day. During this chaotic period of his life, the U.S. Congress modified the Pledge of Allegiance to include the words "under God" and prove that U.S. citizens differed from godless communists. Lateiner did not believe the alteration appropriate and thus did not pledge with the two offending words, then or later. His silence was not noticed at the time.

Owing to his parents' marital difficulties, his mother returned to New York City, with her children, on the HMS *Queen Elizabeth*. For some months, Don attended a public school in Manhattan, where he lived in a hotel and learned to sew. He attended a total of five different schools in fifth grade. His parents were divorced when he was in sixth grade at Central School in Mamaroneck; in a state of emotional turbulence, he was nearly expelled for insubordination there, but he was granted a reprieve because the incident occurred on the last day of the school year.

At Mamaroneck Junior and Senior High School, Lateiner studied French from seventh grade onward and Russian in eleventh and twelfth grades. Despite his *nomen omen* name, he studied no Latin, even though his homeroom teacher, Mrs. Leone Roselle, was very knowledgeable—a Columbia PhD, he was told. She was willing to teach Lateiner and his salutatorian-to-be friend Susan Adler (later the wife of classicist Victor Bers) ancient Greek during her lunch period, but the school authorities forbade it, allegedly because it violated union rules. Don's favorite subject was history. At sixteen, Lateiner, accompanying his father on an around-the-world business trip to New Zealand, first saw Thermopylae (after traveling through the former Yugoslavia at one hundred miles an hour in an Austin-Healy 3000 Mark II) and the Parthenon (on foot). On that trip, Lateiner confirmed his disinclinations about entering his father's lucrative business in industrial safety training yet did not suspect that teaching was his future.

Lateiner seized the present by engaging in conspicuous and principled

---

1.   This campus in the mountains was a Jewish children's refuge during World War II.

political resistance throughout his high school career. He organized objections to Christmas trees displayed in his public school, though he ultimately abandoned that battle, to the disgust of hard-liners, and also despaired of another effort against collectivization concerning what he calls "the robotic fealty-recital embodied in the Pledge of Allegiance." He sat down during recitations of the New York State Regents' Prayer. He was president of the Forum Club, a group that precociously debated both serious and frivolous issues. He joined in picketing the New Rochelle Woolworth's in support of efforts to integrate lunch counters in the retail company's Southern five-and-ten-cent stores. As the 1962 Mamaroneck Senior High School yearbook, the *Mahiscan*, testifies, he was voted the "most individualistic" in his class. At his graduation, the principal, Dr. Joseph McClain, refused to shake Lateiner's hand as he ritually, if reluctantly, delivered Lateiner's diploma. On that day, June 25, 1962, the U.S. Supreme Court handed down its six-to-one decision in *Engel v. Vitale* declaring unconstitutional the twenty-two-word, allegedly nondenominational Regents' Prayer (Justice Black writing for the majority). Lateiner felt vindicated and pleased by Principal McClain's snub. He thought the night too good to waste on attending the senior prom.

For his higher education, Lateiner selected the University of Chicago, because of its reputation (in his opinion undeserved) for nurturing intellectuals and idealists. His uncle Robert Goldwin sarcastically recommended that Donald might prefer to attend a college in Hawaii or Florida that catered to his fantasy interests in surfing and lounging. Donald's stated goal in life at that time was to become a "beach bum." Both Uncle Bob Lateiner and Uncle Bob Goldwin disapproved of Alfred Lateiner's indifference to Judaism—in thought, appearance, and practice—and, *inter alia,* to Alfred's sharing his subscription to *Playboy* with young "Donnie."

At Chicago, Lateiner was granted sophomore standing by placement exam before his first week of classes and studied ancient history (with S. I. Oost) along with medieval history (with several scholars he found less than stimulating). The eccentric but effective Oost wondered aloud in his ancient history survey course whether Lateiner wished to emulate Hitler, after the sophomore appeared with a typical, closely clipped, Viennese mustache. Lateiner's wearing a black armband during the Cuban missile crisis did not affect the course of human events. Among those who entered Chicago with him were Victor Bers, from neighboring New Rochelle, and Susan Adler, his Mamaroneck classmate, with whom he was dawdling on the November afternoon when the announcement came that President Kennedy had fallen to an assassin's bullet in Dallas.

After one year of Russian, during which his instructor, a native of Moscow, insulted Lateiner for his Polish accent (an accurate observation, since Lateiner's post-Sputnik Russian teacher in high school was a native Pole), Don abandoned the lovely language of that politically and religiously oppressed nation. He then began his lifelong study of ancient Greek, under James Redfield in the University of Chicago's night school. In his third and final year, he read Thucydides, his reason for learning Greek, in a tutorial with Redfield (wrongly receiving a grade of F from Chicago's uninformed classics faculty),[2] Demosthenes with a visiting instructor, and Herodotus with Anne P. Burnett. Burnett gave him a B+ but told him that she owed him a better grade to be delivered in a future class, despite the fact that he was about to graduate in the next week of that quarter, on the first of June, his twenty-first birthday. His success at Chicago including winning second prize in a university poetry competition. Having been graduated in 1965, becoming the first university graduate in his direct family line and completing his degree program a year before the rest of his entering class, Lateiner was granted a deferment from military service as the United States ratcheted up commitments in the Vietnam War. After that, the Congress and Selective Service draft boards seldom granted deferments for graduate studies in the humanities.

Vocational Formation: Philology Meets History

At Cornell University in the summer of 1965, Lateiner at last began to learn Latin with the Wheelock textbook, mostly on his own; the first work of continuous Latin text he tackled was the linguistically complex and psychologically convoluted preface to Livy's history. According to Donald, his tutor Nick Rudall played "this grim joke" because Lateiner was a "peregrine from the somewhat different wavelength of the history department." After studying only six weeks of Latin, Lateiner opined, "Either Wheelock does not teach this language or Livy wrote in another, similar [one]." He then studied Ci-

---

2.   Since Redfield taught for the Committee on Social Thought, the classics faculty was clueless about Lateiner's independent study. After a sleepless night, Lateiner stormed into Redfield's office. The professor laughed, and the grade was changed to an A in short order. The final exam required him to translate Thucydides' "Stasis on Corcyra."

cero with Ancil Payne (a very learned graduate student, who apparently did not finish his PhD degree), Lucretius and Cicero's *Paradoxa* with Philip DeLacy, and Plautus with Pietro Pucci. Ned Spofford (who, Lateiner reports, refused to finish his PhD on Theocritus at Harvard "for perfectionist reasons") offered Donald tutorials on Horace's *Satires* and Aristophanes. Lateiner continued Greek with the aged but congenial Harry Caplan (Demosthenes) and James Hutton (a Renaissance scholar oddly reading Homer). Lateiner was registered with the ancient history program, having gone to Cornell to study with the young Donald Kagan. After Kagan was awarded a year's fellowship at the Center for Hellenic Studies in Washington, DC, Zvi Yavetz replaced him, as a visiting faculty member.[3] With this learned Roman historian, Lateiner wrote his MA thesis in 1967 on the politics of Cato the Younger. On his master's oral exam, he failed to answer a softball question posed by the medievalist James J. John: who was the teacher of the Middle Ages?

Lateiner argued with Gordon Kirkwood about the war in Vietnam. Don supported the war at that time and briefly considered serving in the army to gain relevant military experience, like Thucydides. During the summer of 1966, he hitchhiked all over Western Europe—Britain, then the Netherlands, Belgium, Germany, Italy, and France. He was trying to forget a girlfriend who had wisely chosen to marry someone else in her hurry to be married. The preexisting quarrels between the classics and history departments at Cornell (revealed to graduate students such as Don only by rumor) and his growing interest in ancient languages led Lateiner to explore graduate school options elsewhere, in the land of late sixties California.

Lateiner was awarded a Ford Fellowship in Classics at Stanford, and in the summer of 1967, he drove himself west to study with A. E. Raubitschek, who had fled Nazi-occupied Vienna in 1938. Don's emigration westward enabled him to study topography, epigraphy, and Thucydides with Raubitschek. Lateiner never took a formal course from Lionel I. C. Pearson, but that master of Attic oratory served helpfully on Donald's dissertation committee. In Lateiner's first year, Brooks Otis taught the survey course in Roman republican poetry. When Otis remarked in class that Lucilius' one-foot recita-

---

3.   Yavetz, a teenaged wartime immigrant to Israel who barely escaped from Czernowitz (the Hapsburg Empire's Ostmark, where some of Lateiner's ancestors had also lived), remained a friend. In 2011, when Lateiner traveled to Israel for a conference at the Hebrew University in Jerusalem honoring the late Martin Ostwald, Lateiner visited Yavetz in Tel Aviv, shortly before he died.

tions were a "great feat," nobody but Don laughed. Bumped up beyond his linguistic competence, Lateiner also studied Greek composition with Raubitschek. He was fortunate, in his two years of classes, to study Homer and Homeric antiquities with T. B. L. Webster (who, Donald says, "stifled" his interest in the "poet of poets"), as well as Ovid with Gregson Davis. He heard Herman Fraenkel lecture on Pindar and Greek pronouns and attended one of Moses I. Finley's Sather lectures in nearby Berkeley.

At Stanford, for not entirely foolish reasons, Don gave up the study of Roman history. Nineteen new students received full Ford Fellowships in the fall of 1967, the year that Lateiner entered the program, but many never finished their doctorates, seduced by the siren charms of laid-back California. Among his prized colleagues were William Beck, later placed in charge of the *Lexicon der frühgriechischen Epos*; Susan Stephens, who eventually returned to teach and serve as dean at Stanford; and the brilliant but shy David Cole, who failed to obtain a classics position in the "job crash" of the early seventies. During the riots in the spring of 1969, before he left for the American School of Classical Studies at Athens (ASCSA), Lateiner taught Greek history for one semester at San Francisco State University, where students, angry at the management style of S. I. Hayakawa, tried to shut down the institution. There he received his first envelope addressed, precociously and therefore incorrectly, to "Professor Donald Lateiner." The message disappointingly began, "Dear Pig Lateiner. Stop crossing the picket lines and support the strike, or your tires will be slashed." He did not stop teaching, and his tires were not slashed.

In 1969, Professor Mabel Lang of Bryn Mawr College set the ASCSA qualifying exams. Before sitting for the exams, Lateiner, who hoped to win an ASCSA fellowship to obtain firsthand experience of Greek material conditions and Greek history on site, asked Raubitschek whether those taking the exam on Greek sight translation were allowed to use dictionaries. Responding first with "No" and then with "I don't know," Raubitschek invited Lateiner to use his office telephone to call Lang, who exploded in incredulous fury at the question. While Raubitschek merely chuckled at Lateiner's traumatized reaction, Don was convinced that this interchange had destroyed his chances to win a fellowship, before he had endured eight-hour exams in literature, history, and archaeology. Some months later, just before the final quarterly exam in an ancient art course taught by Raubitschek's wife, Isabelle, Don learned from his fellow Stanford student Sharon Herbert, later of the University of Michigan, that she had been awarded an ASCSA fellow-ship. Because he had been told that it was rare for two students from the same graduate institution to win ACSCA fellowships, Lateiner assumed that his fears had been proven correct. He biked home after his art exam, in a rush and a huff, to find a telegram announcing the brief but good news that he had won the school's Thomas Day Seymour Fellowship.

Benjamin Merritt, who had been Raubitschek's mentor at the Institute for Advanced Study and was retired and serving as visiting professor at the the ASCSA, did not inspire Don to pursue a career in epigraphy. Don shared the awe that his fellow ASCSA students felt for the legendary topographer Eugene Vanderpool. Lateiner toyed with the idea of writing a dissertation on ancient Greek fortifications. But life in Greece, then ruled by the junta of the colonels, held less appeal than a return to Stanford. At the ASCSA, he met fellow philhellene Rachel Kitzinger, who had recently graduated from Swarthmore and later taught Greek and Latin first at Amherst and then long at Vassar. They continued their topographical archaeological studies together, traveling to Crete and Istanbul over winter break, later to Samos (then airport-free), and in springtime, after the end of the school year, from Siracusa to Selinunte in Sicily and Paris. In his absence, Vietnam War protestors had partially trashed the Stanford University Library's card catalog, an act that mitigated henceforth Lateiner's tendencies toward radical actions and reinforced his liberal beliefs, ones inclined to conserve laboriously accumulated knowledge and data.

After returning to Stanford, Lateiner researched and wrote his dissertation on Lysias and Athenian politics, consciously avoiding his first love, Thucydides, "in order," Donald reports, "not to taint the historiographer with [the] intellectual pains of dissertation-writing" that Raubitschek was bound to inflict. For Lateiner, this process included enduring many of Raubitschek's sarcastic comments in the margin of his handwritten drafts on lined yellow paper.[4] Moreover, a fellow classicist who had served as the thesis typist publicly threw the work—at this point completed and many times corrected—at Lateiner, only to be forced to pick up the pages and recollate them. On June 1, 1971, at his PhD oral exam, Lateiner failed to answer a ques-

---

4.   Raubitschek preferred that chapters be presented in this form, claiming that they then did not have the appearance of authority possessed by typewritten drafts. For further details about this painful dissertation process, see annotations in *Autobiography of Antony Erich Raubitschek*, ed. D. Lateiner.

tion posed by the outside examiner, an electronic engineer: who was Archytas of Tarentum? During this academic period, Don played on the classics department's baseball team and hitchhiked to Seattle.

Initiation into the Professoriate

The market in teaching classics turned sour in 1971, depressing Don, now ornamented with a PhD. But Brooks Otis, at that point the chairman of the classics department at Stanford, agreed to write him a letter of recommendation. When they met in the chair's office, the chain-smoking Otis oddly wrote Lateiner's name and the place where he was to send the letter on a matchbook, used the last match, and then tossed the matchbook away. Don figured out a delicate way to salvage an awkward moment as well as the matchbook and thus save his precarious career. That winter, he interviewed with Penn State at the annual meeting of the American Historical Association and with the University of Pennsylvania at the annual meeting of the American Philological Association. Penn, as the latter was then known, was interested. Don's former teacher Philip DeLacy was chair of Penn's Department of Classical Studies. While being interviewed in Philadelphia for a Penn position teaching ancient history, Don recited several of Catullus' lyrics by heart, and so he obtained a coveted Ivy League tenure track position in the Department of Classical Studies and the Ancient History Graduate Group. No other offer came his way that year.

In August 1972, Lateiner moved to Philadelphia, aided by his dearest Stanford friend and roommate, Brian Howard, the seventh Apple employee. Donald occupied an apartment at 4418 Spruce Street, in the same building as DeLacy and another classics colleague, J. Douglas Minyard.[5] At Penn, DeLacy informed the new assistant professor that because he was the new first-year hire, he would teach seven semester courses, although the teaching load for all other classics faculty was six. Interpreting his teaching load as an initiation, a jolly rite of passage, Don set to work conscientiously.

That year, he gladly taught Ovid in Latin, a survey in Roman history (he

---

5.   By chance, this building was located one block away from where Don's future wife, Philadelphia native and Stanford alumna Marianne Gabel, then lived. The two had met the previous spring in Palo Alto, when Marianne had visited her alma mater. Mutual friends had invited them to help cut back an overgrown bougainvillea bush.

was replacing Robert E. A. Palmer), and too many other courses, including one on the Attic orators. He was pleased to have Martin Ostwald and Michael Jameson as Greek history colleagues. His fellow junior colleague Nancy Zumwalt was not, however, renewed. Doug Minyard, himself a Penn PhD, was denied tenure. For those who could read, the writing was on the wall. Lateiner foolishly wrote articles on Catullus, Ovid, Thucydides, and Herodotus for pleasure, rather than dutifully composing a book or revising his dissertation as a monograph—a requirement for tenure, it turned out (although the dice were perhaps already loaded against him). Don had little time for extended research, although he published his first articles on Catullus, Ovid, Thucydides, and Herodotus as well as on archaic and classical Greek history. His senior colleague Lloyd Daly invited Lateiner to work with him on an annotated English translation of several *bioi* by Plutarch. He declined this kind offer—one of several mistakes the young assistant professor made.

Lateiner taught Greek, Latin, and ancient history at all levels, graduate and undergraduate. He directed dissertations, among them those of Donald Engels, Joe Patwell, and Rosaria Munson; Munson's dissertation, conceived and written only after Don had left Penn and gone to Ohio Wesleyan, was generously undersigned by the supportive Martin Ostwald. In 1976, Lateiner married Marianne Gabel, a former winner of the Philadelphia Latin Prize and student at Penn Law School. Their first son, Ulysses, was born in 1978 in Philadelphia.

Lateiner asked his department for an unpaid leave for his fifth year, realizing that he needed to finish his book on Herodotus if he hoped for tenure. The new chair, Robert E. A. Palmer, told him that his teaching was too valuable to spare. This flattery diverted the naive assistant professor, who, in any case, had no other options. In the 1970s, Penn did not provide untenured faculty with sabbaticals, nor did the institution make TIAA-CREF contributions to untenured faculty members.

The University of Pennsylvania Department of Classical Studies denied Lateiner tenure twice, in the regular cycle and again when he appealed the following year. A recently hired German Vergilianist in the department was unfriendly toward Donald.[6] A Bronze Age expert was also hostile. Palmer

---

6. He had lamented to Lateiner, when Donald's dinner guest and while admiring Marianne's dinner service, that all of his family's linen and china had been destroyed by the Allies' bombing of Hamburg. The Nazis of this scholar's youth had cheerfully murdered some of Lateiner's relatives, Jews stranded in their homelands of Austria and Poland, a fact to which the learned critic seemed oblivious. He had, moreover, served on the Eastern front only, as most German soldiers said they did.

seemed variably and unpredictably friendly and hostile. Wesley Smith, Don's sometime tennis partner, did not stand up well to bullying, and Martin Ostwald served only half-time at Penn. Michael Jameson had left for Stanford at an awkward time for Lateiner's tenure prospects. Jameson's replacement in Greek history, A. John Graham from Manchester, was too new to promote Lateiner's candidacy energetically, if he had wished to do so. Don remained friends with Graham and Ostwald until their deaths in 2006 and 2010.

Lateiner had published a number of well-received articles and had written a book manuscript on the historical method of Herodotus. Nevertheless, the manuscript had not yet been accepted by a university press, so Palmer had declared "insufficient grounds for granting tenure." Donald had profitably spent seven years on the East Coast and believed that, with his academic record, it would not be difficult to land a job comparable to a position at Penn.

From the Delaware River to Delaware, Ohio

In late 1978, Lateiner was thrown back on the job market for the 1979–80 academic year. He had seventeen promising interviews at the annual meeting of the American Philological Association, in Vancouver, but received no offers through them. Some colleagues suspected that the problems lurked in his letters of evaluation. In May 1979, Ohio Wesleyan University (OWU) advertised for a classics position. Its previous occupant had appealed a denial of tenure and lost. Lateiner was hired there and gratefully taught Greek, Latin, great books, folklore, and Greek history at OWU for the next thirty-four years. Eventually he became chair of the Humanities-Classics Department (serving for several terms) and John R. Wright Professor of Greek.

In 1982, Lateiner's second son, Abraham, was born. After settling in the town of Delaware, Ohio, Don began to participate in library "Freedom to Read" days (perhaps in subconscious homage to his formative and liberating childhood experiences at the Larchmont library), once acting out several parts in a lascivious scene from Aristophanes' *Lysistrata*. In consecutive years, he organized three oral marathon readings in English of the entire *Odyssey*, Ovid's *Metamorphoses*, and Vergil's *Aeneid*, lasting—from start to finish—a little over twelve hours each.

In 1984, the entire Lateiner family decamped from Ohio for a semester, settling in among the Italian hills of Oltrarno, near Florence. On the Arno River's other bank, near the Piazza Savonarola, Donald taught archaeology and Etruscan and Roman history at Syracuse in Florence and led field trips to Fiesole, Chiusi, Ostia, and Rome. In 1988 and 2000, he organized and led study trips to Greece, Crete, and Turkey, codirected by Carolyn Dewald and Daniel Levine.[7] In 1999, he enjoyed a three-week stint as senior scholar at the Center for Hellenic Studies in Washington, DC, where he lectured on Athenian insults and researched the topic of ominous names in ancient Greek and Roman historiography.

Lateiner was invited to teach Greek history and Herodotus as Benedict Distinguished Visiting Professor at Carleton College in the spring of 2001. The dean there, wanting to match Don's regular salary as OWU full professor, laughed at the OWU figure and upped his salary, making it more or less equivalent to the pay of an assistant professor at Carleton. After Lateiner returned from Carleton to OWU, in the week before the terrorist attacks in the United States on September 11, 2001, a student in his Greek literature class wondered why the Homeric Greeks and Trojans placed so much importance on recovering dead bodies; later in the term, the sadder but wiser class revisited that troubling question. Lateiner was awarded the Ohio Humanities Council's Bjornson Prize for Service to the Humanities in 2003 and Ohio Wesleyan's first Welch Award for Scholarly Achievement in 2013.

For twenty-seven of his years at OWU, Lateiner had no permanent colleague in classics or ancient history, so he taught many language courses as overloads. He chaired both the Humanities-Classics Department and the Ancient, Medieval, and Renaissance Studies interdisciplinary program. In Delaware, Ohio, he convened a medieval Latin reading group for a decade and a Byzantine Greek reading group for a few years. He induced the Humanities-Classics program to lure scholars whose specialties were not the Western great books but others, including Slavic, Arabic, and Oriental literatures. He eventually received stellar, though not tenure-track, teaching assistance in classics—most notably from Stephanie Winder, Herman Pontes, and Brad Cook. The Humanities-Classics Department finally won a permanent second classics position in 2005.

In addition, Don taught comparative courses. One of them, entitled Myth, Legend, and Folklore, examined classical, biblical, African, Native American, and Afro-American texts along with customs, folksay, and material artifacts. As a historian, Lateiner had always disregarded—indeed, neglected—

---

7.   The Herodotus Hotel in Halicarnassus (Bodrum) was disappointingly full when Herodotus specialist Lateiner requested accommodation in 2000.

classical mythology, but the title of this course inspired him to read comparative texts, displacing the classical myths from an undeserved and misleading, isolated pedestal. His functionalist approach proved enlightening and successful for him, his research, and his students.

Don also enjoyed creating and teaching a course on great books that was titled Love and Sexuality in Literature and the Arts. The syllabi for that course included early chapters of Genesis, the Song of Songs, selections from Paul and Augustine, Heloise's correspondence, Castiglione, Boccaccio, *Measure for Measure*, Benjamin Constant, D. H. Lawrence, Robert Johnson, Fats Waller, Milan Kundera, Robert Mapplethorpe, and Isabella Allende, with improvised additions from newspaper and magazine advertising copy and popular American song lyrics. He enriched the Ohio Wesleyan curriculum by introducing such innovative courses as Ancient Novels, Athenian History 600–400 BCE, and Women in Antiquity, all of which sadly vanished from the offerings when he retired in 2013. He developed a course in Mediterranean archaeology that looked at Greek and Roman materials from the Bronze Age to the age of Constantine, as well as a comparative course in epic that included—in addition to classical epics—*Gilgamesh* and *Beowulf*. He also regularly taught two courses: Greek and Roman Literature and Thought in Translation. As noted, he taught Latin and Greek at all levels, every year offering elementary Latin and Greek. The authors he most frequently taught in advanced classes and tutorials were Cicero, Ovid, Homer, Plato, and the Attic orators. His courses featured other literary genres and authors in response to student requests (e.g., Sappho, Aristophanes, biblical Greek, Longus, Martial, Apuleius). He never taught Aeschylus in Greek, and he only taught Vergil and Lucretius in Latin once each. Lateiner decided to retire from active teaching after the spring of 2013, in order to complete several scholarly projects.

Professional Citizenship, Research Achievements

Lateiner has been elected to and served on the Nominating, Publications, and Professional Matters Committees of the American Philological Association (APA). He was the longtime institutional representative to the Managing Committee of the ASCSA, also serving on its Committee on Committees and its Summer School and Publications Committees. Furthermore, he was both treasurer and president of the Friends of Ancient History. After serving as vice president and president of the Columbus, Ohio, chapter of the Archaeological Institute of America (AIA), Don joined the AIA's Education Committee; he has also been elected to committees for the Classical Association of the Middle West and South (CAMWS) and of the Ohio Classical Conference. In 2001, he organized the Ohio Classical Conference's Latin Day at OWU, providing a program, a venue, and assistance from soup to Latin-inscribed pencils. He is a life member of the APA, AIA, and CAMWS.

Don's publications, brilliant and original contributions to multiple areas of scholarly inquiry, embody—no less than do his teaching repertory and range of service endeavors—the "infinite variety" referenced in the first paragraph of this biographical sketch. They include investigations of Herodotus' methods and Homer's gestures, three other volumes of essays that he coedited, annotated editions of the two great Greek historians, over seventy articles, and more than 120 reviews of books (see this volume's bibliography of his works). He has presented papers at over sixty-five institutions in North America and Europe, often illustrated and frequently describing and explaining familiar and unfamiliar nonverbal behaviors in ancient literature and art, such as gestural insults, expressions of disgust, and kissing.

Don's research encompasses six different fields. He was initially drawn to Greek historiography—to Thucydides while still in high school and to Herodotus much later, after realizing how misguided most of the criticism on the "father of history" had been. He has published nine articles on Thucydides, a book (*Historical Method*) and eighteen articles on Herodotus, and other studies in fifth-century political and social history and further fields in historiography (e.g., "Tears in Greek Historiography from Herodotus to Polybius," with an appendix on Plutarch). For the Barnes and Noble Classics series, he published edited and annotated complete editions of the histories written by Herodotus and Thucydides. His first article on Latin poetry concerned obscenity in Catullus, but his interests then shifted to Ovidian elegy (*Amores* 2.9) and the poetics of Ovid's epic *Metamorphoses*, producing ten articles on Latin poetry, among them his iconic essay on mimetic syntax. Having compared Herodotus' deployment of nonverbal behaviors to those of Homer, as an influential comparand, he explored the amazing richness of Homer's traditional and unique gestures (idiogests), postures, and descriptions of exhibited emotions; this research led to ten articles and his book on Homeric nonverbal behaviors, *Sardonic Smile*. Meanwhile, his courses Women in Antiquity and Ancient Novels stimulated research in these areas, singly and in combination, producing eight articles, among them "Mothers in Ovid's *Metamorphoses*," "Blushes in the Ancient Novels," "Insults in the Latin Novels," and "Gendered Places in Two Later Ancient Novels (*Aithiopika, Historia Apollonii*)." He has also coedited three volumes—*Selected Papers of Lionel Pearson, Thucydides and Herodotus,* and *Domina Illustris,* this last in honor of yours truly. As I write, he is in the process of publishing, with extensive annotation, the autobiography of his mentor A. E. Raubitschek. Essays by Lateiner in the history of classical scholarship examine the careers of Vassar College Latin professor Elizabeth Hazleton Haight and his Ohio Wesleyan predecessors.

Don's scholarship has, *inter multas alias res,* pioneered the reexamination and reevaluation of Herodotus as more than a raconteur and dupe—indeed, as a serious political thinker and dependable historian. More recently, Lateiner has opened up an entirely new subfield of scholarly inquiry in classics, with his interdisciplinary, groundbreaking research on nonverbal behaviors, proxemics, and, especially, emotions and their gendered "leakages" (in the form of blushes and tears) as reported in several genres of ancient literature, among them historical narratives, epics, and novels. It merits note and wonder that Don taught for thirty-four years while shouldering a heavy instructional and administrative burden at an undergraduate liberal arts college where he was the only full-time classicist, and that he only spent a few years, during the early part of his career, teaching at an institution with a graduate program in classical studies, where he taught more courses and a wider range of courses than his classics colleagues at the time. He has produced more copious and more significant scholarship, and influenced more—and more appreciative—scholars in our profession from all over the globe than has many a classics colleague ensconced in a department at a "Research I" university offering a PhD in classics.

At Ease and at Leisure

Lateiner indulges in many of his favorite pastimes at his summer home in Deer Isle, Maine, which once belonged to the family of the children's book author Robert McCloskey, best known for *Blueberries for Sal, One Morning in Maine,* and *Make Way for Ducklings.* They include reading in English to his bilingual granddaughter Estella (born in 2010 to Abraham Lateiner and his Peruvian wife, Erika Ramos), kayaking on Eggemoggin Reach, deck repair at the cottage itself, and chainsawing fir trees killed by balsam woolly adelgid in the gout phase. He listens to Beethoven's piano sonatas, Schubert's String Quartet in D minor, Bach's Brandenburg concertos, Louis Armstrong, Son House, and Muddy Waters and their epigones, the Rolling Stones. He loves to read Greek prose and poetry, Sterne, Melville, Conrad, Cavafy, and Woody Allen. He enjoys observing politics in one-party, Republican Delaware County in Ohio and listening to colleagues "discourse up" on the foibles of our profession. I am among the most grateful and fortunate of those colleagues to whom he listens. I cherish not only Don's unflagging support of me as teacher, scholar, and professional activist but also the connections he forged between me and several members of his extraordinary extended family, particularly his great-aunt Lena Rosenblatt Gitter (1905–2000). An early childhood educator who worked with Maria Montessori before fleeing Nazi-occupied Vienna in 1938, "Tante Lena" enriched and helped transform many a young and not-too-young life on both sides of the Atlantic, that of our distinguished classicist and ancient historian colleague Erich Gruen as well as Don's and my own.

Don concludes his autobiographical memoir by observing that he tries to encourage other students of life, literature, and social history to pay more attention to gestures, postures, proxemics, chronemics, and paralinguistics—how they say what they say. He has plans for monographs on Ovid's poetics and nonverbal behaviors in Heliodorus. May he continue to encourage his fellow students, fulfill his scholarly plans, and keep saying what he says in the ways that he says it, as his and my beloved Catullus might have said it, *perennius uno saeclo.*

Introduction

Christina A. Clark and Edith Foster

Don Lateiner is a famously versatile scholar, whose publications extend over the entire field of Greco-Roman classics. But every body of work, no matter how multifaceted it ultimately turns out to be, must begin in one specific place. Don began with an idea that seems obvious to us today but was much less so at the time: namely, that one might read ancient historiography just as carefully as ancient tragedy or epic, looking closely at the historians' language. Thus, for many who study historiography, his presence as a scholarly voice begins with two articles published in 1977. "Heralds and Corpses in Thucydides" and "No Laughing Matter: A Literary Tactic in Herodotus" soon became and have remained often assigned and frequently cited articles. Don's close reading of the texts, combined with synoptic views of characteristic but previously little-noticed themes, made these articles into instant classics.

Looking back at his articles from the 1970s and 1980s, Don's progress toward a monograph that would address the traditional questions of historiography from the point of view of a close reading of Herodotus seems clearer to us than it could have seemed to Don at the time. The first publication of *The Historical Method of Herodotus*, by the University of Toronto Press in 1989, was a watershed moment. Herodotus had had few defenders until that time, but Don's work cleared the way for Herodotus to stand beside Thucydides as an author worthy of close analysis. The creative effect of this book, which raised as many questions as it answered, was enormous, and since then, Don's work on ancient Greek historiography has remained at the successive centers of contemporary research.

Ancient Greek Historiography

Following the arc of Lateiner's career, the first part of this volume contains essays on historiography. Jeffrey Rusten's essay on Thucydides' use of the word *kinesis* (chapter 1) challenges our reading of one of the most famous words in the first chapter of Thucydides. Translations of the word *kinesis* (1.1.2) have been mostly metaphorical; common English translations are "up-heaval" or "disturbance." Do these translations make sense of Thucydides' Greek? Basing his presentation on a thorough examination of Thucydides' use of *kin-* words and a careful explanation of the initial sentences of Thucydides, Rusten argues that they do not and that *kinesis* is more accurately and meaningfully translated "mobilization." Rusten's essay therefore challenges romantic and metaphysically oriented interpretations of the opening paragraphs of Thucydides. It does not, however, deny the symbolic level in Thucydides' writing.

Rosaria Munson's essay (chapter 2) responds closely to Rusten's themes, since it asks whether, in Thucydides, the physical world is a "sender of signs." Munson reflects on Thucydides' records of natural events and disasters, particularly the plague, situating her analysis through a comparison to Herodotus: "The human and the natural world are ontologically mediated by a rational divine principle, whose intentions are difficult but nevertheless possible, at least retrospectively, to access. Thucydides, however, never in his own voice explains events in terms of transcendent mediation, so that the meaning of the concomitance of war and natural phenomena appears to lie beyond the reach of the historian's opinion." Munson argues that the concomitance she mentions is palpable.

Edith Foster (chapter 3), who also focuses on the character of Thucydides' text, discusses a particular Thucydidean narrative strategy, the use of a verb in the present tense where a past tense is expected; grammarians call this substitution of one tense for another an occurrence of the "historical present tense." Book 8 of Thucydides displays a superabundant use of the historical present tense, which often seems to mark an action that will not succeed or the initiation of a series of actions that will not attain their intended end. Foster's essay argues that the historical present is a species of narrator intervention, serving to emphasize events that are "good to think with" rather than simply events that are important for the war.

Hans-Peter Stahl (chapter 4) offers another close reading of the historians and their techniques. Stahl shows how Herodotus and Thucydides showcase the passionate bases on which political actors make life-and-death decisions. His comparison between the decisions of Herodotus' Croesus and Thucydides' Athenians shows that the two historians' explanations of the progress of human decisions are structurally similar. In particular, in both historians, opportunities to learn both from warnings and also from experience are ignored, as overconfidence and the "desire for more" (*pleonexia*) cause optimistic overreaching in characters who are not able to control their passions.

Carolyn Dewald and Rachel Kitzinger (chapter 5) examine Herodotus' depictions of characters who refuse to speak or who enjoin others to silence. They then analyze the crucial silence of those female characters of Sophoclean plays who are speechless at critical moments in the action of a play. Turning back to the historian, they consider Herodotus' narratorial silences and relate his silences as a narrator to that of Sophocles' characters.

Deborah Boedeker (chapter 6) discusses Herodotus' stories of herald murder and their continuation in Thucydides. Herodotus relates that the Spartans and Athenians threw Persian envoys into a pit and a well, respectively. Their acts of herald murder unleashed a set of consequences that lasted until the Peloponnesian War, and Thucydides tells the story of the Athenians' murder of the Spartan descendants of those who had tried but failed to expiate the herald murder reported in Herodotus. Boedeker analyzes the stories and their religious context in both historians, drawing out the connections between them.

Daniel Tompkins (chapter 7) offers a catalog of the Gorgianic figures in the Thucydidean speeches of the Syracusan statesman and general Hermocrates. He argues, against an established scholarly consensus, that the Gorgianic figures were politically strategic elements of the speeches, rather than being merely decorative. Concerning Hermocrates' speech at Gela in book 4 of Thucydides, Tompkins writes, "Far from being ornamental, then, the Gorgianic features are *constitutive*, marking moments of intense thinking, and pivotal to Hermocrates' mission of changing Sicilian cities' *ways of thinking*, their attitudes toward cooperation." Tompkins offers a commonsense argument about why Thucydides chose to include these figures in his accounts of Hermocrates' speeches: first, because Hermocrates really chose to use them; second, because when he did, they worked.

John Marincola (chapter 8) takes up the theme of gender and historiography when he asks why one historian castigates another for being overemotional. He looks at Polybius' charges against Phylarchus and Timaeus, both of whom Polybius calls "ignoble and womanish" in their presentation of excessively moving or sensational scenes from history. Marincola shows how Polybius marginalizes these competitors by asserting that their writings educate readers not to manly restraint but, rather, to womanish weakness. Polybius' criticisms of his competitors imply that only authors such as himself, who wrote to educate men properly, produce useful and appropriate histories. By contrast, his criticisms disqualify the writings of Phylarchus and Timaeus as harmful for weak men and uninteresting for those already educated.

Emotion and Nonverbal Behavior

Several of the essays on historiography in part 1 (e.g., those by Boedeker, Dewald and Kitzinger, Marincola, and Stahl) grapple with gestural language or emotion while also treating historiographical questions. The essays in the second part of this volume focus on these nonverbal topics, which represent the second, but perhaps now more famous, emphasis of Don's work.

A very brief introduction to Don's work on nonverbal behavior must suffice; for a list of Don's dozens of essays, please refer to this volume's bibliography of his works. "Teeth in Homer," which appeared in the *Liverpool Classical Monthly* in 1989, established him as one of the first classicists to draw on sociological and anthropological research to explore the representation of nonverbal behavior in ancient literary texts. The year 1992 saw the publication of his "Affect Displays in the Epic Poetry of Homer, Vergil, and Ovid," a broad overview of how ancient epic poets depicted nonverbal behaviors such as blushes, pallor, and tears. Three years later, in 1995, Lateiner published the influential *Sardonic Smile: Nonverbal Behavior in Homeric Epic* with the University of Michigan Press, and dozens of articles focusing on different categories of nonverbal behavior in various ancient literary genres followed at a steady pace. The scholars represented in this volume find themselves operating in a field strengthened and, in good measure, created by Don's seminal contributions.

The essays in part 2 of this volume therefore focus directly on gesture, motion, and emotion in literature and art and demonstrate the rewards of close and careful attention to nonverbal codes and conventions. Christina Clark (chapter 9) examines Lucan's treatment of Pompey's death in book 8 of the *Bellum Ciuile*, arguing that this treatment serves as a capstone to a process begun in book 1, where the narrator asserts that "rivalry in masculinity [*uirtus*] spurred them [Pompey and Caesar] on." Arguing that the poet definitively subverts Pompey's *uirtus* in book 8 by stripping him of power over his own body in the extremity of death, Clark shows how Lucan uses nonverbal behavior to create our final, vivid, and defining impression of Pompey.

Carolin Hahnemann (chapter 10) focuses on the confrontation between Phaedra and her stepson, Hippolytus, in Seneca's *Phaedra*. This confrontation involves a variety of nonverbal behaviors that form a parallel to the verbal text. For instance, Phaedra prostrates herself before Hippolytus as she declares her love, supplicating him. Tracing the important role that Theseus' sword continues to play up to the tragedy's end, Hahnemann argues that this symbolic object and emphatic displays of nonverbal behavior are central to a plot in which much (especially on Phaedra's side) is left unspoken.

Ellen Finkelpearl (chapter 11) explores the representation of animal emotion in Roman imperial texts. She reviews Aristotelian and Stoic debates concerning the emotional capacities of animals, focusing on examples from Pliny the Elder and Aelian, who share "a quest to enter the animal mind." Finkelpearl shows that by coupling their attributions of animal emotion with representations of other cognitive and social acts, "the authors challenge assumptions about animal abilities and engage subtly with philosophical debates," ultimately defending the ability of animals to feel a wide variety of emotions.

Hanna Roisman (chapter 12) offers an overview of Lucian's *Dialogues of the Courtesans*, arguing that "their attempt to present the lives and conduct of the courtesans from the courtesans' own perspective" is nearly unique in ancient literature. She shows that Lucian addresses a variety of the courtesan's common problems and concerns, often in a comic way but always sympathetically. Roisman argues that Lucian's depictions of courtesans, which are more favorable than those found in other texts and focus on the courtesans' own experience and emotions, correct an increasingly negative picture of this profession during the Second Sophistic.

Judith Hallett (chapter 13) analyzes Ovid's account of Apollo and Daphne in book 1 of the *Metamorphoses*. In the first twenty-two lines of this episode, Ovid lays out his key concepts of love/resistance and art/movement by means of significant word choice, placement, and repetition. Moreover, by representing Cupid's two arrows, Ovid emphasizes the theme of duality and doubling that is present throughout the narrative. Hallett's close analysis of Ovid's portrayal of love as a physically and psychologically mobile force explores these lines through the "Lateinerian lens" that results from full consultation of both verbal and nonverbal evidence.

Eliot Wirshbo (chapter 14) shows how the repetitive verbal behavior of the Homeric poet(s) depicts the unchanging patterns of human behavior with presentations of both sides of significant actions and characters, reflecting principles also explained by Herodotus' Solon. He argues against interpretations that homogenize the contradictions created by this type of presentation, showing that the resulting disjunctions must be appreciated in order to understand the poem's characterizations.

James Morrison (chapter 15) explores shipwreck stories in Homer's *Odyssey* and J. M. Coetzee's novel *Foe*, looking particularly at the way each poet deploys "first- and third-person narratives, distinct audiences, and a different status for each shipwreck story: actual, recollected, fictional—and figurative." Focusing on the way shipwreck survivors assume the role of storyteller in both works, Morrison seeks to highlight "a psychological truth" about shipwreck survivors' need for narrative control.

Bruce Heiden (chapter 16) examines "a network of relationships" between Aristophanes' *Clouds* and Plato's *Symposium*. For Heiden, *Clouds*, like the *Symposium*, "is a meditation on eros, justice, and scientific expertise," showing "a city that sorely needs someone to teach its citizens justice and to correct their eros." As examples of the connections between the two works, Heiden shows the relations between the speeches of Plato's *Symposium* and the themes of the *Clouds* and discusses Aristophanes' theatrical bout of hiccups in the *Symposium*, which is both comic and a comment on the philosophical content of the previous speeches.

The last two essays in this volume, by Daniel Levine and Brad Cook, ring back to the topic of movement initiated in Jeffrey Rusten's opening essay, tracking translation, reinterpretation, or misinterpretation as traditional images or themes change through time. Daniel Levine (chapter 17) considers two questions arising from the depictions of Hephaestus in Birth of Athena scenes on four sixth-century Attic black-figure vases: "(1) why do some Athenian artists depict Hephaestus wearing winged shoes in some of the earliest scenes, and (2) what is the source of the literary tradition that Hermes acted as midwife for Athena's birth?" Furnished with Judith Levine's detailed illustrations, the essay not only displays a careful reading of the gestural language of vases but also opens up the possibility that such a reading can correct both literary and artistic misreading of these scenes.

Brad Cook (chapter 18) demonstrates how significant objects within the Alexander Romance reveal much about the linguistic and cultural challenges facing redactors of this multicultural work. Tracing the transformations of significant objects such as papyrus, pepper, or cheese in three Alexander narratives, Cook illustrates how these objects are adjusted, translated, and enhanced as the narrative travels over time and space.

PART 1

Ancient Greek Historiography

CHAPTER 1

Kinesis in the Preface to Thucydides

Jeffrey Rusten

"For this was the very greatest *kinesis* for the Greeks and for a considerable portion of barbarians—thus for virtually most of humanity."[1] This is the most quoted sentence of Thucydides' preface, but the precise translation of its subject presents translators with a difficult choice. The neutral meaning of the verbal abstract *kinesis* is "moving" or "movement." It seems likely that Thucydides, who often adapts or even coins abstracts ending in -σις to present specialized concepts, has applied it with special significance here. But the two other occurrences of *kinesis* in his work do not suffice to define it conclusively;[2] as a result, translators are reduced to deductions from its immediate context or from possible connections with other parts of the work. Of the two current interpretations, one postulates *kinesis* as a technical term, with human beings as its agents; the second, held by many more scholars (including myself in earlier work), views it as a metaphor that involves humanity as its victims and that recurs as an idea (though not represented by the word itself) in 1.23.1–3. In this essay, I shall argue that Thucydides uses *kinesis* in 1.1.2 to refer to a prewar "mobilization" that surpasses all previous ones, an assertion defended in 1.2–19, and that the premise of 1.23.2–3 is entirely different.

---

1. 1.1.2. This and all other translations are my own. This essay, offered to an insightful reader of Thucydidean pathos (Lateiner 1977), comes out of my work preparing a commentary on book 1 of Thucydides in the Greek and Latin Classics series of Cambridge University Press. For their helpful suggestions, I am indebted to the editors of that series and to Simon Hornblower, Cynthia King, Hayden Pelliccia, and Hunter R. Rawlings III.
2. One refers to the movement of body parts and objects (5.1–4), and the other ("to prevent their enemies from being in movement") has a range of possible specifications (3.75.1). The semantics of the verb κινεῖν will be discussed below.

I

I will begin with the conventional view.

Near the end of his preface (1.1–23), after concluding his argument about the inferiority of all previous Greek power (1.2–21.1) and his statements on the methods and aims of his upcoming account (1.21.2–22), Thucydides unexpectedly evokes the Persian War—which he has largely omitted in his discussion of previous power.[3]

τῶν δὲ πρότερον ἔργων μέγιστον ἐπράχθη τὸ Μηδικόν, καὶ τοῦτο ὅμως δυοῖν ναυμαχίαιν καὶ πεζομαχίαιν ταχεῖαν τὴν κρίσιν ἔσχεν. τούτου δὲ τοῦ πολέμου μῆκός τε μέγα προύβη, παθήματά τε ξυνηνέχθη γενέσθαι ἐν αὐτῶι τῆι Ἑλλάδι οἷα οὐχ ἕτερα ἐν ἴσωι χρόνωι. οὔτε γὰρ πόλεις τοσαίδε ληφθεῖσαι ἠρημώθησαν, αἱ μὲν ὑπὸ βαρβάρων, αἱ δ' ὑπὸ σφῶν αὐτῶν ἀντιπολεμούντων (εἰσὶ δ' αἳ καὶ οἰκήτορας μετέβαλον ἁλισκόμεναι), οὔτε φυγαὶ τοσαίδε ἀνθρώπων καὶ φόνος, ὁ μὲν κατ' αὐτὸν τὸν πόλεμον, ὁ δὲ διὰ τὸ στασιάζειν. τά τε πρότερον ἀκοῆι μὲν λεγόμενα, ἔργωι δὲ σπανιώτερον βεβαιούμενα οὐκ ἄπιστα κατέστη, σεισμῶν τε πέρι, οἳ ἐπὶ πλεῖστον ἅμα μέρος γῆς καὶ ἰσχυρότατοι οἱ αὐτοὶ ἐπέσχον, ἡλίου τε ἐκλείψεις, αἳ πυκνότεραι παρὰ τὰ ἐκ τοῦ πρὶν χρόνου μνημονευόμενα ξυνέβησαν, αὐχμοί τε ἔστι παρ' οἷς μεγάλοι καὶ ἀπ' αὐτῶν καὶ λιμοὶ καὶ ἡ οὐχ ἥκιστα βλάψασα καὶ μέρος τι φθείρασα ἡ λοιμώδης νόσος· ταῦτα γὰρ πάντα μετὰ τοῦδε τοῦ πολέμου ἅμα ξυνεπέθετο.

[The greatest of earlier actions was the Persian, yet this nonetheless had a quick judgment in two naval battles and infantry battles. But this war's length proved great, and during it there came to pass sufferings for Greece like no others in an equal time period. For so many cities were never captured and emptied, some by barbarians, some by Greeks themselves fighting against each other (and some cities were sold into captivity and received new populations); nor were there so many instances of men driven into exile, or slaughtered either in the war itself or because of factional conflict. Reports once spread as rumors, but seldom confirmed as fact, became credible, about earthquakes which not only affected most territories but were also of the greatest intensity, eclipses of the sun which happened more frequently than had been remembered previously,

---

3.   He mentioned it only in 1.18.2–3, as a stage in the growing power of Athens and Sparta.

great droughts in some areas and as a result famines. Most destructive and fatal to a considerable number was the pestilential plague. All these things accompanied this war.] (1.23.1–3)

Noting the Persian War's brevity, Thucydides uses this fact to pivot back[4] to a new aspect of "this war," the Peloponnesian one: that it was very long and contained in it sufferings (*pathemata*) of the sort that had been previously only rumored but were now easily credited and that were qualitatively unequal even to its long time period (i.e., worse than would be expected over twenty-seven years). He subdivides these sufferings into those caused by humans (depopulation of cities, murders, and exiles) and natural ones (earthquakes, eclipses, droughts, famines, and the Athenian plague).

The topics of the war's length and its sufferings and catastrophes are introduced for the first time at this point in the work, and they will recur occasionally in the war narrative.[5] But numerous scholars, prompted by the mention of earthquakes and other natural events here and by two uses of the passive ἐκινήθη later in Thucydides, referring once to an earthquake (2.8.3: ἔτι δὲ Δῆλος <u>ἐκινήθη</u> ὀλίγον πρὸ τούτων, πρότερον οὔπω σεισθεῖσα ἀφ' οὗ Ἕλληνες μέμνηνται) and once to the condition of Greece during wartime (3.82.1: πᾶν ὡς εἰπεῖν τὸ Ἑλληνικὸν <u>ἐκινήθη</u>), have felt that one very significant link with the preceding chapters is likely: they suppose that 1.23.2–3 not only recalls the "very greatest κίνησις" mentioned in 1.1.2 (even though no forms of κιν- occur in the later passage) but retrospectively helps us translate the earlier word as "upheaval." For a recent example, see Meier 2005: 333–34 (translation mine):

> In my view, hidden behind this notion of *kinesis* can only be a reference to the Thucydidean concept of war, a concept that—corresponding to a current model of warfare in premodern societies—understands war not only as a military conflict among humans, but also as a disturbance in nature.[6]

---

4.   It might seem that 1.23.1–3 is a continuation of 1.2–19, in that it initially asserts the greater magnitude of the Peloponnesian War over the Persian War also. But in fact the function of the Persian War here is to be a foil, and the premise of 1.23.2–3 is entirely different from that of 1.2–19; see below.

5.   On the *pathemata*, see esp. Lateiner 1977; Stahl 2003: 29–30; Parry 1981: 94, 114; Munson in this volume. On the war's length, see Rawlings 1981: ch. 1.

6.   "Meines Erachtens kann sich hinter dem Begriff *kinesis* einzig ein Hinweis auf die thukydideische Konzeption des Krieges verbergen, eine Konzeption, die—entsprechend einem geläufigen Muster der Wahrnehmung von Krieg in vormodernen Gesellschaften—diesen

Gomme (1937: 120) finds in *kinesis* a blending of the military preparations observed in Thucydides' first sentence and the *pathemata* of chapter 23:

hence what is relevant is, exactly, the scale of the war—the number of states and peoples engaged in it, victims of it, its duration, and its intensity—the amount of material and moral damage done. It was the greatest *kinesis* that had ever been.

See also Gomme's commentary on 1.23.1 (1945: 151):

Thucydides is concerned with war as a *kinesis*, a destructive agency.

The *pathemata-kinesis* link is accepted by the great majority of scholars,[7] and there seems to be wide agreement that the most evocative translation of *kinesis* is "disturbance" (Lattimore 1998; Hammond 2009) or "upheaval," "Aufruhr" or "Erschütterung." It is imposed on its victims from outside, and they suffer it passively.

II

These discussions of *kinesis* seldom consider its immediate context in the second sentence of the preface. When viewed from this perspective, the word (in a sentence introduced with γάρ) suggests an entirely different set of possibilities (1.1.1–2).

Θουκυδίδης Ἀθηναῖος ξυνέγραψε τὸν πόλεμον τῶν Πελοποννησίων καὶ Ἀθηναίων, ὡς ἐπολέμησαν πρὸς ἀλλήλους, ἀρξάμενος εὐθὺς καθισταμένου καὶ ἐλπίσας μέγαν τε ἔσεσθαι καὶ ἀξιολογώτατον τῶν προγεγενημένων, τεκμαιρόμενος ὅτι ἀκμάζοντές τε ἦσαν ἐς αὐτὸν ἀμφότεροι παρασκευῆι τῆι πάσηι καὶ τὸ ἄλλο Ἑλληνικὸν ὁρῶν ξυνιστάμενον πρὸς ἑκατέρους τὸ μὲν εὐθύς, τὸ δὲ καὶ διανοούμενον. κίνησις γὰρ αὕτη μεγίστη δὴ τοῖς Ἕλλησιν ἐγένετο καὶ μέρει τινὶ τῶν βαρβάρων, ὡς δὲ εἰπεῖν καὶ ἐπὶ πλεῖστον ἀνθρώπων.

---

nicht nur als militärische Auseinandersetzung unter den Menschen versteht, sondern auch als Aufruhr der Natur."

7.   Price 2001: 207–9; Lateiner 1977; Stahl 2003: 29–30; Parry 1981: 94, 114. But Schmid 1998 and Hrezo 2000 discuss *kinesis* solely in generalities.

[Thucydides of Athens composed the war the Peloponnesians and Athenians fought against each other. He started to work as soon as it broke out, since he foresaw it would be important and most noteworthy of all before it. This realization was based on the peak of every aspect of preparedness reached by both entrants and the observation that the remaining Greek peoples were joining one side or the other, either from its outbreak or planning it later. For this was the very largest *kinesis* for Greeks as well as a significant number of non-Greeks, extending over more or less the most population.]

Latacz 1994 (first published in 1980) offers an exhaustive account of the controversy over the meaning of *kinesis* in this sentence among German-speaking scholars from Ullrich to Erbse. Three questions arise:[8]

What is the exact function of γάϱ—that is, what does this sentence add to the previous one?

If *kinesis* refers to what has gone before (as αὕτη and γάϱ would both suggest), exactly how does it do so?[9]

What is the purpose and significance of the reference to barbarian involvement (μέϱει τινὶ τῶν βαϱβάϱων . . . ἐπὶ πλεῖστον ἀνθϱώπων), which is not found in the first sentence?

Apart from unprofitable speculations,[10] most scholars have contented themselves with the following answers (which Latacz finds unsatisfactory):

The word γάϱ is here "explicative," not directly causal, or else the "expectation" about the future in the opening sentence is converted into "confirmed fact" in the second one.[11]

---

8. I have altered Latacz's formulation of these questions by combining two of them into the first here and adding the question of the barbarian reference, which he downplays, although it seems to me (and most commentators) an important issue.

9. Even Connor (1984: 21 with n. 4), who does not link it with *pathemata*, translates it "movement or dislocation" and thinks it "obscure and surprising in this context."

10. These include speculations on whether this sentence was written "early" or "late," as well as the bizarre suggestion of Schwartz (1929: 177) that *kinesis* designates the Trojan War.

11. Price (2001: 207), the only "upheaval" advocate to note its context at all, expresses nicely what needs to be supplied to make γάϱ work in this case: "[Thucydides] says that he started writing with the expectation that the war would be 'the most worthy to be told' of all wars up to that time. *By the end of the war this initial impression, if that is what it was, proved more correct than he could have known,* 'for [the war] was the greatest *kinesis* to befall the Hellenes and a considerable portion of the non-Hellenes, so to speak most of mankind'" (emphasis mine).

The word *kinesis* is a general restatement of the contents of the previous sentence, an equivalent of πόλεμος.

The reference to barbarians refers to the eventual extension of the war to tribes in Thrace and Northwest Greece and to areas like Sicily and the Black Sea.[12]

Latacz himself, in the second part of his article, offers his own interpretation of the meaning of *kinesis* (unaware that it closely resembles a proposal put forward by Hammond in 1952 and rarely mentioned since).[13] He proposes to approach the interpretation of 1.1.2 by comparing other sentences in Thucydides with similar structures, of which there are quite a few, but two are most instructive.[14] The first is a sentence from the description of the battle of Sybota (1.50.1):

> they could not easily tell who was on the winning side and who among the losers; for this had been the very greatest Greek-against-Greek sea battle, in numbers of ships, of all those before it [ναυμαχία γὰρ αὕτη Ἕλλησι πρὸς Ἕλληνας νεῶν πλήθει μεγίστη δὴ τῶν πρὸ αὐτῆς γεγένηται].

The second is a sentence in book 3 where an Ambracian herald collapses in inarticulate grief when he learns of his side's massive losses (3.113.6):

> for this was the very greatest misery, among all that occurred in this war, for a single Greek city in the space of so many days [πάθος γὰρ τοῦτο μιᾷ πόλει Ἑλληνίδι ἐν ἴσαις ἡμέραις μέγιστον δὴ τῶν κατὰ τὸν πόλεμον τόνδε ἐγένετο].

Latacz (1994: 417–21) notes that each case explains (γὰρ) an extraordinary result in the previous sentence (referenced with a form of οὗτος), one that

---

12. For the clarification of this question in the more extensive description of prewar preparations in 2.7–8, see Rusten 2013 and n. 25 below.
13. Correspondingly, Latacz's own argument remains unknown to English-speaking scholars; even among German ones, Meier knows of it but cites it very briefly, without acknowledging that Latacz's interpretation of *kinesis* is very much in opposition to his own. Schmid (1998) adapts Latacz's proposal so broadly as to deprive it of any usefulness.
14. Latacz's list of parallels (derived, as he notes, from Classen-Steup on 1.1.2) includes also 1.50.2, 5.60.3, 6.31.1, 7.87.5, 1.2.6, 2.31.2, and 7.29.5. Hammond (1952: 132) had done the same. Unless I misunderstand, Connor (1984: 21n4) rejects Hammond's suggestion because of his "mistaken notion of how Thucydidean ring compositions work"; but Hammond's argument is based on the same parallel sentences used by Latacz and cited above.

readers might be tempted to disbelieve (could there have been such confusion at Sybota, could the Ambracian herald really have reacted so strongly, and could Thucydides really have predicted that a great war was about to happen?), is explained (γάρ) by asserting the unparalleled conditions surrounding it.

From these parallels, Latacz argues about 1.1.2 that (1) γάρ clearly has its normal explanatory function and (2) κίνησις—admittedly tougher to define than πάθος or ναυμαχία—cannot be identical with the war but must refer to the conditions that led to his prediction: namely, the two-part observation of the combatants' peak of military resources (πάσηι, ἀκμάζοντές, ἀμφότεροι) and Panhellenic participation (τὸ ἄλλο Ἑλληνικόν).[15] He thus translates *kinesis* as *Vorkriegsbewegung*, "prewar movement," such an uncompelling translation that it is perhaps not surprising that it has not caught on.[16]

In support of his interpretation, Latacz noted that attestations of κινεῖν in Thucydides are predominantly military;[17] considering that Thucydides is writing about a war, that fact might not be considered particularly surprising. But there is a much more precise significance of this "movement": out of twenty-six occurrences of κινεῖν in Thucydides, the same specific meaning predominates for at least twenty-two of them, which is "to convert (something) to offensive[18] use in warfare" or (if used absolutely, without an object) "to initiate offensive action in warfare."[19] An appropriate English equivalent is, in most cases, "mobilize."[20]

---

15. It is important to note that each of the participles in the opening sentence proceeds in reverse chronological order, something I was very proud to observe in the manuscript of my commentary on book 1 but now discover that Latacz (1994: 415) had already noted.

16. Similarly difficult to grasp easily is the following argument by Hammond (1952: 132): "When we take this sentence in relation to 1.1.1 and ask what the movement was, the answer is clearly the movement which culminated in the contestants (the Peloponnesians and the Athenians) reaching their acme of power, and in the other Greek powers aligning themselves on one side or the other at the beginning of the war."

17. Latacz 1994: 421, but without details. Hammond (1952: 132) goes off the track by assuming that κινεῖσθαι is primarily a political, rather than a military, term.

18. It is sometimes used of a vigorous defense (e.g., the material converted into the Themistoclean wall), but the distinction between offense and defense is very important in instances such as 1.105.4, 2.24.1, and 3.16.1.

19. The only exceptions are apparent ones, for the earthquake at Delos in 2.8, stasis in 3.82.1 (see below), and the movement of soldiers in retreat (at 2.81.8 of a force pinned down by slingers and at 7.15.4 of the delay of Nicias' escape from Syracuse, both times opposed to ἡσυχάζειν). In assembling my list, I have used not only 1843: s.v. κινεῖν (Bétant's attempt to organize his entry by the place from which things are moved produces no coherent account of the verb's usage) but also Stork 2008.

20. Here is the entry from Dictionary.com: "1) to assemble or marshal (armed forces, military reserves, or civilian persons of military age) into readiness for active service. 2) to organize or adapt (industries, transportation facilities, etc.) for service to the government in time of

I have organized the following list of occurrences by the verb's object, that is, the thing converted (or not converted) to offensive military use:

Military Objects (converted from defensive to offensive action)

Army: 1.105.4, 5.10.5
Navy: 3.16.1, 7.4.4, 8.100.2
ὅπλα: 1.81.1
πόλεμος: 6.34.3

Nonmilitary Objects (converted from peacetime to wartime use)

χρήματα: 1.143.1, 2.24.1, 6.70.4, 8.15.1[21]
ὕδωρ: 4.98.5 (water from the sanctuary at Delium)
πάντα: 1.93.2 (grave monuments and other materials for the Themistoclean wall)

The following occurrences of the verb are absolute (denoting movement from rest into a war attitude, sometimes with internal accusative or *passive):

Mobilize (or "be mobilized" for attacks against external enemies):
  *4.55.4, *5.8.1, 5.25.1, *6.67.2
Mobilize for a coup within one's own city: 4.76.4 (linked with 4.89.2),
  6.36.2, *8.48.1, 8.71.2

In the light of this special meaning, let us revisit and examine more closely the interpretation of a passage that was cited in support of *kinesis* as a metaphor for "upheaval." Here is its complete context in the analysis of the conditions of stasis (3.82.1):

Οὕτως ὠμὴ <ἡ> στάσις προυχώρησε, καὶ ἔδοξε μᾶλλον, διότι ἐν τοῖς πρώτη ἐγένετο, ἐπεὶ ὕστερόν γε καὶ πᾶν ὡς εἰπεῖν τὸ Ἑλληνικὸν ἐκινήθη, διαφορῶν οὐσῶν ἑκασταχοῦ τοῖς τε τῶν δήμων προστάταις τοὺς Ἀθηναίους ἐπάγεσθαι καὶ τοῖς ὀλίγοις τοὺς Λακεδαιμονίους. καὶ ἐν μὲν εἰρήνῃ οὐκ ἂν ἐχόντων πρόφασιν οὐδ' ἑτοίμων παρακαλεῖν αὐτούς, πολεμουμένων δὲ καὶ ξυμμαχίας ἅμα ἑκατέροις τῇ τῶν ἐναντίων κακώσει καὶ σφίσιν αὐτοῖς ἐκ

---

war. 3) to marshal, bring together, prepare (power, force, wealth, etc.) for action, especially of a vigorous nature: to mobilize one's energy."

21. On this usage of κινεῖν (perhaps taken from decrees), see Kallet-Marx 1993: 95 and n. 155, 110, 185; Classen-Steup on 1.93.2.

τοῦ αὐτοῦ προσποιήσει ῥᾳδίως αἱ ἐπαγωγαὶ τοῖς νεωτερίζειν τι βουλομένοις ἐπορίζοντο.

[This was the savagery reached by factional conflict, its impact heightened by being the very first instance; later virtually all of Greece was *mobilized*, and in every individual place there were disputes between the champions of the people and the oligarchs on whether to seek Athenian or Spartan protection. In peacetime, they would have had neither an excuse nor the inclination to call upon them, but in wartime, with alternative systems of alliance in place, agitators had the obvious option of appealing for intervention, and at one stroke reinforcing their own positions and crippling their opponents'.]

From the context of the analysis, we can see that ἐκινήθη refers to the mobilization that affected all Greece; it is contrasted with ἐν μὲν εἰρήνῃ and rephrased with πολεμουμένων δὲ καὶ ξυμμαχίας ἅμα ἑκατέροις. *Kinesis* here connotes not an earthquake-like upheaval or human suffering[22] but, rather, the onset of a state of war over all of Greece at the initiative of the two opponents, and it repeats some of the leading ideas of 1.1.1–2 (ἀμφότεροι . . . τὸ ἄλλο Ἑλληνικὸν ὁρῶν ξυνιστάμενον πρὸς ἑκατέρους . . . κίνησις τοῖς Ἕλλησιν). It is thus the twenty-third instance of the military sense of κινεῖν cataloged above.

Let us revisit the translation of the entire first chapter of the preface with this meaning of *kinesis* and extend that meaning to the following sentences as well (1.1.1–3):

Θουκυδίδης Ἀθηναῖος ξυνέγραψε τὸν πόλεμον τῶν Πελοποννησίων καὶ Ἀθηναίων, ὡς ἐπολέμησαν πρὸς ἀλλήλους, ἀρξάμενος εὐθὺς καθισταμένου καὶ ἐλπίσας μέγαν τε ἔσεσθαι καὶ ἀξιολογώτατον τῶν προγεγενημένων, τεκμαιρόμενος ὅτι ἀκμάζοντές τε ἦσαν ἐς αὐτὸν ἀμφότεροι παρασκευῆι τῆι πάσηι καὶ τὸ ἄλλο Ἑλληνικὸν ὁρῶν ξυνιστάμενον πρὸς ἑκατέρους τὸ μὲν εὐθύς, τὸ δὲ καὶ διανοούμενον. κίνησις γὰρ αὕτη μεγίστη δὴ τοῖς Ἕλλησιν ἐγένετο καὶ μέρει τινὶ τῶν βαρβάρων, ὡς δὲ εἰπεῖν καὶ ἐπὶ πλεῖστον ἀνθρώπων. τὰ γὰρ πρὸ αὐτῶν καὶ τὰ ἔτι παλαίτερα σαφῶς μὲν εὑρεῖν διὰ

---

22. The consequent human suffering will be introduced in the very next sentence, καὶ ἐπέπεσε πολλὰ καὶ χαλεπά, with the same verb used for the plague (2.48.3, 3.87.1). The contrast between peacetime and a state of war is continued in the metaphor of war as the "violent teacher" that brutalizes civic behavior beyond the norm (3.82.2; cf. Poverty's teaching a man against his will at Thgn. 1.387–92).

χρόνου πλῆθος ἀδύνατα ἦν, ἐκ δὲ τεκμηρίων ὧν ἐπὶ μακρότατον σκοποῦντί μοι πιστεῦσαι ξυμβαίνει οὐ μεγάλα νομίζω γενέσθαι οὔτε κατὰ τοὺς πολέμους οὔτε ἐς τὰ ἄλλα.

[Thucydides of Athens composed the war the Peloponnesians and Athenians fought against each other. He started to work as soon as it broke out, since he foresaw it would be important and most noteworthy of all before it. This realization was based on the peak of every aspect of preparedness reached by both entrants and the observation that the remaining Greek peoples were joining one side or the other, either from its outbreak or planning it later. For this was in fact the largest *mobilization* for Greeks as well as a component of non-Greeks, extending over more or less the entire population.[23] For preceding ones, including those of the more distant past, although impossible to determine adequately after so much time, were nonetheless important neither in wars nor for other ends. This belief is based on my study as far back as possible, and the deductions I concluded were convincing.]

Kinesis is neither the war itself nor the upheaval inflicted by it on humanity but the mobilization that Thucydides observed at war's outbreak (ἀκμάζοντές ... παρασκευῆι τῆι πάσηι καὶ τὸ ἄλλο Ἑλληνικὸν . . . ξυνιστάμενον πρὸς ἑκατέρους). He asserts that this mobilization of manpower, money, and materials at the war's outset surpasses all previous Greek mobilizations,[24] and he undertakes the defense of this assertion in chapters 2–19.

III

That is my argument in sum. There are, however, two important issues that I may seem to have slighted or undervalued in reaching the above conclusion but whose relevance to the meaning of *kinesis* is great.

---

23. The datives are not agents in this sentence (the implied agents are the Athenians and Spartans) but, rather, datives of reference. The superlative ἐπὶ πλεῖστον references τῶν προγεγενημένων above, "the most people of any previous conflict."

24. τὰ πρὸ αὐτῶν means "mobilizations before this mobilization," with a change of gender and number very characteristic of Thucydides, noted already by Hammond (1952: 132). Cf. 18.2: Ἀθηναίους καὶ Λακεδαιμονίους . . . ταῦτα; 21.2: τὸν παρόντα (πόλεμον) . . . τὰ ἀρχαῖα; 23.2: (ἐκλείψεις) παρὰ τὰ ἐκ τοῦ πρὶν χρόνου μνημονευόμενα; 2.43.1: τὴν δύναμιν . . . αὐτά.

The first is the sole remaining instance of κινεῖν, meaning "disturb," used of an earthquake at Delos in 2.8.3, where the application of ἐκινήθη to an earthquake might be thought to cast doubt on my argument. But the reverse is the case: the customary clear difference between κινεῖν and σείειν raises revealing questions about the interpretation of 2.8.3. Because space here is limited, I refer the reader to my lengthy treatment of the "Delian earthquake" in the *Journal of Hellenic Studies* (Rusten 2013). Building there on work by Philip Stadter and Angelos Chaniotis on earthquakes of largely symbolic value, I argue that the phrase Δῆλος ἐκινήθη comes into existence from a chain of intertexts including Pindar fr. 33c–d, a Delphic oracle quoted by Herodotus 6.98.4, and the (interreferential but mutually incompatible) statements on the earthquake's date by Herodotus and Thucydides. The oracle's κινήσω is unlikely to have been applied to an earthquake except by hermeneutic license; in fact, archaeological and geological evidence has established that Delos, in contrast to Greece in general and Santorini in particular, was free of earthquakes in antiquity (and subsequently).

Though Thucydides, like Herodotus, glosses ἐκινήθη as a prewar earthquake, he has placed it in the context of a last-minute review of preparations (2.7–8) on the very eve of war. There, not only does the prewar κίνησις of Delos repeat the prewar κίνησις of 1.1.2, but other mobilization language from that section recurs. This vivid depiction of furious activity on the very eve of war evokes what Thucydides observed in 1.1; and so, relying on its technical meaning for him as well as the well-known omen of the "movement" of Delos, he adopts, for different reasons, the oracle's term *kinesis*.[25]

The second unresolved issue is this: if the resonance of *kinesis* within Thucydides' work is seen as more likely to be backward to the prewar mobilization (in 1.1.1) and forward to the positive—if naive—prewar excitement of 2.7–8, where does this leave the powerfully negative catalog of *pathemata* of 23.2–3?[26]

Part of the answer lies in the recognition that the *pathemata* list belongs to a very different part of the preface. Chapters 1–19 (with 20–21.1 as a pendant)

---

25. In this passage of book 2, we also find the clarification of the third problem of the sentence in 1.1.2 noted above, concerning the role in the *kinesis* of "a large part of the barbarians, . . . most of mankind" (μέρει τινὶ τῶν βαρβάρων, ὡς δὲ εἰπεῖν καὶ ἐπὶ πλεῖστον ἀνθρώπων)—namely, the embassies sent far and wide, including to the Persians and other barbarians, to acquire aid and allies in 2.7.1.

26. Decades ago, it would have been tempting to explain such contrasts in terms of "early" and "late" passages.

constitute an argument about the superiority of resources available in the Peloponnesian war compared to all the Greek past. The following four sections of 21.2–23.6—on methods of the speeches and narrative, aims of the work, sufferings during the war, and organization of the prewar narrative—are united by the repetition of οὗτος ὁ πόλεμος and τὰ ἔργα and by the future tenses in 21.1 (δηλώσει) and 22.4 (φανεῖται, βουλήσονται, ἕξει) that mark these chapters as characterizing the upcoming narrative.

As such, chapter 23 does not confirm or reflect or link to any of the overt themes of 1.2–19—κίνησις, ἀκμή, παρασκευή (money, ships, walls); rather, it subverts them, partly by stressing supernatural events,[27] but especially by revealing that the upcoming war will contain unmatched examples of the failures of the denigrated predecessor-enterprises in 1.1–19[28]—lack of food (1.5.1, 1.11.1–2), a war that goes on too long (1.11.1, 1.12.2), stasis (1.2.4, 1.12.2), murders (1.2.4), exiles (1.12.2), and cities emptied of their populations (1.10.2).

Dionysius of Halicarnassus has two contradictory things to say about chapter 23: he criticizes Thucydides for introducing so much misery at the beginning of his account and depressing his readers (*Pomp.* 3), yet he also admires the passage greatly (*Dem.* 40). I would maintain that it is important not to assimilate *pathemata* in chapter 23 to *kinesis* at 1.1.2, not only because it misreads the context of the earlier passage, but also because it masks a more interesting and more characteristically Thucydidean connection between the two, the juxtaposition of optimistically confident rational sections with highly pessimistic ones: the funeral oration followed by the plague, Pericles' last speech followed by the analysis of the reasons for Athenian failure, the Melian dialogue and Sicilian debate followed by the disaster at Syracuse. To the potential of prewar *kinesis* of 1.1, the *pathemata* of 1.23.2–3 provide a devastating and, within the preface at least, unanswered reply.[29]

Works Cited

Bétant, E. A. 1843. *Lexicon Thucydideum*. Geneva: É. Carey.

Classen, J., and Steup, J. 1892–1922. *Thukydides*. Berlin: Weidmann.

---

27. Because Thucydides removes any possible divine agency for these, they appear all the more irrational. Cf. Meier 2005; Strasburger 1982.
28. On the often-overlooked sufferings that accompany the "optimistic" survey of Greek progress in 1.1–19, see Foster 2010: ch. 1; den Boer 1977.
29. Two well-known essays arguing for "two voices" in Vergil and Thucydides are Parry 1963 and Perry 1937.

Connor, W. R. 1984. *Thucydides*. Princeton: Princeton University Press.

den Boer, W. 1977. *Progress in the Greece of Thucydides*. Mededeelingen, Koninklijke Nederlandse Akademie van Wetenschappen, Afd. Letterkunde 40. Amsterdam: North-Holland.

Foster, E. 2010. *Thucydides, Pericles, and Periclean Imperialism*. New York: Cambridge University Press.

Gomme, A. W. 1937. "The Greatest War in Greek History." In *Essays in Greek History and Literature*, 116–25. Oxford: Blackwell.

Gomme, A. W. 1945. *A Historical Commentary on Thucydides*. Vol. 1. Oxford: Clarendon. First published 1937.

Hammond, M., and Rhodes, P. J. 2009. *The Peloponnesian War*. Oxford World's Classics. Oxford: Oxford University Press.

Hammond, N. G. L. 1952. "The Arrangement of Thought in the Proem and in Other Parts of Thucydides I." *CQ* 2: 127–41.

Hrezo, M. 2000. "Thucydides, Plato, and the Kinesis of Cities and Souls." In L. Gustafson, ed., *Thucydides' Theory of International Relations: A Lasting Possession*, 42–63. Baton Rouge: Louisiana State University Press.

Kallet-Marx, L. 1993. *Money, Expense, and Naval Power in Thucydides 1–5.24*. Berkeley: University of California Press.

Latacz, J. 1994. "Die rätselhafte grosse Bewegung: Zum Eingang des Thukydideischen Geschichtswerks." In F. Graf et al., eds., *Erschliessung der Antike: Kleine Schriften zur Literatur der Griechen und Römer*, 399–426. Stuttgart: Teubner. Originally published in *Würzburger Jahrbücher für die Altertumswissenschaft* 6 (1980): 77–99.

Lateiner, D. 1977. "Pathos in Thucydides." *Antichthon* 11: 42–51.

Lattimore, S. 1998. *Thucydides, The Peloponnesian War*. Indianapolis: Hackett.

Meier, M. 2005. "'Die grösste Erschütterung für die Griechen': Krieg und Naturkatastrophen im Geschichtswerk des Thukydides." *Klio* 87: 329–45.

Parry, A. 1963. "The Two Voices of Virgil's 'Aeneid.'" *Arion* 2: 66–80.

Parry, A. 1981. *Logos and Ergon in Thucydides*. Salem, NH: Ayer.

Perry, B. E. 1937. "The Early Greek Capacity for Viewing Things Separately." *TAPA* 68: 403–27.

Price, J. J. 1997. "A Puzzle in Thucydides 1.18." *Mnemosyne* 50: 665–76.

Price, J. J. 2001. *Thucydides and Internal War*. Cambridge: Cambridge University Press.

Rawlings, H. R. 1981. *The Structure of Thucydides' History*. Princeton: Princeton University Press.

Rusten, J. S. 2013. "Δῆλος ἐκινήθη: An 'Imaginary Earthquake' on Delos in Herodotus and Thucydides." *JHS* 133: 135–45.

Schmid, A. 1998. "Kinesis, Physis, Politik: 'Anschauungsform' bei Thukydides." *Würzburger Jahrbücher für die Altertumswissenschaft* 22: 47–72.

Schwartz, E. 1929. *Das Geschichtswerk des Thukydides*. Bonn: F. Cohen.

Stahl, H-P. 2003. *Thucydides: Man's Place in History*. Swansea: Classical Press of Wales.

Stork, P. 2008. *Index of Verb Forms in Thucydides*. Leiden: Brill.

Strasburger, H. 1982. "Die Wesensbestimmung der Geschichte durch die antike Geschichtsschreibung." In W. Schmitthenner and R. Zoepffel, eds., *Studien zur alten Geschichte*, 963–1016. 3rd ed., with addenda. Georg Olms: Hildesheim. Originally published in *Sitzungsberichte der wissenschaftlichen Gesellschaft an der Johann-Wolfgang-Goethe-Universität*, vol. 5, no. 3 (Frankfurt am Main, 1966 Franz Steiner Verlag).

CHAPTER 2

Natural Upheavals in Thucydides (and Herodotus)

Rosaria Vignolo Munson

To my favorite historian and a master of nonverbal communication, I dedicate this inquiry: is the physical world a sender of signs? I am sure that Donald Lateiner has his own answers, just as Herodotus and Thucydides had theirs. These authors were free from our environmental guilt and less bombarded than we are by the spectacle of humanitarian tragedies in every corner of the earth. Both of them, however, mention natural cataclysms in connection with human actions and sociopolitical turmoil, most especially war. It is the thesis of this essay that, despite major differences, shared cultural assumptions emerge from the relations Herodotus and Thucydides establish between the natural and the human spheres.

1. *World of Men and World of Nature*

In his introductory sentence, Thucydides calls the Peloponnesian War and its preliminary a κίνησις . . . μεγίστη for the Greek and partly for the non-Greek world (1.1.2). For most scholars (e.g., Hornblower 1991: 6), this is a reference to the "convulsion" caused by the war, and although Jeff Rusten makes a powerful argument (in this volume) that κίνησις here means "mobilization,"[1]

---

1. Elsewhere in Thucydides, *kine-* words refer, in fact, to unproblematic material transports. In one case, *kineô*, while retaining its literal sense, is used somewhat abnormally (or, as Rusten shows, poetically) to denote a geological movement (2.8.3; see below, sec. 3).

it would be a mistake to strip the term of all metaphorical undertones. In Aristotle's (in itself metaphorical) definition, *metaphora* consists in "the carrying over [*epiphora*] of the name [*onoma*] of something to something else" (*Poetics* 21.1457b6–7). In Thucydides, however, the metaphorical conflation between the political and the physical realms carries over well beyond the level of the single "name" κίνησις at 1.1.2. It reappears in a different form in the second introduction of book 1, where Thucydides adds to the survey of various sufferings brought about by the war a parallel list of natural upheavals that occurred in the same period (1.23):

> This war went on for a great length of time, and the sufferings [παθήματα] that happened to Greece during it were not comparable to any in an equal amount of time. For never had so many cities ever been taken and evacuated, some by barbarians, others by the parties themselves who were at war with one another (in some cases cities that were captured even changed their inhabitants), never had there been so many banishments and bloodshed, partly during the war itself and partly as a result of civil struggle [ὁ μὲν κατ' αὐτὸν τὸν πόλεμον, ὁ δὲ διὰ τὸ στασιάζειν].
>
> Phenomena that were previously reported, but more rarely confirmed as facts, became believable, concerning <u>earthquakes</u> of the greatest magnitude, which involved most of the world, and <u>eclipses of the sun</u>, which occurred more frequently than those remembered from earlier times, as well as <u>droughts</u>, sometimes severe and, as a result of these also <u>famines</u>; and, not least damaging and destructive far and wide, the <u>pestilential disease</u>. All these things happened at the same time as the war [<u>σεισμῶν</u> τε πέρι, οἳ ἐπὶ πλεῖστον ἅμα μέρος γῆς καὶ ἰσχυρότατοι οἱ αὐτοὶ ἐπέσχον, <u>ἡλίου τε ἐκλείψεις</u>, αἳ πυκνότεραι παρὰ τὰ ἐκ τοῦ πρὶν χρόνου μνημονευόμενα ξυνέβησαν, <u>αὐχμοί</u> τε ἔστι παρ' οἷς μεγάλοι καὶ ἀπ' αὐτῶν καὶ <u>λιμοὶ</u> καὶ ἡ οὐχ ἥκιστα βλάψασα καὶ μέρος τι φθείρασα ἡ λοιμώδης νόσος· ταῦτα γὰρ πάντα μετὰ τοῦδε τοῦ πολέμου ἅμα ξυνεπέθετο]. (1.23.1–3)[2]

What we may call the "subsidiary term" of the κίνησις metaphor at 1.1.2 (the natural realm) is here deployed as a literal reality side by side with the primary term (human society).[3] The man-made παθήματα fall outside the

---

2.   Unless otherwise specified, the translations in this essay are mine.
3.   I borrow the terms from Black 1962: 39–40.

routine effects of ancient warfare, just as the concurrent natural events in the next sentence are presented as abnormal. The earthquakes are of unprecedented intensity and extend to "a great part [μέρος] of the earth" (1.23.3), just as, according to the opening chapter, the war involved "Greek states as well as a portion [μέρει] of the barbarians and, so to speak, most of the world" (1.1.2). Here the earthquakes are the objective correlative of the figurative κίνησις of the war (1.2.1), while eclipses, droughts, and famines, with their connotation of disappearance or lack, correspond to the exiles and depopulation of cities. The summary of natural phenomena enhances the central theme of tremendous suffering. It is not clear, however, what kind of relation, other than contemporaneousness (πολέμου ἅμα ξυνεπέθετο), it means to establish.[4]

2. Earthquakes and Eclipses in Thucydides

Aside from the plague in Athens, to which Thucydides will devote some of his most famous pages, how frequently and in what contexts does his narrative include natural events? One item that receives great emphasis in the list, namely famines produced by droughts, occurs nowhere else—a point to which we will return later.[5] By contrast, we find earthquakes in all but one book of the *History*. The most important is arguably the great earthquake that struck Laconia (c. 464 BCE), first mentioned in its proper chronological place as a well-known disaster ("*the* earthquake," 1.101.2) and referred to retrospectively four additional times by the narrator or speakers. This earthquake had severe material and political consequences as well as troubling the Spartans on religious grounds, but it occurred thirty years or so before the outbreak of the Peloponnesian War.[6] Within the period Thucydides has bracketed at 1.23.3, he briefly records six more.[7] The first is an earthquake at Delos, mentioned not for its material consequences but because people considered it to have been a sign of the imminence of the great war.[8] Subsequently, in the

---

4. Cf. Gomme 1945: 51; Oost 1975; Hornblower 1991: 62–63.
5. The term αὐχμός only appears at 1.23.3. On the use of λιμός at 2.54.3, see below, sec. 4. Elsewhere in Thucydides, λιμός refers not to a natural event but to a circumstantial shortage of food.
6. For the Spartans' religious interpretation, see 1.128.1. That earthquake is also mentioned at 2.27.2, 4.56, and 3.54.5. On its historical significance, see Cartledge 2002: 186–91.
7. Thuc. 2.8.2, 3.87 and 89 (several episodes of the same seismic phenomenon), 4.52.1, 5.45.4, 6.95.1, 8.6.5.
8. 2.28.2. See below, sec. 3.

fifth and sixth years of the conflict, an objectively catastrophic series of shocks affected large areas of central Greece over a long period of time, from the winter of 427/26 (3.87.4) to the summer of 426 (3.89). Thucydides first reports their inception in a chapter where he notes the return of the plague to Athens that same year and provides a summary count of its disastrous casualties (3.87.1–3). In the following summer, with the disease still raging in the city, the earthquakes prevented the annual Peloponnesian invasion of Attica, and "at about the same time," inundations (ἐπίκλυσεις) struck Orobiae in Euboea, leaving part of the city under water and killing some of the inhabitants. The tsunami damaged an Athenian fort and wrecked one of two ships at Atalanta, an island off the coast of Opuntian Locris; at Peparethus, where there was no flooding, fortifications and buildings were destroyed (3.89.1–5). Thucydides concludes this account by expressing the opinion that the earthquake caused the tsunamis and that one phenomenon would not have happened without the other. The formulation is emphatic (αἴτιον δ' ἔγωγε νομίζω . . . μοι δοκεῖ), as if designed to counter the idea of a mysterious coincidence.

While the earthquakes and inundations of 427/26 are causally related, the recrudescence of the plague in Athens in the same period is an independent event, and the coincidence seems to matter.[9] Similarly, the summer of 424 is marked by both an earthquake and an eclipse of the sun. Thucydides records both events in a single sentence; he provides no particular setting, no description, and no account of damages, and he establishes no connection to the subsequent account of military operations (4.52.1).[10] By contrast, the remaining earthquakes of the *History* are integrated into the narrative and affect the action, although not always in dramatic ways. In the summer of 420, seismic episodes interrupt two different assemblies, thereby preventing, first, the Athenians (5.45.4) and, subsequently, the Corinthians (5.50.5) from being persuaded to break up relations with Sparta and make an alliance with Argos. In the summer of 414, an earthquake forces the Spartan expedition against Argos to turn back (6.95.1); another one in the following winter causes the Spartans to scale down their support of revolting Chios (8.6.5). This second earth-

---

9. Hornblower 1991: 495. For the spring of 426, Thucydides records also an eruption of Mount Etna (only the third since the Greeks settled in Sicily) at the time of a surge in the Athenian anti-Syracusan operations (3.116.1–2).

10. This may be simply an extension of the indication of time introducing the eighth year of the war ("that was the summer when . . ."). See Dewald 2005: 42, 50–53, for the narrative discontinuity created by this type of introduction.

quake is evidently the same that Thucydides, in a later passage, calls "the greatest in living memory" (μέγιστός γε δὴ ὧν μεμνήμεθα γενόμενος), noting that it left Meropid Cos ruined and vulnerable to Spartan attacks (8.41.2).

Natural phenomena that produce human suffering, weaken a state, or destroy infrastructures are evidently pertinent to Thucydides' narrative of the war. When they impede military or political actions, the text does not always make clear whether the disruption was due to material danger or to the fact that historical agents interpreted them as signs.[11] Solar eclipses must have had considerable psychological impact, which made them worth recording.[12] But Thucydides' statement that they "occurred more frequently than those remembered from earlier times" (1.23.3) is an exaggeration, even if one counts all of the solar eclipses that scientists today attribute to that period.[13] Thucydides, at any rate, only mentions two: the eclipse of 424, as we have already seen (4.52.1), and another in the summer of 431 (2.28.1), when "the sun took the shape of a crescent and the sky was dark enough that some stars became visible." By specifying that both happened at the new moon, "which is apparently the only time when this is even possible" (2.28.1), Thucydides is noticing an element of regularity in planetary conjunction.[14] At the same time, standing as they do on their own, divorced from the narrative of the war, the two reports have no apparent raison d'être other than timing and coincidence. While the solar eclipse in 424 coincides with an earthquake, the one that occurred in the summer of 431—when the Peloponnesians will invade Attica for the first time and the Athenians will be forced to evacuate their country homes and farms—counts as one of the natural phenomena that preceded—and, according to some people, announced—the beginning of the war (2.8.3).

The most consequential eclipse in Thucydides' narrative is, of course, the lunar eclipse of 413 BCE, which was interpreted as a divine sign, inducing the Athenians to delay their withdrawal from Syracuse (7.50). The omission of

---

11. The unclear cases are at 3.89.1, 5.45.4, and 5.50.5.
12. As Lloyd remarks (1989: 331), eclipses frightened many people even after the correct explanation for their occurrence was available. According to Plut. *Per.* 35, the eclipse of 431 (reported at Thuc. 2.28.1) occurred when the Athenian naval expedition to the Peloponnese was about to sail; Pericles allayed the panic of the crews by persuading them that it was a natural phenomenon.
13. See the chart provided in Stephenson and Fatoohi 2001, with exact dates.
14. The scientific information may have come from Anaxagoras (see DK 59 A 42; Guthrie 1965: 304–8), who, according to Plut. *Per.* 23, also studied lunar eclipses.

lunar eclipses from the list of phenomena at 1.23.3, unless it is due to the chronology of composition, might confirm how much Thucydides wanted to distance himself from that spectacular case of irrational thinking. On that occasion, what we read of the disastrous results of Nicias' trust in "divination and such" (to use the dismissive Thucydidean phrase) reinforces much other evidence presented in the *History* that to derive divine guidance from the physical world is impossible.[15] My goal here, however, is not to evaluate the role of religion in Thucydides or his religious views[16] but, rather, to explore in what terms a text that declines to consider transcendent causation and that regularly devalues human attempts to traffic with it also shows an interest in the correlation between the social and the natural spheres. To that end and for the sake of comparison, it will be useful to give a synthetic account of Herodotus' inquiry into the natural world as a bearer of divine signs.

3. Herodotus and Thucydides on the (One and Only) Earthquake of Delos

Even though Thucydides sometimes mentions natural events seemingly for their own sake, he does so only as part of his narrative of the war. Not so Herodotus, who also discusses synchronically the "nature" (*phusis*) of lands, rivers, seas, climate, animals, and plants.[17] In his cautiously expressed view, this entire natural apparatus "somehow" (κως) shows evidence of having been put in place by a transcendent intelligence—"the providence of the divine" (τοῦ θείου ἡ προνοίη, 3.108.2)—so as to function teleologically according to material and empirically observable laws. When Herodotus reports how Thales of Miletus had predicted the eclipse of the sun that interrupted a battle between Lydians and Medes (1.74), he places the phenomenon in the realm of physical science, somewhat as when Thucydides notes the normalcy

15. Thuc. 7.50.4: θειασμῷ τε καὶ τῷ τοιούτῳ; cf. 2.47.4: ἱεροῖς . . . ἢ . . . μαντείοις καὶ τοῖς τοιούτοις. On Nicias and the lunar eclipse, see Plut. *Nic.* 23; Flower 2009: 13–15. Greek cities housed various types of religious professions, more or less respected (see Flower 2008: 58–71). Thucydides often devalues their activity (see 2.8.2, 2.21.3, 8.1.1) as well as anyone's dogmatic interpretation of oracles (see 5.24.3; cf. below, sec. 4, on 2.17.2 and 2.54).
16. On Thucydides and religion, see esp. Furley 2006; Rubel 2000: 123–34; Jordan 1987; Marinatos 1981; Oost 1975. Regardless of belief, Thucydides considers the decline of traditional religious customs such as oaths or funerary rituals as a symptom of social deterioration; see, recently, Lateiner 2012, esp. 169–70.
17. Thucydides only uses the word *phusis* (nature) in reference to human beings.

of solar eclipses "at the new moon" (2.28.1, 4.52.1; see above, sec. 2). We could indeed cite several passages from Herodotus that concentrate on natural processes, without at the same time denying a different level of reality.[18] Here Herodotus' position appears not so radically different from that of the Hippocratic author of the treatise *On the Sacred Disease*, who states that epilepsy is no more or less "sacred" than any other diseases. Their causes (προφάσιες) depend on their nature (φύσις); at most, all diseases can be called "divine" (θεῖα) to the extent that nature as a whole is.[19]

In the medical writers, however, stipulations of this sort appear in contexts that emphasize their proactive disregard for metaphysical issues. Those writers especially object to religious explanations that interfere with the accurate diagnosis and cure of physical disorders—somewhat as when Thucydides points out cases of the activity of diviners influencing strategy.[20] Herodotus' notions of causality differentiate him sharply both from the medical writers and from his colleague Thucydides: he considers it part of his task to inquire whether or not specific natural phenomena or pathologies that happened in the past for natural reasons can *also* be shown to manifest a divine intention. On the one hand, for example, Herodotus, much like the Hippocratic author, seems to regard the "sacred disease" of Cambyses as not particularly sacred, but rather as a congenital disability that, in turn, could well have been the natural cause of his mental insanity. But on the other hand, he also reports as not implausible the Egyptians' opinion that Cambyses' madness flared up as a result of his killing of the Apis bull (3.30.1; cf. 3.33).[21]

In Herodotus, diseases and material disasters, if they appear to come from the gods, may either be designed to produce particular effects (e.g., punishment) or simply signal that something else will happen in the human world.[22] As he generalizes from the sufferings of Chios during the Ionian Revolt,

---

18. E.g., Hdt. 2.11–13 (the alluvial formation of the Egyptian delta), 2.20–27 (causes of the floods of the Nile), 7.129.4 (geology of the Peneius valley).

19. *Morb. Sacr.* 1.10–12, 2.1–7; cf. *Aer* 22.1–10. Aristotle considers nature as δαιμονία, ἀλλ' οὐ θεία (*Div. Somn.* 463b12). On the causes of the plague in Athens as noted by Thucydides and others, see below, n. 41 and corresponding text. On the intersection of Herodotus and the medical writers, see Lateiner 1986; Thomas 2000: 28–74.

20. See above, n. 15 and corresponding text; Lloyd 1979: 15–58; Lloyd 1986: 40–42, 128.

21. Munson 1991; for divinely induced diseases in Herodotus, see, e.g., 1.19, 4.205, and esp. 1.105.4, where the supernatural explanation of the Scythian "female disease" contrasts with that provided for the same condition by the Hippoc. *Aer* 22. See also Demont 1988. The first attested case of disease as punishment is the plague described in *Iliad* 1.

22. For divine intervention and communication in Herodotus, see Munson 2001: 183–206.

There tend to be predicting signs somehow when great misfortunes are about to strike a city or a people. And, as a matter of fact, before these events also the Chians received great signs. (6.27.1–3)

Here, the "great misfortunes" (μεγάλα κακά) are hardships that "brought the city to its knees" as a result of war, while the "great signs" (σημήια μεγάλα) are a series of prior catastrophes, including an earthquake and a plague epidemic. As at 3.108.2, the particle κως expresses that we are on speculative territory. Nevertheless, here and elsewhere, Herodotus presents the time coincidence of material and political events as empirical evidence of their mutual connection.[23]

Like Thucydides, Herodotus places himself in the midst of a period characterized by geopolitical turmoil that began with an exceptional natural event: the shaking of Delos. He reports that at the time of Darius' expedition against Athens and Eretria in 490 BCE, when the Persian fleet under the command of Datis proceeded west from Delos, an earthquake shook the island. According to Herodotus, nothing of the sort ever happened before or after "in my time":

> After he sailed away from there, Delos was shaken, as the Delians say, and this earthquake was the first and the last to my times. 2. And no doubt this was a prodigy that the god manifested to men of the evils that were going to happen [μετὰ δὲ τοῦτον ἐνθεῦτεν ἐξαναχθέντα Δῆλος ἐκινήθη, ὡς ἔλεγον οἱ Δήλιοι, καὶ πρῶτα καὶ ὕστατα μέχρι ἐμέο σεισθεῖσα. Καὶ τοῦτο μέν κου τέρας ἀνθρώποισι τῶν μελλόντων ἔσεσθαι κακῶν ἔφηνε ὁ θεός].
> For in the times of Darius, the son of Hystaspes, Xerxes, the son of Darius, and Artaxerxes, son of Xerxes, in these three consecutive generations, more evils happened to Greece than during the other twenty generations that preceded Darius, some [of these evils] deriving to Greece from the Persians, others from the leaders themselves as they were fighting over the hegemony. 3. So it was not at all out of order that Delos was shaken, having previously been unshaken [κινηθῆναι Δῆλον τὸ πρὶν ἐοῦσαν ἀκίνητον]. And in an oracle, the following

---

23. For coincidence as evidence of divine influence, see esp. 7.137.1: δῆλον ὦν μοι ὅτι θεῖον ἐγένετο τὸ πρῆγμα; also 2.120.5, where the general rule that becomes "clear" is that the gods inflict great punishments on great injustices (καταφανὲς . . . ὡς τῶν μεγάλων ἀδικημάτων μεγάλαι εἰσὶ καὶ αἱ τιμωρίαι παρὰ τῶν θεῶν). Besides the one Herodotus records at 6.98 (discussed below), a divinely motivated earthquake also occurs at 5.85.1–2 (c. 490 BCE) and 8.64.1–2 (480 BCE).

had been written about it: I shall shake Delos, although she is unshaken [κινήσω καὶ Δῆλον ἀκίνητόν περ ἐοῦσαν]. (Hdt. 6.98.1–3)

For Herodotus, the earthquake of Delos "no doubt" (κου) verifies the general principle that the gods "somehow" (κως) send "great signs" in anticipation of "great evils" (6.27.1). That most fifth-century audiences would have agreed with his notion of divine communication through nature is confirmed by the passage in which Thucydides himself records an earthquake of Delos as the first in the period bracketed at 1.23.3 (see above, sec. 1). It is this seismic event (and not one that Herodotus assigns to 490) that Thucydides maintains was the first ever in the history of the island. At the time, all of Greece was "up in the air" (μετέωρος) in anticipation of the coming conflict, and "many oracles were recited, and oracle interpreters chanted many predictions":

ἔτι δὲ Δῆλος ἐκινήθη ὀλίγον πρὸ τούτων, πρότερον οὔπω σεισθεῖσα ἀφ' οὗ Ἕλληνες μέμνηνται· ἐλέγετο δὲ καὶ ἐδόκει ἐπὶ τοῖς μέλλουσι γενήσεσθαι σημῆναι. εἴ τέ τι ἄλλο τοιουτότροπον ξυνέβη γενέσθαι, πάντα ἀνεζητεῖτο.

[Moreover, shortly before this, Delos was shaken having never before experienced an earthquake in the memory of the Greeks. [Or so, at least] it was being reported, and it seemed to have been a sign for things that were going to happen, and if something else of this kind happened to occur, it was examined in all its aspects.] (2.8.3)

Herodotus' and Thucydides' texts use similar formulations, and their intertextuality is not in doubt.[24] It is clear from Thucydides that people in mainland Greece in 431 BCE believed Delos to have experienced an unprecedented earthquake "shortly before" and that many interpreted that earthquake as having been a sign that the conflict for which they were eagerly preparing would soon break out.[25] Herodotus, for his part, places the unique event two

24. For different scholarly opinions, see Nenci 1998: 256–58 with bibliography; Scott 2005: 345–48. Guidoboni, Comastri, and Traina (1994), who underline that assessing ancient testimony about earthquakes is difficult because earthquakes greatly vary in intensity and magnitude (12–13), survey ancient naturalistic theories and religious thought on earthquakes (42–54).
25. According to Lewis 1960, the epigraphic evidence shows that the Athenians voted the construction of a shrine to Delian Apollo at Phaleron at this time, perhaps as a response to the earthquake.

generations earlier, appealing to a tradition preserved by the Delians. Unless he wrote his passage before 431 and never revised it, or unless he was in Thurii at the time of what he would regard as a second Delos earthquake, Herodotus may be objecting to the widespread view that Thucydides records, if not specifically to Thucydides. This does not mean that Herodotus denies that there was an earthquake that portended the coming of the Peloponnesian War; he simply places such an event earlier and assigns to it a much longer prophetic range, one extending for three generations, from the Persian Wars to all the subsequent struggles of Greeks against Greeks for hegemonic power (Hdt. 6.98.2), including those of the Pentecontaetia and at least part of what we now call the Archidamian War. This passage represents an important expression of Herodotus' overarching view that the events leading to the Persian Wars represented the "beginning of evils" (Hdt. 5.97.3) and that the Persian Wars, in turn, produced the inter-Greek wars, all in the course of a continuous historical period of "evils" that lasted down to his own times.[26]

Thucydides, of course, divides time differently. While he recognizes the chain of causes and consequences from the Persian Wars to the Peloponnesian War, he essentially conceives of the Pentecontaetia as the great divide between the two conflicts. Like Herodotus, he is clearly aware of the significance of Delos as a symbol of stability and as a geographical marker (center or boundary) of the political life of the Greeks.[27] The placement of the earthquake in the historical context he has chosen is consistent with this periodization. Whether or not Delos could have experienced more than one seismic episode,[28] Thucydides here also underlines that this was the first ever, thereby confirming the poetic tradition about the hitherto "unshakable" nature of Delos, a tradition that was vulnerable to rationalistic challenges even in antiquity.[29] Although he is poised between *ergon* and *logos*—between the earthquake

---

26. Munson 2001: 201–6.
27. Cf. Stadter 1992; Hornblower 1992: 193–96; Nenci 1998: 257–58.
28. See Nenci 1998: 157, citing Guidoboni, Comastro, and Traina 1994. Rusten 2013, however, presents archeological evidence on the nonseismic nature of Delos.
29. Like the oracle in Herodotus 6.98.3, Pindar (fr. 33c 3–4) calls Delos ἀκίνητον, although his use of the term no doubt means "no longer floating": see Verg. *Aen.* 3.77; cf. *Hymn. Hom. Ap.* III 14–18 and Callim. *Hymn* 4.51–54. See Williams 2006: 141–42 on Seneca's polemic against the myth of an unshakeable Delos. The priesthood of Delos encouraged this idea of an unshakeable island, yet in the tradition of Delphi, earthquakes represent a way in which Apollo defends his sanctuary against enemy attacks; see Hdt. 8.37.3 and other sources on Delphi and Delos in Panessa 1991: 1.318–26, 338–41. Rusten (2013) argues that the earthquake(s) of Delos in Herodotus and Thucydides are fictional events entirely derived from the poetic tradition.

itself and the memory, reports, or religious interpretations of others (μέμνηνται; ἐλέγετο δὲ καὶ ἐδόκει)—he includes the event as a matter of fact among those that "happened at the same time" (ξυνέβη γενέσθαι, 2.8.3; cf. πολέμου ἅμα ξυνεπέθετο, 1.23.3), "things previously spoken about by hearsay [ἀκοῇ μὲν λεγόμενα], but more rarely confirmed in fact" (ἔργῳ δὲ . . . βεβαιούμενα, 1.23.3). The first cosmic convulsion (ἐκινήθη)[30] occurred just before the greatest metaphorical κίνησις (Thuc. 1.1.2) and coincided with what Thucydides (differently than Herodotus) regarded as the "beginning of evils" in the human sphere (Thuc. 2.12.3; cf. Hdt. 5.99).

4. The Plague

The preceding brief survey is enough to show that for Herodotus the human and the natural world are ontologically mediated by a rational divine principle, whose intentions are difficult but nevertheless possible, at least retrospectively, to access. Thucydides, however, never, in his own voice, explains events in terms of transcendent mediation, so that the meaning of the concomitance of war and natural phenomena appears to lie beyond the reach of the historian's opinion. The unintelligibility of Thucydides' text in this area has led some readers to conclude that there is nothing to understand except for the author's rhetorical aim to enhance, with rumbles and growls, what he advertises at the outset as the most sensational war narrative of all times.[31] More useful is the notion of metaphor invoked at the beginning of this discussion, not merely as a verbal or literary trope, but as a conceptual framework and a cognitive tool, which borrows one domain to make sense of another.[32] Thucydides' two domains are the natural and the political worlds presented side by side at 1.23, where the list of different types of natural disasters—all made up of plural terms—culminates in the verbal crescendo of ἡ οὐχ ἥκιστα βλάψασα καὶ μέρος τι φθείρασα ἡ λοιμώδης νόσος, parallel to the singular *phonos*, the loss of life due to war and *stasis*.[33] Likewise, in

---

30. For Thucydides' unique use of *kine-* in this passage, see Rusten's essay in this volume and Rusten 2013.
31. Most scholars who hold this position focus on 1.23 and/or the description of the plague. See, e.g., Woodman 1988: 28–40; Bellemore and Plant 1994. Morgan 1994 also implies a purely literary aim. *Contra* Foster 2010: 42.
32. See above, sec. 1 and n. 3; Black 1962: 25–47; Black 1979. See also Lloyd 1989: 172–214.
33. For the traditional association between pestilence (*loimos*) and civil war, see Demont 1990: 153–55.

the historical narrative, the driving force of Thucydides' tracking of specific earthquakes, inundations, and eclipses is arguably the experience of the plague that ravaged Athens in 430–26, again abruptly mentioned at the outset as *the* disease (ἡ νόσος, 2.47.3), a phenomenon unparalleled in the memory of men (according to a formulation that recalls his report of the Delian earthquake)[34] and so singular and exclusive that, at the time, it obliterated and absorbed all others (2.49.1).[35]

For the Athenians, the trauma of that epidemic was strictly intertwined with the pragmatic discomfort and the anxieties of a city at war. From this time on, literary sources, especially drama, show a marked increase in the use of nosological references and in the metaphorical application of the notion of disease to dysfunctions of the body politic.[36] Thucydides' description of the plague and his structural placement of the episode as a sort of factual response to the theoretical formulation of the *Epitaphios* signals a profound malaise with the internal state of the polis and the external role of Athens in the geopolitical world. It is not merely that the plague, like war and stasis, brings disruption in the social fabric of the community, that is, that *nosos* extinguishes *nomos* (2.52–53).[37] The plague, rather, represents the objective correlative of war. It cuts short and, in a sense, replaces or parallels the Spartan invasion, and like that invasion, it comes from the outside; it travels through a great part of the non-Greek world (cf. 1.1.2), "invades" Greece, reaches Peiraeus, and finally settles in Athens (2.48.1). At the level of the individual person, its δύναμις (2.48.3) follows an opposite course, from the head to the extremities, as it "invades" and "conquers" the space of the body (2.49.2).[38]

Cognitive metaphors work, however, not simply on the basis of analogy

---

34. Cf. οὕτως ἀνθρώπων οὐδαμοῦ ἐμνημονεύετο γενέσθαι (2.47.3) with πρότερον οὔπω σεισθεῖσα ἀφ' οὗ Ἕλληνες μέμνηνται (2.8.3).

35. See, most recently, Kallet 2013.

36. The connection between the "literal" plague in Soph. *OT* (see esp. 25–28) and the historical plague in Athens has been famously argued in Knox 1956, even though we have no external evidence for dating the play. Many other metaphorical disease references in tragedy are cited in Mitchell-Boyask 2008 and Brock 2000: 27. On the city as a diseased body, see Thuc. 6.14; Kallet 2013, n. 5 with bibliography.

37. Finley (1967: 159–60) compares Thucydides' description of the social effect of the plague with his account of the stasis in Corcyra (3.82–83; cf. 3.75.4). The contrast between Pericles' praise of the Athenian citizen's *autarkia* in the *Funeral Oration* (2.41.1) and Thucydides' observation that "no physical constitution was *autarkes*" (2.51.3) establishes another connection. Herodotus applies nosological language to political discord at 6.100.1 and 7.157.2, and he uses a mixed metaphor of rottenness (σαθρόν) and shaking (διασείσειν) at 6.109.5 (Brock 2004: 169).

38. See Parry 1969 for the metaphorical language in Thucydides' description.

but according to a set of complex interrelations.[39] In many respects, the plague is not at all like the war. Its attack is "sudden" and "without cause" (ἐξαπιναίως, 2.48.1; ἐξαίφνης . . . ἀπ' οὐδεμιᾶς προφάσεως, 2.49.2). Thucydides' self-confidence in identifying *aitiai* and *prophaseis* of war for the benefit of posterity (1.22.4–23.6) contrasts with his insistence on the mysteriousness of the disease. He will only be able to provide future readers with a minute and accurate description of symptoms, leaving it to others, be they doctors or laymen, to opine on "their adequate causes" (τὰς αἰτίας . . . ἱκανάς, 2.48.3).[40] He dismisses the rumor about the Peloponnesians poisoning the Peiraeus wells (2.48.2), and he relegates to the role of aggravating factor the overcrowding in the city as a result of the war policy.[41] In the absence of satisfactory natural explanations, the questions raised by the text (what is it, why here, and why now?) connect the biological and the political body in an utterly aporetic way.

The plague just "strikes";[42] Thucydides has called it ἡ λοιμώδης νόσος (1.23.3), recalling the Homeric λοιμός (*Il.* 1.61), and Pericles includes it among things *daimonia* (2.64.2). This last identification may be in itself a metaphor (denoting an "act of god," as in modern legal terminology), but many of Pericles' fellow citizens would have taken it more literally.[43] Some connected it with the Delphic oracle in which Apollo had promised to assist the Spartans in the Peloponnesian War (Thuc. 2.54.4; cf. 1.118.3, 1.123).[44] Thucydides, who never attributes the plague to the gods, reports, at any rate, that the remedies of cult were just as ineffective as the resources of medicine or other human *technai* (2.47.4).[45] However, he confirms the factual "basis" of the divine-as-

39. Cf. Richards 1936: 89–112; Black 1962: 35–44.
40. Thomas 2006; Kallet 2013: 358–59. *Aition* and *prophasis* are also part of the vocabulary of causation of medical writers: see above, sec. 3; Lloyd 1979: 51–58.
41. Thuc. 2.52.1; cf. 2.54.5. Contrast Diod. 12.45.1–2; Plut. *Per.* 34.4. Thucydides is aware of person-to-person contagion (see Holladay and Poole 1979: 295–98) but is silent on environmental causes; cf. Diodorus 12.45 and 58, citing crowding, rain, foul air, spoiled crops, and lack of wind. See Longrigg 2000; Allison 1983. The reading of 1.23.3 (ἀπ' αὐτῶν καὶ λιμοί, καὶ ἡ οὐχ ἥκιστα βλάψασα καὶ μέρος τι φθείρασα ἡ λοιμώδης νόσος) as meaning that both the famines and the plague derived from droughts (Demont 1990: 149; Demont 2013: 81–84) is not supported by Thucydides' narrative of the plague.
42. Cf. Parry 1969: 114 on the verb ἐγκατασκῆψαι (2.47.3) in Aesch. *Pers.* 414 and Soph. *Trach.* 1087.
43. In the fifth century, δαιμόνιος (which does not occur anywhere else in Thucydides) is occasionally used as synonymous with θεῖος (e.g., Hdt. 2.120.5), but see the distinction made by Aristotle at *Div. Somn.* 463b12, cited above, in n. 19.
44. See Thuc. 2.54.4–5. Cf. Diod. Sic. 12.58.6; Paus. 1.3.4.
45. Thucydides does not even deign to mention Pericles' hereditary pollution (1.126–27) as an alleged cause of the plague, although Demont (2013: 77–78) sees the words Thucydides attributes to Pericles at 2.64.1 as an allusion to public opinion on this matter. Thucydides is

cause theory by reporting that the beginning of the plague coincided with the Spartan invasion of Attica (ἐσβεβληκότων . . . τῶν Πελοποννησίων) and by insisting on the extent to which the disease targeted only the Athenians both at home and abroad (2.54.5, 2.57, 2.58.2–3).

On the basis of this and other evidence, Lisa Kallet (2013) has recently argued that Thucydides' entire 430 BCE narrative is designed to suggest to his readers the possibility that Apollo indeed caused the plague. This view seems too specific and leaves unanswered the more general question of whether Thucydides also sees the other natural phenomena he records as possibly responding to human activity. Nevertheless, Kallet's discussion of the plague narrative confirms Thucydides' sensitivity to a mysterious causal relation between the natural and the human worlds at a level that is not merely empirical. This inclination emerges even as Thucydides criticizes the procrustean Athenian attempts, at the time of the plague, to read the thought of the divine:

ἐν δὲ τῷ κακῷ οἷα εἰκὸς ἀνεμνήσθησαν καὶ τοῦδε τοῦ ἔπους, φάσκοντες οἱ πρεσβύτεροι πάλαι ᾄδεσθαι

'ἥξει Δωριακὸς πόλεμος καὶ λοιμὸς ἅμ' αὐτῷ.'

(3) ἐγένετο μὲν οὖν ἔρις τοῖς ἀνθρώποις μὴ λοιμὸν ὠνομάσθαι ἐν τῷ ἔπει ὑπὸ τῶν παλαιῶν, ἀλλὰ λιμόν, ἐνίκησε δὲ ἐπὶ τοῦ παρόντος εἰκότως λοιμὸν εἰρῆσθαι· οἱ γὰρ ἄνθρωποι πρὸς ἃ ἔπασχον τὴν μνήμην ἐποιοῦντο. ἢν δέ γε οἶμαί ποτε ἄλλος πόλεμος καταλάβῃ Δωρικὸς τοῦδε ὕστερος καὶ ξυμβῇ γενέσθαι λιμόν, κατὰ τὸ εἰκὸς οὕτως ᾄσονται.

[Among other things which, of course [οἷα εἰκός], they remembered in the midst of their misfortune, was also the following verse, with the elders claiming that it was sung long ago:

---

also silent about various religious remedies, like the importation of Asclepius' cult from Epidaurus to Athens in 420 (*IG* II2 4960). He avoids connecting the plague with the Athenian purification of Delos in 426, which was carried out, he says, "according to some oracle" (3.104). Diodorus (12.58.6) regards it as an attempt to appease Apollo, who had promised, from Delphi, to help Sparta in the war (Thuc. 1.118.3; cf. 2.54.2), and most scholars agree that this was at least one of the motives. Cf. Hornblower 1992: 195; Flower 2009: 5–9. *Contra* Mikalson 1984: 221–22.

'A Dorian war will come and with it pestilence [λοιμόν]'.

Although a dispute arose among people as to whether in the verse the ancients had really said 'pestilence' [λοιμόν] or 'famine' [λιμόν], in the present situation—of course [εἰκότως]—the version with 'pestilence' won, for people adapted their memory to what they were suffering at the time. I think that if ever another Dorian war comes upon them after this one, and if a famine happens at the same time, they will of course [κατὰ τὸ εἰκὸς] sing the verse in that way.] (2.54.2–3)

While Thucydides' "of course" discourse displays condescension toward popular piety, this passage does not constitute a crystal clear display of rationalism either. In an earlier narrative of how Athenians from the countryside crammed into the city according to Pericles' policy and took habitation wherever they could, Thucydides similarly quotes—and criticizes the ordinary interpretation of—another prediction applicable to the same period, this time a Pythian oracle deploring an eventual occupation of the Pelasgian ground (2.17.1–2). That oracle proved true, Thucydides maintains, not because the sacrilegious occupation caused misfortunes for the state (as most people would say), but in the sense that the necessity of the occupation was caused by the unfortunate advent of the war (2.17.1–2). Now, *this* is a rationalistic explanation. It denies the common assumption that infractions of cult are punished by the gods (consistently with Thucydides' position that cult does not buy divine favors), while at the same time contributing to the pragmatic assimilation of war and plague: the hardships of the war here cause a violation of religious *nomos*, very much in the same way as the hardships of the plague unsettle funerals and other rituals (2.52–53).

On this model, Thucydides might have rationalized the prediction that "with a Dorian war will come pestilence" by emphasizing the role of war logistics in producing the pestilence or, for that matter, *limoi*, in the sense of shortages of food.[46] He does not do so, as we have seen, perhaps rather preferring to imply causes bigger and more fundamental than these material explanations. For him, the prophecy is "true"—or at least interesting— because it formulates the concomitance of suffering caused by humans and suffering caused by nature, be it pestilence or famine. Thucydides' implicit

---

46. See above, n. 4.

recognition of the essential equivalence of the two different versions of the prophecy may give us the key to why the last items leading up to the λοιμώδης νόσος (pestilential disease) in his list of unparalleled natural disasters that "happened at the same time" as the war (1.23.3) are famines (λιμοί) that were a natural phenomenon caused by droughts (αὐχμοί), even though, in the narrative of the war, he never mentions them again as actually having occurred.[47] The author of the ancient prediction "With war will come pestilence/famine" need not have had special access to the gods. He might have been one of those poets who envisioned famine, pestilence, and war as parallel responses to impairments in the political sphere:

πολλάκι καὶ ξύμπασα πόλις κακοῦ ἀνδρὸς ἀπηύρα,
ὅστις ἀλιτραίνῃ καὶ ἀτάσθαλα μηχανάαται.
τοῖσιν δ᾽ οὐρανόθεν μέγ᾽ ἐπήγαγε πῆμα Κρονίων,
λιμὸν ὁμοῦ καὶ λοιμόν, ἀποφθινύθουσι δὲ λαοί·
[οὐδὲ γυναῖκες τίκτουσιν, μινύθουσι δὲ οἶκοι
Ζηνὸς φραδμοσύνῃσιν Ὀλυμπίου· ἄλλοτε δ᾽ αὖτε]
ἢ τῶν γε στρατὸν εὐρὺν ἀπώλεσεν ἢ ὅ γε τεῖχος
ἢ νέας ἐν πόντῳ Κρονίδης ἀποτείνυται αὐτῶν.

[Often even a whole city suffers because of an evil man who sins and devises wicked deeds. Upon them Cronus' son brings forth woe from the sky, famine together with pestilence, and the people die away; the women do not give birth, and the households are diminished by the plans of Olympian Zeus. And at another time Cronus' son destroys their broad army and their wall, or he takes vengeance upon the ships on the sea.] (Hes. Op. 238–47, trans. G. Most)

Heirs of the tradition that produced these lines are both Herodotus, who puts a just divine principle in charge of causation, and Thucydides, who does not.[48] Thucydides replaces this principle with the professed ignorance of scientists and other intellectuals, including himself.[49] The ignorance he acknowledges is different from the religious simplemindedness he attributes to

47. Oracles and other texts that associate *limos* and *loimos* (or hesitate between them) are collected by Demont 1990.
48. See, e.g., the famines in Herodotus 6.139.1 and 9.93.3. At the metaphorical level, Herodotus talks of family lines as of plants extirpated "from the roots" as a result of cosmic balance or *tisis* (see Lateiner 1989: 142–44).
49. Cf. ἀγνοίᾳ at 2.47.4 with σκοπῶν, προειδώς, and μὴ ἀγνοεῖν at 2.48.3.

most people, but it nevertheless finds meaning in coincidence and implies between cosmic and human behavior a sort of synergy that lies beyond the sphere of what one can analyze, predict, and know. Like the river Scamander faced with the onslaughts of Achilles, nature itself reflects or reacts to human overreaching.[50]

Works Cited

Allison, J. 1983. "Pericles' Policy and the Plague." *Historia* 32.1: 14–23.

Bellemore, J., and Plant, I. M. 1994. "Thucydides, Rhetoric, and Plague in Athens." *Athenaeum* 82: 385–401.

Black, M. 1962. *Models and Metaphors: Studies in Language and Philosophy.* Ithaca: Cornell University Press.

Black, M. 1979. "More about Metaphor." In A. Ortony, ed., *Metaphor and Thought*, 19–43. Cambridge: Cambridge University Press.

Brock, R. 2000. "Medical Imagery in the Greek Polis." In Hope and Marshall, 24–33.

Brock, R. 2004. "Political Imagery in Herodotus." In V. Karageorghis and I. Taifacos, eds., *The World of Herodotus*, 169–77. Nicosia: Foundation Anastasios G. Leventis.

Cartledge, P. 2002. *Sparta and Lakonia: A Regional History, 1300–362 BC.* 2nd ed. London: Routledge.

Demont, P. 1988. "Hérodote et les pestilences (Notes sur Hdt. VI, 27; VII, 171; VIII 115–17)." *RPh* 62: 7–13.

Demont, P. 1990. "Les Oracles Delphiques Relatifs au Pestilences et Thucydide." *Kernos* 3: 147–56.

Demont, P. 2013. "The Causes of the Athenian Plague and Thucydides." In A. Tsakmakis and M. Tamiolaki, eds., *Thucydides between History and Literature*, 73–90. Berlin: De Gruyter.

Dewald, C. 2005. *Thucydides' War Narrative.* Berkeley: University of California Press.

Diels, H., and Kranz, W. 1954. *Die Fragmente der Vorsokratiker.* 7th ed. 3 vols. Berlin: Weidmann.

Finley, J. 1967. *Three Essays on Thucydides.* Cambridge, MA: Harvard University Press.

Flower, M. A. 2008. *The Seer in Ancient Greece.* Berkeley: University of California Press.

Flower, M. A. 2009. "Athenian Religion and the Peloponnesian War." In O. Palagia, ed., *Art in Athens during the Peloponnesian War*, 1–23. Cambridge: Cambridge University Press.

---

50. Hom. *Il.* 21.240–324.

Foster, E. 2010. *Thucydides, Pericles, and Periclean Imperialism*. Cambridge: Cambridge University Press.

Furley, W. D. 2006. "Thucydides and Religion." In Rengakos and Tsakmakis, 415–38.

Gomme, A. W. 1945. *A Historical Commentary on Thucydides*. Vol. 1, *Introduction and Commentary on Book I*. Oxford: Oxford University Press.

Gould, J. 2006. "Herodotus and the 'Resurrection.'" In P. Derow and R. Parker, eds., *Herodotus and His World: Essays from a Conference in Memory of George Forrest*, 297–302. Oxford: Oxford University Press.

Guidoboni, E., Comastri, A., and Traina, G. 1994. *Catalogue of Ancient Earthquakes in the Mediterranean Area up to the 10th Century*. Rome: Istituto Nazionale di Geofisica.

Guthrie, W. K. C. 1965. *A History of Greek Philosophy*. Vol. 2, *The Pre-Socratic Tradition from Parmenides to Democritus*. Cambridge: Cambridge University Press.

Holladay, A. J., and Poole, J. C. F. 1979. "Thucydides and the Plague of Athens." *CQ* 29: 282–300.

Hope, V. M., and Marshall, E. eds. 2000. *Death and Disease in the Ancient City*. London: Routledge.

Hornblower, S. 1991. *A Commentary on Thucydides*. Vol. 1, *Books I–III*. Oxford: Oxford University Press.

Hornblower, S. 1992. "The Religious Dimension of the Peloponnesian War, or What Thucydides Does Not Tell Us." *HSCP* 94: 169–97.

How, W. W., and Wells, J. 1912. *A Commentary on Herodotus*. 2 vols. Oxford: Clarendon.

Jordan, B. 1986. "Religion in Thucydides." *TAPA* 116: 119–47.

Kallet, L. 2013. "Thucydides, Apollo, the Plague, and the War." *AJP* 134: 355–82.

Knox, B. 1956. "The Date of the *Oedipus Tyrannus* of Sophocles." *AJP* 77: 137–47.

Kosak, J. C. 2000. "*POLIS NOUSOUSA*: Greek Ideas about the City and Disease in the Fifth Century BC." In Hope and Marshall, 30–53.

Lateiner, D. 1986. "The Empirical Element in the Methods of Early Greek Medical Writers and Herodotus: A Shared Epistemological Response." *Antichthon* 20: 1–20.

Lateiner, D. 1989. *The Historical Method of Herodotus*. Toronto: University of Toronto Press.

Lateiner, D. 2012. "Oaths: Theory and Practice in the Histories of Herodotus and Thucydides." In E. Foster and D. Lateiner, eds., *Thucydides and Herodotus*, 154–84. Oxford: Oxford University Press.

Lewis, D. M. 1960. "Apollo Delios." *ABSA* 55: 190–94.

Lloyd, G. E. R. 1979. *Magic, Reason, and Experience: Studies in the Origins and Development of Greek Science*. Cambridge: Cambridge University Press.

Lloyd, G. E. R. 1989. *The Revolution of Wisdom: Studies in the Claims and Practice of Ancient Greek Science*. Berkeley: University of California Press.

Longrigg, J. 2000. "Death and Epidemic Disease in Classical Athens." In Hope and Marshall, 55–64.

Marinatos, N. 1981. "Thucydides and Oracles." *JHS* 101: 138–40.

Mikalson, J. D. 1984. "Religion and the Plague in Athens." In A. Boegehold et al., *Studies Presented to Sterling Dow on His Eightieth Birthday*, 218–25. Durham: Duke University Press.

Mitchell-Boyask, R. 2008. *Plague and the Athenian Imagination: Drama, History, and the Cult of Asclepius*. Cambridge: Cambridge University Press.

Momigliano, A. 1930. "Erodoto e Tucidide sul terremoto di Delo." *SIFC* 8: 87–89.

Morgan, T. E. 1994. "Plague or Poetry? Thucydides on the Epidemic at Athens." *TAPA* 124: 197–209.

Most, G. W. 2006. *Hesiod, Theogony, Works and Days, and Testimonia*. Cambridge, MA: Harvard University Press.

Munson, R. V. 1991. "The Madness of Cambyses." *Arethusa* 24: 43–63.

Nenci, G. 1998. *Erodoto, Le Storie, Libro VI: La Battaglia di Maratona*. Milan: Mondadori.

Oost, S. I. 1975. "Thucydides and the Irrational: Sundry Passages." *CP* 70.3: 186–96.

Panessa, G. 1991. *Fonti greche e latine per la storia dell'ambiente e del clima nel mondo Greco*. Pisa: Scuola Normale Superiore.

Rengakos, A., and Tsakmakis, A., eds. 2006. *Brill's Companion to Thucydides*. Leiden: Brill.

Richards, I. A. 1936. *The Philosophy of Rhetoric*. Oxford: Oxford University Press.

Rubel, A. 2000. *Die Stadt in Angst: Religion und Politik in Athen während des Peloponnisischen Krieges*. Darmstadt: Wissenschaftliche Buchgesellschaft.

Rusten J. S. 1990. *Thucydides, The Peloponnesian War, Book II*. Cambridge: Cambridge University Press.

Rusten J. S. 2013. "ΔΗΛΟΣ ἘΚΙΝΗΘΗ: An Imaginary Earthquake on Delos." *JHS* 133: 135–45.

Scott, L. 2005. *Historical Commentary on Herodotus Book 6*. Leiden: Brill.

Stadter, P. 1992. "Herodotus and the Athenian *archê*." *ASNP*, 3rd ser., 22: 781–809.

Stephenson, F. R., and Fatoohi, L. 2001. "The Eclipses Recorded by Thucydides." *Zeitschrift für Alte Geschichte* 50.2: 245–53.

Thomas, R. 2000. *Herodotus in Context: Ethnography, Science and the Art of Persuasion*. Cambridge: Cambridge University Press.

Thomas, R. 2006. "Thucydides' Intellectual Milieu and the Plague." In Rengakos and Tsakmakis, 87–108.

Woodman, A. 1988. *Rhetoric in Classical Historiography*. London: Croom Helm.

Williams, G. D. 2006. "Greco-Roman Seismology and Seneca on Earthquakes in *Natural Questions* 6." *JRS* 96: 124–46.

CHAPTER 3

Action and Consequences

The Historical Present Tense in the Opening Narrative of Book 8 of Thucydides

Edith Foster

The debate concerning the form and even the authenticity of book 8 of Thucydides is nearly as old as scholarship on Thucydides.[1] To my knowledge, however, no scholar has analyzed one striking linguistic feature of that book: namely, the frequency of the historical present tense, which occurs about 147 times in book 8.[2] This total displays a startling contrast between book 8 and the other books of Thucydides' text. For instance, Thucydides uses the historical present tense (hereafter HP) about forty-three times in book 5, about thirty-six times in book 6, and about sixty-three times in book 7.[3] In total, we find approximately 578 occurrences of the HP in Thucydides,

---

1. Cf. Hornblower 2008: 1–4 with 32–35; Rood 1998: 251–53. The author wishes to thank Tobias Joho for reading a draft of this paper, and especially Donald Lateiner—to whom this essay and volume are affectionately dedicated.
2. Rood (1998: 259–60 with n. 34) remarks on its frequency and use in battle narratives.
3. All books of Thucydides exhibit fewer instances of the HP per chapter length than book 8. Thucydides uses the HP about sixty-five times in book 1, about sixty-one times in book 2, about ninety-eight times in book 3, and about sixty-six times in book 4. It may be objected that book 8 contains no speeches and that this book, which is nearly entirely narrative, simply has more room available for the HP, which does not occur in direct speeches. However, at 106 narrative chapters, book 8 has fewer narrative chapters than, for instance, book 4 (featuring about 121 narrative chapters and sixty-six instances of the HP) or book 5, which also has no speeches but has far fewer instances of the HP (there are about 110 narrative chapters and forty-three instances of the HP).

about one-quarter of which are found in book 8.[4] Since it would be impossible to discuss all of book 8 in one short chapter, this essay discusses the first narrative of book 8, that is, the story of the winter of 413 and the summer of 412, which includes forty-three uses of the HP. I argue that Thucydides employs the HP in two main ways in these chapters. First, he uses it to mark a political action or decision whose outcome(s) we should notice. Second (in a contrasting use), he uses it to mark the main events and damage of ongoing battles. Other uses, especially characterization, will be mentioned in passing; indeed, the HP seems to be primarily a nudge to the reader to pay attention to something, and the variety of political and military considerations that we might pass over unless reminded, particularly in a narrative of this density, seems nearly unlimited. The final section of this essay offers some suggestions about why the HP appears so frequently in book 8.

What is the historical present tense? The use of the HP as a literary device begins with Herodotus. Homer did not employ this technique, in which a verb in the present indicative intrudes on a historical narration in order to emphasize a particular action. The HP is common in English narrations, as when someone might say, "We were driving along, and everything was going smoothly, when suddenly the car next to us *crashes* into the ditch." In Greek, occurrences of the HP stand out because they are surrounded by verbs in the aorist and imperfect. Verbs in the historical present are also recognizable in other ways. Historical presents nearly always occur in the third-person singular or plural and are nearly always "telic"; that is, they denote an action completed within a well-understood time. The HP does not occur in speeches, direct or indirect, and only rarely occurs in passages where Thucydides is assessing or explaining a situation in his own voice.[5] Moreover, the vocabulary of the HP in Thucydides is limited: many of the verbs Thucydides uses in the HP are among the verbs students learn in their first semester of Greek.[6]

4. Much of the information in this paragraph is derived from the indispensable appendixes provided in Lallot et al. 2011, esp. app. 2 (pp. 301–17). However, I have noted instances of the historical present not recorded in these appendixes (e.g., μεταπέμπεται at 8.5.1 and ἐκπορθεῖ at 8.41.2), and the figures I have provided above for each book remain approximate.

5. Again, the information in this paragraph was gathered from the comprehensive descriptions in Lallot et al. 2011, particularly 1–17 (Rijksbaron) and 19–36 (Lallot).

6. For a description of the thirteen Thucydidean verbs most commonly used in the HP, see Lallot 2011: 22–24. The top four HP verbs are ἀφικνέομαι, πέμπω, αἱρέω, and πείθω. No scholarly studies compare this vocabulary to Herodotus' HP vocabulary. Donald Lateiner

The intrusion of the present tense is one of many devices Thucydides uses to draw our attention to particular events in the narrative, and although this essay isolates the HP, that focus should not be taken to argue that this device is more important than others.[7] However, since the HP is especially common in book 8, an attempt at explication seems useful. In my view, Rijksbaron (2011) is somewhat off the mark in concluding about Thucydides' text as a whole that "the primary function of the HP is to mark events that were, according to Thucydides, of decisive (crucial, central) importance for the development of the war" (17). Despite the extraordinary frequency of the HP in book 8, for instance, Thucydides does not employ it in his descriptions of many of book 8's most important events. Thus, the story of the oligarchical revolution at Athens, including the suspenseful passage in which the Spartan king Agis waits at the gates of Athens, hoping to take over the city during its period of civil strife (8.65–71), features no verbs in the HP. Again, the narrative that treats the establishment of the five thousand (8.89–94) includes only one verb in the HP (at 92.4, where Alexicles is arrested). We therefore cannot, for instance, search out HP verbs in Thucydides to find out which events in the war he considered decisive, and I argue that Thucydides does not use the HP for demonstrating the importance of an event for the war; rather, it is one way of pointing out to the reader that he or she needs to attend to an action. Why the action is worth attention is ultimately for the reader to decide.

As mentioned, this essay analyzes Thucydides' use of the HP in chapters 1–28 of book 8, which include forty-three uses of the HP. This is the same number of occurrences as in all of book 5 and more occurrences than in all of book 6, which features thirty-six uses of the HP. The chapters under discussion thus furnish a rich sample of material for analysis. A brief introductory review of these chapters will help to situate this essay's examination.

Chapters 1 and 2 of book 8 explain the contrasting passions of the combatants after Athens' defeat in Sicily. The Athenians experience fear and panic

---

asked the following in his remarks on this essay: "Since Herodotus was first to develop the HP, could some/many of Thucydides' uses be considered his Herodotean mood or dramatic style, as in the Themistokles and Pausanias excurses (which are very rich in the use of the HP)?"

7.   Other devices of emphasis include, for instance, the so-called vivid subjunctive (which is, however, fundamentally different from the HP in that it also occurs in the direct speeches— i.e., in character text, whereas the historical present is reserved for narrator text), the use of superlatives and special adverbs, manipulation of word order, direct narrator intrusions, and many others. On narrator intrusions and their relation to the HP, see the conclusion of this essay.

(8.1.2, 4), while high hopes of victory and of the subsequent secure leadership of all Greece (8.2.4) characterize the Spartan side. As Tim Rood has argued in detail, the ensuing narrative shows how the expectations of the Spartans and their allies are thwarted.[8] Chapters 3–11 show how the Spartans' initial plans to cause revolts in Ionia and capture Athens' empire are stalled and then dashed by their naval defeat at Speiraeum. This story includes ten verbs in the HP. The first four point out decisions or actions that will be thwarted, and the final six, all of which are deployed in chapter 11, emphasize the main events of Sparta's naval defeat. A second set of explanations begins with the account of the revolt of Chios (8.12) and ends with the revolt of Mytilene (8.22), the high-water mark of the Ionian revolts against Athens in 412 BCE. These ten chapters include sixteen verbs in the HP. Most striking here are the five uses of the HP to mark the inception of revolts that will ultimately fail, and the persistent use of the HP to mark the damage of the small naval battles that punctuate the continuous struggle between Athens, on the one hand, and Sparta and her Ionian allies, on the other. Finally, the last section of this narrative (8.23–28) shows how the Spartans lose Lesbos, which had also revolted from Athens, but hold on to Miletus, since the Athenians, who had just won a land battle for possession of the city, flee a freshly arriving Spartan fleet. These six chapters include seventeen verbs in the HP. For example, five HP verbs are found in chapter 23 and mark the Spartans' belated and insufficient attempts to retain Lesbos; another four occur in chapter 25 and mark Athens' quickly abandoned victory at Miletus. The narration of the events of the summer of 412 ends with Thucydides' description of the Spartan campaign on behalf of Tissaphernes against Amorges, an enemy of the Persian king.

As this brief review makes clear, many HP verbs in these chapters mark the initial stages of actions that will fail or suffer a reversal of some kind, and many also mark the ongoing events of battles. Nearly all inevitably also contribute to characterization, since the decisions or actions marked with the HP must reveal something about the character of the historical agent(s). A closer analysis of the first section of the narrative (8.1–11) helps to elucidate these functions of the HP.

The first HP verbs in book 8 mark the independent political decisions of the Spartan king Agis. The Euboeans apply to him for support in their in-

---

8.   Cf. Rood 1998: 251–53.

tended revolt against Athens, and Agis summons (HP μεταπέμπεται, 5.1) his fellow Spartans Alcamenes and Melanthus to lead them. But he changes his mind after the arrival of envoys from the Lesbians: a verb in the HP marks the fact that he is persuaded (ἀναπείθεται, 5.2) to support the Lesbians instead, so that Alcamenes will now be sent to Lesbos. Sentence 5.3, which is devoid of verbs in the HP, contains an emphatic authorial description of Agis' independent power as the commander at Decelea, a Spartan-occupied fort north of Athens.[9]

Meanwhile, messengers from the Chians, the Erythraeans, and the Persian satrap Tissaphernes seek support at Sparta. Their actions are not marked with the HP. Instead, Thucydides uses the HP to mark the arrival (ἀφικνοῦνται, 6.1) of competing messengers from the satrap Pharnabazus, who wants to accomplish the same basic aims as Tissaphernes—namely, to make the Spartans Persian allies and to eliminate the Athenians from his district, since they impede his collection of tribute (6.1; cf. 5.4–5). In the event, the Spartans are influenced by Alcibiades, who supports Tissaphernes, so that they spurn Pharnabazus' embassy and vote to send forty ships to Chios, with ten going ahead under Melanchridas. But due to an earthquake they subsequently change their minds, and decide to send Chalcideus with a reduced advance force of five ships (6.4–5). No verbs in the HP mark either these decisions or their revision after the earthquake.

The next HP verb of this section occurs at 7.1, which also marks the beginning of the summer of 412 BC. At Chian urging, the Spartans send (HP ἀποπέμπουσιν) three Spartiates to Corinth to make arrangements for bringing their entire navy (thirty-nine ships) over to the Aegean side of the Isthmus of Corinth. No more HP verbs appear for about two pages of the Oxford Classical Text of Thucydides, although important events are proceeding: in chapters 7–10.3, Agis abandons his own plans in order to join the common policies of the Spartans, and the Corinthians delay the departure of the Spartan navy until after the Isthmian games, during which the suspicious Athenians confirm that the Chians are planning to revolt. The Spartans, who have conceived contempt for Athens' present weakness, allow this delay to happen and even divide up their fleet, making it easier for the Athenians to attack them (cf. 8.3–4).

By contrast, six HP verbs occur in the eleven lines from 10.3–11.1, where

---

9.   See n. 11 on the role of the HP in characterization.

thirty-seven Athenian ships pursue (HP καταδώκουσιν) twenty-one Peloponnesian ships to Speiraeum. (Speiraeum was a deserted harbor on the Aegean side of the Isthmus of Corinth and was near the spot where the Spartans planned to marshal and dispatch their navy toward Asia Minor.) The Spartans lose (HP ἀπολλύασι) one ship at sea but anchor (HP ὁρμίζουσιν) the other twenty. The Athenians then attack by land and sea, seriously damaging (HP κατατραυματίζουσιν) most of the beached ships, and they kill (HP ἀποκτείνουσιν) the Spartan admiral Alcamenes. Finally, they blockade the area, anchor (HP ὁρμίζονται) on an island close by, and send for help to Athens.

To review, of ten verbs in the HP in chapters 5–12, the first four indicate political decisions and events. Two emphasize Agis' decisions, neither of which are realized; one emphasizes the arrival of the messengers from Pharnabazus, who leave without accomplishing their aims;[10] and a fourth emphasizes the fact that the Spartans send messengers to Corinth to arrange for moving their fleet, an aim the Corinthians thwart until the Athenians are both well informed and well prepared to attack. The remaining verbs in the HP pertain to the battle at Speiraeum. These verbs contrast to the previous HP verbs: in the battle narrative, the HP outlines the dire facts that constitute the reversal of the Spartans' hopes and expectations, spotlighting Athenian agency, Spartan losses, and, finally, the Athenian blockade. In the battle narrative, the HP emphasizes not anticipated outcomes but outcomes themselves. As we shall see, this contrast between the functions of HP verbs in the larger political narrative and in the battle narratives is persistent.

In general, analysis of the next section of book 8 confirms these initial observations. The narrative between 8.12 and 8.22 begins with the revolt of Chios and ends with the revolt of Mytilene. It features sixteen HP verbs, most of which emphasize political actions, although some illuminate the material damage of small naval battles. Several occurrences of the HP in these chapters seem to pertain particularly to Alcibiades.

Let us look first at the main story of the Ionian revolts. After the disaster at Speiraeum, Alcibiades persuades (HP πείθει) the discouraged Spartans nevertheless to send himself and Chalcideus to Chios with five ships (12.1).[11]

---

10. Pharnabazus' unsuccessful messengers leave, with their money (fifteen talents), in 8.1; one difference between them and Tissaphernes is that while the former promised money, Pharnabazus' ambassadors had actually brought money.

11. As we have already seen in respect to the verbs associated with King Agis (5.1 and 2), the

Another HP verb marks Alcibiades' and Chalcideus' sudden arrival at Chios (HP ἀφικνοῦνται . . . αἰφνίδιοι, 14.1), and the next two HP verbs after that mark the results of his crucial diplomatic successes, as the Chians and Ery-thraeans revolt (HP ἀφίστανται, 14.2) and then cause the Clazomenians to revolt (HP ἀφιστᾶσιν, 14.3). A final HP verb of this account marks the arrival at Athens of the news of these revolts (HP ἀφικνεῖται, 15.1). Thucydides re-lates that the Athenians decide, in response, to expend their emergency fund of one thousand talents. They then set about organizing a navy in order to reclaim Chios. These decisions, both of which begin processes that will be realized, are not marked with HP verbs.

The subsequent arrival of the Athenian general Strombichides at Samos with eight ships (HP ἀφικνεῖται, 16.1) is marked with the HP, although his escape from the twenty-three ships of the Spartan Chalcideus is not, and nei-ther is Chalcideus' capture of Teos and the destruction of its wall (16.2–3).[12] The next HP verb occurs when Chalcideus and Alcibiades cleverly arm their Peloponnesian sailors and leave them on Chios (καταλιμπάνουσιν, 17.1), filling their ships with Chians instead.[13] Alcibiades and his Chian forces are subsequently successful in causing Miletus to revolt (HP ἀφιστᾶσι, 17.3). The Spartans then make a treaty with the Persian king that essentially annuls the Greek victory in the Persian Wars and will cause them much trouble later on (18; cf. 37, 43–44).[14]

Finally, Thucydides' fast-paced description of political upheaval in Ionia ends with a political revolution in Athens' favor and further revolts against Athens. The compressed story, in chapter 21, of the revolution in which the Samians, with Athenian help, throw off their oligarchs, become a democracy, and draw closer to Athens, which grants them autonomy, is not marked with

HP sometimes supports characterization. Alcibiades' actions get more HP emphasis than those of any other leader in book 8. In addition to the HP verbs in chapters 12–17, which emphasize Alcibiades' powers of persuasion, his cleverness (see n. 13 below), and his quick movements, an HP verb occurs at 45.1 where he flees to Tissaphernes because of Spartan death threats (HP ὑποχωρεῖ). At 50.4, he sends (HP πέμπει) a letter to friendly Athenian commanders on Samos, asking that his accuser, Phrynichus, be murdered. At 56.2, he resorts to a strategy (HP τρέπεται ἐπὶ τοιόνδε εἶδος) to protect himself from the suspicion that he is not influential with Tissaphernes. Where the initial HP verbs used of Alcibiades had emphasized his powerful but ultimately futile machinations, the final three instances seem to emphasize his increasingly desperate and isolated situation.

12. Meaning "he [or it] arrived," ἀφικνεῖται is the most common HP verb in Thucydides and seems well suited to creating reader anticipation.
13. A *hapax legomenon* in Thucydides, καταλιμπάνουσιν emphasizes both the moment and Alcibiades' cleverness; cf. n. 11.
14. This agreement is summarized as documentary evidence in chapter 18. Like speeches and other quotations, documentary evidence includes no use of the HP.

verbs in the HP. By contrast, when the Chians undertake their campaign to Lesbos, the HP is employed (στρατεύονται, 22.1). With Spartan support on the continent, the Chians bring Methymna to revolt (HP ἀφιστᾶσι, 22.2). Then, leaving four of their thirteen ships to guard Methymna (HP καταλείπονται, 22.2). They then go on to bring over Mytilene (HP ἀφιστᾶσιν, 22.2). The revolts against Athens have now reached their furthest extent.

This section of narrative focuses on revolts and political revolutions. The HP does not mark every political revolution (especially not the events on Samos, but cf. also the revolts of Lebedos and Haerae at 19.4 and the revolt of Eresus at 23.4). The main, doomed Ionian revolts are so marked, however, and cause a remarkable density of the HP. The verb ἀφίστημι, in its active ("to cause to revolt") or middle ("to revolt") forms, is used eleven times in the HP in Thucydides. Eight of those uses are in book 8, and five of those are in the chapters I just reviewed (14.2, 14.3, 17.3, 22.2 *bis*; cf. 62.1, 80.3, 100.3).[15] This is striking, particularly considering how many revolts are described in Thucydides' *History* as a whole and how little the HP has been used to emphasize them. In book 8, the HP marks swiftly undertaken and subsequently defeated revolts: it is possibly important to recall that Thucydides is in fact reminding his readers, who know how things will end, of this series of hopeful beginnings.

As our analysis of the next section of this narrative will show, the reconquest of these cities is not marked with the HP; except for the battle narratives, Thucydides does not seem to use the HP to mark verbs of finished stories and endings of stories. For instance, the story of Teos—captured by Chalcideus, further destroyed by Tissaphernes, and recaptured by Athens—is entirely completed in the chapters I just reviewed (16–20) and includes no verbs in the HP, despite the reversals portrayed. Likewise, as has been mentioned, the account of the successful revolution on Samos in chapter 21 includes no use of the HP, despite its dramatic events and the questions it raises for the coming narrative. By contrast, the HP seems to mark actions—particularly political actions—that stand at the beginning of some kind of process, usually (though not always) a problematic one; note that Thucydides marked Strombichides' arrival on Samos (16.1) with the HP and that the subsequent revolt did succeed.

Before moving on to the final narratives of the summer of 412, one more

---

15. The other uses of ἀφίστημι in the HP in Thucydides are at 1.58.1 (revolt of Potideia), 4.123.1 (revolt of Mende to Spartans), and 5.31.5 (revolt of Elis to Argos).

observation about the use of the HP in chapters 12–22 seems pertinent: in these chapters, HP verbs again mark the events and damage of small naval battles. In chapter 19, for instance, Thucydides relates that a fleet of ten Chian vessels catches sight of (HP καθορθῶσιν, 19.1) a fleet of eleven Athenian ships. One Chian ship flees. The Athenians capture (HP λαμβάνουσι, 19.3) four empty ships, but the five remaining Chian ships escape to Teos (HP καταφεύγουσιν, 19.3). Likewise, during this same time, the Peloponnesians who are blockaded at Speiraeum finally break out, capturing four Athenian ships (HP λαμβάνουσι, 20.1). Given a context in which all of Ionia is in revolt, Thucydides' insistence on spotlighting the regular reversals and damage of small naval battles seems puzzling.[16] One possible consideration is that the HP here points up the inescapable facts of a wearing war of attrition.

The final stories of the summer of 412 begin in chapter 23, which features five uses of the HP, three of which again feature the verb ἀφικνεῖται. The action is typically complicated. The Spartan Astyochus finally arrives at Chios (HP ἀφικνεῖται, 23.1) from Greece, with four ships, not the "many ships" Alcibiades had promised (cf. 14.2). After three days, Astyochus sails to Lesbos. He arrives at Pyrrha (HP ἀφικνεῖται, 23.2) and then, on the next day, at Eresus, where he learns (HP πυνθάνεται, 23.2) what the reader simultaneously learns, namely that Mytilene had fallen to the Athenians on the previous day.[17] He causes Eresus to revolt (no HP), sends (HP παραπέμπει, 23.4) reinforcements and a commander to Antissa and Methymna, and tries to support the revolts himself. But he finds "everything opposed to him" on Lesbos (23.5) and withdraws to Chios, whence he plans to set out for the Hellespont. Afterward, six more ships from Greece arrive (HP ἀφικνοῦνται, 23.6) to strengthen his side. In his absence, the Athenians take back Lesbos and return exiles to Clazomenae, which then also reverts to Athens.

The hopeful verb ἀφικνεῖται thus appears in the HP three times in this chapter. But the Spartans arrive everywhere too late and with forces that are too small to affect events. The HP πυνθάνεται in 23.2, at which point Astyochus and the reader simultaneously learn that the game is essentially already

---

16. Further instances of Thucydides' use of the HP to mark the events of apparently unimportant sea battles occur, for instance, in chapter 34, where three Athenian ships are wrecked while chasing three Chian longboats in a storm. The Athenians from these ships die, are captured, or escape. This event is marked with eight HP verbs in seven lines of text. At 8.39.3, the Spartans capture and burn three empty Athenian ships, an event marked with two verbs in the HP.

17. Cf. Rood 1998: 259.

over, displays this point. By contrast to the HP verbs that mark the Spartans' futile island hopping, no successful Athenian actions portrayed in chapter 23 (e.g., their retaking of Lesbos and Clazomenae) are marked with verbs in the HP. The chapter nicely demonstrates that the HP emphasizes not necessarily "important" events (e.g., the reconquest of these peoples) but, rather, actions that are important to learn from and that readers might have too easily ignored, particularly as they prove futile.

The Athenians do get an HP verb at the beginning of the next chapter, when, mounting an attack on Miletus, they kill (HP ἀποκτείνουσι, 24.1) the Spartan Chalcideus. After this, they attack Chios from many sides, and the Chians lose several battles in a row, suffering heavy losses, until they no longer dare to emerge from their city. The Athenians proceed to waste Chian land, pristine since the Persian Wars, an action not marked by any verbs in the HP but emphasized by a substantial pause in the narrative, since Thucydides here offers a narratorial assessment of the Chian revolt and describes how the city was splitting into pro-Athenian and pro-Spartan factions.

The events of the subsequent battle at Miletus display several HP verbs. The Athenians now send a large expedition of thirty-five hundred infantry and forty-eight ships to Samos and, from there, to Miletus. At Miletus, the Milesians, the Peloponnesians, and Tissaphernes attack the Athenians. In the battle, the Athenians' Argive allies, who have conceived contempt for the Milesians (25.3), fall into disorder and lose (HP νικῶνται, 25.3). Nearly three hundred of their men are killed (HP διαφθείρονται, 25.3). By contrast, the Athenians win and take control of the countryside; they "place their weapons" (HP ὅπλα τίθενται, 25.4), i.e., take an armed rest from fighting, near the city of Miletus itself. A few hours later, however, the arrival of a large Spartan and Sicilian navy (fifty-five ships) is announced (HP ἀγγέλλεται, 26.1). The commanders of this Spartan navy do not know the outcome of the battle but soon learn this (HP πυνθάνονται, 26.3) from Alcibiades, who urges the Spartans and their allies to save Miletus, which they determine to do with the coming dawn (27.1).

The Spartans' decision to fight for Miletus is not marked with the HP, and neither are the passages in which Phrynichus, the Athenian naval commander, refuses to risk Athens' navy in a battle with this newly arrived Spartan force.[18] Thucydides relates that the Athenians left Miletus immediately,

---

18. They do, however, feature a speech in indirect discourse, the first lengthy speech of book 8.

and that the Spartans put in the next morning at the same place from which the Athenians had set out at dawn (HP ἐπικατάγονται, 28.1).

In his dramatic relation of the battle at Miletus, as in other battle narratives, Thucydides employs the HP at successive important reversals or events.[19] The Argives are defeated and suffer losses, the Athenians establish themselves at Miletus, the game-changing news arrives, Alcibiades reveals the course of events to the Spartans, and they arrive the next morning at the Athenians' heels. It is perhaps well to note once again that Thucydides has many devices for establishing emphasis and that I have here isolated one, in order to analyze its functions. Other devices—such as foreshadowing, changes of pace, or the use of striking vocabulary—abound in Thucydides' *History*. Particularly noteworthy is the frequency of narratorial intrusion in these chapters of book 8. Since an occurrence of the HP is essentially a type of narratorial intrusion into the reader's sphere, it should be analyzed in conjunction with them.[20]

The narrative of the summer of 412 concludes with the relation of a Spartan action that needs to be brought into closer relation with further events in book 8 and that I will therefore not attempt to analyze here.[21] So far, my review of these chapters shows that the HP frequently marks the inception of a series of actions that lead to some kind of setback. This was perhaps especially clear with the five uses of the HP to mark revolts against Athens, but it pertained to a large number of other actions as well. Since the narrative as a whole shows the failure of Spartan hopes, the failed actions were usually undertaken by the Spartans and their allies. A corresponding disproportion

---

19. Cf. the similarly dense use of the HP in the action passages of the Athenian-Spartan battle in the Hellespont at 8.102–6.
20. On narrator interventions in book 8 of Thucydides, cf. esp. Gribble 1998: 63ff.; Rood 1998: 344n5.
21. The story transpires in approximately the following way: After failing to meet the Athenian forces at Miletus, the Spartan navy sails south, and Tissaphernes convinces them (HP πείθει, 28.2) to attack Iasus, where Amorges (a bastard son of the Persian satrap Pissouthnes) has rebelled against the king. They capture (HP αἱροῦσιν, 28.2) Iasus and hand over (HP παραδιδόασιν, 28.3) Amorges to Tissaphernes to send to the king. We may wonder whether these uses of the HP—and perhaps the whole story—are included in order to display the fact that the Spartans have now clearly helped Tissaphernes, who will ultimately betray them. Remembering this incident will help the reader to understand their later enmity. Two other forward-looking HP verbs appear in this section: as their last recorded deed of this summer, the Spartans send (HP ἀποστέλλουσι, 28.5) Pedaritus as the infantry commander of their forces and make (HP καθιστᾶσιν, 28.5) Philippus commander at Miletus. Discussing the consequences of these appointments would require analysis of further sections of book 8.

between the HP verbs marking Spartan and Athenian actions occurs: of forty-three HP verbs in this section of the text, all but seven active HP verbs marked actions of the Spartans (including Alcibiades) and their Chian allies.

I also noted that many HP verbs in these chapters marked the events of battle narratives and that these seem to be the only kind of completed story where Thucydides used the HP. Other completed stories were entirely devoid of the HP; moreover, the HP did not mark the completion of event sequences whose beginnings Thucydides had marked with the HP.

The analysis in this essay allows for only tentative conclusions about book 8 as a whole. However, some observations about the preponderance of the HP in this book can be attempted. First, we found that two types of narrative tended to employ the HP in greater frequency: (1) dense narratives of political events featuring frequent reversals and (2) compressed battle narratives. These types of narratives are famously characteristic of book 8, a fact that has been used to support the view that it is less perfect, compositionally, than the other books of the *History*.[22]

In fact, however, Thucydides generally uses the HP with these types of narrative. Book 3, for instance, contains the second greatest density of occurrences of the HP in Thucydides, and there the HP also occurs mainly in political stories with complicated individual reversals and outcomes. (For instance, we find fourteen uses of the HP between 3.2.3 and 3.8.1, where Thucydides is describing the revolt of Lesbos and the swift failure and death of Asopion, son of Phormio, and twenty-three uses of the HP between 3.69.1 and 3.81.1, where Thucydides is describing the revolution at Corcyra.) This observation perhaps offers a basis for considering the abundant use of the HP in book 8 in the context of the larger *History*. The suggestion is that the type of narrative Thucydides thought was appropriate to swiftly changing political and military events is responsible for the frequency of his use of the HP in book 8 and that a decision to use this (well-established) style of narration more frequently may have led to the denser use of the HP analyzed in this essay.[23]

As for the battle narratives, it is interesting to note that the great set battle

---

22. Cf., e.g., Andrewes in Gomme, Andrewes, and Dover 1981: 399–400; Connor 1984: 210–11; Rusten 1989: 4.
23. Gribble (1998: 66) argues that Thucydides' more frequent recourse to narrator interventions in book 8 "is consistent with the general tendency of book 8, which is not to introduce new techniques for structuring the narrative, but to have more frequent recourse to techniques already familiar from the earlier books." Cf. Hornblower 2008: 923.

narratives of book 7 rarely use the HP. For instance, the HP occurs only twice in the first battle of book 7, in which Gylippus takes Plymmerion (7.21–24), and once more in the second battle, in which the Athenians combat the reinforced ships of their Syracusan and Corinthian enemies (7.36–41); it does not occur at all in Thucydides' long depiction of the final battle in the harbor at Syracuse (7.59.2–7.71). By contrast, the narratives of the sporadic encounters between the major battles sometimes use the HP quite extensively. (For instance, the narrative of Athenian maneuvering in Sicily before Gylippus' arrival displays fourteen uses of the HP in eight chapters, between 6.97.2 and 6.104.2; Demosthenes' operations on his way to Sicily show twenty uses of the HP in eight chapters, from (7.25.1 to 7.34.5); and the swiftly concluded skirmishes after Demosthenes' arrival in Sicily display eight HP verbs between 7.50.4 and 7.53.2.) Thus, in books 6 and 7, as well as in book 8, the HP is frequently used to emphasize the actions of compressed battle narratives. The long battle narratives, which contain speeches in direct and indirect discourse and drawn out scenes of action, use different strategies for emphasis.[24] Once again, therefore, Thucydides' use of the HP in the battle narratives of book 8 seems similar to his practices in the rest of the *History*. The difference to the other books is that, like Xenophon in the *Hellenica*, Thucydides has chosen to use short battle narratives, rather than long elaborate depictions such as we find in book 7, to describe the endless fighting in Ionia. Overall, a comparison to the rest of the *History*, in regard to the HP, seems to reflect a choice to use a few types of narration more intensely.

On the whole, in these chapters Thucydides often used the HP to engage the reader in political actions or decisions whose consequences will be instructive. Like a brief flash of light, the use of the HP attracts attention to an initiating moment of some kind. But we noticed that this did not seem to be the case in the battle narratives, where the HP spotlighted events and their consequent damage. Other verbs marked with the HP were more inscrutable, showing Agis' authority or Alcibiades' cleverness, and would require a reading of (at least) all of book 8 to understand fully. However, the HP is often not that hard to construe, if we analyze it in a "readerly" way, proceeding through the narrative as a reader does. Moreover, the significant frequency of narratorial intrusion in these sections of the text helps to guide us; in a way, the HP is just one more such intrusion, a flag or signal from the narrator to wake up.

---

24. Cf. the analyses in de Romilly 2012: ch. 2.

Works Cited

Classen, J., and Steup, J. 1892–1922. *Thukydides*. Berlin: Weidmann.

Connor, W. R. 1984. *Thucydides*. Princeton: Princeton University Press.

Gomme, A. W., Andrewes, A., and Dover, K. J. 1981. *A Historical Commentary on Thucydides*. Vol. V. Oxford: Oxford University Press.

Gribble, D. 1998. "Narrator Interventions in Thucydides." *JHS* 118: 41–67.

Hornblower, S. 2008. *A Commentary on Thucydides*. Vol. 3. Oxford: Oxford University Press.

Lallot, J. 2011. "Vue Cavalière sur les emplois du présent historique dans les *Histoires* de Thucydide." In Lallot et al., 19–36.

Lallot, J., Rijksbaron, A., Jacquinod, B., and Buijs, M., eds. 2011. *The Historical Present in Thucydides*. Leiden: Brill. Also published in French as *Le présent historique chez Thucydide*.

Rijksbaron, A. 2011. "Introduction." In Lallot et al., 1–18.

Romilly, J. 2012. *The Mind of Thucydides*. Trans. E. T. Rawlings. Ithaca: Cornell University Press.

Rood, T. 1998. *Thucydides: Narrative and Explanation*. Oxford: Oxford University Press.

Rusten, J. 1989. *Thucydides, The Peloponnesian War, Book II*. Cambridge: Cambridge University Press.

Svensson, Arvid. 1930. *Zum Gebrauch der erzählenden Tempora im Griechischen*. Lund: H. Ohlssohn.

CHAPTER 4

Herodotus and Thucydides on Not Learning from Mistakes

Hans-Peter Stahl

Herodotus, the so-called "father of history," populates his work with fabulous stories, oracular predictions, acts of divine retribution, and minuscule happenings, whereas the "founder of scientific historiography" (as Thucydides has been called) bans all transcendental influence and, in a severe restriction to the warranted factual, foregoes the flourishes of meandering tales.

Though on the surface incompatible, the two approaches do not preclude some basic affinity of outlook.[1] Where Herodotus sees a constantly turning "wheel of human affairs" (1.207.2), with its inherent ups and downs, Thucydides offers insight not only into past events but also toward a recurring future that will, "according to the human condition,"[2] turn out to be "such and similar" (1.22.4). And as Herodotus describes cities both large and small alike because of their changing fates over time (1.5.3–4), Thucydides also reports—most densely, perhaps, when summarizing the early history of Greece—of communities overturned in reversals of fortune. So the instability of human affairs can safely be stated to be a constant denominator in both authors.

My topic in this essay is the irrational and incorrigible optimism that human participants in such processes display at bifurcation points. I shall start

---

1. On areas of affinity between the two authors, see Stahl 2012, esp. 150–51.
2. What Thucydides refers to as τὸ ἀνθρώπινον comprises both human nature and "the external circumstances affecting human existence" (Stahl 2003: 29).

out by comparing King Croesus' increasingly confident and warlike behavior (beginning with his dismissal of wise Solon's arguments) with the Athenians' decision after their Pylos victory in 425 BCE to reject Sparta's peace offer in favor of continued military action. In either instance, the authors make it clear that ensuing responses to events issue from a state of mind that negates earlier experience.

I

When Solon arrives at the Lydian court in Sardis, King Croesus is at the height of his power, having conquered most of Asia Minor west of the Halys River. However, Herodotus has informed his reader beforehand of a neglected Delphic prophecy (1.13.2) according to which revenge will fall on Croesus for an ancestor's act of usurpation. Although he has therefore reported that the end of Croesus' career is predetermined by destiny, the conversation of Solon and the king moves mostly along empirical lines.

Upon having had his treasures shown to Solon, Croesus, appealing to Solon's wisdom and his far-reaching travels, asks his guest whom he, based on his wealth of information, considers the happiest (most fortunate) man? Solon (arguing like a second Herodotus) disappoints his host first by "sincerely" naming an Athenian blessed with healthy and noble offspring, a comfortable standard of living, and a glorious death on the field of honor. Without thinking of applying the answer to his own family circumstance, Croesus pushes for the second place, only to be acquainted with two young men of satisfactory means and great physical strength, athletic prizewinners who themselves go under the yoke and pull the chariot when their mother has to travel to the neighboring Hera festival but the oxen have not come in time. When the joyful mother asks the goddess to grant her sons what is best for man, the two fall asleep in the shrine and do not wake again. Solon calls this "the best end of life" (31.3) and a divine sign that it is better for man to be dead than to live.

Croesus, still without insight, and indignant about being ranked behind common people in terms of happiness, now must listen to a lecture of general impact and scope: "You ask me about *human affairs*, me who is one who *knows* that the divine is all jealous and causing trouble" (32.1). Solon here echoes his creator, who at the outset presented himself as "*knowing* that human good fortune [εὐδαιμονίη at 1.5.4, the same word Croesus claims for his own status at 32.1] nowhere remains stable."

Solon then proceeds, in terms of statistical probability rather than theology, to explain that on every single day of a seventy-year life (he arrives at over twenty-six thousand days), something new may happen, and in particular many things "that one would rather not see or experience." "So, oh Croesus," he concludes, "man is totally (mis-) chance" [συμφορή]" (32.2–4). Once one brackets the background transcendence, what one finds here is surprisingly close to Thucydidean chance, τύχη, and its ability of striking unexpectedly at any time. And like men in Thucydides' world, so the Herodotean Croesus is not (yet) ready to learn from his wise guest and to open his eyes to the consequences of what has been presented to him. Accordingly, he will have to go through what he "would rather not see or experience."

Solon continues by saying that wealth (as well as a powerful kingdom) does not make a man happier than his counterpart of moderate means can be, unless luck (or τύχη, "chance," 32.5) attends him so that he keeps all his goods and ends his life well. It is significant that the continued good life— and not its opposite—is connected to chance (in this case, luck): often, after granting men a glimpse of happiness, "god destroys them, root and branch" (32.9). King Croesus, unenlightened and not amused, sovereignly decides against accepting his guest's lesson and even thinks him thoroughly stupid (ἀμαθέα, "not learned," 33) for exhorting him "to look at the end of everything while regarding lightly the goods that are present" (33). Croesus is about to experience a terrible retribution for deeming himself the "happiest of all men" (34.1); namely, he has to experience the death of his elder son, a youth far distinguished among his contemporaries.[3] Quite in character, Croesus—vainly, of course—has first tried to fend off the misfortune by manipulating the dream oracle about this son's impending death (34–45). But now he realizes that a god—the same god who sent the dream—is the cause of his loss (45.2). So has Croesus learned a lesson?

After two years of inactivity (κατῆστο, 46.1), spent in deep mourning (ἐν πένθεϊ μεγάλη), Croesus is stirred to military action when Cyrus, king of Persia, conquers the Medes, ruled by Croesus' brother-in-law Astyages (46.1).

---

3. He could easily have measured his condition by taking Solon's example of parents with healthy offspring as an eye-opener, having himself a son who was "disabled" (διεφθαρμένον, 38.2) by being mute and dumb. After all, in Greek, "root and branch" (32.9) includes your offspring (cf. Soph. *El.* 764–765).

Intending to check Cyrus' power, Croesus first tests a number of oracles for their reliability and bestows massive amounts of gold and silver on the winner, that is, Delphi (and also Theban Amphiaraus). The self-assured spirit of manipulating (or, better, bribing) the oracle is the same he displayed when trying to circumvent the dream about his son's impending misfortune. The result is Delphi's (and Amphiaraus') well-known answer that if Croesus attacked Persia, he would destroy a great empire (53.3) — which, of course, will turn out to be his own realm.

Two more causes for concern pronounced in vain to Croesus I mention in passing only: Delphi's warning of the mule on the Persian throne (55) — which complements the neglected oracle (13.2) about doom coming in Croesus' generation — and wise Sandanis' reminder that nothing will be gained from a victory over poverty-stricken Persia (71.2–4).

Herodotus' final summary of Croesus' motives for war is of interest here because of the reversed priorities: revenge for his brother-in-law now comes last. First is desire for expansion or "greed for land" (γῆς ἱμέρῳ), and second is "highest trust in the oracle" (73.1). Overall, then, his decision flows from an irrational drive and a wish-directed (mis-) interpretation of the oracle — an understanding that self-assuredly believes in the manageability of potential obstacles. Croesus did not learn from the mistake he made earlier, when he believed he could cheat the dream about his son's doom but (45.2) had to acknowledge afterward that "the god" of the dream was the cause of his son's death.

Only one more facet of Herodotus' Croesus figure must be singled out here: defeated and put on a pyre by Cyrus, Croesus invokes the name of Solon three times (86.3); he even repeats Solon's (empirical) argument and acknowledges Solon's pronouncement ("spoken under divine influence") that "no one alive is happy." Further, he wishes that every ruler could have a conversation with Solon (86.4). Recounting his own encounter with wise Solon in detail, Croesus not only stresses "that for himself all things turned out precisely as that one had said" but also that Solon spoke "with regard to all mankind and especially those who seem to themselves to be happy" (86.5). In Croesus' judgment, Solon has moved from foolish (33) to wise, and Croesus, seemingly "having learned his lesson," now appears to endorse his literary creator's tenet of the instability of human affairs.

Starting after Croesus' two-year despondency over the death of his favorite son, the reader (or hearer) has by now, for the second time, been led around full circle, from Croesus' initial self-reliance despite select examples and obstacles pointed out to him, followed by overblown greed and unreasonable hope for wish fulfillment, to Croesus' second irremediable loss and insightful acceptance of the position initially rejected. Learning appears to be a painful process.

However, when asked by Cyrus "who induced him to become his enemy"? Croesus—while admitting that the man is foolish (ἀνόητος) who chooses war over peace—transfers the responsibility for his decision away from himself to "the god of the Greeks," that is, Apollo in Delphi (87.3). Clearly, Croesus still has more to learn:[4] it will take another pronouncement from Delphi for Croesus to acknowledge "that the mistake was his own and not the god's" (91.6).

II

As a comparable development in the work of Thucydides, I single out the Athenians' conduct after their victory at Pylos in 425 BCE. The facts, briefly stated, are as follows: Demosthenes, a former general, receives special permission for operations around the Peloponnesus (4.2.4). His plan[5] is to fortify the uninhabited headland of Pylos on the west coast of the Peloponnesus, with the intent of settling Messenians there so that they may continuously harass the Spartan countryside. Though his goal is, in the end, successfully realized (41.2), there are unexpected developments along the way. Not only do these developments threaten to overthrow his plans—chance (τύχη) and human whim repeatedly interfere—but on the other hand they also exceed the terms of the original plan to such an extent that they lead to a Spartan peace offer that, if accepted, would end the Peloponnesian War.

The initial stumbling block for Demosthenes is that the Spartans take his occupation of Pylos so seriously that they send ships and land troops to the area. In preparation for attacking the Athenians, a group of more than four hundred Spartiates occupy the island (i.e., Sphacteria) in front of the only

---

4.   For details on the whole Croesus story, see Stahl 1975; Stahl 2012: 147 with n. 23. For Croesus' "learning," see also n. 5 below.

5.   Demosthenes, it is true, has learned from his catastrophic earlier campaign and now seeks to apply the lesson learned, but he will be overruled by unforeseen developments. See Stahl 2003: ch. 7; Roisman 1993: passim. On Thucydides' view of the operations around Pylos, see Stahl, loc. cit.

natural harbor. However, events turn in Demosthenes' favor when the Athenian fleet manages to cut the island off from the forces on the mainland and to neutralize the Spartan fleet. Sparta, worried about the elite troops who are now trapped on the island, sends ambassadors to Athens to sue for peace. Their speech (4.17–20) contains elements that are well comparable to Solon's arguments before Croesus.

Having no trump card in their hands, the ambassadors drive home the point that the Athenians' situation is not as rosy as they may think. They even assign the Athenian success a negative tinge by saying, "It is possible for you to settle your present good luck well" (17.4), giving their εὐτυχία a transient quality similar to that Solon had assigned to Croesus' εὐδαιμονίη.

And like Solon's reference to the constant threat of some calamity happening on every day over a lifetime, the Spartans, too, appeal to the experience (cf. δι' ἐμπειρίαν) of reversals for better and worse shared by themselves and the Athenians, experience that ought to lead the Athenians to a solid distrust of success (17.5). The Spartans' specific paradigm for their general point is their own present calamity (18.1), which they call ξυμφοραί (18.1), using the same word that Solon used to characterize man's condition in general.

The Spartan ambassadors point out that their own unexpected misfortune has resulted not from lack of power or arrogance motivated by a sudden increase in power (the Athenians' present situation) but from misjudging what is always latently present (ἀπὸ δὲ τῶν αἰεὶ ὑπαρχόντων γνώμη σφαλέντες, 18.2). They argue that the Athenians should not expect, because of the present strength of their city, that the factor of chance, τύχη, will also always be on their side. This sounds like an echo of Solon's warning that the continuation of the good life depends on chance, τύχη.

Sound-minded men, the ambassadors say, safely place success (or "the good things") in the realm of uncertainty and do not believe that war makes itself available to them as they wish to take hold of it but as *chances* (τύχαι) lead them (18.4). So, they argue, Athens should preserve its reputation for strength and intelligence by concluding a peace treaty and in this way avoid the possibility that, in case of a later reversal, the city-state's present success will also be ascribed to chance, τύχη (18.5).

So far the ambassadors' analysis of the mindset the Athenian victory calls for. They enhance their explanation by cautioning the Athenians that, so far, nothing irremediable (ἀνήκεστον, 20.1) has happened. They emphasize that matters "are still undecided" (ἔτι δ' ὄντων ἀκρίτων) at present and that the choice of peace over war lies before them ("let us choose peace instead of war!" 20.2)—a choice whose importance, one recalls, Croesus understood only after losing his war against Cyrus: at that point, he still ascribed the mistake of his decision to the god of Delphi.

III

Having outlined for the Athenians of 425 BCE a choice in terms not dissimilar to the ones with which Herodotus confronted his Croesus before his attack on Persia, Thucydides, like his predecessor in this also, has raised the reader's interest in their decision. For a reader acquainted with both texts, the question that arises at this point is whether the younger historian can report a different type of human behavior. Thucydides answers: the Athenians "believing that, as long as [or since] they were holding the men on the island, the peace treaty would now be available to them *whenever* they wished to conclude it with them [sc. the Spartans], were reaching out for more" (21.2).

Were they right in their belief that they were "holding" (ἔχοντες) the men on the island? Or is the status of the men like the transient status of the treasures on which Croesus based his happiness? Obviously, the Athenians are unwilling to open their eyes to the Spartan arguments, and the appeal that they may risk their reputation for strength and intelligence is in vain. Thucydides would hardly have described Athens' incomprehension by laying out the details of the alternative route they do not follow if he did not, again similar to Herodotus, view such unenlightened behavior as a significant factor in the workings of history.

But they wanted more. Under the leadership of Cleon, demagogue par excellence, Athens not only demands surrender of the Spartiates but also adds a number of territorial demands—a point against which the Spartan ambassadors had expressly warned, advising that they should not act like people who, being unused to it, receive some good: "For they always *want more* in their hope, because of being unexpectedly lucky also in what they have" (17.4). (As an aside, let the irony be stated that Cleon's behavior indirectly confirms the very insight he pronounced earlier [3.39.4]: unexpected success leads states to insolence, and humans more easily shake off a failure than preserve a situation of good fortune.)

Soon the presumed Athenian pawn proves illusory. The blockade of the island of Sphacteria is not completely enforceable, and the Athenian fleet is worn down by extended siege operations that offer no prospect of compelling the Spartiates to capitulate. The long duration of the siege, taking place against the Athenians' original calculation (παρὰ λόγον, 26.4), causes despondency among the troops (26.4)—and at home. When, in addition, the Spartans no longer kept asking for negotiations, "they felt regret that they had not accepted the peace treaty" (27.2). If one looks for a comparable point in Croesus' psychological development, one probably would have to think of the two years of insightful (1.45.2) mourning (46.1) into which the paralyzing experience of his son's death had cast him.

But as Croesus is wakened from his dormancy to new activity by the expectation of successfully checking Persian expansion, so the Athenians, through Cleon's (and Demosthenes') unexpected coup of bringing home almost three hundred Spartiates from the island as prisoners, experience an invigorating renewal of the good fortune they originally believed to reap when "holding the men on the island." Will they decide more wisely this time when the Spartans once more come seeking to negotiate a return of Pylos and of the prisoners? Thucydides reports that "*they wanted more* and sent them away without achieving their objective, though they came many times" (4.41.4). Apparently, the Athenians have not learned from their earlier mistake.

One remembers that Croesus' first priority at the point when he attacked Cyrus had been desire for expansion ("greed for land"). So, too, the Athenians' renewed "desire for more" manifests itself in a number of successful campaigns, mostly around the Peloponnesus. Their exuberance about these successes even leads them to punish the generals who had agreed to the peace accord at Gela, for accepting bribes and not bringing affairs in Sicily under control (65.3)! And as Herodotus had detailed Croesus' unheeding second confidence, because of which he again tried to manipulate a divine voice, this time that of the Delphic oracle, so Thucydides describes the Athenians' post-Pylos delusion "that nothing would place itself in their way," ascribing it "to their unexpected success in the majority of their undertakings" (65.4)—a direct reference to the reminder pronounced by the Spartan envoys at Athens to settle their present good luck well and their warning not to act like people who, unaccustomed to good luck, "in their hope always desire more"(17.4; ἐλπίδι is reflected in 65.4 by ἰσχὺν τῆς ἐλπίδος). We note that Herodotus placed his notice of Croesus' decision to dismiss Solon's wise arguments immediately after the list of Croesus' successful conquests (1.28).

As Croesus must once more, in defeat, face the consequences of having been overconfident, so the Athenians again, after major defeats at Delium and Amphipolis, find themselves in the same depressed mood as before: "holding no longer the firm trust in their strength, because of which they earlier kept rejecting the peace treaty in the belief, caused by their good luck at that time, that they would {continue to} prevail" (5.14.1); they now "felt regret because, after the events at Pylos, they had not concluded the treaty, though the opportunity had certainly offered itself"(14.2). In terms of the Herodotean Croesus-on-the-pyre, one feels tempted to call this the Athenians' "Oh, Solon!" moment. Thucydides' report is perhaps even more poignant than that of Herodotus, because he uses exactly the same word to characterize the Athenians' despondency on both occasions: "They felt regret" (μετεμέλοντο, 4.27.2 = 5.14.2). Athens, too, has not learned from its earlier experience.

For my enterprise of explicating human resistance to learning from mistakes as perceived by the two historians, it is a welcome confirmation to see that, notwithstanding the historically different situations of Croesus and Athens, both authors can observe and describe humans going through the same self-destructive double sequence of decision making in unheeding confidence followed by despondency, where, in either sequence, the second instance of despondency results from not having taken to heart the lesson offered by the first cycle of pride, error, and regret.

IV

The outcome of the foregoing comparison supplies an indication of important anthropological parallels in Herodotus and Thucydides. However, since historical processes do not regularly tend to evolve in precise repetitions, it would be expecting too much if one searched for more instances of closely parallel sequences of unenlightened, elated decisions each followed by regretful (pseudo) "learning." Already in Croesus' case, there is an overshooting development. Claiming to have learned, from his own calamity (τὰ δὲ μοι παθήματα ἐόντα ἀχάριτα μαθήματα γέγονε, 1.207.1), a lesson about "the wheel of human affairs" (κύκλος τῶν ἀνθρωπηίων ἐστὶ πρηγμάτων, 207.2), Croesus magisterially instructs (μάθε) his conqueror and new advisee, King Cyrus of Persia, to disregard the unanimous advice of his chiefs and to do battle with the Massagetae beyond the river Araxes. Accepting this recommendation (and a substratagem likewise devised by Croesus), Cyrus is defeated and killed. Croesus' claim to have learned from his experience (the outcome is his—by now—third experience of a devastating blow) has, after his Solonic "conversion" on the pyre, for the second time yielded to renewed confidence and unenlightened self-certainty, again resulting in a decision with a calamitous outcome.[6]

There is, as indicated above, no direct parallel in Thucydides for this scene in which a person believes he has learned from his experience but then repeats his mistake. But there is a comparable instance, in which the Athenians again err, at a time after they have recovered from the pessimism that led them to conclude the peace of 422/1 BCE. As Croesus rejects the advice of Cyrus' chiefs, so the assembly at Athens, when deciding on the Sicilian expedition, dismisses the serious concerns outlined by the general Nicias, who, in his earlier speech, had enjoined them "to preserve what is in your hands . . . and not to risk what you have for what is *invisible* and future" (τά τε ὑπάρχοντα σῴζειν . . . καὶ μὴ τοῖς ἑτοίμοις περὶ τῶν ἀφανῶν καὶ

---

6. I should deal with an alleged problem in my interpretation of 1.207 (as outlined in Stahl 1975). Shapiro (1994) raises a serious (if valid) objection against this interpretation: "If Stahl's examples are examined closely" (349f.), it will turn out that wisdom, "once gained," is "very difficult to lose" (355) or "is not forgotten" (354). About Croesus', the alleged learner's, advice to Cyrus, Shapiro asserts, "Since he [sc. Croesus] tries to minimize any possible losses that might ensue from a defeat, it seems that Croesus gives Cyrus good advice, consistent with *Solonian wisdom*" (351; my italics). I here offer two points in response:

   (1) It is questionable that one may cite Herodotus' warner sage Solon as an advocate for downplaying the risk inherent in crossing the Araxes in order to invade another country: Herodotus' other *paradeigmata* of the Halys, Danube, and Hellespont ("the river motif"; see Immerwahr 1966: 293 with n. 162) portray such an act, in itself, as hubris that carries severe consequences.

   (2) While quoting 1.207.1 (where Croesus claims to have learned from his suffering), Shapiro skips 1.207.2–3., where Croesus claims knowledge (which Cyrus is to "learn," μάθε) about the "wheel of human affairs" that "does not let the same men always be fortunate" (translation from Stahl 1975: 24). Based thereon (cf. ἤδη ὦν, "consequently," 207.3; Stahl 1975: 24), Croesus presumptuously proceeds to give his pernicious ("wise"?) advice, against the opinion of all of Cyrus' chiefs, on how to deal with the affair at hand (τοῦ προκειμένου πρήγματος is an individualizing instance of τῶν ἀνθρωπηίων . . . πρηγμάτων). Herodotus' literary focus is on Croesus' baneful role in the downfall of Cyrus, the successful conqueror who also will not "always be fortunate" but is about to experience his eventual defeat and death (see Stahl 1975: 21–22). The erroneous character of Croesus' well-meaning advice is confirmed by a "detail" in book 3, where Croesus is blamed by Cambyses for having given pernicious advice to his father, Cyrus (Stahl 1975: 25; see also Stahl 2012: 147n23).

μελλόντων κινδυνεύειν, 6.9.3). Yet they, even more eager after Nicias' second speech than before (πολὺ δὲ μᾶλλον ὥρμηντο), transform his concerns into an argument favoring the enterprise: "for it seemed he had given good advice and now there would be safety even in abundance" (6.24.2). In rejecting Nicias' fact-based warnings and accepting Alcibiades' bogus projections, the Athenians do—and herein lies the irony—repeat the miscalculation of the doomed Melians, who set hope over facts despite having been warned by their Athenian attackers as follows: "you judge the future to be clearer than what lies before your eyes, and what is *invisible* you by wishful thinking envisage as already taking place" (τὰ μὲν μέλλοντα τῶν ὁρωμένων σαφέστερα κρίνετε, τὰ δὲ ἀφανῆ τῷ βούλεσθαι ὡς γιγνόμενα ἤδη θεᾶσθε, 5.113). The recurring key terms ("future," "invisible") show that the assembled Athenians themselves have not internalized the lesson that their own negotiators in vain tried to impress on the doomed Melians;[7] that is, the Athenians repeat the fateful mistake[8] committed by their empire's most recent victims—after all, the massacre of Melos had happened only a few months ago at most, "in the same winter" (6.1.1). So again there is regret (about having undertaken the Sicilian campaign: τῆς στρατείας ὁ μετάμελος, 7.55.1; cf. κατάμεμψις σφῶν αὐτῶν, 75.4; see also the panicky reaction in Athens 8.1), which will play its part here as it did in the Pylos development.

Wish-dictated suspension of rational reasoning is seen to be a resilient historical phenomenon in both Thucydides and Herodotus, as is experience-defying self-confidence that rises up again after (most often, self-inflicted) calamity, leaving far behind earlier remorse and lessons soon again unlearned.

This essay is for my friend and colleague Donald Lateiner, whose work testifies to the power of emotion.

---

7.   In view of the interrelatedness ("Fernbeziehungen"; see Rengakos 1996) of many Thucydidean speeches, the naive view that the Athenians could not have heard the arguments their generals had presented to the Melian councilors is not valid in a case of comparable contexts. So the statement made in the text above about the Athenians not having taken to heart the lesson of Melos is valid even if they have not expressly claimed (as Croesus does) to have learned from mistakes (here mistakes of a people they just recently brought under their sway).

8.   Under the conditions outlined in 6.1–24, the Sicilian undertaking originates from a blind, rationality-defying decision. That, nevertheless, there later were points in the war where the tide might have turned in favor of the Athenian expeditionary forces is one of Thucydides' insights into the unpredictability of history. If one were to maintain that the catastrophic outcome of the expedition was unavoidable and clear from the beginning, one would overlook the emphasis on game-changing details in the historian's narrative of events. See Stahl 2003: 200.

Works Cited

Grethlein, J. 2009. "How Not to Do History: Xerxes in Herodotus' *Histories*." *AJPh* 130: 195–218.

Immerwahr, H. R. 1966. *Form and Thought in Herodotus*. Cleveland: Press of Western Reserve University.

Lateiner, D. 1989. *The Historical Method of Herodotus*. Phoenix Supplementary Volumes 23. Toronto: University of Toronto Press.

Pelling, C. B. R. 2006. "Educating Croesus: Talking and Learning in Herodotus' Lydian *Logos*." *ClAnt* 25: 141–77.

Rengakos, A. 1996. "Fernbeziehungen zwischen den Thukydideischen Reden." *Hermes* 124: 396–417.

Roisman, J. 1993. *The General Demosthenes and His Use of Military Surprise*. Historia Einzelschriften 78. Stuttgart: Franz Steiner Verlag.

Shapiro, S. O. 1994. "Learning through Suffering: Human Wisdom in Herodotus." *CJ* 89: 349–55.

Stahl, H. P. 1975. "Learning through Suffering? Croesus' Conversations in the History of Herodotus." *YClSt* 24: 1–36.

Stahl, H. P. 2003. *Thucydides: Man's Place in History*. 2nd. ed. Swansea: Classical Press of Wales.

Stahl, H. P. 2012. "Herodotus and Thucydides on Blind Decisions Preceding Military Action." In E. Foster and D. Lateiner, eds., *Thucydides and Herodotus*, 125–53. Oxford: Oxford University Press.

CHAPTER 5

Speaking Silences in Herodotus and Sophocles

Carolyn Dewald and Rachel Kitzinger

Donald Lateiner's *The Historical Method of Herodotus*, published in 1989, was a groundbreaking work. It was one of a handful of books on Herodotus, mostly written in the late 1980s, that explored the degree of Herodotus' explicit authorial control over his vast and vastly heterogeneous narrative material.[1] *Historical Method* in particular put to rest conclusively the notion that in Herodotus, the "father of history," we had an amiable storyteller who did not quite know what he had invented, or a strolling flaneur, making up material to entertain his audiences. To use Lateiner's own words, Herodotus wrote his long text in all thoughtful seriousness, in the service of "the creation of a secular meaning for mankind's immediate past."[2] He did so by collecting and writing down *logoi*, stories and data culled from his many human sources.

In this essay, we record several ways in which we have learned from Don Lateiner (henceforth DL), both in his fundamental work on Herodotus and in his equally pioneering work on nonverbal communication as a part of ancient literature. Here we argue two ideas, both, in effect, responses to DL's combined work on Herodotus and on nonverbal proxemics. First, we extend the idea of Herodotus' authorial control over his human sources to include a brief exploration of the way that actors within Herodotus' narrative themselves extend a comparable control over others by acting with nonverbal ef-

---

1. These include Boedeker 1987, Darbo-Peschanski 1987, Gould 1989, Hartog 1980, Hunter 1982, Lang 1984, and Waters 1985. Influential pioneering works that should be recognized as anticipating this move are Immerwahr 1966, Fornara 1971, and, of course, Jacoby 1913.
2. Lateiner 1989: 56.

fect, either trying to inflict silence or quiet on one another or imposing it on themselves. On a level within the text that can act almost as a mise-en-scène, this set of social moves shows that one of Herodotus' most pervasive beliefs concerns the social and political power of speech: the way that the choice of speaking or silence is often highly fraught, filled with consequences for the speaker and for others. The significance of Herodotus' own role as the careful gatekeeper of his *logoi*, developed by DL, is enhanced when we see the politics of enjoined silences—how and when silence is explicitly enacted by or imposed on people within the text. Thus the choice of what to report and what to repress, a role Herodotus considers important for the historian, is associated within the text to the acquisition and loss of power on the political stage. The parallel invites the reader to be aware of the control that Herodotus exerts over *logoi* as an exercise of power with which the reader may either collude or argue.

We go on then to a second theme, one that acts in darker counterpoint to the first one. Taking off from DL's work on Penelope's silence in the *Odyssey*,[3] we look at silence as a kind of darkened glass through which we can dimly picture things that shape human lives yet have no presence in the language of public discourse. We explore several instances within Attic drama where Sophocles, Herodotus' coeval, presents women who keep silent at a crucial moment in the action, although they are clearly present on stage. In these cases, beyond immense human sorrow, the silence makes us aware of the presence of something that needs to be communicated but is literally unspeakable, at least in the context of public discourse, the medium of tragedy.

Both Sophocles and Herodotus are intensely attentive to the social and political functions of speech. Some aspects of human existence, however, can only be signaled by an absence of language and therefore challenge not only the adequacy of the political and social world to define what it is to be human but also the capacity of the author to make these aspects explicitly a part of the story he is telling. In Sophocles' dramas, a character's silence can make the audience aware of something that must be understood but that cannot be spoken. Sometimes, critics who discuss silence, in a particular passage or in general, assume that it must always be associated with secrecy, deception, or the expression of emotion.[4] In exploring these quite different examples in

---

3. Lateiner 1995: 258, 276.
4. This assumption is expressed, for example, by Nicole Loraux (1987: 21), when she says of the silences of Deianeira, Jocasta, and Eurydice before their suicides, "These silences,

Herodotus and Sophocles, however, we hope to demonstrate that silence is a rich but not self-explanatory category of human communication.

Given the differences between Herodotus' and Sophocles' use of silence that emerge in the first two parts of this essay, we go on to explore whether these two masters of language (who are, by repute, close friends) share the view that silence can be the only way to "talk about" certain aspects of the human condition, so that, rather than suppressing language, silence is a substitute for it. Since the words of Herodotus' text are not enacted, like the words spoken onstage, the presence of this kind of silence is harder to detect in Herodotus than it is in Sophocles. As DL himself says, when something as subtle as the absence of an expected move (or expected words) occurs, it is hard to see and harder still to consider as data in an academic argument, in which evidence in theory should be citable and even quantifiable.[5] But silences that are not an aspect of control and power in the *Histories*, though rare, are important. The comparison with Sophocles suggests that sometimes the silence that falls around a character in Herodotus is not just about grief (or any other strong emotion experienced by the protagonist) or about strategic calculations in the trade of power. It points rather to a larger silence that lies under and about the doings and sayings of human beings in their ordinary lives. Through this silence, Herodotus "speaks" directly to his readers and requires us to consider what meanings it might convey, just as the silence of Sophocles' characters baffles the stage audience but allows the poet to draw the theater audience's attention—and perhaps its understanding—to what is not being or cannot be said. At such moments, both writers self-consciously mark the limits of language itself for conveying what matters on the political and public stage.

I

In part 2 of *Historical Method*, DL describes how carefully Herodotus manages the rhetoric surrounding his presentation of material, mostly called *logoi*, that his informants have conveyed to him. He does so, DL argues, as part of his

---

which are heard as expressions of anguish, precede an action that the woman wants to hide from view."

5. Lateiner 1989: 246n6: "the topic of omissions does not allow convenient limits or strictly verifiable instances."

interest in exploring issues of truth, reliability, and accuracy. By collecting Herodotus' explicit discussions of intentional omissions, controversies among his informants, doubts about the veracity of oral information he has received, and disagreements with written sources, DL makes clear how carefully Herodotus has established himself as a gatekeeper for his many informants, determining when and precisely how he allows them to speak. Herodotus' rhetoric of control is necessary because "the *logos* itself is part of *ta genomena*."[6] Especially concerning issues of geography, quantified data, and partisanship in his informants or uncertainty over their motives, as well as when the information conveyed seems unbelievable, involves religion, or is insignificant, Herodotus has even learned (perhaps from the Egyptians?) the art of *damnatio memoriae*—how to consign an act to oblivion by explicitly passing it over in silence.[7]

The world within Herodotus' text shows the same issues of power and control operating particularly clearly when people either are told to be still or enforce stillness and silence on themselves.[8] The simplest scenes to think about represent people in power who impose silence on others: Cleisthenes the tyrant calls for silence so that he can make a pronouncement to his daughters' suitors (6.130.1); Demaratus commands silence from the Athenian Dicaeus when they see the inexplicable chain of dust from Eleusis (8.65); more generally, Xerxes' herald tells the Argives to sit down quietly (ἡσυχίην ἔχοντας κατῆσθαι, 7.150.2)—a predictable political request rather than purely a matter of nonspeech. Characters in Herodotus who are enjoined to silence, either explicitly or tacitly, anticipate that move and either acquiesce or refuse it: after his captivity, Croesus deferentially asks Cyrus if he wants him to keep quiet (1.88.2); Demaratus tells Xerxes in the run-up to Thermopylae that he will hold his peace and not continue advice giving, if that is what Xerxes desires (7.104.5). Both on the Persian side and on the Greek one, the expectation of obsequious silence can be thwarted: Artabanus breaks the courtiers' silence after Mardonius' speech advocating invasion of Greece,

---

6. Lateiner 1989: 62. More broadly, "the very composition of the *Histories* attests to a limited confidence in the reliability and durability of ordinary testimony, as well as elicited oral accounts and even written ones" (99).
7. Lateiner 1989: 69. For Herodotus' suppression of women's names, see Larson 2006.
8. Montiglio (2000: 154–157) places Herodotus' representations of group silence in a larger Athenian oratorical context: "The image of an orderly and silent listening in practice seems to be at odds with the egalitarian representation of an assembly in which every citizen is virtually called to speak his mind" (157).

with some necessary prudential calculations that he can get away with because he is Xerxes' uncle (7.10.2); his son, Trinantaechmes, carries on the family tradition by blurting out to his cousin, again the now higher-ranking Mardonius, that the Greeks are awesome to make the prize of victory in the Olympic games a mere garland, rather than money (8.26.3). Even more tellingly, in terms of Greek politics, when Adeimantus the Corinthian tries to establish dominance and enforce silence on Themistocles the Athenian, because the Athenians have now become stateless after Xerxes' burning of the city, Themistocles refuses the imposition of silence, which is also an attempt at controlling him. He first lashes out, but then verbally seizes control of the whole situation. Themistocles' defiant and impassioned speech is what persuades the Spartan commander to fight the decisive sea battle off Salamis (8.61.1).

Almost as politically revealing are the places where an individual resists saying something because he or she feels it will bring on trouble. It is not always possible to be completely sure here that one has read the ancient setting correctly, but both the fragile self-control of the angry overlord and the submissive silence of the underling who has internalized the master's commands are surely present on a number of occasions. Socles the Corinthian is the only one who dares to countermand the obsequious (and, it turns out, dismayed) silence that descends when the Peloponnesians hear the Spartan demand that Athens have its tyrant restored (5.92.1, 93.2); Cleisthenes the tyrant, in the episode mentioned above, keeps quiet himself for a while, not wanting to rebuke the increasingly inebriated and enthusiastic Hippocleides (6.129.4); the Peloponnesians who hear that Eurybiades has decided to fight at Salamis think he is crazy but mutter their thoughts to themselves privately (σιγῇ), until their discontent finally bursts out (8.74.2). The Athenians angrily tell Gelon that they had been willing to keep quiet until he threatened their command of the Greek navy (7.161.2); the assembled Persian and Greek commanders are silent when Mardonius asks them to speak up about negative Greek oracles (9.42.1, 2).[9] In these cases, the eventual breaking of the silence both reveals the difficulty of sustaining it and leads to consequences that are

---

9.   Two instances where a courtier's compliant answer to an intolerable abuse of power by his overlord come to almost the same thing occur in 1.119.7, where Harpagus, gathering up the pieces of his son's cannibalized body, replies that the king can do no wrong, and 3.35.4, where a fearful Prexaspes, whose son, the royal cupbearer, has just been shot by Cambyses, congratulates the king on the accuracy of his aim.

often the point of the narrative but that would not be evident without the initial silence.

These two kinds of silence, both the enjoined and the self-enforced, acknowledge the constructive aspects of silence as a part of political communities. But there is another kind of silence that Herodotus tells us people keep or choose not to keep in the *Histories*, one that is more toxic, since silence implies or expressly signifies deliberate and hostile secrecy.[10] The Babylonians, Herodotus tells us, are not permitted to walk silently past their sick compatriots but must speak out whatever they know that might help cure them (1.197); one of Darius' talking points about the superiority of monarchy is that a monarch is effective because he can be trusted to keep his plans secret (3.82.2). Keeping their actions secret from the Ethiopians, the Egyptians feed their exiled king (2.140); both Evenius and his fellow Apollonians resort to secrecy, Evenius to try to hide the killing of the sheep, the Apollonians to hide the fact that they must make whatever reparation he demands for the fact that they have blinded him (9.93.2, 94). Alexander the Macedonian has to give gifts to the Persian investigator so that the deaths of prominent Persians at his father's house are kept secret (5.21.2), and Alexander himself begs the Athenians to keep secret the fact that he is warning them that the battle of Plataea is about to begin (9.44.1).[11] Themistocles is a mastermind at exploiting the possibilities of a secretive silence: before the battle of Salamis he has his trusty slave Sicinnus secretly deliver to the Persians his tricky recommendation to come at dawn (8.75), and the Persians themselves, thinking they are part of a secret plot when they are really its dupes, work silently and secretly all night to maneuver their ships into position (8.76.3). After the Persian defeat at Salamis, Themistocles tells Sicinnus and other slaves whose silence could be trusted to hurry to King Xerxes and claim credit for Themistocles for allowing Xerxes to flee home (8.110.2).[12] Two women are dangerously silent and secretive in the *Histories*: the unnamed wife of Candaules at its beginning (1.11.1) and Amestris, wife of Xerxes, at its end (9.110.1). Each of them holds

---

10. See also Montiglio 2000: 282, who again locates this theme in the context of uneasiness about silence and secrecy in classical Athens.
11. Both these secrets seem to be part of a larger Macedonian revisionist history after the Persian loss in 479, to show that the Macedonians were really on the Greek side all along.
12. We learn from Thucydides 1.138.4 and Plutarch *Them.* 31.4–5 that Themistocles was a great keeper of secrets. Even at the end of his life, the Athenians remained unsure how he died or whether to consider the possibility that he committed suicide as the act of an Athenian patriot or an obedient Persian underling.

her peace when her royal husband has transgressed against her, and each fashions a plot that succeeds because it has remained hidden until its successful implementation.[13] Such passages demonstrate that Herodotus himself is acutely aware of the impact of silence as part of a community's politics; who speaks and what and when they can speak profoundly affect the outcome of an important chain of events.

II

In part 1 of *Historical Method*, DL discusses the ways that the depiction of various characters' actions—including nonverbal gestures, such as the imposition of silence—are a crucial part of Herodotus' own analysis both of character as a historical force and of causal sequences.[14] This anticipates DL's work on Homeric epic and particularly the *Odyssey* in *Sardonic Smile*, where DL shows how nonverbal communication and proxemics, in particular, are essential to the way Homer tells his story. As nonverbal communication, silence plays an interesting role in Herodotus, because, as we have seen, the absence of language as a stratagem in political discourse is as significant as its presence. DL's work on silence in the *Odyssey* reveals that in that poem too, silence is closely related to the stratagems of power. In this section, we explore how silence may also be an indication of the failure of public discourse to articulate a more complex human reality, if not a political one. We see the germ of this possibility in the way DL has discussed Penelope's silence in particular.

DL shows how both Penelope and Odysseus make brilliant use of nonverbal communication to regain control over their home, the culmination of the narrative's goal.[15] Odysseus uses body language and verbal silence to bait the suitors and expose their general unfitness for the role they aspire to; Penelope has all along shown her cunning ability to employ silence and secrecy in delaying the suitors and undermining their designs against her and her son.[16] But, as DL has shown us, in Penelope in particular we also see that her

---

13. This is part of a larger theme, concerning tricks and secrets in Herodotus, some of which are constructed or decoded by clever people. See Lateiner 1987: 98–99, 115–16; Dewald 1993; Hollmann 2011.
14. Lateiner 1989: 20, 24–30.
15. Lateiner 1995: 167–289.
16. Lateiner 1995: 119–29, 243–79.

use of silence protects her own place in the world. She engages in silence in a way that the other characters—including her husband—do not understand. As soon as Odysseus enters his house, she shows by her actions that she is the gatekeeper of her own secrets; she is not willing to relinquish or explain them until she has forced Odysseus suddenly to abandon his own silence, in his outraged outburst about his bed. As she ultimately explains to her infuriated husband, her final trick has only worked because she and her faithful handmaid have kept silent all these years about the secret of the bed—it is something not even a god would know, if he tried to trick her by taking on Odysseus' identity. At the end, Penelope forces Odysseus to speak out his truth, by obdurately remaining true to her reality: she is a wife waiting for her husband. By preserving the secret of the bed through her silence, she symbolically maintains a place for Odysseus' return, a place that also preserves her position in the world.[17]

A woman's silence in relation to her own, threatened reality, which DL has allowed us to appreciate in the *Odyssey*, has interesting parallels in Sophocles' plays.[18] Three women, Jocasta, Eurydice, and Deianeira, all keep silence before they exit to destroy themselves,[19] and their silences are commented on with perplexity by someone on stage. As we shall see, their silences mark an understanding of their own reality that cannot be shared, for a variety of reasons, with those around them. These women's silence is disturbing to others, and the theater audience is thereby invited to struggle with its meaning, to imagine what they are not finding words for.

To help us understand the silences of these women, we might consider first an even more enigmatic form of silent presence, to which no one on stage draws attention: Tecmessa's silence in the final 250 lines of the *Ajax*. If Teucer had not announced her entrance onto the stage, we would have no reason to know from the text that she is present. Her silence, then, is absolute. Yet she is physically, visually present to "adorn" Ajax's tomb, as Teucer says (1168—

---

17. Lateiner 1995: 272–78.
18. Kirk Ormand (1999: 160), for example, sees a parallel between the unbounded nature of silence and the reality of marriage for Sophoclean women as a "state of perpetual and unfulfilled longing" that silence is "both a result and emblem of." We question whether the silence belongs not just to the female characters' understanding of their reality but also to Sophocles' understanding of what his language, fashioned by the conventions of the public stage on which tragedy is enacted, can express.
19. See Montiglio 2000: 238–42 for a discussion of these three women's silence in relation to their suicides. See Rood 2010: 355n13 for further bibliography.

70).[20] All Teucer's instructions about the protection of the body and its removal, however, are directed only at Eurysaces. Tecmessa's silent presence is never referred to. One might argue that she is merely there as the mother of Eurysaces, who is too young to be present on his own, and that she simply helps him perform the actions Teucer tells him to perform. But her prominence as a witness to and interpreter of the action in the first two-thirds of the play has given her voice a central role, and her silence now establishes a striking contrast that seems to beg the audience to question what that silence signals.[21] As Teucer and Agamemnon argue about the public recognition of Ajax's τίμη, does Tecmessa's silence remind the audience both of Ajax's private struggle to find a way to tolerate his own life and of his failure to do so?[22] In the public wrangling over what a life means, does Tecmessa's silence remind us that Ajax has failed, in the face of his public dishonor, to value the private self in its web of relationships? Tecmessa's silence seems to say both that there is no language available on the tragic stage to make these considerations part of the agon and that they must not be forgotten. Her silence prevents the burial of Ajax with which the play closes from achieving the kind of clean, unambiguous closure that a burial might easily represent.[23]

III

The final scenes of the *Ajax* make of Ajax's dead body an object whose significance Agamemnon, Odysseus, and Teucer struggle with each other to define. Eurysaces' silent presence is that of a suppliant, suggesting the possibility of divine investment in the dead Ajax, in contrast to Athena's interest in the living Ajax, with which the play begins. But Tecmessa's unmarked silence bears witness to a world that the men's words do not acknowledge—not just the private world of the family, which Tecmessa has tried to persuade Ajax to

---

20. All citations of Sophocles' text are from Lloyd-Jones' and Wilson's 1990 Oxford Classical Texts edition.
21. Finglass (2011: 466) comments that "a silent entry is unusual for a character as important as Tecmessa." Earlier (416), he suggests that her silent presence on stage is a reminder to Teucer that he must protect Ajax's wife, as well as his son.
22. In this way, Tecmessa's silence prolongs the unknowable, unspoken truth masked by Ajax's deception speech, itself a kind of silence.
23. In this way, the end of the *Ajax* has similarities to the burial of Patroclus at the end of the *Iliad*. The exclusion of Odysseus from Ajax's burial adds, we argue, to the unanswered questions that Tecmessa's silence raises.

take into account, but the internal world of Ajax's shame, righteous outrage, madness, and helplessness, whose weight finally he could not bear. Keeping Tecmessa's silence in mind, let us look at instances where silence is marked and puzzled over by the onstage audience: the final silences of Eurydice, Jocasta, and Deianeira. These moments help us to understand Tecmessa's silence—and perhaps women's silence generally in Sophocles—as the expression not only of a private, personal life but also of a consciousness for which there are no words.[24]

Eurydice's silence in *Antigone* is perhaps the most straightforward of the three, in that she comes on stage only to hear the story of Haimon's death and to respond with silence before killing herself off stage. As the receiver of the messenger's speech, she registers the emotional impact of Haimon's death, just as Haimon has registered the impact of Antigone's. Eurydice's silent response mirrors Haimon's silence in his encounter with Creon at Antigone's "tomb," and their silence leads the audience to feel that Creon has wrought unspeakable devastation, before Creon himself appears, singing in an attempt to fill the silence.

What deepens the meaning of Eurydice's silence is the discussion about it that the chorus and the messenger have after her exit. While the messenger suggests that her silent departure is an act of discretion, to express her private grief (1249) away from a public audience, the chorus replies that excessive silence, like excessive sound, is a burden (βαρύ, 1251). Excessive silence seems to indicate a state that weighs down those who witness it, precisely because it is one that words cannot articulate; Eurydice's silence, like her suicide, is an ultimate isolation of the self. We hear from the messenger that her suicide was accompanied by the sound of her lamentation for Haimon and Megareus and the cursing of Creon. That Eurydice's only vocal expression after departing in silence is lament and curse reinforces the sense that her feeling and thought form a complex web of internal experience that language cannot encompass. Such silence is felt as a burden because, finally for Sophocles, humans count on words to mediate experience; when language cannot do that, death may be the only alternative.

---

24. Women's silence in tragedy has been associated by several scholars with Pericles' admonition to women not to be the subject of talk, which is also understood to imply their own silence in the public sphere (e.g., Suksi 2001: 33; McClure 1999: 24). The three instances of women's silence we will discuss, however, occur in a context where the stage audience expects speech, not silence, from them, so that, here at least, their silence cannot be read as virtuous reticence.

Jocasta's silence in the *Oedipus Tyrannus* also signals her suicide, as the audience eventually learns, but she announces her silence as a choice not to speak to Oedipus about what she knows (1071—72):

ἰοὺ ἰοὺ δύστηνε· τοῦτο γάρ σ' ἔχω
μόνον προσειπεῖν, ἄλλο δ' οὔποθ' ὕστερον.

[Oh, oh wretched one: I have only this to say
To you, and nothing else ever after.][25]

Δύστηνος (wretched) is the only word she can speak to him. This fact and the fact that there will be no other word to speak in the future imply a limit that she herself places on her speech.[26] She refuses to allow her own existence as her son's lover; she also chooses not to formulate the language that she could use to name their relationship and situation. In Jocasta's case, then, both silence and death erase what is there to be seen and spoken.[27] Jocasta's choice contrasts with Oedipus' insistence on bringing all to light and enduring what he uncovers. Unlike Eurydice's silence, Jocasta's is a refusal to allow language to express what is known and felt, not evidence of language's incapacity to do so.

Yet Jocasta's silence "speaks" the private and intimate sphere of Oedipus' and Jocasta's complex love for each other in a way that language could not. If she were to use language to articulate the truth of that connection, it would lend it the linearity of syntax, the framework of cause and effect. As we learn from the messenger's description of Eurydice's behavior after her silent exit in the *Antigone*, the pain of Haimon's death is connected for Eurydice to the loss of Megareus and to her rage at Creon's decisions that led to both these deaths, in a tangled web of experience that only silence gives us space to imagine. Similarly, Jocasta's silence allows us to sense the terrible tangle of Oedipus' and Jocasta's love and all the web of actions and decisions that created it, without the imposition of the order required by language, particularly the language of public discourse. Oedipus' fantasy, on Jocasta's depar-

---

25. Our translation.
26. Whether her line is read as "I have only this to say" or "I am able to say only this," the sentence implies a choice to stop speaking.
27. Mossman (2012: 504) sees Jocasta's silence here as "performative," stressing her shame and "supplant[ing] the articulacy of the past." She contrasts this silence with Eurydice's, which she sees as the silence of "a conventional and virtuous wife."

ture, that "chance" (τύχη, 1080) is his mother and that the linear passage of time lays out an ordered sequence of greatness and smallness seems to bring a kind of order to the tangled, twisted complexity that Jocasta's silence has allowed the audience to imagine. In the contrast between Jocasta's silence and Oedipus' words, we see that even if language is, in theory, capable of giving some kind of expression to what Jocasta knows, only silence gives presence to an interior experience that cannot be contained in the linearity of cause and effect and the singularity of a narrative that defines things clearly and orders one action after another in time. In this way, rather than hiding the truth of her relationship to Oedipus, Jocasta's silence is the only way that Sophocles has to express it.[28]

The role of silence as a response to the inexpressible, tangled, and nonlinear complexity of an individual's experience and understanding of that experience is most vividly dramatized in Deianeira's response to Hyllus' accusation of murder in the *Trachiniae*.[29] Hyllus has "made sense" of Heracles' suffering by accusing Deianeira and establishing a clear pattern of cause and effect. When Deianeira leaves in silence after listening to Hyllus' account, the chorus fears that her silence expresses agreement with her accuser (814): συνηγορεῖς σιγῶσα τῷ κατηγόρῳ (You agree by your silence with your accuser). The chorus and the audience already know some of the confusion and uncertainty that accompanied Deianeira's use of Nessus' potion, making Hyllus' assignation of blame an inadequate account of what has happened. In appealing to Deianeira to give language to that more complex story, the chorus assumes that there is language she could use. Her silence seems to say that no language she can use in the public world can give an adequate account of what has happened and why. Later, when Hyllus breaks Deianeira's silence and speaks to Heracles of Nessus' potion and Deianeira's lack of ill intention (1126), Heracles immediately displaces both her role in the story and her reasons for action with the narrative of Nessus' revenge. He focuses only on the prediction that he would die at the hand of one not living; in so doing, he creates a linear account of cause and effect, from his killing of Nes-

---

28. Looked at this way, her silence might seem similar to Oedipus' blinding later on; the blinding both cuts Oedipus off from others and indicates a kind of understanding that, like blind Teiresias', cannot be spoken.

29. For a treatment of the many silences in this play, see Rood 2010. Rood reads Deianeira's silence as an unsuccessful attempt to hide herself and her agency, in contrast to Aphrodite's silent and successful agency. We argue that Deianeira's final silence does not conceal her reality but, rather, points to it in the only way possible.

sus to Nessus' revenge (ignoring, of course, the possible reference of the oracle to Deianeira, who also is no longer living). Heracles' new account, which
leaves out so much, seems to reinforce Deianeira's decision that only silence
can give space for all that has taken place.

In the nurse's account of what Deianeira does after she leaves the stage in
silence, however, we learn that, in the isolation and privacy of her home, before her suicide, and in both her movements and her words, she does express
why she has acted. Together, the touching of the objects she has used to create her household, her address to the women who have created it with her,
and her words to her marriage bed constitute the world she has tried to protect, the private world of the house, which she cannot speak of in the male,
public world, knowing that the latter does not recognize the former's value or
meaning. Her silence in the public world is the only way to point to the existence of a whole sphere of motivation, feeling, action, and reasoning that
would make her story understandable.

In these three instances of women's silence, we can see Sophocles' ac-
knowledgment that the world the language of the tragic stage depicts leaves
out of view and consideration an interior world whose unspoken complexities change the shape of what we must take into account if we are to be fully
human.[30] These examples in Sophoclean tragedy allow us to go back to
Herodotus and consider characters in the *Histories* whose silences are not
explicitly political, to see whether they, too, point to some of the issues that
Sophocles' women on stage have made visible.

IV

It is well known that dramatic silences mark some of the most famous passages in Herodotus. When Harpagus gathers up the remains of his cannibalized son (1.119.7), when Adrastus waits until all is silent and still around
Atys' tomb to kill himself (1.45.3), or when Psammenitus bows down in silence when he sees his daughter and son led captive before him (3.14.3–4), we

---

30. Blok (2001: 100–101) notes the association of women's silence with privacy and the protection of the *oikos* from public scrutiny and gossip. In the cases we have discussed, the association of silence and privacy serves, we argue, to point to the private—personal and famil-
ial—as a factor that must be taken into account, not hidden, in order to understand the
play. See Kitzinger 2012 for discussion of the private and public in the *Women of Trachis*.

can echo Denniston's remark on the occasional "hushed intensity in [Herodotus'] style which recalls Homer, Malory, or the English Bible."[31] DL identifies such passages as marking "a sorrow so profound and isolating that impulsive and conventional communicative signals are altogether insufficient."[32] But building on our observations of Sophocles' female silences, we can perhaps extend our analysis a bit, to include in our understanding of such passages not just the depiction of a character's private, overwhelming and inexpressible emotion but also Herodotus' attempt to acknowledge for us, his audience, the impossibility of capturing in words a different, more complex meaning to which the character's silence points. This, too, is part of the "secular meaning of the past" that Herodotus has given us in the *Histories*. Like the dramatist Sophocles, Herodotus can directly address his readers through the medium of a character's depicted silence, and he can use that silence to ask us to engage with multiple, complex meanings that the passage at hand generates but that have not been and cannot be put into words.

We will focus here only on the first historical character mentioned in the *Histories*, Croesus, and on two of the very last ones, Artayctes and Xanthippus. Croesus' reign is marked by some fraught silences. One of Croesus' sons is mute—perhaps a deaf-mute (1.34)—and, after a life of silence, suddenly speaks out when Croesus' own life is at stake (1.85.5). After his capture, Croesus stands mutely on his pyre (1.86.3−4), only breaking his long silence to call out Solon's name thrice, then only explaining why he has done so when he is threatened with violence. Much explanation ensues, both on Croesus' part (1.87–90) and on the part of the Delphic oracle when Croesus has challenged Apollo's oracular integrity (1.91). But all this speaking does little good—the warning that Delphi had given to Gyges several generations earlier has certainly gone unheeded, and both Croesus and Cyrus forget the lesson of Solon's message, that the value of a life cannot be assessed until it is ended.[33] So a question arises: is speaking of any use, when the kind of understanding that Croesus' silence on the pyre indicates cannot be sustained or integrated into further action? Perhaps that silence is all that can express, for

---

31. Denniston 1952: 5.
32. Lateiner 2009: 113. See also Lateiner 1989: 28.
33. For Croesus's later errors of judgment and dubious values, see 1.155, 1.207, 3.36; for Cyrus, 1.204. Of Croesus, Stahl (2001: 102) comments, ". . . the twofold, riddling silence of King Croesus . . . gives . . . the reader pause to ponder another two *fermatas*; they gather up the sum of past mistakes; either one also forms the prelude to increasing insight but will eventually result in a new chain of human errors which again will involve Croesus."

the historian and his readers, what it means to come to terms with the human condition, as the anonymous Persian describes to his Orchomenan dinner mate before the battle of Plataea (9.16.4–5): ξεῖνε, ὅ τι δεῖ γενέσθαι ἐκ τοῦ θεοῦ ἀμήχανον ἀποτρέψαι ἀνθρώπῳ· οὐδὲ γὰρ πιστὰ λέγουσι ἐθέλει πείθεσθαι οὐδείς. . . . ἐχθίστη δὲ ὀδύνη ἐστὶ τῶν ἐν ἀνθρώποισι αὕτη, πολλὰ φρονέοντα μηδενὸς κρατέειν (Friend, an event which has been decreed by the god cannot be averted by man, for no one is willing to believe even those who tell the truth. . . . There's no more terrible pain a man can endure than to see clearly and be able to control nothing).[34] "Control," we argue, includes the role that public and political speech plays throughout the *Histories*; sometimes speech, like other action, simply fails in the face of a complex and brutal reality.

The very last episode in the *Histories*, concerning the fifth-century Persian invasion of Greece, is a horrible one. Artayctes, the Persian ruler of Sestus, has been captured and tries to deliver a very chatty apology and an offer of money, in order to spare his own life and that of his son (9.120.2–3). The people of Elaeus, however, demand his death, and Xanthippus, the father of Pericles, the Athenian commander in the region, gives it to them. He has Artayctes crucified and his son stoned to death before Artayctes' eyes (9.120.4). Neither Artayctes nor Xanthippus has more to say, and Herodotus' own silence as narrator at this point is also deafening.[35] Are we to see in Xanthippus' cruelty simply the triumph of the Greek cause? Or are we being led to understand that the Athenians are embarking on a road that will lead in the future to the Chersonese again and to their own defeat in 404? Or are we here exposed to something bleaker altogether about the nature of human political communities in war?[36] We are not told. Instead, a bald and banal wrap-up follows, and an anecdote from the time of Cyrus ends the *Histories*.

Why does the master of *logoi* end his narrative of the war with an event so brutal that it cries out for an explanation that releases the reader from it, then offer instead only silence? One of the things Don Lateiner's work has led us

34. Translation from Waterfield 1998: 547, slightly changed.
35. Lateiner (1989: 133) comments on Herodotus' "superhuman silences about future events" at the close of the *Histories*. See also Strid 2006: 399. For some of the larger implications to which Herodotus' silence points, see Boedeker 1988; Dewald 1997.
36. Thucydides' phrase is that war is a *biaios didaskalos*, a violent teacher and teacher of violence (3.82.2). Murray (1988: 471) points to the failed Ionian revolt of 499–494 as perhaps distinctively marking Herodotus' narratives about East Greece, as well as his sense of "Delphic moralizing" in general, with the profound pessimism of a defeated and traumatized people.

to think about is that in both Herodotus and Sophocles, silence can reveal characters who occupy the communicative space but are not able to put into words the complexities of reality as they understand it or to share that consciousness with others. By asking who has the power to use language and by questioning the ability of language to communicate all realities, both authors self-consciously acknowledge the limits to what the language of their art can achieve. The historian and his readers, like the poet and his audience, look across at each other, acknowledging through their silences the depths of what it is to be human in what cannot be spoken.

Works Cited

Blok, J. 2001. "Women's Speech in Classical Athens." In A. Lardinois and L. Mc-Clure, eds., *Making Silence Speak: Women's Voices in Greek Literature and Society*, 95–116. Princeton: Princeton University Press.

Boedeker, D., ed. 1987. "Herodotus and the Invention of History." Special volume, *Arethusa* 20.

Boedeker, D. 1988. "Protesilaos and the End of Herodotus' *Histories*." CA 7: 30–48.

Darbo-Peschanski, C. 1987. *Le discours du particulier: Essai sur l'enquête hérodotéenne*. Paris: Éditions du Seuil.

Denniston, J. 1952. *Greek Prose Style*. Oxford: Clarendon.

Dewald, C. 1993. "Reading the World: The Interpretation of Objects in Herodotus' *Histories*." In R. Rosen and J. Farrell, eds., *Nomodeiktes: Greek Studies in Honor of Martin Ostwald*, 55–70. Ann Arbor: University of Michigan Press.

Dewald, C. 1997. "Wanton Kings, Pickled Heroes, and Gnomic Founding Fathers: Strategies of Meaning at the End of Herodotus' Histories." In D. H. Roberts, F. M. Dunn, and D. Fowler, eds., *Classical Closure: Reading the End in Greek and Latin Literature*, 62–82. Princeton: Princeton University Press.

Finglass, P. 2011. *Sophocles, Ajax*. Cambridge Classical Texts and Commentaries 48. Cambridge: Cambridge University Press.

Fornara, C. 1971. *Herodotus: An Interpretive Essay*. Oxford: Clarendon.

Gould, J. 1989. *Herodotus*. London: Weidenfeld and Nicolson.

Hartog, F. 1980. *Le miroir d'Hérodote: Essai sur la représentation de l'autre*. Paris: Gallimard.

Hollmann, A. 2011. *The Master of Signs: Signs and the Interpretation of Signs in Herodotus' Histories*. Hellenic Studies 48. Washington, DC: Center for Hellenic Studies.

Hunter, V. 1982. *Past and Process in Herodotus and Thucydides*. Princeton: Princeton University Press.

Immerwahr, H. 1966. *Form and Thought in Herodotus*. Cleveland: Press of Western Reserve University. Reprint, Scholars Press, 1986. Atlanta, GA.

Jacoby, F. 1913. "Herodotos." *RE* Suppl. 2: 205–520. Reprinted in *Griechische Historiker* (Stuttgart: Alfred Druckenmüller, 1956).

Jäkel, S., and Timonen, A. eds. *The Language of Silence*. Vol. 1. Turku: Turun Yliopisto.

Kitzinger, R. 2012. "The Divided Worlds of Sophocles' *Women of Trachis*." In K. Ormand, ed., *A Companion for Sophocles*, 111–25. Chichester, West Sussex: Wiley Blackwell.

Lang, M. 1984. *Herodotean Narrative and Discourse*. Cambridge, MA: Harvard University Press.

Larson, S. 2006. "Kandaules' Wife, Masistes' Wife: Herodotus' Narrative Strategy in Suppressing Names of Women (Hdt. 1.8–12 and 9.108–13)." *CJ* 101: 225–44.

Lateiner, D. 1989. *The Historical Method of Herodotus*. Toronto: University of Toronto Press.

Lateiner, D. 1995. *Sardonic Smile: Nonverbal Behavior in Homeric Epic*. Ann Arbor: University of Michigan Press.

Lateiner, D. 2009. "Tears and Crying in Hellenic Historiography: Dacryology from Herodotus to Polybius." In T. Fögen, ed., *Tears in the Graeco-Roman World*, 105–34. Berlin: De Gruyter.

Loraux, N. 1987. *Tragic Ways of Killing a Woman*. Cambridge, MA: Harvard University Press.

McClure, L. 1999. *Spoken Like a Woman: Speech and Gender in Athenian Drama*. Princeton: Princeton University Press.

Montiglio, S. 2000. *Silence in the Land of Logos*. Princeton: Princeton University Press.

Mossman, J. 2012. "Women's Voices in Sophocles." In A. Markantonatos, ed., *Brill's Companion to Sophocles*, 491–506. Leiden: Brill.

Murray, O. 1988. "The Ionian Revolt." In John Boardman, N. G. L. Hammond, D. M. Lewis, and M. Ostwald, eds., *The Cambridge Ancient History*, vol. 4, *Persia, Greece, and the Western Mediterranean*, 461–90. 2nd ed. Cambridge: Cambridge University Press.

Ormand, K. 1999. *Exchange and the Maiden: Marriage in Sophoclean Tragedy*. Austin: University of Texas Press.

Rood, N. 2010. "Four Silences in Sophocles' *Trachiniae*." *Arethusa* 43: 345–64.

Stahl, H.-P. 2001. "On the Sadness of Silence in Ancient Literature." In Jäkel and Timonen, 86–104.

Strid, O. 2006. "Voiceless Victims, Memorable Deaths in Herodotus." *CQ* 56: 393–403.

Suksi, A. 2001. "Silence in Sophocles." In Jäkel and Timonen, 31–40.

Waterfield, R., and Dewald, C. 1998. *Herodotus, The Histories*. Oxford: Oxford University Press.

Waters, K. 1985. *Herodotos the Historian: His Problems, Methods, and Originality*. Norman: University of Oklahoma Press.

CHAPTER 6

Two Tales of Spartan Envoys

Deborah Boedeker

Among his many contributions to scholarship in Greek and Roman literature, Don Lateiner has pioneered the study of nonverbal communication in
ancient texts: gestures, postures, facial expressions, bodily reactions, and
other wordless acts, both intentional and involuntary. His work in this area
adds a rich dimension to our understanding of narrative techniques, not least
in Herodotus. In Don's words, through gestures, "concepts are given substance. There is an intangible eloquence to gesture, an intangible rhetoric,
that sometimes seems to correlate to true meaning more directly than
words."[1] This essay begins with a Herodotean story that features two Spartans' refusal to perform a gesture of deference at the Persian court (7.134–37),
a passage Don himself noted in an influential article.[2] I then briefly consider
a related passage in Thucydides, which mentions the silence later imposed
by Athens on captured Spartan envoys. My analysis is not restricted to nonverbal communication, but I hope to show that its "intangible rhetoric" enriches the reading of both these passages.

I

As he began his attack on mainland Greece, Xerxes sent heralds (κήρυκες) to
demand earth and water of cities that had not yet submitted to him, but he

---

1. Lateiner 1987: 102.
2. Lateiner 1987: 91–92.

sent none to Athens or Sparta (Hdt. 7.133.1). Herodotus recalls that Darius had similarly requested tokens of submission (as described in 6.48), but mentions here for the first time that at both those cities the heralds had been killed:

πρότερον Δαρείου πέμψαντος ἐπ' αὐτὸ τοῦτο, οἱ μὲν αὐτῶν τοὺς αἰτέοντας ἐς τὸ βάραθρον οἱ δ' ἐς φρέαρ ἐμβαλόντες ἐκέλευον γῆν τε καὶ ὕδωρ ἐκ τούτων φέρειν παρὰ βασιλέα. τούτων μὲν εἵνεκα οὐκ ἔπεμψε Ξέρξης τοὺς αἰτήσοντας·

[Previously Darius had sent men for the same purpose. The [Athenians] threw those making this request into the pit, and the [Spartans] threw them into a well, telling them to take earth and water from those places for the king. For this reason Xerxes did not send men to make the request.] (7.133.1)[3]

In this story, significantly, the Persian king's messengers are described, from a Greek perspective, as κήρυκες, "heralds." These officials, in some cases hereditary (as for instance at the Eleusinian Mysteries), served in various kinds of public business: they might voice announcements at certain rituals or assemblies, and state heralds were sent to make proclamations such as the start of wars or truces.[4] Their traditional inviolability is reflected in the myth of the Heraclids,[5] according to which the Athenians killed an Argive herald (sometimes named Copreus) who was demanding return of the suppliants; the Athenians atoned for the crime with a long-standing ephebic ritual.[6] Diodorus (30.18.2) lists "Do not put a herald to death" (κήρυκα μὴ ἀναιρεῖν) as one of very few laws that prevailed in the generally lawless world of war.[7] Herald murder was a rare and serious crime; apart from Darius' heralds, only one other case is attested in historical times: an Athenian herald, Anthemocritus, was killed by Megarians shortly before the Peloponnesian War for a proclamation barring territorial access. According to Pausanias, his murder roused the wrath of the Two Goddesses against the Megar-

3. All translations in this essay are my own.
4. See Lateiner 1977 on heralds in Thucydides, who often proclaim truces for burying the dead.
5. The myth is strikingly reflected in Eur. *Heracl.* 270–73.
6. On Copreus, see Wéry 1966: 483–84; Mariggiò 2007: 197.
7. Cited in Pritchett 1991: 203.

ians down to his own time: "To them alone of Greeks not even the Emperor
Hadrian could bring more prosperity" (1.36.3).[8]
Herodotus accordingly associates the murder of Darius' heralds with an
expectation of divine retribution:

ὅ τι δὲ τοῖσι Ἀθηναίοισι ταῦτα ποιήσασι τοὺς κήρυκας συνήνεικε ἀνεθέλητον
γενέσθαι, οὐκ ἔχω εἶπαί τι, πλὴν ὅτι σφέων ἡ χώρη καὶ ἡ πόλις ἐδηιώθη.
ἀλλὰ τοῦτο οὐ διὰ ταύτην τὴν αἰτίην δοκέω γενέσθαι.

[What unwelcome consequence came about for the Athenians who did those
things to the heralds I am not able to say, except that their territory and city
were destroyed—but I do not think that happened for this reason.] (7.133.2)

I will return to the vexed question of Athens' punishment. In Sparta, however,
the consequences were more readily perceived. Herodotus continues:

τοῖσι δὲ ὦν Λακεδαιμονίοισι μῆνις κατέσκηψε Ταλθυβίου τοῦ Ἀγαμέμνονος
κήρυκος. ἐν γὰρ Σπάρτῃ ἐστὶ Ταλθυβίου ἱρόν, εἰσὶ δὲ καὶ ἀπόγονοι
Ταλθυβιάδαι καλεόμενοι, τοῖσι αἱ κηρυκηίαι αἱ ἐκ Σπάρτης πᾶσαι γέρας
δέδονται. μετὰ δὲ ταῦτα τοῖσι Σπαρτιήτῃσι καλλιερῆσαι θυομένοισι οὐκ
ἐδύνατο·

[On the Lacedaemonians, in any case, fell the wrath of Talthybius the herald of
Agamemnon. For in Sparta there is a shrine of Talthybius,[9] and descendants
called Talthybiads have the honor of serving on all heraldic missions from
Sparta. But after these things, when the Spartans sacrificed they could not get
favorable omens.] (7.134.1)

As this state of affairs persisted, the distressed Spartans "held many assemblies, asking publicly whether one of the Lacedaemonians would be willing to die for Sparta." At last, two noble Spartiates, Boulis and Sperthias,

---

8. See Mosley 1973: 85; Gourmelen 2007: 21, citing also Plut. *Per.* 30. On the date of the inci-
    dent, see Dover 1966.
9. See Paus. 3.12.7 and 7.24.1 for the cult of Talthybius at Sparta and also at Aegae in
    Achaea.

volunteered to journey to the Persian court (where Xerxes had succeeded to the kingship in 486) and to offer their lives in expiation. The narrator comments, "The daring deed [τόλμα] of these men was worthy of wonder [θώματος ἀξίη]; so also were their words" (7.134.2–3).

As the story proceeds, the two Spartiates were entertained en route by Hydarnes, the Persian commander in coastal Asia Minor (and soon to be leader of the Immortals at Thermopylae: 7.211). Their host encouraged them to become "friends" of Xerxes and enjoy, as he did, the wealth and power the king offered to brave men (ἄνδρας ἀγαθούς): they would be made rulers in Greece (7.135.2). The Spartans replied that since Hydarnes knew only how to be a slave (δοῦλος), he was not in a position to offer such advice. Had he ever experienced freedom, he would tell them to fight for it "not only with swords but with axes" (7.135.3).

When they arrived at Susa, Boulis and Sperthias continued to project Spartan values. Before their verbal exchange with Xerxes, all we learn of their visit is that they refused to prostrate themselves before the king, even when his bodyguards tried to force them. The Spartans explained their refusal to the guards (and to Herodotus' audience), saying that they would not fall down before the king even if they were pushed headfirst, for it was not their custom (ἐν νόμῳ) to bow (προσκυνέειν) to a human being, nor was that the purpose of their journey (7.136.1). Thus Sperthias and Boulis once more combined daring action with admirable words.

Lateiner cites this passage as an example of Herodotus' interest in culture-specific behavior: "Herodotus associates the protocols, the elaborate titles and gestures of politesse with oriental, centralized autocracies. . . . When the Spartan heralds refuse to genuflect before the King of Kings, the incident exemplifies not lack of manners, discourtesy or ignorance of hierarchical deference cues, but self-respect, subordination to an idea greater than a man, and the clash of fundamental *nomoi*."[10] Their bold refusal signifies not that the Spartans misunderstood the Persian act of *proskynesis* but that the two cultures differed in the deference considered appropriate to show any human being.[11]

---

10. Lateiner 1987: 91–92, mentioning the protocols that Deioces established to distance himself from his subjects (1.99), as well as Darius' later measures to restrict access (3.84); these can be seen as background to the *proskynesis* episode.
11. For "divine" respect directed toward a mortal by Greeks, see Herodotus' comment that Athenians foolishly worshipped Phye, a mere human being, as if she were really Athena (1.60.4–5).

Indeed, no Greeks in the *Histories* ever "bow down" (προσκυνέω) to mortal or immortal. All those who do are subjects of eastern dynasties: Median Harpagus to Astyages (1.119.1); low-ranked Persians to their betters (1.134.1); Egyptians to each other, by lowering a hand to the knee—the only example not based on differences of rank (2.80.2); Egyptians to a statue of Summer (2.121.1); the coconspirators to their new king Darius (3.86.2); Persian councilors to Xerxes (7.13.3); Xerxes' noble Persian shipmates to him before casting themselves into the sea to save his life (8.118.4). Even when in an ethnographic context Herodotus says that Spartans, but no other Greeks, resemble Egyptians in their gestures of respect for elders, he specifies that no Greeks bow down when they meet, as Egyptians do (2.80.1–2).

After Sperthias and Boulis laconically explained their attitude toward *proskynesis*, they told Xerxes that they were sent to "pay the penalty for the Persian heralds killed in Sparta," but he refused to take their lives (7.136.2). Herodotus comments that the king did this magnanimously (ὑπὸ μεγαλοφροσύνης), and indeed their release accords with the respect for valorous adversaries elsewhere attributed to Persians (see esp. 7.238.2).[12] Hydarnes had told them that the king recognized them as "brave men" (ἄνδρες ἀγαθοί, 7.135.2); sparing their lives could be understood partly as his response to their courage.[13]

Xerxes' magnanimity, however, was double-edged. He said he would not be like the Lacedaemonians. By killing heralds, they had shattered the laws [νόμινα] of all mankind, and he would not do the things he blamed them for doing.[14] He would not kill them in return [ἀνταποκτείνας] and thus release the Lacedaemonians from blame [αἰτίης]" (7.136.2). Whether we understand this blame to refer to the wrath of Talthybius or, more generally, to "the laws of all mankind," Xerxes' remark emphasized that Sparta was not exonerated.[15]

---

12. This characteristic is attributed to Persians most explicitly in 7.238. Cf. Lateiner 1987: 92; Gourmelen 2007: 33. A striking example of Persians honoring courageous enemies is the treatment of Pytheas of Aegina, who fought fiercely at Artemisium (7.181). A marked exception is Xerxes' mutilation of the corpse of Leonidas (7.238); see Lateiner 1987: 92 for further examples.

13. Writing of this episode, Lateiner (1989: 160–61) points out that Herodotus has enclosed "a dramatic endorsement" of Greek values "within an inner frame of Persian hospitality and moral dignity."

14. Sperthias and Boulis, however, are not identified as κήρυκες; he refers to their sons with the more general term ἀγγέλους, "messengers" (7.137); Thucydides calls them πρέσβεις, "ambassadors" (2.67, discussed below).

15. A little later (7.146), Xerxes also spared three Greek spies who were discovered at Sardis; before they could be executed, he ordered that they be allowed to look around and then

The mission of Sperthias and Boulis lulled Talthybius' wrath for half a century, but according to the Spartans themselves, he was not finally appeased until their war with Athens (in 430 BCE and the latest datable event in the *Histories*):

οὕτω ἡ Ταλθυβίου **μῆνις** καὶ ταῦτα ποιησάντων Σπαρτιητέων ἐπαύσατο τὸ παραυτίκα, καίπερ ἀπονοστησάντων ἐς Σπάρτην Σπερθίεώ τε καὶ Βούλιος. χρόνῳ δὲ μετέπειτα πολλῷ ἐπηγέρθη κατὰ τὸν Πελοποννησίων καὶ Ἀθηναίων πόλεμον, ὡς λέγουσι Λακεδαιμόνιοι. τοῦτο μοι ἐν τοῖσι **θειότατον** φαίνεται γενέσθαι. ὅτι μὲν γὰρ **κατέσκηψε** ἐς ἀγγέλους ἡ Ταλθυβίου **μῆνις** οὐδὲ ἐπαύσατο πρὶν ἢ ἐξῆλθε, τὸ δίκαιον οὕτω ἔφερε· τὸ δὲ συμπεσεῖν ἐς τοὺς παῖδας τῶν ἀνδρῶν τούτων τῶν ἀναβάντων πρὸς βασιλέα διὰ τὴν **μῆνιν**, ἐς Νικόλαν τε τὸν Βούλιος καὶ ἐς Ἀνήριστον τὸν Σπερθίεω . . . δῆλον ὦν μοι ὅτι **θεῖον** ἐγένετο τὸ πρῆγμα ἐκ τῆς **μήνιος·**

[So the **wrath** of Talthybius ceased for the time being, since the Spartans had taken these measures, even though Sperthias and Boulis returned home to Sparta. But much later it was roused again, during the war between the Peloponnesians and the Athenians, as the Lacedaemonians tell. In these matters this seems to me to be **extremely supernatural**: on the one hand, it was by justice that the **wrath** of Talthybius **struck down upon** messengers and did not cease until it was accomplished; but on the other hand, that it fell upon the sons of those men who had gone up to the king because of the **wrath**, that is, against Boulis' son Nikolaos and Sperthias' son Aneristus . . . makes it clear to me that the event was **supernatural**, coming from the **wrath**.] (7.137.1–2)

This passage abounds in poetic/religious language. Talthybius' wrath (μῆνις) is mentioned four times, more than in all the rest of the *Histories* combined.[16] Similarly, the poetic compound κατασκήπτω, "strike (down)," appears in Herodotus only three times, always of a divine force: it is used twice of Talthybius' wrath (here and at 7.134.1) and once, in direct discourse, of the danger that would threaten Xerxes and his army if the miraculous cloud of dust from Eleusis should "strike down" on the Peloponnese (8.65.3).

---

freed. Here, too, benevolence had an ulterior motive: the spies would bring home frightening information about Persian might.

16. Elsewhere, μῆνις and μηνίω are used only of Minos' posthumous wrath against the Cretans (7.169.2); the wrath of Laphystian Zeus against descendants of Phrixus (7.197); and the Spartans' wrath against Aristodemus, who returned alive from Thermopylae (7.229.2).

Further, not only did "justice" (τὸ δίκαιον) direct the wrath against messengers (ἀγγέλους), but in an "extremely supernatural" manner against the
sons of the very men who had tried to appease Talthybius. Only here is the
superlative θειότατον attested in the *Histories*.[17] Very seldom does Herodotus use his own voice[18] to ascribe an event to a named god or hero, as he does
here; this passage is connected to a specific divinity more insistently than any
other in the *Histories*.[19]

Talthybius acted through human agents. The Lacedaemonians sent Nicolaus and Aneristus as messengers (ἄγγελοι) to Asia (7.137.3). Along the way,
they were arrested in Thrace; "betrayed by Sitalces, son of Tereus king of the
Thracians, and by Nymphodoros, son of Pytheas, a man of Abdera"; and
taken back to Attica, where "they died at the hands of the Athenians
[ἀπέθανον ὑπὸ Ἀθηναίων], along with a Corinthian man, Aristeas the son
of Adeimantus" (7.137.2–3).[20] The Athenians who killed Nicolaus and Aneristus at last stilled Talthybius' wrath against Sparta, but as far as they themselves were aware, they were simply putting to death three enemy agents
apprehended on a mission to Asia.

II

Killing Persian heralds demanded retribution, and Sparta paid for it in a
(Spartan) tale that spans six decades. It is then all the more remarkable that
Herodotus so conspicuously leaves open (as we have seen) the question of
how Athens atoned for its violation:

> ὅτι δὲ τοῖσι Ἀθηναίοισι ταῦτα ποιήσασι τοὺς κήρυκας συνήνεικε ἀνεθέλητον
> γενέσθαι, οὐκ ἔχω εἶπαί τι, πλὴν ὅτι σφέων ἡ χώρη καὶ ἡ πόλις ἐδηιώθη.
> ἀλλὰ τοῦτο οὐ διὰ ταύτην τὴν αἰτίην δοκέω γενέσθαι.

[What unwelcome consequence came about for the Athenians who did those
things to the heralds I am not able to say, except that their territory and city
were destroyed—but I do not think that happened for this reason.] (7.133.2)

17. θειός, in all its forms, is used thirty times in the *Histories*, including the two instances here
    in 7.137.
18. See Munson 2001: 192.
19. Compare Demeter in 9.65.2 and 9.100–101 and Poseidon in 8.129. Cf. Harrison 2000: 65–67;
    Boedeker 2007; Mikalson 2003: 86, 96–97.
20. Athenians also assisted with divine vengeance against Artayktes, Persian governor of the
    Chersonese, by crucifying him after the siege of Sestos to help the local Greeks avenge their
    hero-god Protesilaus for the outrages Artayktes had committed against his shrine (9.120.4).
    Cf. Boedeker 1988; Dewald 1997.

This comment begs for explanation.[21] As to why Herodotus or his audience believes Athens was destroyed, a common suggestion is that it was in retaliation for the burning of Cybele's temple in Sardis, related in 5.102.[22] Laurent Gourmelen, noting that the herald killing immediately precedes the famous praise of Athens (7.139), concludes that Herodotus' Athenian bias explains why the city was not punished.[23] To attribute such a bias to the historian is controversial; the preponderance of recent work (with which I agree) favors a more balanced view, including the notion that Herodotus subtly admonishes the imperial Athens of his own day.[24] Louise Marie Wéry examines the episode in detail from the perspective of "international and divine law" protecting heralds.[25] Arguing that Athens would have been too prudent to break such a law, she favors Plutarch's version (*Them.* 6), according to which not actual heralds but only an interpreter was murdered.[26]

My concern here, however, is more the structure of Herodotus' *logos* than its historicity, about which serious questions can be raised.[27] In his account, both cities killed Darius' heralds in remarkably similar ways (7.133.1). The cult of Talthybius at Sparta provides the narrator (and doubtless his Lacedaemonian sources) with a ready mechanism for that city's punishment, but Herodotus declares himself unable to say how Athens suffered.

Rosaria Munson speculates that Herodotus might have seen Athens paying for the crime in his own time, with the plague and Spartan devastation of Attic lands (she does not suggest that he attributed the whole Peloponnesian War to the herald-murder)[28]—an intriguing possibility. Even more significant, I find, is the speaker's professed ignorance (οὐκ ἔχω εἰπαί τι, 133.2). Herodotus typically does not present himself as an omniscient narrator;[29] here, after suggesting that some "unwelcome consequence" should punish Athens, he leaves his audience to ponder what, if anything, that consequence

---

21. See Lanski 2013: 120.
22. See, most recently, Gourmelen 2007: 23.
23. Gourmelen 2007: 23.
24. Cf. Moles 2002.
25. Wéry 1966.
26. Wéry 1966: 475–79, but disagreeing with Plutarch's connecting the incident to the second Persian War. Wéry raises the possibility that the Athenian herald-murder was fabricated by Spartans wanting to share the guilt, and she argues, against Pausanias (3.12.7), that Miltiades alone was responsible and paid for the crime (Wéry 1966: 474–75). See also Sealey 1976; Mikalson 2003: 51–52.
27. See esp. Mariggiò 2007.
28. Munson 2001: 193–94.
29. For a concise discussion, see Lateiner 1989: 32, 59–64.

was. Lateiner has shown how silence can be a powerful form of communication;[30] so too, Herodotus' aporia may be more engaging than a straightforward answer.

Munson also discusses the "painful discrepancy" between the mission of Sperthias and Boulis and that of their sons, for "the bare mention of this second set of Spartan envoys to Persia would have been enough" to remind the audience of "the changed circumstances of their own time."[31] Analogously, Pericles Georges points to Herodotus' sharp contrast between "the unflinching heroism of the Athenians" in the Persian War and the behavior of the Athenian demos in his own time.[32] These attractive readings show how the contemporary situation can color the main narrative of the *Histories*. The narrator himself, however, emphasizes continuity rather than contrasts, by focusing his story on the wrath of Talthybius. By their deaths, Nicolaus and Aneristus unwittingly accomplished at the hands of the Athenians what their fathers, though willing, were unable to do at the hands of Xerxes.

III

From a very different perspective, without mentioning Talthybius, Sperthias, or Boulis, Thucydides also recounts the deaths of Nikolas and Aneristus. He begins with a longer list of those who were arrested in Thrace—"Aristeus the Corinthian; Aneristus, Nicolaus, and Pratodamos, envoys [*presbeis*] from Lacedaemon; Timagoras the Tegean, and Pollis of Argos, acting privately." He then adds the shocking fact that they were heading for Asia in order "to persuade the [Persian] king to furnish money and join in the war" (2.67.1). Thucydides' account of the arrest follows the same general lines as Herodotus', but with greater detail and a fuller, more politically oriented account of those involved (2.67.2–3).[33]

Thucydides then turns to the captives' arrival at Athens. Aristeus had previously caused Athens great harm, and since the Athenians feared (δείσαντες)

---

30. E.g., Lateiner 1995: 201–2; see also the contribution of Dewald and Kitzinger in the present volume.
31. Munson 2001: 193. Note, too, that Herodotus explicitly mentions the Peloponnesian War (7.137.1).
32. Georges 1994: 161.
33. Dewald (2005: 70–71) notes the elaborate complex of factors cited in 2.67, from the political situation in Thrace to Athenian motives for killing the prisoners.

what he might do if he escaped, they "killed them all that very day, without trial and wanting to say something, and threw them into a pit" (ἀκρίτους καὶ βουλομένους ἔστιν ἃ εἰπεῖν αὐθημερὸν ἀπέκτειναν πάντας καὶ ἐς φάραγγα ἐσέβαλον). The Athenians justified their actions (δικαιοῦντες) on the grounds that the Spartans had used such tactics first: they killed and threw into pits all the Athenians and their allies whom they captured on merchant ships (2.67.4). Thucydides concludes the chapter by verifying this charge and adding an important detail: "**For indeed [γὰρ δὴ]** at the start of the war the Lacedaemonians destroyed [διέφθειρον] as enemies all those they caught at sea, both the allies of the Athenians **and those on neither side** [καὶ τοὺς μετὰ Ἀθηναίων ξυμπολεμοῦντας **καὶ τοὺς μηδὲ μεθ' ἑτέρων**]" (2.67.4).

Commentators rightly find 2.67.4 a troubling passage; for A. J. Gomme and others, the executions were extreme or unwise;[34] the killing of prisoners, however, was by no means an uncommon practice.[35] For Simon Hornblower, Thucydides displays "indignation and shame" over the treatment of the captives, particularly because "the Athenian democratic constitution . . . gave the opportunity for those who 'wanted to say/speak' [a phrase ironically echoed in βουλομένους ἔστιν ἃ εἰπεῖν, 2.67.4] to do so."[36] In a general discussion of Athenian uneasiness with silence and secrecy, Silvia Montiglio similarly asserts that "the silence of power . . . was at odds with . . . Athens' alleged openness vis-à-vis citizens and foreigners alike,"[37] although she provides little evidence for the rights of foreigners.[38] P. J. Rhodes, however, noting that only citizens, metics, and certain specified others "were in law entitled to a trial in Athens" (and that heralds, but not envoys, were protected), concludes that the captives in 2.67 "had no legal grounds for complaint."[39] Rhodes' point is well taken, but we cannot overlook Thucydides' conspicuous reference to the fact that the captives were not allowed to have their say. The enforced silence powerfully signifies their abjection and frustration.

Thucydides' story is not a pretty one; it illustrates well his bitter generalization at 3.82.2 that "war is a harsh teacher, which puts most men's tempera-

---

34. E.g., Gomme 1956: 201 (citing Marchant).
35. Pritchett 1991: 205–23.
36. Hornblower 1991: 351.
37. Montiglio 2000: 281.
38. Montiglio (2000: 282) mentions only Andocides *On the Peace* 33–34: there should be no secrets or lies when the assembly negotiates peace for all the Greeks.
39. Rhodes 1988: 248.

ments on the level of their circumstances" (ὁ δὲ πόλεμος . . . βίαιος διδάσκαλος καὶ πρὸς τὰ παρόντα τὰς ὀργὰς τῶν πολλῶν ὁμοιοῖ).[40] Athens can hardly be praised for its harsh, peremptory execution of the captured envoys and desecration of their bodies. Thucydides' entire chapter, however, is framed by the misdeeds of Athens' enemies, from their mission to seek alliance with Persia to Sparta's wholesale killing and desecration of merchants captured at sea, including (in Thucydides' own words, not his Athenians') those from neutral cities (τοὺς μηδὲ μεθ' ἑτέρων).

These two versions of the "same" story present virtually a case study of the famous (but sometimes superficial) differences between Herodotean and Thucydidean historiography—for example, Herodotus' discursiveness and his openness to the working of divine justice through time versus Thucydides' secularism[41] and interest in the details of power politics. For all these differences, however, both writers are skilled in deploying nonverbal communication as a literary device. Herodotus makes Sperthias and Boulis's refusal to bow to Xerxes into an eloquent contrast of Hellenic with despotic (especially Persian) values, one entirely consistent with all other references to *proskynesis* in the *Histories*. Moreover, the narrator himself incorporates a pregnant silence into his discourse, by highlighting his inability to tell what punishment Athens suffered for murdering the heralds.

Thucydides, for his part, complicates his story of Athenian behavior toward the captives by declaring that the prisoners were executed summarily even though they "wanted to speak." With this remark, he makes their execution more controversial than it need have been. After all, as the Athenians maintain and as Thucydides agrees, Sparta had used the same tactics on merchants from enemy and even neutral cities. Moreover, killing captives was not unusual; as noncitizens, they had no right to a trial, and one of the prisoners was considered especially dangerous. These passages provide another example of what Don Lateiner has richly demonstrated: judicious use of nonverbal communication can ineffably enrich a narrative and engage its perceptive readers.

---

40. I am grateful to Carolyn Dewald for reminding me of this formulation.
41. Hornblower (1992: 152) notes that Thucydides "corrects" Herodotus' account by removing religious motivation. The relationship between the Herodotean and Thucydidean accounts of this tale are explored in a rich and provocative paper by Elizabeth Irwin (2013) that came to my attention too late to be incorporated into this discussion.

Works Cited

Boedeker, D. 1988. "Protesilaos and the End of Herodotus' *Histories*." *CA* 7: 30–48.

Boedeker, D. 2007. "The View from Eleusis: Demeter in the Persian Wars." In E. Bridges, E. Hall, and P. J. Rhodes, eds., *Cultural Responses to the Persian Wars: Antiquity to the Third Millennium*, 65–82. Oxford: Oxford University Press.

Dewald, C. 1997. "Wanton Kings, Pickled Heroes, and Gnomic Founding Fathers: Strategies of Meaning at the End of Herodotus' *Histories*." In D. H. Roberts, F. M. Dunn, and D. P. Fowler, eds., *Classical Closure: Reading the End in Greek and Latin Literature*, 62–82. Princeton: Princeton University Press.

Dewald, C. 2005. *Thucydides' War Narrative: A Structural Study*. Berkeley: University of California Press.

Dover, K. J. 1966. "Anthemocritus and the Megarians." *AJP* 87: 203–9.

Georges, P. 1994. *Barbarian Asia and the Greek Experience: From the Archaic Period to the Age of Xenophon*. Baltimore: Johns Hopkins University Press.

Gomme, A. W. 1956. *A Historical Commentary on Thucydides*. Vol. 2, *The Ten Years' War: Books II–III*. Oxford: Clarendon.

Gourmelen, L. 2007. "Le meurtre des hérauts perses (Hérodote VII, 133–137): Écrire et réécrire l'Histoire." In G. Jacquin, ed., *Récits d'ambassades et figures du messager*, 21–45. Rennes: Presses Universitaires de Rennes.

Harrison, T. 2000. *Divinity and History: The Religion of Herodotus*. Oxford: Clarendon.

Hodkinson, S. 2000. *Property and Wealth in Classical Sparta*. London: University of Wales Press.

Hornblower, S. 1991. *A Commentary on Thucydides*. Vol. 1, *Books I–III*. Oxford: Clarendon.

Hornblower, S. 1992. "Thucydides' Use of Herodotus." In J. M. Sanders, ed., *ΦΙΛΟΛΑΚΩΝ: Laconian Studies in Honour of Hector Catling*, 141–54. London: British School at Athens.

Irwin, E. 2013. "The Significance of Talthybius' Wrath (Hdt. 7.133–7)," in K. Geus, E. Irwin, and T. Poiss (eds.), *Herodots Wege des Erzählens: Topos und Logos in den Historien*. Frankfurt 2013: 223–60.

Lanski, A. 2013. "Narratological Function of Messengers in Herodotus." PhD diss., University of Illinois at Urbana-Champaign.

Lateiner, D. 1977. "Heralds and Corpses in Thucydides." *CW* 71: 97–106.

Lateiner, D. 1987. "Nonverbal Communication in the *Histories* of Herodotus." In D. Boedeker, ed., "Herodotus and the Invention of History," special volume, *Arethusa* 20: 83–107.

Lateiner, D. 1989. *The Historical Method of Herodotus*. Toronto: University of Toronto Press.

Lateiner, D. 1995. *Sardonic Smile: Nonverbal Behavior in Homeric Epic*. Ann Arbor: University of Michigan Press.

Marrigiò, V. A. 2007. "Le voyage en Asie des Spartiates Sperthias et Boulis." *Les Études Classiques* 75: 193–205.

Mikalson, J. D. 2003. *Herodotus and Religion in the Persian Wars.* Chapel Hill: University of North Carolina Press.

Moles, J. 2002. "Herodotus and Athens." In E. J. Bakker, I. de Jong, and H. van Wees, eds., *Brill's Companion to Herodotus*, 33–52. Leiden: Brill.

Montiglio, S. 2000. *Silence in the Land of Logos.* Princeton: Princeton University Press.

Mosley, D. J. 1973. *Envoys and Diplomacy in Ancient Greece.* Historia Einzelschriften 22. Wiesbaden: Franz Steiner Verlag.

Munson, R. V. 2001. *Telling Wonders: Ethnographic and Political Discourse in the Work of Herodotus.* Ann Arbor: University of Michigan Press.

Pritchett, W. K. 1991. *The Greek State at War.* Pt. 5. Berkeley: University of California Press.

Rhodes, P. J. 1988. *Thucydides, History II.* Warminster: Aris and Phillips.

Sealey, R. 1976. "The Pit and the Well: The Persian Heralds of 491 BC." *CJ* 72: 13–20.

Wéry, L. M. 1966. "Le Meurtre des hérauts de Darius en 491 et l'inviolabilité du héraut." *L'Antiquité Classique* 35: 468–86.

CHAPTER 7

Gorgias in the Real World

Hermocrates on Interstate *Stasis* and the Defense of Sicily

Daniel P. Tompkins

As Athens threatened Sicily, first in 427 and then in 415 BCE, the Syracusan leader Hermocrates vigorously organized resistance, urging military alliances in Gela, Syracuse, and Camarina.[1] In this essay, I argue three points:

1. Hermocrates' style differs from those of other Thucydidean speakers in its use of stylistic innovations that are generally attributed to his fellow Sicilian and contemporary Gorgias of Leontini. This sort of stylistic differentiation has not been widely noticed in Thucydidean scholarship.[2]
2. Whereas Gorgias delivered both deliberate and display speeches, Hermocrates' focus is consistently deliberative, and the Gorgianic features of his speeches are not, as often claimed, merely ornamental but constitutive: they are concentrated nodes of political discourse that advance the speaker's argument about matters of life and death.

---

1. I am grateful to Professors Paula Debnar and Paul Cartledge for their extremely valuable advice during the composition of this essay, which was first conceived as an effort to inventory and discuss Hermocrates' use of Gorgianic innovations, frequently noticed but seldom analyzed by scholars. When the essay was in its final draft stage, Professor Debnar provided a copy of Jessica Miner's unpublished Smith College senior thesis on Hermocrates' style, which covered nearly the same ground as my draft written fifteen years earlier. After consulting Miner's fine study, I changed course and composed a new essay emphasizing Hermocrates' diplomatic skills. Hermocrates' Thucydidean speeches occur at 4.59–64 (Gela, 425), 6.33–34 (Syracuse), and 6.76–80 (Camarina, 415).
2. See n. 9 for further detail.

3. In Thucydides' portrayal, Hermocrates uses language adroitly and force-fully, seeking both to influence Sicilian defense strategy and to forge a new Sicilian consciousness.

Hermocrates' success, like all successes in Thucydides, is qualified. Within two years of his first speech, his own city nearly gave Athens an opening at Leontini and Camarina (5.4–6, 6.8.2), and neither of his later speeches is fully persuasive.[3] But he emerges as the successful leader of Sicilian defense.

The Innovations of Gorgias

In 427 BCE, the great sophist Gorgias of Leontini arrived in Athens as a member of the fateful embassy that first invited Athenian forces to Sicily. Gorgias' highly stylized prose at once drew attention:

Πρῶτος ἐχρήσατο γὰρ τοῖς λέξεως σχηματισμοῖς περισσοτέροις καὶ τῆι φιλοτεχνίαι διαφέρουσιν, ἀντιθέτοις καὶ ἰσοκώλοις καὶ παρίσοις καὶ ὁμοιοτελεύτοις καὶ τισιν ἑτέροις τοιούτοις, ἃ τότε μὲν διὰ τὸ ξένον τῆς κατασκευῆς ἀποδοχῆς ἠξιοῦτο, νῦν δὲ περιεργίαν ἔχειν δοκεῖ καὶ φαίνεται καταγέλαστα πλεονάκις καὶ κατακόρως τιθέμενα.

[He was the first to use figures of speech that were rather unusual, strange, and ingenious: antitheses, balanced clauses, equal numbers of syllables, similar endings, and other things of this sort, which at that time were considered worthy of reception because of the alien quality of construction, but now seem to have an overdone quality and often appear laughable and excessively used.][4] (Diod. Sic. 12.53.4)

Eric Robinson notes that "the transition to democracy [in Syracuse in 466 BCE] enabled, or indeed necessitated," the development of rhetoric.[5] More-

---

3. Unless otherwise noted, all numerical references are to books and chapters in Thucydides. At Syracuse, debate ends with a general announcing that the military leaders will make policy (6.41). Hermocrates is arguably more persuasive in his two indirect speeches, at 6.72 and 7.21, than in the direct ones. Camarina waits over a year to send aid (7.33.1). Dover notes (ad loc.) that the growing likelihood of Syracusan victory "achieved what rhetoric could not."
4. All translations in this essay are my own.
5. See Robinson 2000: 203. Corax and Tisias are said to have led this development in Syra-cuse. A "garrulous and fabulizing" Christian source, the *Prolegomena Artis Rhetoricae*, hi-

over, verbal communication and persuasion are equally essential in discussions between states—that is, for diplomacy—since the parties must come to agreement. It is not surprising, then, to find Thucydides' Hermocrates, a democratic leader in democratic Syracuse, deploying Gorgianic devices of persuasion in both civic and interstate discussions, as in the following examples:[6]

Antitheses, especially short, staccato formations, sometimes with isocolon or comparison: ξύμπαντες μέν ἐπιβουλευόμεθα, κατὰ πόλεις δὲ διέσταμεν, "We are plotted against all together but have stood apart, city by city" (4.61.1); ὑπεριδεῖν . . . προϊδεῖν, "to overlook . . . to foresee" (4.62.2); οὐκ ἀξυνετωτέρου, κακοξυνετωτέρου δέ, "not less intelligent but more evilly intentioned" (6.76.4); οὐ περὶ τῶν ὀνομάτων, ἀλλὰ περὶ τῶν ἔργων, "not about names, but about things" (6.78.3); ξυστῶμεν . . . διαστῶμεν, "[if] we unite . . . if we stand apart" (6.79.3).[7]

"Doubling" of nouns or adjectives with changes of case (polyptoton): ἰδιώτην ἰδιώτῃ, "private citizen with private citizen," and πόλιν πόλει, "city with city" (4.61.2); πόλεμος πολέμῳ, "war with war" (4.61.7); οἰκείους οἰκείων, "kinsmen to kinsmen" (4.64.3); τούς προεπιχειροῦντας ἢ τοῖς γε ἐπιχειροῦσι προδηλοῦντας, "people who attack in advance demonstrating beforehand to those attacking" (6.34.7); κατοικίσαι . . . ἐξοικίσαι, "to restore . . . to disestablish" (6.76.2); ὄντες Χαλκιδῆς Χαλκιδέας ὄντας, "who are Chalcidians who are Chalcidians" (6.79.2).

Rhyme: εὐπρεπῶς . . . εὐλόγως, "speciously . . . with good reason" (4.61.7); ἀλόγως . . . εὐλόγῳ, "irrationally . . . with good reason" (6.79.2).

Verbal repetition: σῴζοι . . . σωτηρίαν, "preserve . . . safety" (6.78.3); ξυναλλαγῶν, "reconciliations" (4.59.3); καταλλαγῆναι, "to reconcile" (4.61.2); ἀπαλλαγή, "reconciliation" (4.61.7); διαλλακτάς, "reconcilers" (4.64.4).[8]

The question that now arises is what role these features play in Hermocrates' speeches.

---

lariously reports that the Syracusan tyranny that preceded democracy was so "savage" that "the citizens were forbidden to speak, and so being obliged to communicate by pantomime invented the art of dancing" (Hinks 1940: 67); underneath the hilarity lies the serious reminder that democracy requires verbal communication.

6. See also Miner 1997: 25–36. Miner notes (28–29, 34) Hermocrates' restraint in using Gorgianic innovations.

7. Miner 1997: 38–39: "The effective initial [not y but x] construction appears more frequently in Hermocrates' speeches than in those of any other speaker."

8. See Miner 1997: 30–34 for further discussion.

Fatal Cleopatras, Lethal Predators

The example passages cited in the preceding section all conform to Diodorus' description of "Gorgianic" innovations. Hermocrates' distinctive manner of speaking here sets him apart from other Thucydidean speakers, just as Nicias, Alcibiades, Archidamus, and Pericles are distinguished by their own word choice and syntax.[9] It is equally important to notice that Hermocrates' language supports, rather than subverts, his diplomatic work.

Far from being ornamental, then, the Gorgianic features are constitutive, marking moments of intense thinking and pivotal to Hermocrates' mission of changing the Sicilian cities' ways of thinking, their attitudes toward cooperation. Consider this passage from Hermocrates' initial appeal at Gela (425 BCE):

καίτοι τῇ ἑαυτῶν ἑκάστους, εἰ σωφρονοῦμεν, χρὴ τὰ μὴ προσήκοντα ἐπικτωμένους μᾶλλον ἢ τὰ ἑτοῖμα βλάπτοντας ξυμμάχους τε ἐπάγεσθαι καὶ τοὺς κινδύνους προσλαμβάνειν, νομίσαι τε στάσιν μάλιστα φθείρειν τὰς πόλεις καὶ τὴν Σικελίαν, ἧς γε οἱ ἔνοικοι ξύμπαντες μὲν ἐπιβουλευόμεθα, κατὰ πόλεις δὲ διέσταμεν.

[Further, if we are prudent, rather than harming what we have, we should each of us bring in allies and take on dangers while adding to our possessions, and should consider that faction does extreme damage to the cities and to Sicily: all we who live here are the victims of plots, but have stood apart city by city.] (4.61.1)

Gomme declared the last clause (ξύμπαντες ... διέσταμεν, "we have all stood apart") truly Gorgianic, noting that like 4.61.7, it is "highly artificial" and has "only rhetorical point." Gomme stresses the obvious rhetorical balancing of this clause but ignores the clause's traction on the narrative.

Every word of 4.61.1 conveys something significant. For instance, as Jonathan Price notes, with ξύμπαντες, "all together," Hermocrates "insists on the necessity of Sicilian unity by stressing not only the danger from Athens but also common Sicilian interests . . . ; he repeats the phrase 'all Sicily' . . . (4.59.1, 60.1, 61.2) as if it were a natural unit, in much the same way that Thucydides

---

9. See Tompkins 1972, 1994, and 2013. Representing a largely tacit consensus, K. J. Dover (1973: 23) held that "all the Thucydidean speeches are composed in his own form of literary Attic. . . . There is very little individual characterization of speeches."

uses the term Hellas in the Archaeology."[10] The πᾶσα Σικελία theme binds
this suite of speeches, including the last (though there the theme is slightly
undermined by a chauvinistic Dorian appeal to Camarina: 6.77.1). Likewise,
ἐπιβουλευόμεθα, "we are plotted against," recurs as Athens is portrayed as
again "plotting against" Sicily a decade later (4.60.1, 4.64.5, 6.33.5, 6.80.3). The
"division" indicated by διέσταμεν, "we have stood apart," appears in the
discussion of events ten years later as well: τοὺς μὲν λόγοις ἡμῶν διιστάναι,
"to set some of us apart with words" (6.77.2); οὐ γὰρ ἦν ἡμεῖς ξυστῶμεν
πάντες δεινή ἐστιν, ἀλλ' ἤν, ὅπερ οὗτοι σπεύδουσι, τἀναντία διαστῶμεν,
"for it is not terrible if we all stand together but if—which they desire—we,
on the other hand, stand separately" (6.79.3).

"Division" (διέσταμεν, διιστάναι, διαστῶμεν) echoes στάσιν, "civil
war," two lines above. Also, στάσιν, again, is not "artificial" but harshly real.
As was mentioned above, Price perceptively shows that Hermocrates' πᾶσα
Σικελία recalls both Thucydides' use of "Hellas" in the Archaeology and the
unification of the Greek mainland against Persian invaders. By promoting
unity among Sicilians, "Hermocrates won a crucial conceptual battle long
before the huge Athenian armada arrived."[11] The balanced couplet ξύμπαντες
μὲν ἐπιβουλευόμεθα, κατὰ πόλεις δὲ διέσταμεν (all we who live here are
the victims of plots, but have stood apart city by city) may have, as Gomme
says, all the marks of Gorgianic style, but unlike Gorgias' Defense of Helen, it
warns us that lives are at stake.

In his final speech in Thucydides, Hermocrates says,

καὶ εἰ γνώμῃ ἁμάρτοι, τοῖς αὑτοῦ κακοῖς ὀλοφυρθεὶς τάχ' ἂν ἴσως καὶ τοῖς
ἐμοῖς ἀγαθοῖς ποτὲ βουληθείη αὖθις φθονῆσαι. ἀδύνατον δὲ προεμένῳ καὶ
μὴ τοὺς αὐτοὺς κινδύνους οὐ περὶ τῶν ὀνομάτων, ἀλλὰ περὶ τῶν ἔργων,
ἐθελήσαντι προσλαβεῖν · λόγῳ μὲν γὰρ τὴν ἡμετέραν δύναμιν σῴζοι ἄν τις,
ἔργῳ δὲ τὴν αὑτοῦ σωτηρίαν.

[And if he [i.e., a Camarinean leader] should err in his resolve, while he is
mourned for his own woes he might perhaps someday wish again to envy my

10. Price 2007: 170–71.
11. In a footnote (170n89), Price mentions Herodotus' use of στάσις for the potential disagreement over Greek naval command against the Persians (8.3.1). Of course, Herodotus is
speaking metaphorically, since disagreement over leadership hardly equals true "civil
war": the comparison underlines the boldness of Thucydides' usage.

good fortune. That is impossible if he gives up and does not willingly take on the same dangers, not about names but about deeds. For a man would be preserving our power in name, but in reality his own safety.] (6.78.3)

In respect to this passage, Dionysius of Halicarnassus condemns Hermocrates' antithesis, rhyme, and homoioteleuton in a string of pejoratives: for instance, μειρακιώδη, "puerile" (twice); περίεργα, "overwrought" (the same word Diodorus used), and τῶν λεγομένων αἰνιγμά των ἀσαφέστερα, "more obscure than what we call 'enigmas.'"[12] Dionysius dismisses the final clause of 6.78.3 (λόγῳ . . . σωτηρίαν) as οὐδὲ μειρακίῳ προσῆκον, "not even fit for a child."

Gomme and Dionysius judge by a standard that would possibly be appropriate for Gorgias, who contemplated remote fictions like the seduction of Helen. But here, Hermocrates confronts not a fictional enemy but a real and lethal one who threatens to conquer and sack: he is working in a "real world" far different from Gorgias', and in this world of warring men, words like Dionysius' μειρακιώδη, "puerile," suggest a risibly inadequate aesthetic. Indeed, Hermocrates' argument is at its knottiest and most forceful in passages scorned as "overwrought" and "obscure." The balanced and rhyming "Gorgianic" antithesis τοῖς αὑτοῦ κακοῖς ~ τοῖς ἐμοῖς ἀγαθοῖς marks the culmination of a barrage of emphatic possessive and reflexive personal pronouns in this chapter—more than in any other speech in Thucydides. Consider the following examples:

τὸν μὲν Συρακόσιον, ἑαυτὸν δ' οὐ πολέμιον . . . ὑπέρ γε τῆς ἐμῆς . . . οὐ περὶ τῆς ἐμῆς . . . ἐν ἴσῳ δὲ καὶ τῆς ἑαυτοῦ ἅμα ἐν τῇ ἐμῇ μαχούμενος . . . οὐ προδιεφθαρμένου ἐμοῦ, ἔχων δὲ ξύμμαχον ἐμὲ . . . τῇ δ' ἐμῇ προφάσει τὴν ἐκείνου φιλίαν (6.78.1)

τῆς αὑτοῦ ἀσφαλείας (6.78.2)

τοῖς αὑτοῦ κακοῖς . . . τοῖς ἐμοῖς ἀγαθοῖς . . . τὴν αὑτοῦ σωτηρίαν (6.78.3)

As the pronouns reveal, Syracusan and Camarinaean interests are entwined, and the survival of all Sicily requires cooperation:

12. Dion. Hal. Thuc. 48; Pritchett 1975: 38–39.

λόγῳ μὲν γὰρ τὴν ἡμετέραν δύναμιν σῴζοι ἄν τις, ἔργῳ δὲ τὴν αὑτοῦ σωτηρίαν.

[For a man would be preserving *our* power in name, but in reality his *own* safety.] (6.78.3)

Hermocrates' hard work with pronouns has a point: only a fusion of interests, transcending the binary of "my" and "your," will bring survival and "security." Moreover, every noun—even the weather-beaten λόγος/ἔργον and the seemingly redundant σωτηρίαν—is packed with consequence for the same theme. Hermocrates' *polyptota* regularly embed disjunctions (ἰδιώτην ἰδιώτῃ and πόλιν πόλει, 4.61.2; οἰκείους οἰκείων and Δωριᾶ . . . Δωριῶς, 4.64.3; Δωριῆς Δωριῶν, 6.80.3) in appeals for "common" action, "all together," on behalf of "a single land with a single name."

Hermocrates' "Gorgianic" moments, then, compress and compare, showing that Athens is not a "restorer" but a predator, as evil to Greeks as were the Persians (4.60.1), and that Sicilian defense is a shared concern. Sicily must become a community; Athens will never be a "friend"; Camarina's claimed "neutrality" is a fiction that endangers neighbors. Price's keen perception about *stasis* requires emphasis: Hermocrates is the only leader in fifth-century historiography—in all of Herodotus or Thucydides—to conceive of "civil war," *stasis*, as occurring between, rather than within, poleis.[13]

Patricia Parker opens a powerful book on Shakespeare with a critique of Samuel Johnson's condemnation of the dramatist's "quibbles," or plays on words: "A quibble [Johnson said] was to him the fatal Cleopatra for which he lost the world, and was content to lose it." Parker shows that the language that so offends Johnson, "far from being reducible to a trivializing sense of the merely verbal," is embedded in Elizabethan writing and plays rich and meaningfully ambiguous roles within the plays of Shakespeare.[14] Implicitly, she is attacking the form/content dualism that has also been standard for studies on Thucydides' speeches. Thucydidean scholars who condemn the "artificiality" or "reduction and trivialization" of Hermocrates' Gorgianic usages lead us away from the careful analysis demanded by these devices when

---

13. Price 2007: 170–71. Price emphasizes that *stasis* has no "official" definition: speakers have considerable leeway in choosing how to apply the term (personal communication, October 2012).

14. Parker 1996: 5.

they occur in a text that is, after all, about history. In these speeches, defense, not display, is central.

Shaping Policy, Reformulating Identity, Building a Security Community: Hermocrates' Rhetorical Strategy

Hermocrates seeks the obverse of *stasis*: a Sicily sufficiently free from tension to be able to defend itself, or, to use the term Karl Deutsch introduced in 1957, a "security community" in which it is assured that members "will not fight each other physically, but will settle their disputes in some other way."[15] Deutsch's security community is, to some degree, social, and rewards consideration here, although this is not a point to be overstated. Modern theorists often speak of the "shared norms" or the "we-ness" or "shared identity" of a security community. We find Hermocrates edging toward "we-ness," especially when he says that community depends on geography, not ethnicity, though on one occasion he lapses into ethnic parochialism:[16]

. . . ἀλλὰ Δωριῆς ἐλεύθεροι ἀπ' αὐτονόμου τῆς Πελοποννήσου τὴν Σικελίαν οἰκοῦντες.

[. . . but free Dorians, inhabiting Sicily from an autonomous Peloponnese] (6.77.1)

He also admits that the compact among Sicilian states is tenuous:

πρὸς ἀλλήλους δι' ἀντιλογιῶν πειρώμεθα καταλλαγῆναι καί, ἢν ἄρα μὴ προχωρήσῃ ἴσον ἑκάστῳ ἔχοντι ἀπελθεῖν, πάλιν πολεμήσομεν.

[In our debate, we are seeking reconciliation. If this eventuates in each of us departing without a fair share, we shall fight again.] (4.59.4; cf. 4.64.3)

All the same, like other political and diplomatic agents, he seeks to build a security community by using language.[17] In the modern world, this language is as

---

15. Deutsch 1957: 6, quoted in Adler and Barnett 1998: 3.
16. On "we-ness," see Mattern 2005: 16.
17. Cf. Debnar 2002: 198 on Brasidas' appeal to the Chalcidians.

contentious as in Thucydides, and the individuals who use language most effectively are often those who succeed.

"Effective" language means language that makes the agent's proposals appear legitimate and that leaves as little room as possible for the adversary to construct counterarguments. Such language relies on "legitimation strategies" that make a case as strong as possible and include, inter alia, "rhetorical traps" that prevent evasion. Thus Parnell's "calculated ambiguity" won the vote both of supporters of Irish independence and of constitutionalists who wanted to remain part of Britain;[18] to make his case for annexing Schleswig-Holstein, Bismarck simultaneously employed nationalist terms that suited the German confederation and nonnationalist, constitutionalist language when negotiating with Austria and Russia, imperial powers leery of national movements.[19] Dulles, expelling the British from Suez without firing a shot, "used his clout in duplicitous and double-crossing ways," humiliating and infuriating Eden.[20]

Hermocrates does not "double-cross" but does set out "traps." Over the course of three speeches, he presents opponents with hard decisions: they should choose "peace" and "unity" and should side with the "common (or public) good" of "all of Sicily" against a consistently predatory enemy. If Camarina refuses Hermocrates' request and remains allied with Athens, then Athens, as victor, will simply absorb Camarina, whereas Syracuse will enforce retribution (τιμωρίαν, 6.80.4). Either way, he implies, Camarina will suffer the self-enclosed isolation that Aristotle elsewhere (*Pol.* 1253a) compares to that of the single piece in backgammon, ἄζυξ . . . ὥσπερ ἐν πέττοις (unyoked . . . as in draughts).

As Hermocrates frames this case, it is compelling. In actuality, it was qualified. It takes a while for the Syracusans and Camarinaeans to come around, and even when they do, Thucydides remembers the Syracusan tragedy as a victory for Syracuse, not for "all Sicily":

ἀλλ' οὐκ ἐν τούτῳ μόνῳ Λακεδαιμόνιοι Ἀθηναίοις πάντων δὴ ξυμφορώτατοι προσπολεμῆσαι ἐγένοντο, ἀλλὰ καὶ ἐν ἄλλοις πολλοῖς· διάφοροι γὰρ πλεῖστον ὄντες τὸν τρόπον, οἱ μὲν ὀξεῖς, οἱ δὲ βραδεῖς, καὶ οἱ μὲν ἐπιχειρηταί, οἱ δὲ ἄτολμοι, ἄλλως τε καὶ ἐν ἀρχῇ ναυτικῇ πλεῖστα ὠφέλουν. ἔδειξαν δὲ οἱ

18. Goddard 2010: 69.
19. Goddard 2008.
20. Mattern 2005: 142.

Συρακόσιοι· μάλιστα γὰρ ὁμοιότροποι γενόμενοι ἄριστα καὶ προσεπολέμησαν.

[But not on this occasion alone was Sparta the most advantageous opponent of all for Athens, but on many others. That is because these two cities were the most different in character, one swift, the other dilatory, one full of enterprise and the other of timid daring, which especially benefited Athens' naval empire. Syracuse showed this, being similar in character to Athens and thus her best opponent.] (8.96.5)

Thucydides never tells us whether he knew that Hermocrates died in 408 BC while leading an armed effort to restore tyranny to Syracuse. (He was serving his nephew and coinsurgent, who was to become the dread tyrant Dionysius I.)[21] This fact is often omitted from discussions of Hermocrates, and from one point of view, it could be considered a distraction here, since I have sought to demonstrate Hermocrates' effectiveness in rallying Sicilians to the cause of self-defense. But Hermocrates' achievement remains, and in an essay honoring Donald Lateiner, it seems not only appropriate but obligatory to acknowledge that history has jagged edges.

Works Cited

Adler, E., and Barnett, M. 1998. "Security Communities in Theoretical Perspective." In E. Adler and M. Barnett, eds., Security Communities, 3–28. Cambridge: Cambridge University Press.

Debnar, P. 2002. Speaking the Same Language: Speech and Audience in Thucydides' Spartan Debates. Ann Arbor: University of Michigan Press.

Deutsch, K. 1957. Political Community and the North Atlantic Area. Princeton: Princeton University Press.

Goddard, S. 2008. "When Right Makes Might: How Prussia Overturned the European Balance of Power." International Security 33: 110–42.

Goddard, S. 2010. Indivisible Territory and the Politics of Legitimacy: Jerusalem and Northern Ireland. Cambridge: Cambridge University Press.

Gomme, A.W., Andrewes, A., and Dover, K.J. 1945–1981. A Historical Commentary on Thucydides. Oxford: Oxford University Press.

Hinks, D. 1940. "Tisias and Corax and the Invention of Rhetoric." CQ 34: 61–69.

Mattern, J. 2005. Ordering International Politics. New York: Routledge.

---

21. Diod. Sic. 13.63, 75.

Miner, J. 1997. "Gorgiou Kephale: Thucydides' Use of Stylistic Characterization in the Speeches of Hermocrates." Senior Thesis, Smith College.

Parker, P. 1996. *Shakespeare from the Margins: Language, Culture, Context.* Chicago: University of Chicago Press.

Price, J. 2007. *Thucydides and Internal War.* Cambridge: Cambridge University Press.

Pritchett, W. 1975. *Dionysius of Halicarnassus, On Thucydides.* Berkeley: University of California Press.

Robinson, E. 2000. "Democracy in Syracuse, 466–412." *HSCP* 100: 189–205.

Tompkins, D. 1972. "Stylistic Characterization in Thucydides: Nicias and Alcibiades." *Yale Classical Studies* 22: 181–214.

Tompkins, D. 1994. "Archidamus and the Question of Characterization in Thucydides." In R. Rosen and J. Farrell, eds., *Nomodeiktes: Greek Studies in Honor of Martin Ostwald,* 99–111. Ann Arbor: University of Michigan Press.

Tompkins, D. 2013. "The Language of Pericles and Modern International Politics." In M. Tamiolaki and A. Tsakmakis, eds., *Proceedings of the Fourth Annual Alimos Conference on Thucydides.* 447–64. Berlin: De Gruyter.

CHAPTER 8

Manly Matters

Gender, Emotion, and the Writing of History

John Marincola

Donald Lateiner's work has long been concerned with historiography, non-verbal communication, and the emotions. In his early—now landmark—article "Pathos in Thucydides," Lateiner showed how the Athenian historian, often praised by moderns for his "Olympian" detachment, was, in fact, much concerned with the emotions of both the subjects and the audience of his history. Lateiner's important *Arethusa* article of a decade later cataloged and explained the numerous ways in which Herodotus' characters (and also the historian himself) used nonverbal communication. Most recently, Lateiner has examined instances of weeping in the historians from Herodotus to Polybius.[1] Thus emotion and its display in historiographical texts has long been one of the central concerns of his scholarship. My own contribution to this Festschrift tries to build on these important works of the honorand, by starting from one description that is both emotional and nonverbal, Phylarchus' account of the fall of Mantinea in 223 BCE. In particular, I examine Polybius' criticism of this account and of Timaeus' history in general, in which both authors are faulted for revealing an "ignoble and womanish" aspect of their character.

---

1. Lateiner 1977, 1987, and 2009. I do hope that this small contribution may be appreciated by the dedicatee, even if he does not agree with any or all of it. It is offered with gratitude by his long-ago undergraduate student. Like anyone who reads Lateiner's scholarship, I have learned immensely from his careful and painstaking works; like all of his friends, I have had the benefit of his support and encouragement over many, many years.

I

I begin with Polybius' attack on his predecessor Phylarchus, a much-discussed passage.[2] About to narrate the war of the Achaean league with Cleomenes of Sparta in the late third century BCE, Polybius says that he will not be following the historian Phylarchus (as some might expect), because Phylarchus is unreliable. As one of his pieces of evidence for this, he cites Phylarchus' treatment of the fall of Mantinea to the Achaeans in 223 (2.56.6–13):

(6) Wishing to emphasize the cruelty of Antigonus and the Macedonians and also that of Aratus and the Achaeans, he says that the Mantineans, when they fell into the hands of their enemies, were subjected to great misfortunes, and that the calamities which befell the city, the most ancient and the most populous in Arcadia, were so dreadful as to horrify all the Greeks and move them to tears. (7) Eager to arouse the pity of his readers and to make them sympathetic to what is being said, he introduces scenes of women clinging to one another, tearing their hair and baring their breasts, and in addition he describes the tears and lamentations of men and women accompanied by their children and aged parents as they are led away into captivity. (8) Phylarchus does this throughout his history, striving on each occasion to place the horrors before our eyes. (9) Let us ignore for the moment his ignoble and womanish disposition [τὸ μὲν οὖν ἀγεννὲς καὶ γυναικῶδες τῆς αἱρέσεως αὐτοῦ παρείσθω], and consider what is proper and useful to history. (10) The historian must not startle his readers by describing things sensationally [τερατευόμενον], nor should he try, as the tragic poets do, to represent speeches which might have been delivered, or to enumerate all the possible consequences of the events under consideration; he must rather record with fidelity what actually happened and was said, however commonplace this might be. (11) For the aim of tragedy is by no means the same as that of history, but rather the opposite. The tragic poet seeks to thrill and charm his audience for the moment by the most persuasive words possible, but the historian's task is to instruct and persuade serious students for all time by means of the truth of the words and actions he presents, (12) since in the first case the supreme aim is probability, even if what is said is untrue, the purpose being to beguile the spectators, but in the second it is truth, the purpose being to

2.   Not least by me, alas: see Marincola 2003, 2010, and 2013, all with references to earlier literature. The translations of Polybius throughout are those of the revised Loeb, with some modifications; all other translations are my own.

benefit those who love learning. (13) Apart from these considerations, Phylarchus relates most of the reversals in his history without subjoining why things were done and to what end, without which it is impossible to feel pity reasonably or anger appropriately [ὧν χωρὶς οὔτ᾽ ἐλεεῖν εὐλόγως οὔτ᾽ ὀργίζεσθαι καθηκόντως δυνατόν].

It has long been held that this passage exposes and critiques the characteristics of so-called tragic history: namely, the attempt to arouse the reader's emotions, a vivid writing style, and a concern with reversals of fortune. I have argued elsewhere that Polybius is opposed to none of these things and often engages in them himself and that what really is at stake in his attack on Phylarchus is what he considers the falsehood of the account, since Polybius regards tragedy as a genre that is objectively false, while history is, or must strive to be, true.[3]

Within this larger polemic, we may well ask, nonetheless, what is added by accusing Phylarchus of having an "ignoble and womanish nature." The phrase "ignoble and womanish" is not confined to this passage and is used sometimes by Polybius of historical characters, for example, the Bithynian king Prusias II, who comes in for some of Polybius' most virulent criticism. Prusias' undignified behavior before the Roman Senate caused Polybius to say that it was "impossible for anyone after him to surpass him in unmanliness, womanishness, and servility."[4] Undignified behavior may apply in the historical world, but it cannot quite be what Polybius intends here by referring to Phylarchus' "ignoble and womanish nature." Moreover, certain answers that might suggest themselves can also be dismissed at the outset. For example, the notion that Polybius disliked Phylarchus' portrayal of emotions can be countered by two observations. First, Polybius is not opposed to the portrayal of emotions in history, as demonstrated both by his own practice and by his remark, in this very polemic (§13), that Phylarchus failed to include the cause and purpose of individual reversals, without which one cannot feel the proper emotions; this suggests, of course, that with both cause and purpose added, one can and indeed ought to feel pity or anger. Second,

---

3. See Marincola 2003 and 2013. For the bibliography on "tragic history," see Marincola 2013: 74n1.
4. Pol. 30.18.5: ὑπερβολὴν οὐ καταλιπὼν ἀνανδρίας, ἅμα δὲ καὶ γυναικισμοῦ καὶ κολακείας οὐδενὶ τῶν ἐπιγινομένων. See the brief but excellent discussion of this passage in Eckstein 1995: 155–56.

Polybius believes that one ought to feel something about the Mantineans' plight, but it is not pity: rather, because the Mantineans failed to keep faith with the Achaeans and murdered their garrison, one ought to feel satisfaction that they received a just punishment for going back on their word.[5] So it is not a question of avoiding emotion *tout court* here or elsewhere; it is rather a question of raising the appropriate emotion(s).[6]

Tears, of course, could be seen as feminine, but the issue here is more complicated. Every Greek would have been familiar with the copious weeping of the heroes of Homer, but by the classical era, such behavior was not seen as appropriate to the self-control of men.[7] Nonetheless, the histories that have come down to us are hardly devoid of weeping,[8] and in many cases, it is difficult to believe that this is to be interpreted negatively. I will here take just two examples from Polybius. When Scipio Aemilianus weeps at the fall of Carthage and sees in the city's destruction the future of his own city, it is clear that we are meant to admire him, and Polybius himself goes on to say that Aemilianus was a great and accomplished man and one worthy of memory (38.21–22). An earlier Scipio—Africanus—is also portrayed in Polybius as weeping: at the fall of New Carthage in 209, Scipio has the prisoners brought before him. The elderly wife of Mandonius, brother of Andobalus, king of the Ilergetes, falls at his feet, asking that he treat her and her retinue more properly than the Carthaginians had done. He asks her what she is in need of, but she says nothing. He then summons the guards, who say that they have provided for the prisoners, but at this, the woman again falls to her knees and repeats her request. Puzzled, Scipio thinks the guards are lying and so tells the woman that he will appoint different men to see to their interests. Then follows 10.18.12–14:

> The woman, after some hesitation, said, "You mistake my meaning, General, if you think that we are asking you for food." And then Publius, grasping the woman's meaning and seeing before him the youth and beauty of the daughters of Andobalus and those of the other chieftains, was forced to tears, the woman indicating in a few words the character of the danger to which they were ex-

5. Pol. 2.58.11: ὥστ᾽ εἴπερ ἔπαθον ἃ Φύλαρχός φησιν, οὐκ ἔλεον εἰκὸς ἦν συνεξακολουθεῖν αὐτοῖς παρὰ τῶν Ἑλλήνων, ἔπαινον δὲ καὶ συγκατάθεσιν μᾶλλον τοῖς πράττουσι καὶ μεταπορευομένοις τὴν ἀσέβειαν αὐτῶν.
6. Fuller discussion on this topic can be found in Marincola 2013: 80–81, with references there.
7. See van Wees 1999.
8. See the survey in Lateiner 2009.

posed. He now made clear to her that he understood her meaning, and taking her by the right hand, bade her and the rest to be of good cheer, for he would look after them as if they were his own sisters and children.

It is quite clear that Scipio's tears here are, like those of his grandson Aemilianus, the indication of a noble nature. It seems clear also from this scene that Polybius cannot be objecting to Phylarchus' portrayal of scenes of women, even women in the throes of suffering as a result of captivity: it is, of course, true that women can be portrayed as forces of discord, irrationality, and so forth, but a number of women besides the wife of Mandonius come in for praise from Polybius.[9]

But there are distinctions to be made in weeping, and the male/female divide comes into play here, for two things are particularly associated with women and tears: first, they are given to excesses of grief; second, they are thought to delight in grief. The correlation of women (and barbarians) with excessive grief is generally recognized as a feature of Greek thought,[10] and men who engage in such behavior generally earn reproach. This can be seen, surprisingly enough, even when the man at issue is the greatest of Greek heroes, at least as a later age saw it. Zoilus of Amphipolis, the fourth-century BCE critic of Homer, took issue with Homer's portrayal of Achilles' reaction to the news of Patroclus' death. Commenting on *Iliad* 18.22 ("So he spoke, and the black cloud of grief covered him"), the scholiast notes,

> Plato in the third book of his *Republic* [388a] finds fault with those who grieve, saying that they should not do this as if the dead have suffered some terrible thing. And Zoilus says that it is absurd for Achilles to realize this now; for he ought to have known beforehand that dangers in war are common to all, and he should not have supposed that death was a terrible thing; and such excessive grief is womanish [προειδέναι τε γὰρ ἐχρῆν ὅτι κοινοὶ οἱ πολεμικοὶ κίνδυνοι τόν τε θάνατον οὐκ ἐχρῆν δεινὸν ὑπολαμβάνειν τό τε οὕτως ὑπερπενθεῖν γυναικῶδες]. Not even a barbarian nurse would behave like that.[11]

---

9. Consider Polybius' praise of Berenice, daughter of Magas (5.36.1); the wife of Demaratus of Corinth (6.11a.7); the Galatian princess Chiomara (21.38.7); Apollonis, wife of Attalus I (22.20); and the wife of Hasdrubal during the fall of Carthage (38.20). See, further, von Scala 1890: 256–58; Eckstein 1995: 151–56.

10. For women and weeping, see Arnould 1990: 102–8; Holst-Warhaft 1992: chs. 4–5; Loraux 1998: 10–12; Stears 1998. For excessive weeping as characteristic of women and barbarians, see Hall 1989: 44, 83–84.

11. *FGrHist* 71 F 11 = schol. Hom. A Σ 22 (Erbse 4.440).

It is specifically Achilles' "excessive grief" (ὑπερπενθεῖν) that Zoilus characterizes as "womanish," and a similar thing can be seen in a remark from Plutarch's
Life of Solon:

> [Solon] set up a law regulating the appearances of women and their mourning
> and their festivals, prohibiting anything disorderly and licentious. . . . [Other
> laws forbade laceration of the flesh, placing more than three garments in a
> grave, and visiting graves other than those of one's family.] And it has been es-
> tablished in our [Chaeronean] laws that those who do such things will be fined
> by the *gynaikonomoi* on the grounds that they are in the grip of unmanly and
> womanish sufferings and extravagances in their mourning [ὡς ἀνάνδροις καὶ
> γυναικώδεσι τοῖς περὶ τὰ πένθη πάθεσι καὶ ἁμαρτήμασιν ἐνεχομένους].

There is also the notion that women delight more than men in tears and
grief, as can be seen by certain remarks in (especially) the tragedians. Euripides' Electra, for example, tells the chorus of the tears she sheds night and
day, for which she is rebuked by the chorus; in the opening scene, she refers
to "wakening her mourning again" and her "much-teared pleasure." The *Andromache* is even more explicit: "Women's nature is to take pleasure in having
always in their mouths and on their tongues their present evils." And the
chorus in the *Troades* remarks, "How sweet a thing are tears for those who
have fared ill, and songs of lamentation, and music which involves sorrows."[12]

Each of these aspects plays a role in Polybius' characterization. What is
"womanish" in Phylarchus' nature is the excess he displayed in his own
portrayal of the fall of Mantinea, where he, as Polybius says, "introduces
scenes of women clinging to one another, tearing their hair and baring their
breasts, and . . . describes the tears and lamentations of men and women
accompanied by their children and aged parents as they are led away into
captivity" (2.56.7). Placing these δεινά before our eyes encourages a reaction that Polybius thought inappropriate to the situation. It was inappropriate not only because of the factual falsehood (remember, the Mantineans
did not deserve pity) but also because such a portrayal was inimical to the
purposes of history, at least as Polybius conceived them. Here the other element of Polybius' characterization of Phylarchus' nature—that it was "ig-

---

12. Eur. *El.* 125–26: ἴθι τὸν αὐτὸν ἔγειρε γόον / ἄναγε πολύδακρυν ἀδονάν; *Andr.* 93–95:
ἐμπέφυκε γὰρ / γυναιξὶ τέρψις τῶν παρεστώτων κακῶν / ἀνὰ στομ' αἰεὶ καὶ διὰ
γλώσσης ἔχειν; *Tro.* 608–9: ὡς ἡδὺ δάκρυα τοῖς κακῶς πεπραγόσι / θρήνων τ' ὀδυρμοὶ
μοῦσά θ' ἣ λύπας ἔχει.

noble" (ἀγεννές)—is directly relevant. For as Polybius makes clear in the preface of his work, part of history's purpose is to teach all men how to endure their sufferings (1.1.2):

> ... that the truest education and training for a life of political action is the learning that comes from history, and that the clearest and indeed only method of learning how to bear nobly the vicissitudes of fortune [τοῦ δυνάσθαι τὰς τῆς τύχης μεταβολὰς γενναίως ὑποφέρειν] is the recollection of the reversals of others, etc.

The use of "nobly" (γενναίως) here cannot be accidental: for it is a matter not simply of bearing changes of fortune—people must, in the end, bear the fortunes they are given, whether they like them or not—but of bearing them in a particular way. That way clearly must be with the restraint and bearing that was considered appropriate for "men"—not overindulging in grief, not taking pleasure in it, and not displaying it inappropriately.[13]

It is not accidental, therefore, that Polybius has joined "ignoble" and "womanish," because, in this case, they are two sides of the same coin. For Polybius, the kind of portrayal that Phylarchus gave could not serve as a useful exemplum nor help readers master their own emotions, since scenes comprising such lamentations of women and men (or portraying the grief of children and the elderly) cannot teach us anything important about how to conduct ourselves in the real world. To the obvious objection that Polybius himself must have known that Phylarchus' portrayal of the fall of Mantinea mirrored pretty accurately what actually did happen when a city was sacked, he would have responded, I think, "Exactly so: and for just that reason there is no need to dwell on the details; it can add nothing except a kind of (in this case, mis-) identification."

II

Polybius employs this characterization of a predecessor's work as "ignoble and womanish" in a second passage, in the course of one of his attacks on Timaeus of Tauromenium, the great historian of the west and of Sicily, whom Polybius sought to refute and ridicule throughout his book 12. Polybius criti-

---

13. For a discussion of Roman codes of elite manliness, see Clark's essay in this volume.

cizes, among many other things, Timaeus' penchant for dreams and prodigies (12.24.5 = *FGrHist* 566 T 19):[14]

> he exhibits great severity and audacity in accusing others, but his own pronouncements are full of dreams, prodigies, incredible tales, and in short, ignoble superstition and womanish sensationalism [δεισιδαιμονίας ἀγεννοῦς καὶ τερατείας γυναικώδους].

We notice here that same combination of "ignoble and womanish," although the two terms are apportioned separately here. That δεισιδαιμονία can be described as "ignoble" is hardly surprising, since Polybius makes clear that belief in such things is inappropriate for reasonable men, while the ruling elite's use of religion and superstition as ways of controlling the multitude (τὸ πλῆθος) is perfectly acceptable. Thus superstition becomes a quality associated with the lowly and those who cannot govern themselves: δεισιδαιμονία "lui paraît indigne d'une âme bien née, incompatible avec la noblesse et la dignité, conception tout aristocratique"; "seems to him unworthy of a well-born nature, incompatible with nobility and dignity, an idea that is entirely aristocratic."[15]

Τερατεία is a complex term, having mainly to do with marvels or prodigies or portents.[16] In Polybius, it is often associated with falsehood and contrasted, either explicitly or implicitly, with truth. For example, in describing accounts of far-off countries, Polybius distinguishes between writers who have told tall tales and those who have sought to find out the truth (3.58.8–9):

> For it was a difficult matter to see many things at all closely with one's own eyes, owing to some of the countries being utterly barbarous and others quite desolate. . . . Then, even if anyone did see for himself and observe the facts, it was even still more difficult for him to be moderate in his statements, to scorn all talk of marvels and the sensational [καταφρονήσαντα τῆς παραδοξολογίας καὶ τερατείας], and, preferring truth for its own sake, to tell us nothing beyond it.

14. For a discussion of this passage, see Meister 1975: 30–34; on Timaeus' δεισιδαιμονία, see Schepens 1978.
15. Pédech 1961: 119. On Polybius and superstition, see Walbank 1957: 11–12, 741–42; Walbank 1972: 59–60; Pédech 1964: 396–430; Mohm 1977: 108–16.
16. On τερατεία, see Pédech 1961: 119–20; Marincola 2010: 453–54.

Polybius likewise criticizes seafarers' tales (4.42.7):

But I speak [of the Pontus region] especially in view of the falsehoods and sensational tales of seafarers [τῆς τῶν πλοϊζομένων ψευδολογίας καὶ τερατείας], so that we may not be obliged owing to ignorance to listen greedily like children to anything that is told us, but having now some traces of the truth in our minds may be more or less able to form an independent judgment as to the truth or falsehood of the reports made by this or that person.

In his defense of Homeric geography, Polybius again contrasts τερατεία with truth, when he remarks that "it is not like Homer to build an empty narrative full of marvels on no basis of truth."[17]

Polybius also finds fault with historians who introduce τερατεία so as to create a sensationalistic account. In the attack on Phylarchus, for example, Polybius uses the term τερατευόμενον (§10) to indicate something outside the historian's proper remit, and slightly later in his attack, he accuses Phylarchus of writing a sensational narrative (αὐτῆς τῆς τερατείας χάριν, 2.58.11). Similarly, Polybius attacked the historians of the Sicilian king Hieronymus, whom, like Phylarchus, he accuses of introducing sensationalism into their accounts (7.7.1–2):

Some of the historians who have described the fall of Hieronymus have done so at great length and introduced much of the sensational [πολύν τινα πεποίηνται λόγον καὶ πολλήν τινα διατέθεινται τερατείαν], telling of the prodigies that occurred before his reign and the misfortunes of the Syracusans, and describing tragically the cruelty of his character and the impiety of his actions, and finally the strange and terrible nature of the circumstances attending his death, etc.

This kind of sensationalism must be distinguished from what we might designate as appropriate marveling, which would be more akin to admiration and is usually designated by the verb θαυμάζω and its cognates. For example, when Scipio has Carthaginian spies captured and, far from punishing them, shows them all around and then sends them back to their camp, Hannibal is described as so "admiring [θαυμάσας] the daring and magnanimity of Scipio" that he wishes to have a meeting with him (15.5.8). Else-

---

17. Pol. 34.2.1: ἐκ μηδενὸς δὲ ἀληθοῦς ἀνάπτειν κενὴν τερατολογίαν οὐχ Ὁμηρικόν.

where, Polybius says that he will describe the Roman phalanx properly so that his readers may understand its effectiveness (18.28.4–5):

> it will prove useful and beneficial to inquire into the difference [between the Greek phalanx and the Roman formation] . . . so that we may not, like foolish men, talk simply of chance and felicitate the victors without giving the reason for it, but may, knowing the true causes of their success, give them reasoned praise and admiration [ἐπαινῶμεν καὶ θαυμάζωμεν κατὰ λόγον].

This kind of marveling is thus a part of reasoned praise and can lead to appropriate emulation: it is, therefore, quite within the bounds of what is acceptable in history. By comparison, the kind of marvels or sensational matters covered by the term τερατεία is, for Polybius, an abuse by the historian, because their purpose is simply to provoke a response in the reader, without any corresponding benefit other than that of titillation.

In his attack on Timaeus, why does Polybius designate the former's τερατεία specifically as "womanish"? Once again, we must ask what this adds. Here Polybius must be intending to summon up an old topos of gender: namely, the association of women with children's stories, fables, and marvelous and untrue tales. In the *Gorgias*, Socrates urges his listeners not to dismiss his account of the Islands of the Blessed as 'an old wives' tale' (μῦθος . . . ὥσπερ γραός, 527a5), and he had asserted at the outset that the story was true (ὡς ἀληθῆ . . . ὄντα, 523a2). In Euripides' *Heracles*, Megara uses stories to spin out the time for Heracles' children while he is away:

> They seek their father, but I lead them on
> addressing them with tales.[18]

She is encouraged by Amphitryon to do so:

> Be calm and relieve the tear-flowing
> springs of the children, and soothe them with words,
> inventing a tale to delude them, wretched though that be.[19]

---

18. Eur. *Heracl.* 76–77: ζητοῦσι τὸν τεκοντ', ἐγὼ δὲ διαφέρω / λόγοισι μυθεύουσα. For the meaning of μυθεύουσα here, see Wilamowitz 1959: 3.22; Bond 1981: 82–83.

19. Eur. *Heracl.* 98–100: ἀλλ' ἡσύχαζε καὶ δακρυρρόους τέκνων / πηγὰς ἀφαίρει καὶ παρευκήλει λόγοις, / κλέπτουσα μύθοις ἀθλίους κλοπὰς ὅμως.

The "nonsense of old women," γραῶν ὕθλος, is proverbial, of course,[20] and it seems that such characterizations are what Polybius wishes his audience to have in mind.[21] It may be of more than passing significance that one of Timaeus' nicknames was γραοσυλλεκτρία (*FGrHist* 566 T 1)—the image is of an old woman repeating fantastic gossip. Since Polybius has repeatedly averred that history is concerned with truth rather than with fables or fantastic stories, the depiction of Timaeus' "womanish" sensationalism is an attempt to marginalize him and to suggest (again) that such subject matter, while possibly appropriate to other genres, has no place in history, for it can teach us nothing about the actual world and how to conduct ourselves in it.

III

To sum up, Polybius' designation of a person or thing as "womanish" or "ignoble" is an important ancillary part of his overall historiographical strategy. By using such characterizations, he seeks to privilege narratives such as his own, which showed the characters of history behaving in a "manly" and "noble" way when they met with misfortune or reversal—only these kinds of responses, he suggests, are truly appropriate for history. Women are also marginalized by being associated with "old wives' tales," which are the enemies of truth, and truth, in turn, is the goal and essence of history. Seen in this light, the branding of someone or something as "womanish" is not accidental or a mere rhetorical flourish but an important part of Polybius' overall historiographical strategy. In this way, Polybius marks the historian's territory (like the public spaces of an ancient city) as an exclusively male preserve.[22] Moreover, he suggests that just as only a real man is capable of making history, so only a real man is capable of writing history.[23]

20. In addition to the *Gorgias* passage, see Plat. *Rep.* 350e2 (ταῖς γραυσὶ ταῖς τοὺς μύθους λεγούσαις); *Tht.* 176b7 (ὁ λεγόμενος γραῶν ὕθλος); *Hp. mai.* 286a1.
21. That "children's tales" are on Polybius' mind can be seen from his remark in the discussion of the Pontus (quoted above), where he says that he tells the truth "so that we may not be obliged, owing to ignorance, to listen greedily like children to anything that is told us" (ἵνα μὴ παντὶ τῷ λεγομένῳ προσκεχηνέναι παιδικῶς ἀναγκαζώμεθα διὰ τὴν ἀπειρίαν).
22. There is also an important connection, which I cannot explore here, which links "womanishness" on the part of the historian with the historian's flattery of or partiality toward (and thus failure to be independent from) the powerful: see, e.g., Lucian *Hist. conscr.* 8–13, esp. 10 and 12.
23. Presentations of earlier versions of this essay were given at the 2008 annual meeting of the Classical Association, in Liverpool, at a panel organized by Dana Munteanu, as well as at

Works Cited

Arnould, D. 1990. *Le rire et les larmes dans la literature grecque d'Homère à Platon*. Paris: Les Belles Lettres.

Bond, G. W. 1981. *Euripides, Heracles*. Oxford: Clarendon.

Eckstein, A. M. 1995. *Moral Vision in the Histories of Polybius*. Berkeley: University of California Press.

Hall, E. 1989. *Inventing the Barbarian: Greek Self-Definition through Tragedy*. Oxford: Clarendon.

Holst-Warhaft, G. 1992. *Dangerous Voices: Women's Laments and Greek Literature*. London: Routledge.

Lateiner, D. 1977. "Pathos in Thucydides." *Antichthon* 11: 42–51.

Lateiner, D. 1987. "Nonverbal Communication in the *Histories* of Herodotus." *Arethusa* 20: 83–119.

Lateiner, D. 2009. "Tears and Crying in Hellenic Historiography: Dacryology from Herodotus to Polybius." In T. Fögen, ed., *Tears in the Graeco-Roman World*, 105–34. Berlin: De Gruyter.

Loraux, N. 1998. *Mothers in Mourning, with the Essay "Of Amnesty and Its Opposite."* Ithaca: Cornell University Press.

Marincola, J. 2003. "Beyond Pity and Fear: The Emotions of History." *Ancient Society* 33: 285–315.

Marincola, J. 2010. "Aristotle's *Poetics* and Tragic History." In S. Tsitsiridis, ed., *Παραχορήγημα: Studies on Ancient Theatre in Honour of Gregory M. Sifakis*, 445–60. Heraklion: Crete University Press.

Marincola, J. 2013. "Polybius, Phylarchus, and 'Tragic History': A Reconsideration." In B. Gibson and T. Harrison, eds., *Polybius and His World: Essays in Memory of F. W. Walbank*, 73–90. Oxford: Oxford University Press.

Meister, K. 1975. *Historische Kritik bei Polybios*. Wiesbaden. Steiner.

Mohm, S. 1977. "Untersuchungen zu den historiographischen Anschauungen des Polybios." Diss., Saarbrücken.

Pédech, P. 1961. *Polybe, Histoires Livre XII*. Paris: Les Belles Lettres.

Pédech, P. 1964. *La méthode historique de Polybe*. Paris: Les Belles Lettres.

Schepens, G. 1978. "Polybius on Timaeus' Account of Phalaris' Bull: A Case of δεισιδαιμονία." *Ancient Society* 9: 117–48.

Stears, K. 1998. "Death Becomes Her: Gender and Athenian Death Ritual." In S. Blundell, ed., *The Sacred and the Feminine in Ancient Greece*, 113–27. London: Routledge..

the Oxford "Bad Guys" seminar of Trinity Term 2010, organized by Gail Trimble and Christopher Pelling. I am grateful for the invitations of the three scholars, and I thank the audiences at both venues for stimulating and helpful criticism. Remaining errors are, of course, my own.

van Wees, H. 1999. "A Brief History of Tears: Gender Differentiation in Archaic Greece." In L. Foxhall and J. Salmon, eds., *When Men Were Men: Masculinity, Power, and Identity in Ancient Greece*, 10–53. London: Routledge.

von Scala, R. 1890. *Die Studien des Polybios*. Stuttgart: B. G. Teubner.

Walbank, F. W. 1957. *A Historical Commentary on Polybius I*. Oxford: Clarendon.

Walbank, F. W. 1972. *Polybius*. Berkeley: University of California Press.

Wilamowitz-Moellendorff, U. von. 1959. *Euripides, Herakles*. 2nd ed. 3 vols. Darmstadt: Wissenschaftliche Buchgesellschaft. Reprint of 2nd ed., Berlin, 1895.

PART 2

Emotion and Nonverbal Behavior

CHAPTER 9

Masculinity, Nonverbal Behavior, and Pompey's Death in Lucan's *Bellum Ciuile*

Christina A. Clark

Pompey's decapitation comes as no surprise to a reader of Lucan's *Bellum Ciuile*.[1] It is explicitly predicted by a raving matron (1.685–86)[2] and forms the climax to a series of decapitations, such as those of the Sullan proscriptions recalled in book 2 by the old men of Rome, who fear the approach of Caesar and his army. Deaths are often bizarre, gruesome, and grotesque in Lucan's epic, and Pompey's death is no exception.[3] However, Lucan's treatment of Pompey's death is more than this: it serves as a capstone to a process begun in book 1, when the narrator asserts that *stimulos dedit aemula uirtus* ("rivalry

---

1. The dedication of this essay to Donald Lateiner can be but a small token of my gratitude for the inspiration his work provides and for his generous help and friendship over the years. My thanks go as well to Gregory Bucher and Jennifer Larson for reading and commenting on various drafts.

2. The matron foretells a *fluminea deformis truncus harena* ("a maimed trunk on river sand," Housman's text; all translations are my own unless otherwise indicated). As Bowie (1990: 478n67) has shown, Vergil's description of Priam's death in *Aeneid* 2.554–58 evokes Pompey's death "in order that the deaths of Priam and Pompey each should enhance the pathos of the other." Just so, Lucan evokes Vergil's Priam here, to reinforce the message of the oak simile and perhaps to signal that just as Priam's death functions as a sign of Troy's fall (Bowie 1990: 472), Pompey's death symbolizes the fall of republican Rome. See also Narducci's analysis (1973: 321–23).

3. See, e.g., Fuhrmann 1968: 23–66; Henderson 2010: 464–65; Bartsch 1997: 10–47. Bartsch argues that Lucan uses human bodies to express boundary violation. Early examples include the Crassi, a father and son reduced to *trunci* (2.124). One might argue that gruesome deaths are a commonplace in war and thus in epic, yet Lucan's deaths serve other purposes as well. Most (1992: 397–98), investigating the relative frequency of wounds in epic, notes that Lucan outdoes his epic predecessors especially in terms of amputations (see also Most's n. 30, where he collects examples of dismemberment). Friedrich (2003: 48) asserts that decapitation in particular is not common in Homeric warfare. Because decapitations were a feature of the Roman civil wars, their appearance in Lucan's poem is not surprising. However, the manner in which he depicts the decapitations is far from factual accounting.

in masculinity spurred them on," 120), foregrounding masculinity as part of the struggle between Pompey and Caesar.[4] A few lines later, Lucan characterizes the two generals with his famous simile comparing Pompey to an old, weak-rooted, unstable oak and Caesar to a lightning bolt (135–57).[5] This is only the first instance of the techniques he uses to cast doubt on Pompey's ability to perform masculinity successfully, while highlighting Caesar's problematic overperformance. Throughout the epic, Lucan portrays (sometimes extravagantly) his characters' nonverbal behaviors, giving his narrative verisimilitude and vividness, but also characterizing Pompey and Caesar's opposing personalities and actions. In his depiction of Pompey's nonverbal behavior, Lucan sometimes portrays him as the epitome of traditional Roman elite masculinity (e.g., after his defeat at Pharsalus, 7.680–86) yet ultimately undermines him. In the end, the poet definitively subverts Pompey's *uirtus* by stripping him of bodily self-control in the extremity of death. In this essay, I examine Lucan's crafting of Pompey's death in book 8 and argue that the poet shows him not merely as a defeated general but as one losing the main prerequisite for masculinity: *ius sui*, "power over himself."[6]

Pompey's Nonverbal Behavior before and after Pharsalus

Since the oak simile in book 1, the narrator has shown Pompey's inconstancy as a military leader embodying heroic *uirtus* in numerous scenes (e.g., the

4. Green (1991) elucidates Iliadic patterns underlying this assertion and Lucan's epic overall. For discussions of *uirtus* in Roman culture, see McDonnell 2003 and 2009; Fantham 1995; Sklenár 2003. In the scenes I examine, *uirtus* refers to traditional Roman martial masculinity—as defined by McDonnell (2003: 251–58), who notes that Sallust portrays Julius Caesar as the embodiment of traditional martial *uirtus*, and Sklenár (2003: esp. chs. 2 and 4)—and not specifically to Stoic *uirtus*. McDonnell (2006: 296–300) discusses Pompey's conscious embrace of this model of masculinity and his public identification with it.
5. For an extended discussion of this simile, see Rosner-Siegel 1983.
6. At 8.610–12, Pompey, carried away from his fleet and family in a Pharian boat, *perdiderat iam iura sui* (had lost power over himself). He has lost control over where he goes and what is about to happen to him, and he also is about to lose bodily self-control. Roman elite men were expected to exert control over themselves and others. The great legendary exemplum of such control was Mucius Scaevola, who held his hand in fire without physically reacting, having declared, *Romanus sum . . . ciuis . . . et facere et pati fortia Romanum est* ("I am a . . . Roman citizen, . . . and it is the Roman way to act and to endure bravely," Livy 2.12–13). Cicero contrasts this traditional ideal with men who, suffering from *opinio . . . effeminata*, cannot endure a bee sting without crying out (*Tusc.* 2.52). Seneca, Lucan's uncle, also reflects this expectation of male self-control (*quem magis admiraberis, quam qui imperat sibi, quam qui se habet in potestate?* "Whom will you admire more, than he who commands himself, than he who has himself in his own power?" *Ben.* 5.7.5).

contrast between, on the one hand, his aggressive rhetoric when bragging to his troops that the people in Rome flee not in fear of Caesar but in pursuit of himself and, on the other hand, his own flight from Caesar at 2.575–609, where he was *uiribus inpar . . . profugusque per Apulia rura*, "unequal in strength . . . and fled through Apulian fields").[7] Now, as Pompey draws near to his death, at the end of book 7 and start of book 8, Lucan constructs and then deconstructs his masculinity in quick succession. In the aftermath of the general's crushing defeat at Caesar's hands in Pharsalus, the narrator describes Pompey's behavior, which accords with the highest traditional standards of male self-control:

> *tum Magnum concitus aufert*
> *a bello sonipes non tergo tela pauentem*
> *ingentisque animos extrema in fata ferentem.*
> ***non gemitus, non fletus erat***, *saluaque uerendus*
> *maiestate dolor, qualem te, Magne, decebat*
> *Romanis praestare malis.* ***non inpare uoltu***
> *aspicis Emathiam: nec te uidere superbum*
> *prospera bellorum nec fractum aduersa uidebunt;*

> [Then a steed is spurred to carry Magnus from
> the battle, not fearing weapons from the rear
> but going to meet his final destiny with enormous courage.
> **No sorrowing, no tears were there**; his grief deserves respect,
> with dignity maintained, a grief exactly fitting for you
> to show in Roman hardships, Magnus. **With unchanged face**[8]
> you gaze upon Emathia: success in war never
> saw you proud, adversity will never see you broken . . .]

(7.677–84, trans. Braund)

---

7. For Roman constructions of masculinity calling for control of the bodily display of emotion, consult Braund 2002: chs. 5–6; Walters 1997; Williams 1999: ch. 4. Elite men competed with one another in the social performance of masculinity in politics, war, and other arenas: see Gleason 1990; Barton 1994, 1999, and 2002; Alston 1997; Gunderson 2000; Corbeill 2004: ch. 4.

8. Caesar exhibits such facial self-control when he grants clemency to Pompey's soldiers *uoltuque serenus* (with serene facial expression) after they had slaughtered his own troops, first embraced as brothers (4.363). Bettini (2011: 150) studied the Latin terms for "face" and "facial expression" and concluded that *uultus* denotes the upper part of the face (eyes, eyebrows, forehead) that transmits emotions and reveals personality traits and dispositions. As the focus of interpersonal communication, it is considered an even more direct "language" than speech.

The general maintains control over his gestures and affect displays,[9] not allowing his emotions to show in his nonverbal behavior. The poet expects both internal and external audiences to take note of this excellent performance of social masculinity.[10] Next, as Pompey flees, the narrator turns his attention to Caesar for the rest of the book, ending with a direct address to and passionate question for the gods and a reference to future events of the war.

Book 8 begins abruptly, as Pompey, in flight from battle on his exhausted horse, trembles in response to noises in the forest, fearing attack (*pauet ille fragorem / motorum uentis nemorum, comitumque suorum / qui post terga redit trepidum laterique timentem / exanimat,* "He trembles at the roar of forests moved by winds and any of his comrades who returns behind his back petrifies him, alarmed and fearing for his side," 5–8).[11] His fears stem from his belief that Caesar would serve him just as he would Caesar, by sending men to capture and decapitate him: "he still has a throat worth as much as he himself would give for Caesar's severed head" (*seque . . . tantae mercedis habere / credit adhuc iugulum, quantam pro Caesaris ipse / auolsa ceruice daret,* 10–12, trans. Braund). Pondering his changed luck, he fearfully (*trepidum,* 35) sails aboard a tiny boat (38–39) to Lesbos, where his fearful (*trepida formidine,* 44) wife Cornelia waits for him. The picture Lucan paints is a far cry from the scene immediately after Pharsalus. Instead of exhibiting a dignified, controlled demeanor, Pompey is "disfigured by pallor, the white hair covering his face, his clothing dirtied by black dust" (*deformem pallore*

---

9. These are autonomic responses of the nervous system and "types of impulsive but not entirely uncontrollable emotional responses, such as weeping" (Lateiner 1992: 257).

10. As Ormand (2010: 327) notes, "Often in Lucan internal narrators, that is, narrators who are characters acting within the epic, present a visual 'text' that is 'read' by other characters on the scene. Their facial expressions, or, more typical in Lucan, lack of facial expressions, are explicitly described as attempting to convey specific meaning, and as such qualify to be treated as internal narration."

11. "Fear" words with the stem *pau-* convey both the emotion and the physical manifestation of the emotion, violent trembling. *Trepido* also connotes violent trembling (see *OLD* s.v. *trepido* 1 (b); Fowler 2002: 137). Trembling reveals the emotion to others, exposing loss of self-control. Lucretius likens men who fear death to children trembling in fear of the dark (*nam ueluti pueri trepidant atque omnia caecis / in tenebris metuunt, sic nos in luce timemus / interdum, nilo quae sunt metuenda magis quam / quae pueri in tenebris pauitant finguntque futura,* "For even as children tremble and fear everything in blinding darkness, so we sometimes dread in the light things that are no whit more to be feared than what children shudder at in the dark, and imagine will come to pass," 2.55–58, trans. Bailey). According to Fowler (2002: 138), *pauitant* suggests "a violent physical reaction, the exaggerated terror of a small child." Thus, one could argue that by using *pauet* and *trepidum* here, Lucan both emasculates and infantilizes Pompey.

ducem uoltusque prementem / canitiem atque atro squalentis puluere uestes, 56–57, trans. Braund).[12] Pompey's pallor may be due to fatigue and old age, but in epic, pallor traditionally denotes fear and cowardice, and this meaning may thus come to the forefront of readers' minds here, especially given Lucan's emphasis on Pompey's fear in the previous lines.[13] After a tear-filled reunion, the couple leaves Lesbos by ship; on the way to allies in the East, they are met by his supporters, scattered previously by a storm. After some debate, Pompey agrees to sail for Egypt, now ruled by the boy-king Ptolemy, whom the narrator impugns as *semiuir* ("half a man" or "effeminate," 552) while characterizing Pompey in lines 553–54 as *domitor mundi* (conquerer of the world), *triumphator ter Capitolia curru inuectus* (one who celebrates a triumph borne three times by chariot to the Capitol), *regum potens* (having power over kings), and *uindex senatus* (champion of the Senate), descriptions that illustrate the goals of traditional Roman martial masculinity: military accomplishment and successful competition for high political offices.

Pompey's Death

Pompey heads into the trap at Alexandria as *auctor sceptrorum* ("the person responsible for [Ptolemy's] scepter," 573), expecting loyalty from Ptolemy in return.[14] Having come by ship with his wife Cornelia and his son Sextus

---

12. Malamud (2003: 34) argues that Pompey is dressed here as for a funeral. The funereal associations are reinforced by Lucan's limited use of *pallor* in the poem. Of eight instances, five have primary associations with death (3.414, 5.216, 5.628, 6.517, 6.759, 7.129). Thus, the *pallor* of Pompey's face could signal his coming death, much as the *pallor* of the sun over Pharsalus was a divine sign of coming battle (7.200); see Dinter 2005: 298–99 for the corporeality of Lucan's sun.

13. Epic pallor most often denotes fear (e.g., Lucr. 3.154–56, Verg. *Aen.* 2.212; see Lateiner 1992: 260 and 1995: 241). Mackay (1961) notes that Lucan prefers to use "fear" words of mental activity, such as *timeo* and *metuo*, rather than words that include bodily components, such as *pallor*. Thus, while Lucan typically reinforces one "fear" word with another in following lines (310), the fact that this is one of few instances of *pallor* in the epic (312), used after the poet depicts Pompey as manifestly fearful, demands notice. The polysemous *pallor* indicates to internal and external audiences both Pompey's fear and his imminent death. In contrast, when Lucan describes a prophetess as pale, he takes care to clarify that it is not from fear (5.215–16).

14. As Malamud (2003: 32–33) observes, Lucan's account of Pompey's death is influenced by many others: the tradition of Cicero's death in declamatory exercises (Roller 1997: 122–23); the deaths of Turnus, Sulla, and Julius Caesar (Hardie 1993: 38nn45–46).

Pompey, he senses that something is amiss but continues because "it pleases him to prefer death to fear" (*letumque iuuat praeferre timori*, 576).[15] The scene that follows has antecedents in Homeric and Ovidian epic, to which Lucan alludes in order to contrast them with Pompey's dying physical reactions. Pompey's wife Cornelia tries to enter the Egyptian boat with him, and when Pompey orders her to stay where she is and to watch what unfolds, *surda uetanti / tendebat geminas amens Cornelia palmas* ("deaf to him forbidding, out of her mind, Cornelia extended both hands," 582–83).[16] Supplicating him in vain, she hangs over the side of the boat "in stunned fear" (*attonito . . . metu*, 591), unable either to look at or away from what is happening to her husband.

In one of the most famous scenes of the *Iliad*, Hector leaves the battlefield and returns to the city of Troy to fetch his brother Paris and to instruct his mother to offer prayers and gifts to the goddess Athena to stop Diomedes. He finds his wife, Andromache, by the Scaean gates, together with their infant son, Astyanax, and a slave woman. Andromache has run there to watch the battle because she had heard that the Trojans were losing. Homer describes her as being "like a woman gone mad" (*mainomene eikuia*, 6.389). Crying as she stands by her husband, she takes him by the hand, entreating him to stay on the rampart with her, because the Achaeans are massing to kill him, as Achilles had killed her brothers. Hector replies that he cannot do that, because the code of heroic manhood inculcated from boyhood prevents him:

> ἀλλὰ μάλ᾽ αἰνῶς
> αἰδέομαι Τρῶας καὶ Τρῳάδας ἑλκεσιπέπλους,
> αἴ κε κακὸς ὣς νόσφιν ἀλυσκάζω πολέμοιο·
> οὐδέ με θυμὸς ἄνωγεν, ἐπεὶ μάθον ἔμμεναι ἐσθλὸς
> αἰεὶ καὶ πρώτοισι μετὰ Τρώεσσι μάχεσθαι,
> ἀρνύμενος πατρός τε μέγα κλέος ἠδ᾽ ἐμὸν αὐτοῦ.

---

15. Perhaps it pleased Pompey to do so because he had a different audience for his behavior than he had in his flight from battle earlier. Some, such as Sklenár (2003: 107), argue that Pompey here shows progress in his (ultimately unsuccessful) journey toward Stoic *uirtus*.

16. Bruère (1951: 236n107) collects a number of Ovidian parallels for this, such as Ariadne in *Her.* 10.148 and Alcyone at *Met.* 11.726–27. These, of course, also hark back to Priam's appeal to Hector (*Il.* 22.37), discussed in Bowie 1990. Later, Seneca's Phaedra passionately and unsuccessfully supplicates Hippolytus (*Phaed.* 580ff.; see Hahnemann's contribution to this volume).

[I would feel deep shame before the Trojans, and the Trojan women
with trailing garments, if like a coward I were to shrink aside from
the fighting; and the spirit will not let me, since I have learned to be
valiant and to fight always among the foremost ranks of the Trojans,
winning for my own self great glory, and for my father.] (6.441–46, trans.
Lattimore)

The only witnesses here are the slave woman and baby. After Hector explains his behavior according to heroic *habitus*, the couple laughs together over their son's fear of the helmet. Stroking his wife with his hand, Hector reassures her, telling her to go back to the house and to her own work while he returns to the fighting and whatever fate awaits him.

This Homeric intertext prepares us for a display of masculinity before an audience. Unlike Hector and Andromache in this scene, but like Hector and Achilles later, Pompey and Cornelia have a large, public audience.[17] As an elite Roman man, Pompey resembles the rest of his peers in being keenly aware of himself performing in front of an audience on the stage of life, so to speak.[18] As Braund argues, "Pompey's concern with the impression he is making on those around him and with his future reputation (*fama*) is a central element in his characterization by Lucan as a man obsessed with his own name."[19] The Roman fleet is present and anxious as well, but unlike Cornelia, fears not Pompey's death but, instead, that he will unman himself by "kneeling with groveling prayers before a scepter given by his own hand" (*summissis precibus Pompeius adoret / sceptra sua donata manu*, 594–95). It is significant that the fleet fears that Pompey might do such a thing, given both his inconsistent masculinity in the previous books and his lack of control to come.

This scenario of individual *uirtus* on display to both allies and enemies is similar to that of Vulteius and his men in a raft of Caesar's that the Pompeians had caught by trickery at Ilerda (4.465–95). In a hopeless situation, Vulteius seeks *gloria leti* ("the glory of death," 479), pointing out to his men

---

17. In front of the walls of Troy and an audience of Greeks and Trojans, at Achilles' approach, reminding himself of past mistakes and the current need to fight gloriously, Hector shivered (*hele tromos*) and fled from fear (*bê de phobêtheis*) (*Il.* 22.136–37). He thus failed to perform heroic masculinity until later, after Athena's intervention, when he fought Achilles bravely.
18. See Braund 2002: 89; Ormand 2010: 335.
19. Braund 2002: 101.

their opportunity to gain fame through display of traditional martial *uirtus:* *conferta iacent cum corpora campo, / in medium mors omnis abit, perit obruta uirtus: / nos in conspicua sociis hostique carina / constituere dei; praebebunt aequora testes, / praebebunt terrae, summis dabit insula saxis, / spectabunt geminae diuerso litore partes* ("when corpses lie crowded on the field, every individual death is merged into a common one, obscured manliness perishes: the gods have placed us in a vessel in sight of friends and enemies; the sea and land will provide witnesses, the island with highest rocks will give witnesses, both sides will watch from opposite shores," 4.490–95). The *uirtus* displayed here, he says, will win them both glory and notice from Caesar: *magna uirtute merendum est, / Caesar ut amissis inter tot milia paucis / hoc damnum clademque uocet* ("we must earn with great manliness, that with a few among so many thousands lost, Caesar should call this loss a disaster," 512–14). Vulteius successfully inspires himself and his men to feats of heroic manliness;[20] Pompey does not.

Another exemplar of traditional, martial *uirtus* in the *Bellum Ciuile* is the behavior of Caesar's centurion Scaeva when fighting at Dyrrachium, as described in book 6.[21] Caesar had surrounded the city and Pompey's troops with earthworks; when Pompey tries to break through the rampart, Scaeva drives back Pompey's troops with exceptional fighting. Although he is not elite and fights in a typically Lucanian unorthodox manner in what has been characterized as an "anti-*aristeia*," Scaeva nevertheless displays bravery and fortitude to his end, even riddled with spears.[22] When defeated, he assumes the pose of an epic suppliant even as he plans his next attack, carefully schooling his facial expression to fool his enemies (*mitis et a uoltu penitus uirtute remota*, "mildly, and with manliness banished far from his face," 229). At the end of Scaeva's *aristeia*, his men lift him onto their shoulders and revere him as *uiuam magnae speciem Virtutis* ("the living form of great Manliness," 254).[23]

---

20. So notes Sklenár (2003: 31).
21. Bonner (2010: 99) argues that descriptions of the *uir fortis* (brave man) in declamation schools influenced Lucan's description of Scaeva and others.
22. Caesar records Scaeva's bravery at *B. Civ.* 3.53. Sklenár (2003: 45–58) discusses the ways in which Scaeva also subverts heroic *uirtus* in, for example, his lineage and his style of fighting. Henderson (2010: 439–45), Johnson (1987: 57–60), and Gorman (2001: 277–79) examine generic subversion here.
23. In his performance of masculinity, Scaeva, "Caesar's Left Hand" (Henderson 2010: 440), performs as well as Scaevola, "Left-Handed," sharing accomplishments as well as similar names.

Unlike Vulteius and Scaeva, Pompey loses in death one of the main pre-requisites for manhood: self-control. Yet, although his men fear that Pompey will unman himself (593–95), he at first seems to be meeting his death as an elite man should: he covers his face (*inuoluit uoltus*, 614, proleptically recall-ing Caesar's dying gesture[24]), closes his eyes (*lumina pressit*, 615), and holds his breath to keep from crying out and ruining his eternal fame by weeping (*continuitque animam, nequas effundere uoces / uellet et aeternam fletu corrumpere famam*, 616–17; again, sources tell us that Caesar kept silence in the same way after his famous words to Brutus). Indeed, when stabbed, Pompey controls his nonverbal behavior just as Mucius Scaevola did when he held his hand in the fire: "with no groan did he acknowledge the thrust and did not heed the crime; he preserved his body motionless" (*nullo gemitu consensit ad ictum / respexitque nefas, seruatque inmobile corpus*, 619–20).

Like Homeric Hector, Pompey turns his thoughts over in his chest, re-flecting that the eyes of the world and the ages watch his performance (622–24). He exhorts himself to "think of fame" (*nunc consule famae*, 624), begging his pain to suppress moans with more endurance (*tanto patientius, oro, / claude, dolor, gemitus*, 633–34).[25] Hitherto, Pompey has lived his life successfully, but this is his final test, as he reminds himself: *ignorant populi, si non in morte pro-baris, / an scieris aduersa pati* ("The people don't know, if you are not proven in death, whether you know how to endure adversity," 626–27).[26] Therefore, he must not give way to shame (*ne cede pudori*, 627).[27] He expects a display of manliness to win the admiration and love of his wife and son (as well as the world and posterity). Because Roman sons learned *Romanitas* from their fa-thers, Pompey's behavior at death provides a model for his son Sextus to

---

24. Suet. *Iul.* 82; Plut. *Caes.* 66; App. *B. Civ.* 2.16.117. See Bell 1994 for a discussion of accounts of Pompey and Caesar's deaths.

25. Later, Pompeian troops suffering in the desert tried to control such effeminizing paralin-guistics in front of Cato: *puduitque gementem / illo teste mori* ("with him as witness, it shamed them to die groaning," 9.886–87).

26. After Pompey's death, appealing to the same traditional martial code of masculinity, Cato calls to join him in the African desert those Pompeian troops *qui me teste pati uel quae tristis-sima pulchrum / Romanumque putant* ("who think it beautiful and Roman to endure, with me as witness, even the most severe things," 9.391–92). Of course, Cato's fortitude stems not just from traditional codes of masculinity but also from his Stoic beliefs.

27. Kaster (2005: 45–47) discusses the type of *pudor* we see here, a "discreditable 'retraction' of the self," and the theatrical dimension of *pudor* (56–61), when one sees oneself being seen (and judged).

emulate, an additional, unspoken social expectation behind this scene.[28] The general controls his breathing, affect displays, paralinguistics, and facial expression while being stabbed, demonstrating to the internal audience the nonverbal behavior of the ideal elite man performing traditional *uirtus*. At this point, the narrator breaks in, attempting to influence the external audience's perceptions of Pompey: "such control of mind Magnus had, this power he had over his dying spirit" (*talis custodia Magno / mentis erat, ius hoc animi morientis habebat*, 635–36).

The external audience, though, exposed to Pompey's thoughts, receives conflicting messages about his masculinity.[29] Pompey's internal monologue implies that brave self-control is not something that has become natural to him through a lifetime of practice in the "forest of eyes" that was republican Rome.[30] Pompey's thoughts belie the narrator's insistence on Pompey's command of himself, as the behavior of his decapitated head will soon do definitively. Telling us that "those who saw the severed head say that the majestic beauty of his sacred form remained and features calmed by the gods, the last death throes had changed nothing from the appearance and facial expression of the man" (*permansisse decus sacrae uenerabile formae / placatamque*[31] *deis faciem, nil ultima mortis / ex habitu uoltuque uiri mutasse fatentur/ qui lacerum uidere caput*, 664–67), the narrator claims that Pompey's features were unaffected by his dying. But, strikingly, this is not true, as Lucan himself tells us, giving lie to the claims of the internal audience.

After Achillas has stabbed the now *semianimis* ("half alive," 670) Pompey, the Roman soldier Septimius grabs him, uncovers his face, and severs his head with much effort, described in gruesome detail (667–73).[32] Held aloft on a spear, Pompey's head displays nonverbal behavior he had successfully suppressed before, "while his features are alive and sobs of breath impel the mouth to murmur" (*dum uiuunt uoltus atque os*[33] *in murmura pulsant / singultus*

---

28. See, e.g., Pliny *Ep.* 8.14.4–6; Baroin 2011.
29. Against Feeney 2010: 350–51, Ormand (2010: 337) suggests that Lucan evokes the external narratee precisely so that we will read Pompey's death as "falsely stoic."
30. I owe the phrase "the forest of eyes" to Gleason (1990: 389).
31. I here use Shackleton Bailey's emendation (from the 1998 Teubner text) of the manuscript's *iratamque*.
32. The popularity in declamation schools of descriptions of Cicero's murder may have influenced Lucan here (Bonner 1966).
33. Perhaps it is not accidental that the sounds in these words mimic exhalations of breath.

animae, 682–83, trans. Braund).[34] He had suppressed any telltale nonverbal behavior as he was stabbed, but after decapitation, his face reacts, and his mouth releases sounds, undoing his previous manly self-control.[35] He also has opened (*lumina nuda*, 683) his previously tightly closed eyes (*lumina pressit*, 615).[36] The use of the paradoxical word *uiuunt* to describe the action of a dying, decapitated head demands explanation. Elsewhere in the epic, Lucan describes dying body parts as just such: *morientia membra* ("dying limbs," 4.648–51) and *morientia ora* ("dying mouth," 7.609).[37] Given this fact and that Lucan does not characteristically portray wounds and deaths with an eye to verisimilitude, we must ask ourselves what other reasons there might be for Lucan to portray the nonverbal behavior of Pompey's decapitated head in this way.[38]

Other poets show body parts in motion after they have been severed, but they often are continuing the action they were performing beforehand, thus underlining the power and fortitude of the people from whom they have been separated. Four examples from Vergil's *Aeneid* and Ovid's *Metamorphoses* demonstrate this.[39] Vergil provides us with the example of Laris, whose hand, after it has been lopped off in battle, valiantly holds his sword with trembling fingers, (*te decisa suum, Laride, dextra quaerit / semianimesque micant digiti ferrumque retractant*, 10.395–96).[40] In the midst of the battle between Perseus and Phineus, recounted in book 5 of the *Metamor-*

---

34. It is suggestive that Pompey's manly nonverbal behavior after Pharsalus occurs at 7.680–86 while his ultimate unmanly nonverbal behavior occurs at almost the exact lines in book 8 (679–88).

35. Since the head is no longer connected to the torso and, thus, the lungs are no longer able to power such emanations and sounds, it goes without saying that this description is not based on any realistic behavior of decapitated heads.

36. So observes Malamud (2003: 36).

37. Cf. the same manner of description at Ov. *Met.* 5.117: *digitis morientibus* (dying fingers).

38. Sklenár (2003: 22) argues that Lucan's "references to such horrific wounds and deaths as *miracula fati* and *unica leti facies* acknowledge the complete inverisimilitude of his own epic world."

39. I thank Donald Lateiner for directing me to these examples.

40. Lucretius incorporates the epic topos of battlefield dismemberment and mutilation as part of his proof that souls are material and are distributed throughout the body: "Even the head, when from the warm and living trunk lopped off, keeps on the ground the vital countenance and open eyes until it has rendered up all remnants of the soul" (3.654–56). The presence of the soul throughout the body accounts for the movement of body parts even after dismemberment. Scholars such as Johnson (1987) have analyzed Lucan's over-the-top, disgusting, yet sometimes funny death scenes, in which he often inverts subject-object relations (e.g., bodies protect shields at 3.619–20; see Bartsch 1997: ch. 1), veering into the grotesque.

phoses, the aged Emathion "fights" verbally with his tongue as he clings to an altar until Chromis decapitates him.[41] His head falls on the altar, and "his dying tongue denounces them in words of execration" before his soul expires in flames (*atque ibi semianimi uerba exsecrantia lingua edidit,* 5.105–6).[42] Raped Philomela loses not her head but her tongue, which murmurs and writhes on the ground after Tereus severs it to stop her prayers for vengeance (*ipsa iacet terraeque tremens inmurmurat atrae, / utque salire solet mutilatae cauda colubrae, / palpitat et moriens dominae uestigia quaerit,* 6.558–60). Finally, after Orpheus' dismemberment by Ciconian matrons, his tongue makes mournful sounds, an action the narrator calls miraculous (*et mirum! medio dum labitur amne, / flebile nescio quid queritur lyra, flebile lingua / murmurat exanimis,* 11.51–53). Similarly, Lucan makes the tongue of M. Marius Gratidianus, who has been as horribly and completely dismembered as Ovid's Orpheus, writhe on the ground and strike the empty air in silent motion (*exsectaque lingua / palpitat et muto uacuum ferit aera motu,* 2.181–82).[43] This action shows Gratidianus' outrage, enhancing his manly valor. Likewise, when an unnamed Greek continues to fight using what is left of his body after both his arms were severed by a Roman soldier in battle, the narrator remarks: *creuit in aduersis uirtus: plus nobilis irae*

---

41. Malamud (2003: 36), who notes Lucan's double allusion to both Vergil's Priam and Ovid's Emathion in his narrative of Pompey's death, well observes that by naming the elderly victim Emathion, Ovid invites readers to recall Pharsalus and Pompey's defeat. She argues that Lucan took the behavior of Emathion's decapitated head as a model for Pompey's, accounting for the contradiction between what the internal audience claims the dying Pompey looked like and what Lucan describes.

42. As noted previously, Vergil depicts the butchery of Priam at the altar at *Aen.* 2.550–58; Anderson argues that "Ovid destroys the nobility of Vergil's scene by concentrating on the severed head and the incredibly voluble tongue" (1997: 509, ad loc.). Seneca too depicts severed heads emitting sounds. In the *Thyestes* (726–29), Atreus decapitates his brother's son on an altar: *tunc ille ad aras Plisthenem saeuus trahit / adicitque fratri. colla percussa amputat; / ceruice caesa truncus in pronum ruit, / querulum cucurrit murmure incerto caput* ("Then Plisthenes to the altar did that butcher drag and set him near his brother. His head with a blow he severed; down fell the body when the neck was smitten, and the head rolled away, grieving with murmur inarticulate," trans. F. J. Miller). In the *Agamemnon* (901–3), Clytemnestra strikes her husband in such a way that *pendet exigua male / caput amputatum parte et hinc trunco cruor / exundat, illic ora cum fremitu iacent* ("The scarce severed head hangs by a slender part; here blood streams o'er his headless trunk, there lie his moaning lips," trans. F. J. Miller). Unlike those of Emathion, the words of Plisthenes' and Agamemnon's complaining heads lack clarity and force.

43. Quint (1993: 143) argues that by depicting the tongue in this way, Lucan creates emotional distance from the horror of the dismemberment he describes. One might note also that in Lucan, as in Ovid, the tongue *palpitat.*

/ *truncus habet* ("his manliness increased in adversity: his trunk has a greater amount of noble anger," 3.614–15).[44]

Thus, Pompey's loss of self-control after he has been decapitated contrasts markedly with the control displayed by severed body parts elsewhere in Latin epic as well as in the *Bellum Ciuile*. We have many literary examples of men whose dismembered body parts exhibit *uirtus*. Yet Pompey fails to control himself (9.747–48), like Aulus later, who, fighting in the torrid African desert with Cato and the Pompeian army, drinks seawater and his own blood to assuage his thirst, an action that Cato (when offered water in the desert) had previously characterized as effeminate: *mene, inquit, degener unum miles in hac turba uacuum uirtute putasti? / usque adeo mollis primisque caloribus impar / sum uisus?* ("Degenerate soldier, he said, did you take me for the only one devoid of manhood in all this crowd? Did I impress you as so effeminate, so unequal to the first onset of heat?" 9.505–8, trans. Sklenár). Audiences might be tempted to react as Cato did in response to Aulus' (unmanly and un-Stoic) behavior: Cato marched away in disgust.

Even as Pompey's features move and his mouth makes noise, the head's death is heralded by hardening eyes (*lumina nuda rigescunt*, 683). The narrator distances us from what is happening by not allowing us to overhear Pompey's thoughts during and after his decapitation.[45] Lucan follows this shocking description with a reminder of how far Pompey had fallen from the pinnacle of elite male achievement: "this [head] swayed the laws, Campus, and rostra" (*hoc leges Campumque et rostra mouebat*, 685).[46]

Using nonverbal behavior to undermine Pompey's masculinity both during the events leading up to and also during the last moment of his life accords with Lucan's general practice of building up and undercutting Pom-

---

44. Bonner (2010: 99) asserts that Lucan's description here parallels "in exaggeration and absurdity . . . the Greek declamation on Cynegirus," who lost his hand when grasping a Persian ship at the battle of Marathon (Hdt. 6.114).

45. Most 1992: 400. Bartsch (1997: 39) asserts that Lucan takes care at points in his narrative to alienate readers from what is happening, to ensure that we will not pity the characters.

46. Feeney (2010: 354) argues that Pompey "achieves true greatness by and in death," which might be true if the character were judged by "his acceptance of an attitude to death which corresponds to the values asserted by the narrator" (350) and not by his ultimately poor bodily performance of *Romanitas* and masculinity, not to mention Stoicism.

pey.[47] This practice continues even after Pompey's death, as when the poet has Gnaeus Pompey ask about his father, *stat summa caputque / orbis* ("Is he still the head of the world?" 9.123–24), making his decapitation into a grotesque pun.[48] At this point in the narrative, the "oak" has toppled; the general has been defeated in battle, mutilated, and killed, leaving audiences with the image of Pompey's final emasculating failure of bodily control, a control he can never regain. He has indeed proven himself in death. Although his spirit acts at the beginning of book 9, Pompey has definitely lost the contest in masculinity set out at the start of book 1; it is left for Cato and Caesar to contend thereafter.

Works Cited

Alston, R. 1997. "Arms and the Man: Soldiers, Masculinity, and Power in Republican and Imperial Rome." In L. Foxhall and J. Salmon, eds., *When Men Were Men: Masculinity, Power, and Identity in Classical Antiquity*, 205–23. London: Routledge.

Anderson, W. S. 1997. *Ovid's Metamorphoses Books 1–5*. Norman: University of Oklahoma Press.

Baroin, C. V. 2011. "Remembering One's Ancestors, Following in Their Footsteps, Being Like Them: The Role and Forms of Family Memory in the Building of Identity." In V. Dasen and T. Späth, eds., *Children, Memory, and Family Identity in Roman Culture*, 19–48. Oxford: Oxford University Press.

Barton, C. A. 1994. "All Things Beseem the Victor: Paradoxes of Masculinity in Early Imperial Rome." In R. C. Trexler, ed., *Gender Rhetorics: Postures of Dominance and Submission in History*, 83–92. Medieval and Renaissance Texts and Studies 113. Binghampton, NY: Center for Medieval and Renaissance Studies.

Barton, C. A. 1999. "The Roman Blush: The Delicate Matter of Self-Control." In J. I. Porter, ed., *Constructions of the Classical Body*, 212–34. Ann Arbor: University of Michigan Press.

Barton, C. A. 2002. "Being in the Eyes: Shame and Sight in Ancient Rome." In D.

---

47. For discussions of Lucan's inconsistent representations of Pompey, see Ormand 1994; Bartsch 1997: 75–79. O'Hara 2007 studies inconsistency in Roman epic overall.
48. Bartsch (1997: 16n13) notes, "That the head of the world is a headless trunk (or a trunkless head?) is driven home mercilessly in books eight and nine: in only 250 lines, there are seven references to Pompey as a *truncus*—at 8.674, 608, 722, 753, 774; and 9.14 and 53." Dinter (2005: 301–4) discusses Lucan's use of the word *caput* as "one of the master tropes" of his epic.

Fredrick, ed., *The Roman Gaze: Vision, Power, and the Body*, 216–35. Baltimore: Johns Hopkins University Press.

Bartsch, S. 1997. *Ideology in Cold Blood: A Reading of Lucan's Civil War*. Cambridge, MA: Harvard University Press.

Bell, A. A., Jr. 1994. "Fact and Exemplum in Accounts of the Deaths of Pompey and Caesar." *Latomus* 53: 824–36.

Bettini, M. 2011. *The Ears of Hermes: Communication, Imagery, and Identity in the Classical World*. Trans. W. M. Short. Columbus: Ohio State University Press.

Bonner, S. F. 1966. "Lucan and the Declamation Schools." *AJP* 87: 257–89. Reprinted in Tesoriero, 69–106.

Bowie, A. M. 1990. "The Death of Priam: Allegory and History in the *Aeneid*." *CQ* 40.2: 470–81.

Braund, S. 1992. *Lucan, Civil War*. Oxford: Oxford University Press.

Braund, S. 2002. *Latin Literature*. London: Routledge.

Bruère, R. 1951. "Lucan's Cornelia." *CP* 46.4: 221–36.

Corbeill, A. 2004. *Nature Embodied: Gesture in Ancient Rome*. Princeton: Princeton University Press.

Dilke, O. A. W. 1979. "Lucan's Account of the Fall of Pompey." In *Studi su Varrone, sulla retorica, storiografia e poesia Latina: Scritti in onore di Benedetto Riposati*, 1.171–84. Rieti: Centro di studi Varroniani.

Dinter, M. 2005. "Lucan's Epic Body." In C. Walde, ed., *Lucan in the Twenty-First Century*, 295–312. Munich: Saur Verlag.

Fantham, E. 1995. "The Ambiguity of Virtus in Lucan's *Civil War* and Statius' *Thebaid*." *Arachnion: A Journal of Ancient History and Literature on the Web* no. 3.

Feeney, D. 1986. "*Stat Magni Nominis Umbra*: Lucan on the Greatness of Pompeius Magnus." *CQ* 36: 239–43. Reprinted in Tesoriero, 346–54.

Fowler, D. 2002. *Lucretius on Atomic Motion*. Oxford: Oxford University Press.

Friedrich, W.–H. 2003. *Wounding and Death in the Iliad: Homeric Techniques of Description*. Trans. P. Jones and G. Wright. London: Duckworth.

Fuhrmann, M. 1968. "Die Funktion grausiger und ekelhafter Motive in der lateinischen Dichtung." In H. R. Jauss, ed., *Die nicht mehr schönen Künste: Grenzphänomene des ästhetischen*, 23–66. Munich: Fink.

Gleason, M. 1990. "The Semiotics of Gender: Physiognomy and Self-Fashioning in the Second Century C.E." In D. M. Halperin, J. J. Winkler, and F. I. Zeitlin, eds., *Before Sexuality: The Construction of Erotic Experience in the Ancient Greek World*, 389–415. Princeton: Princeton University Press.

Gleason, M. 1995. *Making Men: Sophists and Self-Presentation in Ancient Rome*. Princeton: Princeton University Press.

Gorman, V. 2001. "Lucan's Epic '*Aristeia*' and the Hero of the '*Bellum Ciuile*.'" *CJ* 96.3: 263–90.

Green, C. M. C. 1991. "*Stimulos Dedit Aemula Virtus*: Lucan and Homer Reconsidered." *Phoenix* 45: 230–54. Reprinted in Tesoriero, 149–83.

Griffin. J. 1983. *Homer on Life and Death*. Oxford: Oxford University Press.

Gunderson, E. 2000. *Staging Masculinity: The Rhetoric of Performance in the Roman World*. Ann Arbor: University of Michigan Press.

Hardie, P. 1993. *The Epic Successors of Virgil: A Study in the Dynamics of a Tradition*. Cambridge: Cambridge University Press.

Henderson, J. G. W. 1987. "Lucan: The Word at War." *Ramus* 16: 122–64. Reprinted in Tesoriero, 433–91.

Housman, A. E. 1926–27. *M. Annaei Lucani Belli Civilis Libri Decem*. Oxford: Blackwell.

Johnson, W. R. 1987. *Momentary Monsters: Lucan and His Heroes*. Ithaca: Cornell University Press.

Kaster, R. A. 2005. *Emotion, Restraint, and Community in Ancient Rome*. Oxford: Oxford University Press.

Lateiner, D. 1992. "Affect Displays in the Epic Poetry of Homer, Vergil, and Ovid." In F. Poyatos, ed., *Advances in Nonverbal Communication: Sociocultural, Clinical, Esthetic, and Literary Perspectives*, 255–69. Amsterdam: John Benjamins.

Lateiner, D. 1995. *Sardonic Smile: Nonverbal Behavior in Homeric Epic*. Ann Arbor: University of Michigan Press.

Mackay, L. A. 1961. "The Vocabulary of Fear in Latin Epic Poetry." *TAPA* 92: 308–16.

Malamud, M. 2003. "Pompey's Head and Cato's Snakes." *CP* 98.1: 31–44.

Martindale, C. A. 1993. *Redeeming the Text: Latin Poetry and the Hermeneutics of Reception*. Cambridge: Cambridge University Press.

McDonnell, M. 2003. "Roman Men and Greek Virtue." In R. M. Rosen and I. Sluiter, eds., *Andreia: Studies in Manliness and Courage in Classical Antiquity*, 235–62. Mnemosyne Supplements 238. Leiden: Brill.

McDonnell, M. 2006. *Roman Manliness: "Virtus" and the Roman Republic*. Cambridge: Cambridge University Press.

Most, G. W. 1992. "*Disiecti membra poetae*: The Rhetoric of Dismemberment in Neronian Poetry." In R. Hexter and D. Seldon, eds., *Innovations of Antiquity*, 391–419. London: Routledge.

Narducci, E. 1973. "Il tronco di Pompeo." *Maia* 25: 317–25.

O'Hara, J. J. 2007. *Inconsistency in Roman Epic: Studies in Catullus, Lucretius, Vergil, Ovid, and Lucan*. Cambridge: Cambridge University Press.

Ormand, K. 1994. "Lucan's *auctor vix fidelis*." *CA* 13: 38–55. Reprinted in Tesoriero, 324–45.

Roller, M. 1997. "Color Blindness: Cicero's Death, Declamation, and the Production of History." *CP* 92.2: 109–30.

Rosner–Siegel, J. A. 1983. "The Oak and the Lightning: Lucan, *Bellum Ciuile* 1.135–157." *Athenaeum* 61: 165–77. Reprinted in Tesoriero, 184–200.

Quint, D. 1993. *Epic and Empire*. Princeton: Princeton University Press.

Sklenár, R. 2003. *The Taste for Nothingness: A Study of Virtus and Related Themes in Lucan's Bellum Ciuile*. Ann Arbor: University of Michigan Press.

Tesoriero, C., ed. 2010. *Lucan*. Oxford Readings in Classical Studies. Oxford: Oxford University Press.

Walters, J. 1997. "Invading the Roman Body: Manliness and Impenetrability in Roman Thought." In J. Hallett and M. Skinner, eds., *Roman Sexualities*, 29–43. Princeton: Princeton University Press.

Williams, C. A. 1999. *Roman Homosexuality: Ideologies of Masculinity in Classical Antiquity*. Oxford: Oxford University Press.

CHAPTER 10

Nonverbal Behavior in Seneca's *Phaedra*

Carolin Hahnemann

At the end of his review of Don Lateiner's pioneering exploration of nonverbal behavior in the Homeric epics, Walter Donlan risked a glimpse into the future: "*Sardonic Smile* opens up new dimensions for the study of ancient literature; one may predict that analysis of the nonverbal 'parallel' texts will become increasingly common as a result of this important study."[1] He was right. Although nobody has yet attempted a comprehensive treatment of the subject to supersede Sittl's magnum opus from the end of the nineteenth century, recent years have seen the publication of numerous shorter investigations, often focusing on a particular gesture or on the use of nonverbal behavior in a particular author or genre.[2] The subject's interdisciplinary nature, however, can pose an obstacle to this progress. Since the study of nonverbal behaviors has long been the domain of several fields, there exists no generally accepted terminology. Practitioners in the relevant disciplines—especially behaviorism, social psychology, art history, linguistics, and theater—tend to use different terms to describe the same phenomenon. Even within one discipline, the same term can have different definitions from one scholar to the next. In this essay, I employ several of these taxonomies in an attempt to shed new light on Seneca's *Phaedra*. To this end, I first survey in narrative order the evidence from one scene, the confrontation between Phaedra and Hippolytus at the end of act 2. Then I return to one gesture contained therein—Hippolytus' drawing of his sword—to place it in its thematic

1. Donlan 1996: 79.
2. See Cairns 2005 for a sampling of different approaches.

context, which, I argue, includes not only the other instances of characters handling the sword later in this tragedy but also an event from the play's mythical backdrop. May this attempt to follow in his footsteps—*non passibus aequis*—serve as a token of my appreciation of Don Lateiner as a scholar and a friend.

Methodological Framework

Philosophers of language commonly distinguish three types of elements in analyzing a speech act: verbal, paralinguistic, and kinesic.[3] The verbal and paralinguistic elements are produced by the vocal apparatus, the former referring to what is said (i.e., the utterance's content), the latter to how it is said (i.e., the utterance's pitch, volume, tone of voice, etc.). By contrast, the kinesic elements comprise the accompanying movements produced by the rest of the body, be they small and anatomically focused (like winks, blushes, or finger wagging) or large-scale and complex (like an embrace, a stooped posture, or pacing). In fact, the spectrum of possibilities for kinesics is so vast as to defy a closer definition.[4] In this essay, I use the term *kinesic* interchangeably with the more familiar labels *body language* and *gesture*.[5] Together, the paralinguistic and kinesic elements form the nonverbal portion of a speech act.

Lateiner, who has placed the study of nonverbal behaviors in classical texts at the center of his prolific career, organizes them according to a system of five categories distilled from the work of the psychologists Ekman and Friesen and the anthropologist Hall.[6] He distinguishes between nonverbal behaviors that happen out of awareness (Category B) and those that happen in awareness; these, in turn, can either be expressed in a spontaneous, informal way (Category E) or take a ritualized, conventional shape (Category A). Lateiner's remaining two categories comprise, on the one hand, nonverbal behaviors involving the manipulation of so-called external adaptors (e.g., communicative objects or clothing) and acts of self-grooming (Category C)

---

3. Bußmann, Gerstner-Link, and Lauffer 2008: passim. But some scholars use the term *paralinguistic* to refer to the totality of nonverbal communication.
4. Sittl 1890: 341.
5. So do Sittl, Spitzbarth, and Lateiner, in contrast to common parlance, where the term gesture is usually restricted to movements of the hands and arms.
6. Lateiner 1996: 226–27. Ekman and Friesen (1969) provide a taste of the difficulty inherent in sorting the vast and varied bestiary of nonverbal behaviors into useful categories.

and, on the other hand, nonverbal behaviors depending on proxemics and chronemics, that is, on the social manipulation of space and time (Category D). This last category comes very close to theatrical blocking, the process of determining and recording the positions and movements of the actors.[7] As Lateiner notes, the application of these categories to a text can be cumbersome, since a gesture may fit more than one of his categories.[8]

Whereas much real-life communication happens through nonverbal channels, the verbal record is all we have in the case of ancient drama. How can we know about the attending body language at all? Basically, there are two possible ways. First, an utterance may require a gesture in order to make sense either syntactically or semantically. I call these "completing gestures," to distinguish them from nonverbal behaviors that merely complement or accompany an utterance.[9] The best-known type of a syntactically incomplete sentence is the conditional without apodosis, while semantically incomplete sentences usually involve some form of deixis—either way, the speaker would have supplied the missing information by means of a gesture.[10] However, passages requiring a completing gesture are quite rare, and I am not concerned with them here. By contrast, complementing body language must have abounded throughout the play, but we only know so for sure in those instances when the gesture is described in the text. This, then, is our second way of knowing that a speech act was accompanied by some sort of kinesics. Because dramas consist exclusively of direct speech and choral odes, it is harder for a playwright to integrate descriptions of nonverbal behaviors than for an epic poet or a prose author, who can embed such information in the narrative before and after a speech.[11] It may be no coincidence, then, that the

---

7. Trapido 1985: 87. Fortey and Glucker (1975) provide an annotated set of blocking notes for Seneca's *Phaedra* based on their experience of staging it at the University of Exeter; cf. also Kohn 2012. Since a play constitutes the enactment of a story in a defined physical space, nonverbal behaviors belonging to Category D happen constantly and fluidly, while those belonging to Lateiner's other categories tend to be more circumscribed.

8. Lateiner 1996: 226n3. Thus Phaedra's supplication of Hippolytus belongs to Category D because it hinges on the relative position of the two characters to each other, to Category A because of its ritualized nature, and to Category C if we regard Hippolytus' knees as an external adaptor.

9. Hahnemann 2003: 59–61.

10. Boegehold (1999) analyzes many examples of conditionals without apodosis, among which I find his discussion of Aesch. *Eum.* 885–89 especially persuasive (56–57). For a semantically incomplete sentence, see Ar. *Ran.* 1029.

11. Even within a given genre, however, the frequency of nonverbal behaviors can differ significantly from author to author (cf. Lateiner 1996: 247–52).

sole instance in Seneca's *Phaedra* of a passage combining all three types of elements—verbal, paralinguistic, and kinesic—appears in a section that is akin to epic in nature: the account of Hippolytus' encounter with the monstrous bull in the messenger speech (1064–69).

Otherwise, a search of the *Phaedra* for paralinguistic elements yields rather humdrum results: that the chorus designates a speech by Phaedra as *questus* (404) and one by Theseus as *querelae* (1244) merely confirms a tone of voice we would have inferred from the content of their words anyway, and the same is true of the repeated references to pleading and sobbing (91, 381, 827, 886–87, 990, 1117, 1261, 1263). In addition, there are three times when characters declare themselves too overcome to speak (602, 719, 995). These passages are noteworthy for illustrating an ambiguity often inherent in verbally encoded nonverbal behaviors: they can be interpreted literally, as a stage direction, or metaphorically, as a figure of speech.[12]

In terms of kinesic elements, a search of the *Phaedra* proves more fruitful, because the tragedy contains a number of strikingly detailed descriptions. In the past, scholars have looked to these passages primarily for ammunition in the long-standing debate as to whether Seneca intended his plays for staging or recitation.[13] For the purposes of this essay, however, the question is moot, since this discussion is concerned with not what Seneca wanted his audience to see but what he wanted them to imagine.[14] The two are not the same: even today, a theatrical performance (more than a movie) serves to cue and complement, rather than to replace, the audience's powers of imagination, and the same applies a fortiori in ancient drama, with all its conventions and physical limitations.[15] My goal, then, is to demonstrate that the "parallel text" of body language in Seneca's *Phaedra* is worthy of investigation in its own right. As a test case, I have chosen the confrontation between Phaedra and Hippolytus, which constitutes the fulcrum of the tragic plot.

---

12. The same applies to supplications (Gould 1973: 77, 101n135).
13. Thus, as his final argument against the staging of the plays, Costa (1973: 5–6) lists "the detailed circumstantial descriptions by characters of events or activities on the stage which would have been visible to the audience of an acted play." Other scholars, like Fortey and Glucker (1975), adduce the same evidence in support of the opposite conclusion. See also n. 29 below.
14. See, similarly, Seidensticker 1969: 145–46n23.
15. One of these conventions is the use of masks.

A Sequence of Nonverbal Behaviors: Sen. Phaed. 580–735

The scene begins with an instance of rapid proxemics followed by a spectacular out-of-awareness gesture: after the Nurse's failure to talk Hippolytus out of his austere lifestyle, Phaedra approaches in a hurry (583: *praeceps graditur*), only to collapse in a swoon (585–86: *terrae repente corpus exanimum accidit / et ora morti similis obduxit color*).[16] This display of nonverbal behavior confirms the Nurse's earlier reports of Phaedra's restlessness and failing health (360–83). By contrast, Hippolytus' reaction contradicts his earlier statement that he hates, loathes, and despises all women (559–79), since he now comes to his stepmother's aid by raising her up in his arms (588).[17] Why does he not leave it to the Nurse to support her mistress? Combined with his subsequent inquiries into the cause of Phaedra's distress (591) and readiness to grant her extraordinary request to speak to him in private (601), this action must make us wonder if he really is the ruthless misogynist that he proclaims himself to be.[18]

Phaedra now realizes that her opportunity has come. After some hesitation and some hints, she prostrates herself before Hippolytus to confess her love outright: *en supplex iacet / allapsa genibus regiae proles domus . . . miserere amantis* (666–71). As is normal, the kinesic elements provided here, though plentiful, leave room for variability in the way that different readers/listeners/spectators will imagine the tableau.[19] We can be sure, however, that in contrast to her earlier swoon, Phaedra lowers herself intentionally this time, employing a set of ritualized gestures. Prostrating oneself as a signal of one's inferiority is still intelligible to our modern sensibilities, but touching or kissing another person's knees in token of submission and beseechment is not—unlike the ancients, we do not regard the knees as the body part associated

---

16. Phaedra's behavior fits into Lateiner's Categories B and D, respectively. Her blanching indicates that she is not pretending; cf. Seneca's statement that blushing is an involuntary behavior beyond the scope of the *artifices scaenici* (*Epist.* 11.7).
17. Scherer 1977 (summarized in Bußmann, Gerstner-Link, and Lauffer 2008: 483–84) distinguishes the following four parasemantic functions of nonverbal communication: (1) substitution (e.g., nodding agreement instead of saying "yes"), (2) amplification (e.g., pointing at a place while saying "there"), (3) contradiction (e.g., nodding agreement while saying "no"), and (4) modification (e.g., smiling ironically while expressing agreement). Hippolytus' behavior in this passage fits the third function except that the verbal and nonverbal messages follow one another rather than being conveyed simultaneously.
18. Boyle (1985: 1330) blunts the contradiction when he calls Hippolytus' behavior an act of courtesy and duty.
19. In this case, the uncertainty is compounded by *genibus*, which could indicate either that Phaedra has fallen to her own knees or that she is touching Hippolytus'—a common problem in supplication scenes (Sittl 1890: 156).

with compassion.[20] In other words, supplications, like many ritualized gestures, combine practical content (i.e., elements that are directly intelligible to
the observer regardless of his or her cultural background) with symbolic content (i.e., elements whose meaning is not obvious to people outside the cultural group).[21] Fortunately, however, the mechanics as well as the meaning of
this set of gestures have been studied in depth.[22] Naturally, Phaedra hopes
for a positive outcome of her supplication: that Hippolytus will make a
pledge of love to her.[23] But this is not what happens.[24]

   Phaedra's abject declaration of her passion elicits a verbal outburst from
Hippolytus, who calls on Jove and the Sun to bring the natural order of the
cosmos to a halt and denounces Phaedra as the worst of women (671a–97). In
antiquity, prayers were usually performed with outstretched hands—indeed,
the gesture was thought to be common to all humans, and we possess an
amusing anecdote of an actor being excluded from the competition after he
mistakenly gestured toward the sky when invoking Earth and toward the
ground when invoking Zeus.[25] Consequently, one may plausibly imagine
Hippolytus raising his hands at the beginning of the speech in a complementing gesture.[26] Such an assumption receives support from the consideration
that the ancients gesticulated extensively and that the verbal record of a
drama can reflect only a fraction of the body language accompanying the action as it transpires.[27] Yet positing a specific instance of nonverbal behavior
for a passage that contains no clear trace of it can be dangerous too.[28]

   In addition to explicitly described gestures, a passage may also indicate
indirectly that some nonverbal behavior has taken place. Thus Phaedra's ef-

---

20. Cf. Onians 1988: 174–86; Corbeill 2004: 80–81.
21. For this distinction and terminology, cf. Monahan 1983: 12; see also Boedeker's contribu-
    tion in this volume.
22. E.g., Gould 1973; Naiden 2006, esp. 44–62.
23. Naiden (2006) discusses positive responses to supplication (106–16) and surveys typical
    pledges (116–29).
24. For a similar supplication but with a positive outcome, cf. Sen. *Th.* 517–22. While Atreus,
    albeit treacherously, encourages Thyestes to let go of his knees so that they can embrace,
    Hippolytus perceives Phaedra's touching of his knees itself as an embrace and recoils (cf.
    genibus at *Th.* 522 and *Ph.* 667, 703; *amplexus* at *Th.* 522 and *Ph.* 705).
25. [Arist.] *Mu.* 400A16; Philostr. *VS* 541–42. Cf. Spitzbarth 1946: 18–23; Sittl 1890: 174, 186–90,
    290–91, 294 (Sittl rightly cautions that the gesture is not exclusive to prayer).
26. Fortey and Glucker (1975) direct the actors to raise their arms whenever invoking a deity,
    while Kohn (2012) calls, more vaguely, for "appropriate gestures" (105, 108, 109, 111 bis).
27. At Ar. *Av.* 1507–8, Prometheus asks Peisetaerus to hold his parasol "so that I can talk"; evi-
    dently, he needs both hands to gesticulate. Cf. also Graf 1992.
28. Llewelyn-Jones (2005: 75–76) chides Boegehold for not doing justice to the pervasiveness
    of body language in dramatic discourse, but his own inferences are highly speculative.

fort to clasp Hippolytus' knees *again* (705: *rursum*) shows that he must have
extricated himself from her touch while delivering his tirade. The resulting
sequence of proxemics is very dynamic: Phaedra moves toward Hippolytus
and sinks to the ground; Hippolytus raises her up; Phaedra prostrates herself, clasping his knees; Hippolytus recoils; Phaedra seeks to clasp his knees
again; Hippolytus grabs her with the intention to kill. Seneca describes the
ensuing tableau in shocking detail: Hippolytus draws his sword with his
right hand while twisting Phaedra's head back by the hair with his left, ready
to dispatch her as a human sacrifice for the goddess Diana (706–9):

> stringatur ensis, merita supplicia exigat.
> en impudicum crine contorto caput
> laeua reflexi: iustior numquam focis
> datus tuis est sanguis, arquitenens dea.[29]

When Phaedra expresses joy at the prospect of dying at his hands, Hippolytus decides not to grant her this boon. Instead, throwing away his sword
on the grounds that it, like himself, has become tainted by her touch (713–14),
he rushes off stage (718).[30] Seeing her mistress in so precarious a situation, the
Nurse quickly takes possession of the discarded weapon and exhibits it to the
palace servants in support of her allegation that Hippolytus is guilty of attempted rape (719–32).

A Theme of Nonverbal Behaviors: Hippolytus' Sword

Even after Hippolytus' departure, his sword continues to play an important
role throughout the rest of the tragedy. In the scene I have discussed, he first
drew it as a weapon of execution against Phaedra (706) but then discarded it
as an object of pollution (714), thereby enabling the Nurse to turn it into a
false corpus delicti (729–30). In the next scene, it reappears, this time in Phaedra's hands. She is apparently about to commit suicide with it (866) when

---

29. "Out sword, exact the penalty she deserves! See how with my left hand I hold her head
bent back by the twisted hair. No blood was ever shed with greater justice at your altar,
goddess of the bow." Birt (1911: 345), Zwierlein (1966: 59–60), and Fantham (1982: 41) cite
this passage as evidence for the view that Seneca's dramas were not intended for the stage.
30. Spitzbarth (1946: 69–70) provides a list of objects thrown away in Greek tragedy.

Theseus returns from the underworld. Instead of making a clear accusation in response to his demand that she disclose the identity of the man who has driven her to this extreme, she holds out the sword: *hic dicet ensis* (896). Misled by this evidence, Theseus "recognizes" Hippolytus as her assailant and curses him to death (929–58). Thus the sword, after twice having been pulled back from Phaedra's breast before the fatal blow, now indeed becomes the instrument of Hippolytus' death, albeit indirectly, through her agency. Its role is not finished. As the young man's dismembered remains are brought back to the palace, Phaedra once more takes hold of the sword (1155, 1157), cuts off a lock of hair to place on the corpse as a final gift (1181–82), and then, having made her final confession to Theseus, thrusts the blade into her love-crazed breast (1177, 1193–98).[31]

As this summary shows, the prominence of the sword in the plot of Seneca's *Phaedra* is remarkable. Scholars are well aware of the resulting dramatic ironies as well as the inherent sexual symbolism.[32] By contrast, the implications of the sword's use as a token of (mis)recognition have not yet been fully explored.[33] As a result, Theseus has been harshly criticized for condemning Hippolytus too quickly: "Seneca has contrived matters so as to remove any possible defence of Theseus' actions—Phaedra's accusations are ambiguous and (apart from the sword) without proof. In Seneca, Theseus' rashness and hypocrisy increase his guilt."[34] But what if Theseus was conditioned, by his own past, to trust this particular piece of false evidence? To do justice to Seneca's depiction of Theseus, then, we must take into account a mythical event, which the playwright has woven into his plot through an extensive web of allusions.

When Hippolytus denounces Phaedra as the worst of women, he explicitly compares her to two infamous heroines, Pasiphae and Medea. Like Phaedra, Medea is a granddaughter of the Sun, but in her case, Seneca does not exploit this common ancestry.[35] Instead, he juxtaposes the two women as

---

31. The text does not specify that she uses the sword, but the inference seems logical and can be supported iconographically by the depiction of Orestes cutting a lock of hair as a grave offering on the red-figure *pelike* shown as fig. 93 in Shapiro 1994: 133. (I am grateful to Dr. Oliver Pilz for this reference.)
32. E.g., Segal 1986: 130–79.
33. Seneca is especially fond of symbolic wounds and weapons: see *Th.* 1073; *Oed.* 1034–39; *HO* 845, 869; *Ph.* 106; [*Oct.*] 370. Hähnle (1929) discusses many examples of swords serving as *gnorismata*.
34. Davis 1983: 124 (citing Lefèvre).
35. This omission deserves attention because of the play's focus on heredity: Seneca depicts

contrasting examples of one of his favorite archetypes, the wicked stepmoth-
er.³⁶ No doubt, Medea is best known for (successfully) killing her own children, but the fact that Hippolytus speaks of her as *coniunx Aegei* (563) and as
Colchide nouerca (697) shows that the crime he has in mind is her (unsuccessful) attempt on the life of her stepson, Theseus. The playwright has taken care
to highlight both references: the former constitutes the culmination of Hippolytus' tirade against women, and the latter is preceded by a resounding
literary allusion. In calling any man who has died through a woman's hatred
and treachery "three and four times fortunate," Hippolytus is echoing Aeneas' famous first utterance in Vergil's epic (which, in turn, evokes a speech
by Odysseus in the *Odyssey*).³⁷ While Odysseus and Aeneas yearn for the fate
of their comrades who died heroically on the battlefield, instead of perishing
ignominiously in a shipwreck as they fear they themselves will do, Hippolytus' envy is directed specifically at his father, Theseus, because his stepmother's designs on him were merely murderous rather than erotic.

As the myth of Medea's attempt on Theseus' life is not widely known, it
deserves to be recounted here in a few sentences.³⁸ During a visit to Troezen,
Aegeus has sex with the local princess and leaves a sword as a token of his
paternity in the event that she should bear a son. When Theseus reaches
adulthood, he retrieves the sword and goes to find his father in Athens, killing a host of monsters and marauders along the way. Medea, who is now
living with Aegeus, after having murdered her children with Jason as well as
the king and princess of Corinth, realizes at once that Theseus must be Aegeus' son. Consequently, she persuades the unsuspecting king that the young
man poses a danger to his throne and must be killed (Ov. *Met.* 7.406–7, 419a–
23): "In order that he should die, Medea prepares a draught of aconite, which

Phaedra's and Pasiphae's erotic aberrations as a punishment from Venus after the Sun
betrayed her adulterous affair with Mars. (This congenital explanation dates back to Sosi-
crates *FGrHist* 461 F6 [= schol. Eur. *Hipp.* 47] and Cleo Curiensis *Suppl. Hell.* 339–339A.)

36. References to stepmothers occur at *Ph.* 357, 558, 638, 684, 1192, 1200; *Ag.* 809; *Oed.* 418, 487;
HO passim; and [*Oct.*] 21, 151, 171, 645. Medea refers to Creusa as stepmother to her own
children (*Med.* 847), and Clytaemnestra does the same with Cassandra (*Ag.* 198–99, though
the verse may be interpolated).

37. Sen. *Ph.* 695–97: *O ter quaterque prospero fato dati / quos hausit et peremit et leto dedit / odium
dolusque—genitor, inuideo tibi: / Colchide nouerca maius hoc, maius malum est*; Verg. *Aen.* 1.94–
96: *O terque quaterque beati, / quis ante ora patrum Troiae sub moenibus altis / contigit oppetere!*
Hom. *Od.* 5.306–7: τρὶς μάκαρες Δαναοὶ καὶ τετράκις, οἳ τότ' ὄλοντο / Τροίηι ἐν εὐρείηι,
χάριν Ἀτρεΐδηισι φέροντες.

38. The following synopsis simplifies a mythical sequence with many variants. For an excellent overview of the literary and artistic sources, cf. Gantz 1993: 248–57. Remarkably, in his
Medea, Seneca makes no mention of Aegeus.

long ago she had brought along from the shores of Scythia. . . . Taken in by his consort's guile, the father proffers the poison to his son as if he were an enemy. Theseus, with unwitting hand, had already accepted the cup, when his father recognized his clan's seal on the sword's ivory hilt and dashed the criminal cup from his lips." I quote Ovid's version of the story because of the striking similarity between this recognition and the misrecognition in Seneca's *Phaedra*: in both passages, a father identifies a supposed stranger as his son by means of the ancestral seal on his sword's ivory hilt.[39] Thus the evidence that once saved Theseus' life—a sword, maybe even the same sword—now causes him to condemn his son to death. Instead of realizing that Phaedra, like Medea, is acting as a treacherous stepmother, however, Theseus wrongly links Hippolytus to Medea as a dangerous barbarian because of his descent, asking sarcastically if he was born in Colchis, Medea's ancestral city (907).[40]

Theseus' curse brings about yet another meaningful inversion of the earlier myth. As the references to Sinis (1169, 1224), Sciron (1023, 1225), and Procrustes (1070) underline, the supernatural bull hunts Hippolytus to death on the very road that Theseus had cleared of monsters and marauders during his youthful journey to Athens. Finally, Hippolytus' retracing of his father's steps in reverse leads him to face the monstrous bull from the sea in an explicit attempt to live up to his father's legacy (1067). But in contrast to Theseus, who, upon his arrival in Athens, defeated the Marathonian Bull and the Minotaur, Hippolytus dies.[41]

Given the extent to which Seneca exploits the mirroring effect between the mythical history of father and son, one may wonder if he may have found them thus juxtaposed in two Greek tragedies that were produced as part of the same trilogy. Thus it should be noted that besides Sophocles' *Phaedra* and

---

39. The similarity between the two passages is common knowledge (Mayer and Coffey 1990: 168). Cf. Ov. *Met.* 7.422–23 (the translation provided in the text is my own): *cum pater in capulo gladii cognovit eburno / signa sui generis facinusque excussit ab ore*; Sen. *Ph.* 898–900: *Quod facinus, heu me, cerno? [. . .] regale patriis asperum signis ebur / capulo refulget, gentis Actaeae decus*. The detail of young Theseus' carrying a sword with an ivory hilt upon his arrival in Athens may be as old as Bacchylides (18.48). Hähnle (1929: 29) argues that the engraved design on the hilt originates in drama.

40. Paschalis 1994: 114. More broadly, the reference also belongs to the play's pervasive concern with the contrast between supposedly civilized and barbarian countries (Scott 2011: 100–101).

41. Interestingly, according to some ancient sources, the terror of Marathon was sent by Poseidon and identical with the Cretan bull that aroused Pasiphae's passion (Herter 1973: 1085).

Euripides' *Hippolytus Veiled*—which dealt with the same myth as Seneca's *Phaedra* and have been the subject of much speculation—the corpus of fragmentary tragedies also contains an *Aegeus* by each author, in which they dramatized Theseus' narrow escape from Medea's assassination attempt.[42] In addition, we possess a fragment of unknown provenance containing traces of a messenger report recounting Theseus' confrontation with a beast that has been variously identified as either the Marathonian Bull or the Minotaur (*TrGF* 5.1 F **386b). Although we know excruciatingly little about how the Greek tragedians drew connections between different plays that were performed together, the figure of Theseus, the triangular constellation of father, son, and stepmother, and the use of the sword may have together provided a hinge similar to the links between Aeschylus' *Agamemnon* and *Libation Bearers* or those between the *Alexander* and the *Trojan Women* of Euripides' Trojan trilogy.[43] In the absence of additional evidence, however, such a hypothesis can be nothing more than an intriguing guess, and I offer it not to divert attention away from the Roman tragedy and toward identifying its potential Greek models—the impetus behind many older books on Seneca's dramatic works—but to aid our appreciation of his *Phaedra* as a work of art in its own right. As I hope to have shown, for such an appreciation, especially in terms of plot development and characterization, it is imperative to trace Seneca's sustained and skillful use of a parallel text of nonverbal behaviors.

I would like to thank Scott Smith of the University of New Hampshire and Judson Herrman of Allegheny College for their invaluable help.

Works Cited

Bakewell, G., and J. Sickinger, eds., 2003. *Gestures: Studies in Ancient History, Literature, and Philosophy Presented to Alan Boegehold.* Oxford: Oxbow.

Birt, T. 1911. "Was hat Seneca mit seinen Tragödien gewollt?" *Neue Jahrbücher für das klassische Altertum, Geschichte und deutsche Literatur* 37: 336–64.

Boegehold, A. 1999. *When a Gesture Was Expected.* Princeton: Princeton University Press.

Boyle, A. J. 1985. "In Nature's Bonds: A Study of Seneca's *Phaedra.*" *ANRW* II.32.2: 1284–347.

---

42. Hahnemann 1999. Gibert (1997) surveys the evidence for the *Hippolytus* plays with salutary skepticism, but his voice has not been much heeded.
43. Wilamowitz (1880: 481–84) posits a Euripidean trilogy consisting of *Aegeus, Theseus,* and *Hippolytus Veiled.*

Bremmer, J., and Roodenburg, H. eds. 1992. *A Cultural History of Gesture*. Ithaca, NY: Cornell University Press.

Bußmann, H., Gerstner-Link, C., and Lauffer, H. 2008. *Lexikon der Sprachwissenschaft*. 4th ed. Stuttgart: Kröner Verlag.

Cairns, D. L., ed. 2005. *Body Language in the Greek and Roman World*. Swansea: David Brown.

Corbeill, A. 2004. *Nature Embodied: Gesture in Ancient Rome*. Princeton: Princeton University Press.

Costa, C. D. N. 1973. *Seneca, Medea*. Oxford: Clarendon.

Davis, P. J. 1983. "Vindicat omnes natura sibi: A Reading of Seneca's *Phaedra*." *Ramus* 12: 114–27.

Donlan, W. 1996. Review of *Sardonic Smile: Nonverbal Behavior in Homeric Epic*, by Donald Lateiner. *CJ* 92.1: 77–79.

Ekman, P., and Friesen, W. F. 1969. "The Repertoire of Nonverbal Behavior: Categories, Origins, Usage, and Coding." *Semiotica* 1: 49–98.

Fantham, E. 1982. *Seneca's Troades*. Princeton: Princeton University Press.

Fortey, S., and Glucker, J. 1975. "Actus Tragicus: Seneca on the Stage." *Latomus* 34: 699–715.

Gantz, T. 1993. *Early Greek Myth*. Baltimore: Johns Hopkins University Press.

Gibert, J. 1997. "Euripides' *Hippolytus* Plays: Which Came First?" *CQ* 47: 80–92.

Gould, J. 1973. "Hiketeia." *JHS* 93: 74–103.

Graf, F. 1992. "Gestures and Conventions: The Gestures of Roman Actors and Orators." In Bremmer and Roodenburg, 36–58.

Hahnemann, C. 1999. "Zur Rekonstruktion und Interpretation von Sophokles' *Aigeus*." *Hermes* 127: 385–96.

Hahnemann, C. 2003. "A Gesture in Archilochos 118 (W)?" In Bakewell and Sickinger, 55–62.

Hähnle, A. 1929. *ΓΝΩΡΙΣΜΑΤΑ*. Tübingen: H. Laupp.

Herter, H. 1973. "Theseus." *RE* Suppl. 8: 1045–238.

Lateiner, D. 1995. *Sardonic Smile: Nonverbal Behavior in Homeric Epic*. Ann Arbor: University of Michigan Press.

Lateiner, D. 1996. "Nonverbal Behaviors in Ovid's Poetry, Primarily *Metamorphoses* 14." *CJ* 91.3: 225–53.

Llewellyn-Jones, L. 2005. "Body Language and the Female Role Player in Greek Tragedy and Japanese Kabuki Theatre." In Cairns, 73–105.

Kohn, T. 2012. *The Dramaturgy of Senecan Tragedy*. Ann Arbor: University of Michigan Press.

Mayer, R., and Coffey, M. 1990. *Seneca, Phaedra*. Cambridge: Cambridge University Press.

Monahan, B. 1983. *A Dictionary of Russian Gesture*. Ann Arbor: Hermitage.

Naiden, F. S. 2006. *Ancient Supplication*. Oxford: Oxford University Press.

Onians, R. B. 1988. *The Origins of European Thought about the Body, the Mind, the Soul, the World, Time, and Fate: New Interpretations of Greek, Roman, and Kindred Evi-*

dence, also of Some Basic Jewish and Christian Beliefs. 2nd ed. Cambridge: Cambridge University Press.

Paschalis, M. 1994. "The Bull and the Horse: Animal Theme and Imagery in Seneca's *Phaedra*." *AJP* 115: 105–28.

Segal, C. 1986. *Language and Desire in Seneca's Phaedra*. Princeton: Princeton University Press.

Seidensticker, B. 1969. *Die Gesprächsverdichtung in den Tragödien Senecas*. Heidelberg: C. Winter.

Shapiro, H. A. 1994. *Myth into Art*. London: Routledge.

Sittl, K. 1890. *Die Gebärden der Griechen und Römer*. Leipzig: Teubner.

Smith, R. S. 2011. "*Inhospitalis Taurus* at Seneca *Phaedra* 168." *Mnemosyne* 64: 100–103.

Spitzbarth, A. 1946. *Untersuchungen zur Spieltechnik der griechischen Tragödie*. Zurich: Rhein Verlag.

Trapido, J. ed. 1985. *An International Dictionary of Theatre Language*. Westport, CT: Greenwood.

Wilamowitz-Möllendorff, U. v. 1880. "Exkurse zu Euripides Medea." *Hermes* 15.4: 481–523.

Zwierlein, O. 1966. *Die Rezitationsdramen Senecas*. Meisenheim am Glan: Hain Verlag.

CHAPTER 11

Elephant Tears

Animal Emotion in Pliny and Aelian

Ellen Finkelpearl

Elephants, when withdrawn from the country to which they are accustomed, though tamed at first by captivity and hunger and after that by food and a varied diet, nevertheless do not erase from their memory the spell of the country that fostered them. At any rate, the majority die of grief [λύπη], and some have actually lost their sight through the floods of tears past measuring which they have shed [κλάοντες ἀστακτί]. Aelian *NA* 10.17

According to the Stoics (Posidonius excepted),[1] animals cannot feel emotion. Emotion in the fullest sense is a function of cognition and is bound up with language, and since animals are irrational and inarticulate, they are only capable of impulses, or something "like" emotion. Seneca, in the bluntest statement on the subject, says "mute animals lack human emotions, but they have certain impulses similar to them" (*muta animalia humanis affectibus carent; habent autem similes illis quosdam impulsus, De Ira* 1.3.6).[2] Ancient philosophers more sympathetic to animals dispute Stoic claims; Plutarch says that those

---

1. See Sorabji 2000: 125–29 for the ambiguities.
2. Translations in this essay are from the Loeb editions with modifications. *Ira* proper, for example, is distinguished from *rabies, feritas*, and *incursum*. "First movements" (*impetus, impulsus, motus*) are to be distinguished from genuine emotion or adfectus. Emotions like ira involve four stages, according to Seneca (*De Ira* 2.3–4), the third of which is a voluntary and rational assent of the mind to the appearance of injustice or injury (*species iniuriae*) of which animals, being irrational, are incapable. See Sorabji 1993: 60; Sorabji 2000: 69–75 with passages.

who believe that the lion "as it were" grows angry, and the deer "as it were" is frightened must also say that the animal "as it were" sees, hears, and cries (ὡσανεί, *Sollertia* 961e–f; see also 960f).[3]

Overt pronouncements in Aristotle and the Stoics have tended to dominate the discussion of ancient beliefs about animal emotion, while more literary texts are ignored. It is surprising to read in an essay by the admirable Stephen Newmeyer that Lucretius' sympathetic portrait of the calf at *DRN* 1.259–61 presents "an idea almost unparalleled otherwise in ancient texts, that is, the belief that animals are capable of emotions like sadness and joy, and that they take simple pleasure in their own lives."[4] By following Aristotle in a cognitive and social definition of emotion, David Konstan, in his useful and provocative book *The Emotions of the Ancient Greeks*, excludes animals and children from a share of emotion in the Greek world of the fifth and fourth centuries.[5] Yet other, more imaginative genres—such as animal mirabilia, natural histories, and tales of metamorphosis—reveal a more complicated picture in their free depictions of animals in states of sadness, sympathy, and so on. I submit that these depictions deserve to be taken seriously, as creating an alternative vision of animal life and its relation to ourselves, one that has an eye on the strictures of philosophical ideas that would limit animal abilities.

But what is an emotion?[6] Is it, as William James argued, the immediate, instinctive, physical reaction, consisting of the rapid heartbeat, the sweat, the adrenal rush, the facial expression—a view shared, from an evolutionary perspective, by Darwin? Various neurological studies indicate that emotions are situated in the limbic system and the amygdala, organs that we share with animals, and that emotional responses are subcortical, existing at an early

---

3. See also Porph. 3.19, 3.22.5. Aristotle's view is mixed and self-contradictory, but at *HA* 8.1, he grants animals certain emotions.
4. Newmeyer 2007: 168. The judgment probably springs from his focus on philosophical works.
5. Konstan 2006: xi–xii, 22, not pursued in depth. Konstan admits that there was a different approach to emotion in the Roman world. However, his articles on Plutarch's *Gryllus* (2011) and on eros in animals (2013) also subscribe to the Aristotelian/Stoic views.
6. For full discussion of which affective states qualify as "emotions," see Konstan 2006: ch. 1. Paul Ekman (1998: 390–91), distilling Darwin's long list of emotions, famously offers six basic emotions: anger, disgust, sadness, enjoyment, fear, and surprise—with the possible addition of contempt and shame. Obviously, there are great differences of opinion about whether this list works across cultures and across time. In his survey, for example, Konstan includes anger, satisfaction, shame, envy/indignation, fear, gratitude, love, hatred, pity, jealousy and grief.

mammalian level of the brain.[7] For Aristotle and for neocognitivists, these responses would only be "first movements," or a stage prior to various cognitive
processes, such as appraisal and judgment, that constitute full emotion.

Martha Nussbaum, arguing that animals (real ones) do experience emotions, weighs the views of Chrysippus and Posidonius. The former posits that
emotions involve the acceptance of "proposition-like entities corresponding
to the sentences in a language," which clearly nonlinguistic creatures could
not formulate. The latter insists that animals manifestly have emotions and,
hence, that emotions must be "non-reasoning movements."[8] Nussbaum
points out that even if animals are not capable of all the intellectual operations of humans, they are still capable of intentionality, selective attention,
and appraisal, such that they can have feelings about the way actions and
events contribute to their well-being. Cognitive appraisals need not be objects of reflexive self-consciousness.[9] Hence animals are capable of emotion.
Compare Plutarch (De soll. an. 966b10):

> In general, then, the evidence by which the philosophers demonstrate that
> beasts have their share of reason [μετέχειν λόγου] is their possession of pur-
> pose and preparation and memory and emotions [πάθη] and care for their
> young and gratitude for benefits and hostility to what has hurt them.

While his argument is about reason (logos) rather than emotion (a given for
him), the point is similar: animals may not have the same degree of reason as
humans, but they do engage in mental processes that require some of it.[10]

I have chosen texts of Pliny the Elder and Aelian as my focus here. Despite major differences, their animal narratives (cullings doubtless from the
same compilations, with all the problems that entails) have much in common:
an interest in the wonderful and surprising; a manner of describing animals
that is anthropomorphic but not fantastical, folktale-like but controlled (e.g.,
animals can understand human language but cannot speak); an implicit trust
in animal abilities; an ongoing comparison with the human animal; a belief in

---

7. See Oatley 2004: 67, 71, 73,with reference to, among others, Paul MacLean 1993, "Cerebral
    evolution of emotion," in M. Lewis and J.M. Haviland, eds., Handbook of emotions. New
    York: Guilford: 67–83; Jaak Panksepp 1998. Affective neuroscience: The foundations of human
    and animal emotions. Oxford: Oxford University Press.
8. Nussbaum 2001: 91.
9. Nussbaum 2001: 126.
10. It would be good to know more about Pythagoras concerning animal emotion.

the powers of Nature that questions anthropocentrism; and, above all, a quest to enter the animal mind. There is not enough space here to discuss the nature of their two treatises as a whole or their cultural contexts just this: I do not subscribe to the image of Pliny as a workhorse who collects data indiscriminately and primarily for its usefulness and whose Romanness is manifested in his wakeful industry. I believe in Italo Calvino's Pliny, who combines the obsessive workhorse with "a poetical-philosophical Pliny, with his feeling for the universe and his love of knowledge and mystery,"[11] and in Brian Cummings' Pliny, who respects the elephant as a creature of intelligence within a society that makes sense on its own terms.[12] I subscribe not to the image of an Aelian who tells silly moralistic stories to make humans look bad by comparison but, rather, to the complex, sophisticated, multicultural, political, vaguely postmodern Aelian newly unfolded by Steven Smith.[13] (Aelian is discriminating: at 12.3, he distinguishes his realistic discourse from that of the poet Homer; it is acceptable for Homer to portray a horse speaking, but Aelian himself will not accept the fiction handed down by Egyptians that a lamb was born with eight feet and two tails and that it spoke.)

Emotions Described as Part of a Cognitive Process/Close to Human

This section surveys different emotions in narratives by both Pliny and Aelian, asking how these narratives engage with the debates outlined above. In each case, the authors challenge assumptions about animal abilities and engage subtly with philosophical debates by coupling their attribution of animal emotion with other cognitive and social acts.[14] For example, the elephants in the epigraph to this essay have a homeland, society, and memory, and they shed tears—a physiologically different state from simple sorrow.[15] Further, the ele-

---

11. Calvino 1986: 316–17.
12. Cummings 2004: 176. Cummings notes that Pliny "presents nothing less than the ethnography of the elephant" (173; see, further, 173–77).
13. Smith 2014.
14. The major questions debated by ancient philosophers about animals include whether they are rational, have language, can enter into contracts, are kin, are morally liable and stand in a relation of justice with human beings or have a moral sense in general, and can form social bonds. See, further, Sorabji 1993; Osborne 2007; Newmeyer 2006.
15. More tears occur at NA 12.44: the mares of Libya prance and skip to the sound of the pipe, but

phants have been tricked into embarking on a boat to leave their country; hence the humans have been dishonorable and created a deceptive contract.

Here is Pliny on a grief-stricken panther (*HN* 8.59–60 excerpted):

[She] out of a desire for human aid, lying in the middle of a road, appeared to the father of a certain student of philosophy named Philinus. He began to retreat from fear, but the animal [*feram*] rolled over on her back obviously trying to attract/coax him [*non dubie blandientem*], and tormented by sorrow that was intelligible even in a panther [*seseque conflictantem maerore qui etiam in panthera intellegi possit*]: she had a litter of cubs that had fallen into a pit some distance away. The first result of his compassion [*miserationis*] was not to be frightened, and the next to give her his attention, and he followed where she drew him by lightly touching his clothes with her claws [*uestem unguium leui iniectu*] and when he understood [*intellexit*] the cause of her grief [*doloris*], . . . he got the cubs out of the pit; and the panther with her young escorted him right to the edge of the desert, guiding him with gestures of delight [*laeta atque gestiente*], so that it was easily clear that she was expressing gratitude [*referre gratiam*] and not reckoning on any recompense, which is rare even in a human being.[16]

The panther is driven by maternal instinct to save her cubs, which is unsurprising in an animal, but she also feels deep sorrow, happiness, and gratitude, emotions situated within her obvious attempts to communicate. Lacking language, she uses gesture, which surprisingly constitutes a viable means of communication between her and the philosopher's father (who feels a complementary set of emotions). Pliny is quite insistent about the intelligibility of the gestures, and though the human does the understanding (*intellego* is twice used of the human), the panther effects the skillful communication

---

when the musician plays more vigorously, tears of pleasure stream from their eyes. In Aelian, even animals are prey to complex and contradictory emotions, evoked by the fine arts.

16. I here offer a Lateineresque list of more occurrences of animal sadness. Pliny records numerous examples of the sorrow of loyal dogs at the deaths of their masters: Jason of Lycia's dog starved himself to death (8.144); a dog named Hyrcanus threw himself on King Lysimachus' pyre (8.144); Titus Sabinius' dog, who uttered *maestos ululatus* on the steps of lamentation when his master's body was thrown out, carried food to the mouth of his dead master. (See also *HN* 9.25 and 9.33 on dolphins; 10.155 of a hen.) Cf. Aelian 10.41: Eupolis' dog sang a mournful *threnos* when his master died; 11.13: hunting dogs lamented grievously over the death of Daphnis; 14.10: Mauretanian asses weep over the weakness of their feet; 14.11: a mother cow is distressed over her calf.

and is therefore in possession of a variety of *logos*.[17] Both parties benefit from overcoming the habitual barrier between species.

Anger seems like a simple, primal emotion. Yet Aelian's description of an angry bird goes beyond the kind of instinctive response one expects from an animal (*NA* 5.36):

> There is a bird called *Asterias*, and in Egypt, if tamed, it understands human speech. And if anyone by way of insult calls it "slave," it gets angry [ὀργίζεται]; and if anyone calls it "skulker" [ὄκνον], it takes umbrage [βρενθύεται] and is annoyed [ἀγανακτεῖ], as though [ὡς] it was being jeered at for its low birth and rebuked for its indolence.

A slight to his character incites anger in this intelligent bird who understands human speech. Aelian attributes degrees of anger in proportion to the insult. "Slave" induces ὀργή, but the bird also experiences lesser degrees of anger. In philosophical terms, this passage contradicts the claim that animals feel only *impulsus*, and the bird's understanding that it has been insulted flies in the face of Aristotle's claim that only humans can sense that an insult has occurred.[18]

Both authors provide numerous examples of animals in love with humans or with animals of another species: Sargue fishes intensely love goats (φιλοῦσι ἰσχυρῶς, *NA* 1.23); a dolphin is in love with a beautiful boy (ἐρᾷ ἔρωτα δριμύτατον, *NA* 6.15);[19] another dolphin is in love with a boy and expires after he dies (*NH* 9.8.25); a snake is in love with a girl (ἐρασθῆναι, *NA* 6.17); a horse is in love with his young master (ἐρᾷ δριμύτατα, *NA* 6.44; here the horse tries to mount the boy and has to be sent away); a goose is very much in love with the peripatetic philosopher Lacydes (ἐφίλει ἰσχυρῶς, *NA* 7.41); elephants are in love with a flower seller, a soldier, and a girl selling scents (*amor, amasse, HN* 8.13–14); snakes form couples (*HN* 8.25.85). In all these cases, deep affection is felt by the animal, using the strongest possible words for love: ἔρως, ἐρᾶν; φιλεῖν; *amor, amare*. Animals bestow gifts as an *erastes* would. In several stories, when the beloved dies, the animal wastes away.

---

17. See Osborne 2007: 135–50 for an excellent discussion of Aelian's rendition of "Androcles and the Lion." Osborne combats the accusation of "sentimentality" and the idea that Androcles "is obviously a fairy story and proves nothing about the empirical facts of animal intelligence" (138). Though it is a legend, she contends, the story "makes us rethink the facile inferences from use of speech to moral and intellectual superiority" (139).
18. Konstan 2006: 22, citing Fortenbaugh.
19. For the erotic subtext here, see Smith 2014.

David Konstan has argued that animals cannot have eros, citing the need for a cognitive element, reciprocal feelings, and a difference that he posits between natural sexual urges and something more like our "love."[20] Granting that the kinds of instances cited above do exist, he argues that they are exceptions, mentioned precisely because they are so impossible and out of the ordinary. However, in these authors, tales of animal love are not exceptional; rather, they begin to tell another story about animals, against the grain, in which animals feel deeply and cognitively, like humans but not as stand-ins for humans.[21] Moreover, it is not so clear that the ancient conception of eros is closer to our modern conception of love than to "animalistic" desire, if one considers the baneful *erotes* described by the chorus at *Medea* 627ff., the *furor* of Seneca's Phaedra,[22] or the obsessive un-Epicurean *amor* of Lucretius' book 4. Pliny and Aelian's animals confound our expectations about what animal desire should look like, invoking and yet not exceeding the literature on human obsessive love.[23]

Maternal affection, too, has its complexities. Both Pliny and Aelian describe the mare's love for her foal as a direct chemical result of her eating the black fig-sized substance called "hippomanes" from the foal's forehead at birth. The substance is crucial for the mother-child bond; she will not nurse the foal unless she eats it. Pliny describes the bond with the verb *diligit* (*praeter ceteras fetum diligit*, "the mare loves her offspring more than all other females," *HN* 8.165), but for Aelian the bond is more intense (*NA* 14.18):

> For it is by eating that piece of flesh that the dam begins to love her offspring intensely [φιλεῖν ἰσχυρῶς]. But any man who as a result of some plot tastes of that piece of flesh becomes possessed and consumed by an uncontrollable desire [ἔρωτι ἀκρατεῖ].

---

20. Konstan 2013.
21. Craig Williams' 2013 article on animals in love with humans in *Classical Antiquity* appeared after the completion of this article. Briefly, however, Williams sees the love between humans and animals in these texts as ultimately human-centered as compared with Native American narratives which represent a much more complete symbiosis of the species.
22. For more on Seneca's *Phaedra*, see Hahnemann's essay in this volume.
23. For a useful overview of some ancient discussions of *eros* and related terms, see Brown 1987, 110–18; Brown particularly cautions against the misunderstandings that can result from translating and understanding the terms *eros* and even *amor* to mean "love" in our sense. Obviously, the bibliography on these terms is huge; see, e.g., Sanders et al. 2013, Carson 1986.

Aelian goes on to describe how hippomanes creates erotic frenzy both in humans, making them pursue even the ugliest boys and older women, and in male horses, as some fall madly in love with (ἐρῶσιν καὶ ἐπιμαίνονται) and long to mount a bronze mare at Olympia that has the substance hidden inside (*NA* 14.18). That hippomanes can induce similar feelings of lust in humans and horses implies a continuum of emotive feelings and chemical respons-es.[24] But the description of the mare's maternal bond as rather passionate is curious; maternal love is active and intense rather than simply instinctive.

Fear is mentioned surprisingly rarely. Pliny dwells on the odd things that terrify a lion (*terrent*): wheels turning round, empty chariots, crested combs and crowing of cocks, and especially fires (*HN* 8.52). Aelian describes how the elephant fears pigs, particularly smeared with pitch and burning (*NA* 1.38: ὀρρωδεῖ; 16.36: δέδοικεν), and how lions fear elephants in a herd (*NA* 7.36). The oddity of these objects of fear is testimony to an attempt to under-stand the alien animal mind. Further, both authors attribute awareness and planning even to fish in the grip of fear. Pliny observes (*HN* 9.59) that

> it is an amusing trait [*ridetur*] in the mullet that when frightened [*in metu*] it hides its head and believes [*credentium*] it is entirely concealed.

Aelian notes of anchovies (*NA* 8.18) that

> fish which swim in schools principally eat them, and so when scared [δείσαντα] they rush to one another [συνθεῖ] and as each clings to its neighbor, by their close cohesion they avoid [διαπέφευγε] being easily plotted upon [ἐπιβουλεύεσθαι].

Pliny records amusement over the mullet's naïveté but nonetheless grants him belief. Aelian attributes planning (βουλή) to the anchovy's predators and describes both the anchovy's agency (all the verbs are in the active in-dicative, with no qualifiers) and their position as part of a society. In each case, the fear is followed by an act that involves cognition, and the narrative invites us inside the minds of the sea creatures.

Each of the more cognitive and social emotions of jealousy, gratitude, and

---

24. The distinction between φιλεῖν and ἔρωτι in the passage from Aelian just quoted seems to be due to the nature of the parent-child bond. If anything, it plays up the physical nature of human desire over that of the animal.

shame is complex in itself, involving an understanding of social conventions and bonds. Aelian provides an anecdote in which a goatherd incites the jealousy of a goat by making a very pretty female goat his *eromene*. The goat bides his time and then smashes in the skull of his rival when he is asleep. "From the goat we learn that animals have indeed their share of jealousy [ζηλοτυπίας]," concludes Aelian (*NA* 6.42).[25] Aelian presents the familiar scenario of the third figure watching unwanted attentions toward his love object, and he attributes planning to the goat.

Numerous tales in both Pliny and Aelian (e.g., that of Androcles) tell of animals feeling and expressing gratitude toward their rescuers and recognizing them years later. Pliny describes an eagle that was reared by a maiden and that expressed its gratitude (*retulisse gratiam*) by bringing its prey to the maiden and later throwing itself on her pyre when she died (*HN* 10.18). Aelian directly asserts that animals are good at remembering to be grateful (χάριτος ἀπομνησθῆναι), even better at it than humans,[26] with his proof being that a woman who nursed a young injured stork back to health was, in a year's time, rewarded by his dropping a strange glowing stone in her lap (*NA* 8.22).

Aelian 3.1 tells of a lion's shame. When the lion fails to find prey, his hunger pangs drive him to the house of a Moor, where the wife admonishes him in the Moorish tongue, which lions understand: "Are you not ashamed [αἰδῆ], you, a lion, the king of beasts, to come to my hut and ask a woman to feed you. . . . Whereas, like some sorry lap-dog, you are content to be fed by another." The lion "as though struck in his heart and filled with shame" [ὥσπερ οὖν πληγεὶς τὴν ψυχὴν καὶ ὑποπλησθεὶς αἰδοῦς] quietly and with downcast eyes moves off, overcome by the justice of her words [ἡττηθεὶς τῶν δικαίων]" (*NA* 3.1). Shame is connected with worth and status in the social hierarchy and is constructed as having the same causes as in humans: social humiliation, worth, and honor.[27] The lion assents to the "justice" of the Moorish wife's rebuke and signals his shame by looking down.[28] In short, these

---

25. Konstan (2006: ch. 11) argues that jealousy in our sense is unknown before the Augustan period. The scenario here, post-Augustan, seems to conform to our conceptions of the emotion.

26. Let me not, as a human animal, forget to be grateful to Don Lateiner for many years of encouragement, support, and offbeat humor.

27. See also Pliny *HN* 8.12, on the suicide of a disgraced elephant named Ajax.

28. Aelian and Pliny both portray gesture in animals as sometimes communicative and intentional and ultimately comprehensible to humans. (At *HN* 8.56, it takes a while for the lion to get its point across.) The lion's downward gaze here simply reinforces Aelian's explicit

authors describe a wide range of animal emotions and are insistent on their cognitive and social content and their precise overlap with human feelings— except in the cases where animals are morally superior.

Feeling Like an Animal

What is the use of ὥσπερ in Aelian's lion story above. Determining its exact nuance (and *velut*, in Latin) is important. Elsewhere, Aelian mentions animal shame without any qualifier: the mare is too vain to mate with an ass, so, to produce a mule, first give the mare's mane a very bad trim; then, though at first ashamed (αἰδουμένη), she will consent (*NA* 2.10; cf. 12.16). The rooster defeated in a cockfight hides himself ὑπὸ τῆς αἰδοῦς (*NA* 4.29); again, there are no qualifiers here. Clearly, Aelian has no problem believing or stating that animals feel shame.

Yet Aelian does use ὥσπερ in other similar contexts: at 8.3, a school of dolphins assembles in the sea near the pyre of one Coeranus "as though [ὥσπερ] they were attending his funeral" because he had long ago rescued one of them from a net; an old and feeble lion whose sons have brought him prey licks them "as though [ὥσπερ] he applauded their successful hunting" (9.1). In both cases, Aelian provides long anthropomorphizing descriptions outside of the ὥσπερ clauses, only qualifying what might seem like overly presumptuous interpretations of animal gesture. Likewise, when Pliny is making assumptions about animal intent, he sometimes uses a word like *uelut, similis,* or *quidam* to signal the assumption. For example, in the famous description of the elephants that were displayed by Pompey in the arena and unexpectedly gained the sympathy of the crowd, Pliny uses such a qualifier, saying that the elephants were *misericordiam uulgi inenarrabili habitu quaerentes supplicauere quadam sese lamentatione conplorantes* ("seeking the pity of the crowd by indescribable gestures of entreaty and deploring their fate with *a sort of* wailing," *HN* 8.21).[29]

Beagon argues that Pliny is at pains to represent animal qualities as "very

statement. Gestures are not always anthropomorphic, however; Aelian 8.2 and Pliny 8.147 describe dog gestures with muzzles and tails, and Aelian *NA* 11.31 describes the happiness of a horse prancing and snorting after being cured of an eye ailment by Asclepius.

29. The scene is also described in Dio Cassius 39.38, where the elephants' gestures are described (they raised their trunks to the heavens) and where no qualifiers are used about their lamentation.

close" to human feelings: "[t]his idea of imitation rather than identity is re-flected time and again in Pliny's language. . . . They throw up grass to heaven 'as though' [*uelut*] deputing earth to support their prayers. They possess a 'kind' of justice."[30] Beagon suggests that these qualifiers may "imply Seneca's distinction" between human emotion and animal "impulse."[31] Yet it should already be clear that Pliny does not always qualify and apologize for his an-thropomorphic descriptions of animal acts and feelings (witness the panther story above).[32] At least as often, Pliny dispenses with any qualifier.[33] The use of these qualifying terms does imply some degree of hesitancy to attribute emotion and intent to nonhuman animals. Yet so much else in these authors' depictions of animal feelings defies those Stoic limitations that they cannot be describing only "something like" emotions and certainly are not describing the Stoic ὡσανεί. Nor does the randomness of application suggest anything so formal as "first movements."

Instead, I suggest that Pliny and Aelian use these terms to express the natural groping after the perpetually elusive internal life and subjectivity of the animal. Although both authors repeatedly describe animal feelings with-out any hesitation, both step back cautiously at times, aware that their inter-pretations of gesture or their assumptions about animal society are just that. It is Nagel's "What is it like to be a bat?" dilemma, though, like Elizabeth Costello in *The Lives of Animals*, Pliny and Aelian both seem inclined to feel that it is possible to imagine being a bat (or elephant or anchovy), because "being fully a bat is like being fully human, which is also to be full of being."[34] Arguably, it is in the imagining of the emotions (and, more generally, the "feelings") of animals that we humans can get closest to rupturing the barrier between us. Consider a portion of Aelian's description of the life of a clam (*NA* 15.12):

> [They avoid the wind] but delight [χαίρουσι] in a waveless sea and the pleasant
> and gentle breezes of the zephyrs. And so beneath their influence they quit their
> burrows, with their shells still closed and fast shut, and mount upwards from

---

30. Beagon 1992: 139.
31. Beagon 1992: 139.
32. Overall, Beagon concludes that Pliny is not overly concerned with the fine distinctions sur-rounding human and animal abilities and that he is instead trying to get at the relation between both sets of beings and *Natura*.
33. Surely, the inconsistency of use in both authors is partly dependent on their sources.
34. Coetzee 1999: 33; Nagel 1974.

their recesses and, when the sea is waveless, swim around. And then they open
their coverings and peep forth, like brides looking down from their private
chambers or like rosebuds that, warmed a little, have peeped out of their flower-
cups towards the sun's heat. And so, little by little they gather courage
[ὑποθαρροῦσαι] and are glad to rest quietly [ἀσμένως ἡσυχάζουσι].

This passage, differently from the more anthropomorphizing ones, makes
a real attempt to feel its way into the perspective of a clam (see the full text for
more). Aelian's technique is to mix a straightforward description of the physical acts of the clam with slight attributions of intent and emotion, along with
a startling simile comparing the clam to a human. Martha Nussbaum discusses a similar narrative technique employed in a book by philosopher
George Pitcher about his dogs, suggesting both that Pitcher's ascription of
intent to his own dogs is philosophically responsible when an act clearly contributes to their well-being in ways he knows to be true and that such narrative is a way of getting at animal emotion.[35] In short, while both Pliny and
Aelian may seem excessively anthropomorphizing in granting animals jealousy, shame, and so forth, the narratives of both authors also approach animal emotion from a more animal-centered point of view.

Humans

Pliny and Aelian also say a few explicit things about human and animal emotions, and they diverge from each other here more than in their narrative
passages. In a statement sometimes taken out of context, Pliny says that only
homines experience grief (*uni luctus est datus*) and that no creature has desire
(*cupido*) that is greater, fear (*pavor*) that is more confused, or rage (*rabies*) that
is fiercer (*HN* 7.4–5).[36] Pliny notes that "the first place rightly will be granted
to Man, for whose sake Nature seems to have created all other things" (*HN*
7.1). Yet the grand and central position granted to humans is made ambiguous by Pliny's very contemporary question about the relationship of Man to
Nature; his point here is that only humans live on borrowed resources, with
bodies that do not clothe themselves; only human desires have neurotically
created afflictions like grief, ambition, avarice, and superstition; human life is

---

35. Nussbaum 2001: 119–25, "Animal Emotions in Narrative Form."
36. Konstan (2006: 270n31) takes this as an absolute statement about animal emotion.

more precarious because of our oversensitivity to emotions. Man's dominant status and distance from Nature is an ambiguous blessing.

Elsewhere, Pliny connects facial expression with certain types of emotion. Only humans have a *facies* (other animals have a beak or a snout), and only the brow of the human is an indication of certain emotions; Pliny locates a portion of the *animus* in the eyebrow (*HN* 11.138). The eye is the greatest indication of emotions, particularly for Man (*HN* 11.145). Pliny does not deny animals emotion here; he only grants humans more outward facial expressiveness. Perhaps most important, Pliny is talking here about Man. Manifestly, when he talks about animals, they have intense emotions.[37]

Aelian begins his work declaring that there is nothing remarkable in *anthropoi* being wise and just, since they have been endowed with speech and reason. But that speechless animals (ἄλογοι) should possess many of Man's amazing excellences is huge (μέγα, prologue).[38] Thus, from the beginning, Aelian puts aside the customary privileging of speech and reason. By the end, he expresses pride in writing about foxes and lizards, beetles and snakes, and regrets that he has sometimes shown Man to less advantage (epilogue). But he is repeatedly insistent that certain abilities are a mark of reasoning in humans but a function of φύσις in animals. Animals seem to be capable of reasoning deductively, but *physis* is still the διδάσκαλος ἄμαχος (*NA* 6.59); Aelian questions what should really count as σοφά (6.59),[39] and he escapes the trap of anthropocentrism by downplaying *logos* and emphasizing the value of *physis*. For Aelian, philosophical skepticism over an animal's capacity for emotion is meaningless, because logic, language, and human arts in general are secondary to (and also part of) *physis*.

Conclusions

I have presented the problem of whether animals feel emotion somewhat as a battle between the poets and the philosophers; Pliny and Aelian expend imagination on the inner lives of animals and invite us to believe that they

---

37. Aristotle, too, attributes varying degrees of intelligence to animals, depending on the focus of a given work. In the *Politics*, he insists that Man alone possesses reason (1332b5–6); in the zoological works, he speaks more of a continuum of intelligence from lowest to highest and argues for a kind of kinship, granting certain animals *synesis*, or understanding (*HA* 588a18–19; Newmeyer 2007: 160–61).
38. He also claims for them a share of *logismos* (6.50).
39. See also 5.11, 8.22, 10.5, and passim.

can feel sorrow, shame, and joy, while the Stoics and (less rigidly) Aristotle insist that emotion is a function of cognition inaccessible to animals. Pliny and Aelian are aware of the philosophical arguments and respond implicitly. While neither is directly polemical and while the doctrines of philosophy about animal rationality are largely "arbitrary and irrelevant" (as Cummings says of Pliny),[40] the authors' insistence on situating emotion within other cognitive and linguistic acts indicates an engagement with philosophy and possibly a reformulating of the rules.

The picture should not be binary. Both Pliny and Aelian are (probably) Stoics of some variety.[41] Steven Smith points out that Aelian conventionally refers to animals as ἄλογα but that "one always gets the sense that Aelian is testing the limits of that word."[42] Smith refers to the author's "undoctrinaire relationship with Stoicism," in which the most Stoic feature is the depiction of animals living in harmony with Nature in the face of human perversion of Nature's gift.[43] Pliny and Aelian clearly reject Stoic ideas about animal emotion, but whatever they may say explicitly, they both give Nature a central place and raise potential contradictions in Stoic ideas about nature and animals; more analysis could be done here. In any case, as Coetzee makes clear in *The Lives of Animals*, there is a philosophy and an ethics in the thought experiments that constitute animal narratives.

Works Cited

Beagon, M. 1992. *Roman Nature: The Thought of Pliny the Elder*. Oxford: Oxford University Press.

Beagon, M. 2005. *The Elder Pliny on the Human Animal: Natural History Book 7*. Oxford: Oxford University Press.

Brown, R. 1987. *Lucretius on Love and Sex: A Commentary on De Rerum Natura IV, 1030–1287*. Leiden: Brill.

Calvino, I. 1986. "Man, the Sky, and the Elephant." In *The Uses of Literature*, trans. P. Creagh, 315–30. San Diego: Harcourt Brace Jovanovich.

Carson, A. 1986. *Eros the Bittersweet*. Princeton: Princeton University Press.

Coetzee, J. M. 1999. *The Lives of Animals*. Princeton: Princeton University Press.

Cummings, B. 2004. "Pliny's Literate Elephant and the Idea of Animal Language in

---

40. Cummings 2004: 176.
41. See Smith 2014: ch. 4, on the debates over Aelian's Stoicism; Beagon 2005: 15–16, on Pliny's.
42. Smith 2014: 71.
43. Smith 2014: 72. Smith has much to say about the complexities of Aelian's Stoicism, for which there is no space here.

Renaissance Thought." In E. Fudge, ed., *Renaissance Beasts: Of Animals, Humans, and Other Wonderful Creatures*, 164–85. Urbana: University of Illinois Press.

Darwin, C. 1998. *The Expression of the Emotions in Man and Animals*. 3rd ed., with introduction, afterword and commentary by Paul Ekman. London: HarperCollins. First published 1872.

Ekman, P. 1998. "Afterword." In Darwin, 363–93.

James, W. 1884. "What Is an Emotion?" *Mind* 9: 88–205.

Konstan, D. 2006. *The Emotions of the Ancient Greeks: Studies in Aristotle and Classical Literature*. Toronto: University of Toronto Press.

Konstan, D. 2011. "A Pig Convicts Itself of Unreason: The Implicit Argument of Plutarch's *Gryllus*." *Hyperboreus Studia Classica* 16–17: 371–85.

Konstan, D. 2013. "Between Appetite and Emotion, or Why Can't Animals Have *Erôs*?" In Sanders et al., 13–26.

MacLean, P. 1993. "Cerebral Evolution of Emotion." In M. Lewis and J. Haviland, eds., *Handbook of Emotions*, 67–83. New York: Guilford.

Nagel, T. 1974. "What Is It Like to Be a Bat?" *Philosophical Review* 83.4: 435–50.

Newmeyer, S. 2006. *Animals, Rights, and Reason in Plutarch and Modern Ethics*. New York: Routledge.

Newmeyer, S. 2007. "Animals in Ancient Philosophy: Conceptions and Misconceptions." In L. Kalof, ed., *A Cultural History of Animals in Antiquity*, 151–74. New York: Berg.

Nussbaum, M. 2001. *Upheavals of Thought: The Intelligence of Emotions*. Cambridge: Cambridge University Press.

Oatley, K. 2004. *Emotions: A Brief History*. Oxford: Blackwell.

Osborne, C. 2007. *Dumb Beasts and Dead Philosophers*. Oxford: Oxford University Press.

Panksepp, Jaak. 1998. *Affective Neuroscience: The Foundations of Human and Animal Emotions*. Oxford: Oxford University Press.

Sanders, E., Thumiger, C., Carey, C., and Lowe, N., eds. 2013. *Eros in Ancient Greece*. Oxford: Oxford University Press.

Smith, S. 2014. *Man and Animal in Severan Rome: The Literary Imagination of Claudius Aelianus*. Cambridge: Cambridge University Press.

Sorabji, R. 1993. *Animal Minds and Human Morals: The Origins of the Western Debate*. Ithaca: Cornell University Press.

Sorabji, R. 2000. *Emotion and Peace of Mind: From Stoic Agitation to Christian Temptation*. Oxford: Oxford University Press.

Williams, C. 2013. "When a Dolphin Loves a Boy: Some Greco-Roman and Native American Love Stories." *CA* 32.1: 200–42.

CHAPTER 12

Lucian's Courtesans

Vulnerable Women in
a Difficult Occupation

Hanna M. Roisman

Lucian's *Dialogues of the Courtesans* is a collection of fifteen comic dialogues between courtesans and one or more interlocutors who say little or nothing. As with most of Lucian's works, we do not have any information on when these dialogues were composed, how they fit in with Lucian's artistic development, or how and where they were disseminated.[1] Of Lucian's life, we have similarly limited knowledge. He was born in Samosata, in modern-day Turkey, between 115 and 125 CE, and died after 180 CE. Although he is considered one of the major authors of the Second Sophistic and was a sophist in the early part of his career, Flavius Philostratus does not include him in his *Lives of the Sophists*.[2] Lucian was trained in rhetoric, and for much of his adult life, he earned his living as an itinerant rhetor (although he never refers to himself as such), traveling widely in the Greco-Roman world.[3] It is thus not unlikely that the courtesan dialogues, like the many other dialogues Lucian authored, were composed for oral presentation and delivered, one or more at a time, in the many locales where he taught and lectured.[4]

Judging by the verve of the mimicry in his comic dialogues, it is a literary

---

1. The formidable problems of dating Lucian's works and of tracing his literary development are brought home in Hall 1981: ch. 1.
2. Jones 1986: 6–23, esp. 21–22.
3. He also practiced law in the courts: see *Bis acc.* 32; *Pisc.* 25; Hall 1981: 17; Jones 1986: 12.
4. Jones 1986: 14–15. Gilhuly (2006: 275) similarly suggests that Lucian performed the dialogues.

form Lucian much enjoyed.[5] In three of his extant works—*To One Who Said,* *"You Are a Prometheus in Words"*; *Zeuxis (or Antiochus)*; and *The Double Indict-ment*—he simultaneously boasts of having invented the form and defends it against detractors.[6] His boast is that he combined the ancient genre of dia-logue, the traditional vehicle of philosophy, with comedy, drawn from the theater, to create pleasing, well-crafted pieces, full of stylistic grace. This is the rhetor in him speaking, taking pride in his artistry even as he explains why he abandoned oratory in favor of his new form. His defense, which is also a boast, is that he freed the philosophic dialogue from centuries of en-crustment and made it an attractive vehicle for conveying meaningful thought in an appealing manner. Put differently, he claims that he made phi-losophy appealing and accessible to an audience that had no interest in sterile arguments on esoteric subjects.

Like Lucian's other comic dialogues, *Dialogues of the Courtesans* is an en-tertaining work. As Hall points out, it had to be; Lucian made his living by entertaining his audiences.[7] But along with the humor provided by their sat-ire and the titillation afforded by their mildly salacious subject matter, the dialogues also present a wry and thoughtful look at a social phenomenon. The extent to which the dialogues reflect typical experiences of the courte-san's trade in Lucian's day, as is sometimes claimed,[8] cannot be ascertained. Our perspectives derive from literary sources; during roughly Lucian's pe-riod, for instance, Athenaeus brought together much of what was said about courtesans in his *Deipnosophistae*, or *Symposium*, discussed further at the end of this essay. Also visible in Lucian's dialogues is the influence of New Com-edy, where the figure of the courtesan features prominently.[9] In addition to

---

5. Other comic dialogues by Lucian include *Dialogues of the Gods, Dialogues of the Sea Gods, Dialogues of the Dead, Menippus, The Voyage to the Underworld, The Sale of Lives, Icaromenippus, The Cross-Examination of Zeus, Meeting of the Gods,* and *Dependent Scholars.*

6. For a brief discussion of these three dialogues, see Hopkinson 2008: 109–11. According to Branham (1989: 42), Lucian's comic dialogue is "an incongruous combination of inherently divergent genres." For the question of whether Lucian refers to *Dialogues of the Courtesans* in his *To One Who Said, "You Are a Prometheus in Words,"* see Hall 1981: 28–33; Gilhuly 2006: 276–77.

7. Hall 1981: ch. 1.

8. For the dialogues as realistic sketches of "the varied life of the *hetairae* in its manifold gra-dations," see Hans Licht (the pseudonym under which Paul Brandt published the transla-tion of his *Sittengeschichte Griechenlands*) 1925–28 and 1975: 342. In contrast, my treatment of the dialogues is based on close analysis of the literary values of Lucian's dialogues. The translations offered here are mostly my own, although translations from Athenaeus are from Gulick 1950.

9. Henry 1985: 32–132.

situations, names, and some features of the courtesans' personalities, the dialogues share with the plays of Menander and his Roman adaptors, Plautus
and Terence, a mildly satiric attitude, a focus on ordinary situations, and a
wry and largely sympathetic presentation of women who were at the bottom
of the social ladder and easy to scorn or condemn.[10]

The Form and Character of the Dialogues

Most of the dialogues have two speakers; a few of them have three or four. In
most, one courtesan is troubled or distressed by some problem involving a
client or lover, and her collocutor listens, comments, and sometimes advises
her. A few dialogues feature conversations or arguments between a courtesan and her client, and three are between a courtesan and her mother.

On the whole, the emphasis of the dialogues is more on the courtesans'
plights than on their characters. With only a few exceptions (e.g., Tryphena in
dialogue 11), none of the courtesans stands out as a well-developed or memorable character in her own right. The short length of the dialogues—some no
more than a page and a half—does not allow much character development.
Nor do Lucian's New Comedy models excel in character development. In
any case, this does not seem to have been Lucian's purpose. Yet, like the New
Comedy plays that inspired them, the dialogues present the voices of the
courtesans, showing their experiences, their feelings, and their behaviors as
they ply their trade.

Since the dialogues are, by definition, comic, the courtesans are all
mocked. None is sophisticated, learned, or witty, as, for example, Pericles'
Aspasia is portrayed in our sources (Plut. *Per.* 24, 25, 30, 32). Few are particularly pretty, and some who are mentioned are ugly, old, or both. As we read
the dialogues, we can readily laugh at the silly names Lucian gives some of
the courtesans;[11] at their naïveté, ignorance, and lack of self-awareness; or at

---

10. For Lucian's borrowings from New Comedy, see LeGrand 1907: 184–231. For his combin-
     ing the genres of both New Comedy (Menander, Philemon, Diphilus, etc.) and "mime" in
     Dialogues of the Courtesans, see Sidwell 2004: 155–56. For Lucian's possible use of fifth-
     century comedy in his works, see Sidwell 2000: 137–42, 151–52; Jones (1986: 151) states that
     Lucian was fond of Aristophanes in particular. Lucian's skill in delineating characters has
     brought scholars to ask whether he was familiar with Theophrastus' *Characters*; see Ma-
     cleod 1974. Baldwin 1977.
11. For a comprehensive study of names in these dialogues, see Mras 1916: 325–38, showing
     New Comedy's influence. For naming and the meaning of names in Aristophanes, see Ol-

their nagging and haranguing. But along with the satire, we come away with a sympathetic portrait of vulnerable, struggling women and girls working a demanding—and sometimes heartbreaking—trade.

The women whose voices the dialogues sound are all from the same sector of the sex trade. All are *hetaerae*, courtesans; none is a *pornē* (prostitute) or *pallakē* (concubine). Scholars disagree as to whether the term *hetaera* refers to women in the other two categories as well.[12] It can hardly be by accident, though, that Lucian chose this term for all his speaking characters and studiously avoided the other two designations. A flute girl who appears in dialogue 15 might double as a *pornē* but is not termed as such, and she tells a story about a *hetaera*. The exclusive use of the term *hetaera* to designate the speakers in these dialogues contrasts markedly with the terminology used in Athenaeus' *Deipnosophistae*, which refers to both *hetaerae* and *pornae* and distinguishes between them.[13] Moreover, within the world of the *hetaera*, none of the dialogues feature what might be termed "big-fee" *hetaerae*, who maintained independent and sometimes lavish homes or associated with men of wealth and position and enjoyed a borrowed status and respect.[14] One such *hetaera* is mentioned in dialogue 5, but only as a character who is spoken about.

The Courtesan as Hetaera

In the hierarchy of the sex trade, *hetaerae* were in a relatively good position. Literally, the term refers to female companions. Although they had neither the status nor the protection of *pallakae*, they were a notch above *pornae* in the social hierarchy. Unlike *pornae*, they were paid for social as well as sexual intercourse. They would be hired for an evening or a longer event, not just for sex, and they did not work as brothel slaves or streetwalkers. They were sometimes bound by contract to a single client for a designated period of time, but they could also have more than one client at a time. In any case, they were not forced, by the terms of their employment, to have sex with as many clients as possible for immediate remuneration. Yet Lucian's dialogues show

---

son 1992. For names and nicknames of women, courtesans, and slaves, especially in Athenaeus' *Deipnosophistae*, see McClure 2003a: 60–78.

12. Davidson 1997: 73–108. Whereas McClure (2003a: 11–18) does not recognize a clear distinction between a *pornē* and a *hetaera*, Miner (2003) argues that they are not interchangeable.
13. See Henry 1992: 263.
14. Davidson 1997: 104–7.

the *hetaerae* in a difficult trade, where their clients might be possessive, jealous, violent, or nonpaying or might otherwise mistreat them; where clients they become attached to invariably leave after a while; and where the women's inevitable aging means the loss of their appeal and their income.

Some of the sad realities of the profession of the lower-ranking *hetaera* are highlighted in dialogue 6, between the young Corinna and her mother, mockingly named Crobyle (Κρωβύλη), "Topknot," after a popular fifth-century hairstyle of Athenian male citizens (Thuc. 1.6.3). Crobyle has turned her daughter into a courtesan by hiring her out to a young man for a night in return for a sum amounting to some three months' living expenses.[15] The dialogue consists largely of Crobyle's explaining the profession to Corinna, who is depicted as innocent and naive in the extreme. The first thing we learn about, along with Corinna, is the financial duress that motivated Crobyle—an impoverished widow with no means of adequately supporting herself and her child—to bring her daughter into the degrading trade.[16] Corinna is soon given to understand that her mother expects her to earn enough to look after them both in style. This will require, Corinna learns, that she spend her time "associating with young men, drinking with them, and sleeping with them for pay" (συνοῦσα μὲν τοῖς νεανίσκοις καὶ συμπίνουσα μετ᾽ αὐτῶν καὶ συγκαθεύδουσα ἐπὶ μισθῷ) and that not all of those men will be as young and appealing as the one her mother had procured for her first sexual experience.

As her mother proceeds, Corinna also learns that success in the trade does not come easily. To be successful, her mother informs her, she will have to remake herself in a way that will please men. She must dress nicely, restrain her appetite, cultivate refined table manners, and, above all, be pleasant to all, whatever she thinks of them.[17] Furthermore, she must not cheat her clients, get drunk,[18] be rapacious, speak more than she has to, make fun of

---

15. For mothers in Lucian and New Comedy who bring their daughters into the trade, see Strong 2012: 123–30. For an excellent overview and discussion of mothers in Greek and Latin literature, with an emphasis on mothers in Ovid's *Metamorphoses*, see Lateiner 2006.

16. Obvious in this dialogue is Lucian's social criticism of the structure of a society that forces mothers to prostitute their daughters because of their dire poverty. Some believe that Lucian himself comes from humble origins: for discussions, see Baldwin 1961; Jones 1986: 8–9; Swain 1996: 299, 310.

17. Myrtilus, one of Athenaeus' diners, cites the comic poet Eubulus' praise of a courtesan for eating delicately and not stuffing leeks and onions into her mouth (*Deipn.* 572a). See also, for discussion, Gilhuly 2007: 78; Kurke 1999: 213–17. Kurke observes that excessive consumption of food was a marker of the lower class. Lucian usually connects food with negative characters or conduct, especially in his *Lexiphanes* and *Symposium*.

18. That women were naturally inclined to drunkenness seems to have been an accepted view

anyone, or look at any man other than the one who hired her. The require-
ments border on the unrealistic. The refined table manners—eating daintily
and not gulping even when one is thirsty—are foreign to the poor girls who
go into the trade. The only courtesan in all the dialogues who acts toward the
men as Crobyle would have her daughter do is Lyra, the courtesan Crobyle
holds up as an example for Corinna to follow.

Much of the humor of dialogue 6 lies in Corinna's slow discovery of what
Lucian's more worldly readers surely know about the profession, as well as
in her artless questions, such as whether she must not drink in great gulps
even when she is thirsty and whether she will have to sleep with men who
are not particularly good-looking. Its pathos stems from the difficult life that
awaits the young Corinna in a profession that will never allow her to let
down her guard or be herself and that will require constant tact and skill,
self-discipline, and self-restraint. Moreover, if we take the courtesans in the
other dialogues as indicative, the occupation rewards very few of those who
ply it with the wealth that Crobyle envisions.

Courtesans, Love, and Money

There is more than one way of categorizing, or typing, the courtesans in these
dialogues. Two obvious dichotomies are old versus young and assertive versus nonassertive. The one I will use here to discuss Lucian's characterization
of his courtesans is the broad dichotomy between those courtesans for whom
personal considerations are uppermost and those for whom financial considerations are supreme. The conflict between the two approaches, which is
hinted at in dialogue 6, is salient in the other two mother-daughter dialogues:
dialogue 3, between Philinna and her mother, and dialogue 7, between Musarion and her mother. Like Crobyle, the mothers in these dialogues emphasize the financial aspect of the trade. The daughters, even though they are
more experienced and less compliant than Corinna, insist on a value other
than money.

For Philinna, the value is in being treated decently. Dialogue 3 shows Philinna paying her lover Diphilus back in kind when he mistreats her. As we

---

among the writers of classical antiquity; see Richlin 1984. Athenaeus also held to this view;
see Henry 1992: 259. For *hetaerae* and drunkenness, see Henry 1985: passim. For the image
of *hetaerae* drinking until they die, see Men. *Sam.* 181–82.

gather from her defense of her conduct to her mother, she kissed another man in Diphilus' presence, ignored Diphilus' wishes, and refused to sleep with him in retaliation for his having flirted with a courtesan friend of hers in her presence. When her mother, worried about losing their source of income, reminds her that Diphilus had given them money when they had none, Philinna answers defiantly, "So what? Does that mean I've to put up with such mistreatment by him?" (τί οὖν; ἀνέχωμαι διὰ τοῦτο ὑβριζομένη ὑπ᾿ αὐτοῦ;). In fighting for her dignity, she shows a measure of integrity in a trade where, as indicated in Crobyle's account, falsity is a key to success. For Musarion, whose name suggests the word Muse, the value is love. Musarion gives herself to a young man out of love and accepts no other clients, even though, as her mother points out, he not only fails to pay her but sponges off of her as well.

Much as he does with Corinna, Lucian both satirizes the naïveté of these young courtesans and draws sympathy for their plight. Another example is his depiction of Musarion, whom he shows to be not only naive but also argumentative, brash, and full of misplaced self-assurance. She accepts her man's constant excuses, believes his protestations of love, and trusts his promise that he will marry her when he comes into his inheritance after his father dies. She does not realize that she is being exploited. She does not grasp what his waiting for his father's death says of his character.[19] She does not understand that his young age (he does not yet have a beard) makes him unreliable. For every point her mother makes, she has a ready answer, and foolishly rejects her mother's caution that wealthy young men do not marry poor courtesans. From what we know, the few men who took courtesans as wives were older and usually widowed. But if we laugh at Musarion's overconfidence and misplaced trust, as we do at Corinna's youthful lack of worldly wisdom, we are also aware of the heartbreak that awaits her when her young man matures and moves on—and view his self-centered exploitativeness much more critically than we do her flaws.

Personalization is not limited to young, inexperienced courtesans. Most of the courtesans featured in the dialogues personalize their relationships. This does not mean that they do not charge for their services or that financial considerations are irrelevant.[20] It means that, like Philinna and Musarion, most have only one client at a time and are emotionally involved with him.

---

19. This is a commonplace in Lucian; cf., e.g., *Dialogues of the Dead* 441.
20. For the complexities of *hetaerae* charging for their services, see Davidson 1998: 109–27; Davidson points out that payment often came in gifts rather than money.

When he stops coming, for any number of reasons, they react either with hurt egos (like Philinna) or—if they feel affection or love for the customer—with hurt feelings. Their distress is primarily due not to the financial damage entailed in losing a client—none of the dialogues where the courtesans personalize even mentions this—but to the injury that their man's leaving them does to their egos or to their feelings.

Courtesans and Complaints

Courtesans for whom personal considerations are uppermost can be divided into two subtypes in accord with how they respond when their customer stops coming: those who complain to a friend and/or try to retaliate and those who confront the man directly. The courtesans who respond by complaining and/or retaliating are featured especially in dialogues 1, 4, and 10. Lucian shows them to be particularly helpless in the face of the inevitable lability of their trade, and he depicts them with a mixture of sympathy and satire.

In dialogue 1, the courtesan Glycerion, "Sweetie," is a victim of the competitiveness of the profession, coupled with the tendency of men to always seek new sources of sexual pleasure. When the dialogue opens, we see her angry and upset because of her sudden abandonment by her lover, a soldier, in favor of a fellow courtesan and friend of hers, Gorgona. She was taken by surprise, even though, as her collocutor reminds her, "This is what usually happens among us courtesans" (εἰωθὸς γίγνεσθαι ὑφ᾽ ἡμῶν τῶν ἑταιρῶν); Glycerion herself had similarly stolen a friend's client in the past. Her consternation only increases as her collocutor reminds her of the imperfections in her competition's appearance (e.g., her thin and receding hair, livid lips, scraggy neck, and long nose). Lacking in perspective and self-awareness, Glycerion has no way of understanding or accepting what happened to her. All she can do is complain that her competitor's mother was a witch who had captivated Glycerion's man with magic potions.

The courtesans in dialogues 4 and 10 both have very young lovers—little more than boys—who leave them for reasons connected with their youth. From what we can deduce from Lucian's dialogues and know from other works, young, unmarried men made up a good portion of the courtesan's clientele, so we can assume that the situations depicted in these dialogues were not uncommon. Unlike Glycerion, the courtesans in these dialogues feel affection for their men and suffer from the separation itself, not from the injury it causes to their egos. Like Glycerion, however, neither of them has the resources of mind or temperament to deal adequately with her plight.

In dialogue 4, Melitta's lover was gullible in the way that young people can be and left her for another courtesan when he saw mendacious graffiti on the wall in the Ceramicus stating that Melitta loved Hermotimus and that Hermotimus loved her. Like Glycerion, Melitta puts her faith in witchcraft, which Lucian held in contempt (cf. Epicurus' speech in *Double Indictment*). The only remedy she can think of is to ask her friend to find a witch to bring her man back. The dialogue ends with her eagerly telling her maid to fetch the materials they will need to cast the spell. Neither she nor her friend even thinks of going to tell the young man that she never knew Hermotimus and that he has been misled. Such an explanation might or might not have won him back, but it certainly would have been a more logical, more dignified, and potentially more effective response than witchcraft.[21]

In dialogue 10, the courtesan Drosis, "Dewy," suffers both because of her lover's and her own young age. Like Musarion, she is in love with her young man, though there is no indication that he exploits her. The dialogue opens with her utterly distraught that he had not visited her in three whole days. During those days, she agonized—in the way of an enamored teenager—over what might have kept him away. Did she accidentally cause him pain? Had he fallen in love with someone else? Had his father forbidden him to see her? On the day of the dialogue, she receives a letter from him confirming the last suspicion. The new philosopher-tutor his father had hired forbade him to see her and was keeping a close watch to make sure that he did not. Taking hope from his plea that she remember him, she latches on to the plan suggested by her friend that they accuse the tutor of pederasty. The dialogue ends with the friend planning to write the accusation on the wall in the Ceramicus and with Drosis eagerly looking forward to the completion of the act.

Like the witchcraft in which Melitta had placed her hope, however, Drosis' planned action is unlikely to bring her young man back. Caught up in vindictiveness, Drosis and her friend frame the accusation as an act of retaliation against the tutor, rather than as a means of getting her lover back. Even

---

21. Jones (1986: 47–52, 80, 98) points out that Lucian was well versed in magical practice and exact in its descriptions but, at the same time, mocked magic and people's credulity.

if the accusation gets the tutor fired, there is no saying that the young man's father, who (the dialogue reveals) was aware of the affair and had hired the tutor to put a stop to it, would not find another way of keeping his son in line. From Athenaeus' work, we learn that young men's keeping company with courtesans was viewed with opprobrium on both moral and financial grounds (*Deipn.* 569a–d). From this dialogue, we learn that this young man was rather acquiescent and unlikely to rebel.

Courtesans who confront their lovers are featured in dialogues 2 and 12. In dialogue 2, Myrtion roundly berates her lover Pamphilus for leaving her, eight months pregnant with his child, to marry the daughter of a shipping magnate. In dialogue 12, Ioessa severely rebukes her lover for cold-shouldering her and flirting with another courtesan in her presence. Both women aver that they believed the man's protestations of love, say that they would have been faithful and devoted to him, and declare that they had given themselves to him without demanding payment. Both expatiate at considerable length relative to the short length of the dialogues, depicting themselves as the unjustly wronged woman and characterizing the man as an ungrateful cad. Both speak in irate, spirited tones, very different from the plaintive tones adopted by Glycerion, Melitta, and Drosis. Myrtion, whose pregnancy makes her particularly vulnerable, goes so far as to threaten that if the child is a male, she will name him after his father, so that the boy, when older, will be able to throw his father's betrayal in his face. Both of these courtesans mention the possibility of suicide, albeit more likely as a threat than in earnest.

The responses of these courtesans are also satirized. In both dialogues, the wind is taken out of the courtesans' sails when it becomes apparent that their men had, in fact, not wronged them. Myrtion's man, Pamphilus, had not married (the wedding Myrtion's maid saw was a neighbor's); in the end, he assures her that he has no intention of abandoning her—meaning that he will help her to raise the child. Ioessa's man, Lysias, distanced himself when he mistakenly believed that she had taken another lover; he went back to her when she and her maid convinced him that she had not. In both cases, the courtesans look foolish for going on about what turns out to have been a misapprehension.

Lucian treats the two courtesans differently, however. Dialogue 2 depicts Myrtion with a typical mixture of sympathy, as the weaker party in an uneven relationship, and mockery, for being too eager to believe what she wants. With a child to support, she is the one who needs her man, not the other way around. But her satisfaction with Pamphilus' assurance that he had not married and with his promise not to abandon her is premature. She does not notice that he never promised not to marry in the future. She does not consider that there will be a great deal of family and social pressure on him to do so or that he will cease to support her and their child when he does. In short, she is depicted as foolish and naive. Dialogue 12 is a rare exception to Lucian's generally sympathetic depictions of the *hetaerae*. Ioessa comes across as a sharp-tongued shrew, haranguing her bewildered lover. Her name can be translated as "Poisonous" (ἰόεις, εσσα, εν), and her bitter, undeserved harangue is ugly and repellent.

The Realistic Courtesan

In contrast to the previously discussed dialogues, which feature courtesans who personalize their relationships, five dialogues (5, 8, 9, 14, 15) depict courtesans for whom financial motives are primary—not because they are greedy, which is never suggested, but because they have a realistic appreciation of their need to make a living. In three of these dialogues (9, 14, and 15), the courtesan has chosen to sell her services to the wealthier, higher-class man of two contenders and faces the anger of the poorer, lower-class one.

In dialogue 9, the courtesan Pannychis ("an all-night girl," παννυχίς, ιδος) finds herself at a loss when her soldier returns from the wars just when she is hosting the wealthy merchant who has replaced him. Although it is not said, we may assume that she needed the merchant's trade during the indefinite period when the soldier was away and was not supporting her. Her dilemma is that she does not want to send the wealthy merchant away but is terrified of the jealousy and possible violence of the returning soldier. Moreover, according to Pannychis' maid, the soldier has returned from battle with great riches, so it would not do to send him away either—especially since, as the other dialogues show, the merchant's patronage was unlikely to last forever. In the end, Pannychis avoids making a clear choice. She greets her returning soldier in the presence of her merchant client, abashedly explaining, "It's been a while" (χρόνιος φανείς). Instead of either inviting him in or sending him away, she goes indoors with her maid, leaving the two men to spar over her. It is difficult to know how much Lucian intended us to pity or deride Pannychis for her calculations, fears, and evasions and how much he wanted us to credit her good sense in getting out of harm's way.

The violence of jealous soldiers is attested to in dialogue 15, in which the courtesan Crocalē had turned away a soldier when he could not pay her fee, in favor of a wealthy farmer who could. The soldier burst into the party she was holding, beat up the farmer, and slapped the hired flute girl Parthenis and broke her flute. Only Crocalē, who had the presence of mind to flee to a neighbor's—and the good luck to have been able to do so—escaped uninjured. Had Pannychis, featured in dialogue 9, not gone inside, she might have suffered a fate similar to the flute girl's in dialogue 15.

In dialogue 14, the courtesan Myrtalē turned away a former client, a poor sailor, in favor of a wealthy merchant in his fifties, whose child she is bearing. The dialogue consists of an angry exchange between herself and the sailor, Dorion. First, Dorion enumerates each of the paltry gifts he gave her—which include a pair of shoes, some small coins, onions, cheese, fish, and some cheap jewelry—while Myrtalē reminds him of the services he received for each. Then, Myrtalē enumerates the considerably more substantial gifts—which include jewelry, a carpet, and rent payment—she received from the merchant, after which Dorion brings to her attention the merchant's advanced age and the defects of his physical appearance (e.g., his balding, poor coloring, and bad teeth) and his poor musical talent. Their exchange of words underpins the financial exchange at the heart of the courtesan-client relationship. Dorion acts as though Myrtalē is property he bought; Myrtalē sells herself to a higher bidder. There is no talk of affection on either side. Myrtalē looks after her own interests but is really no worse than Dorion, who has no right to expect any more than he got for the very little he has given.

The Degraded Courtesan

The other two dialogues that depict courtesans for whom financial motives are primary (5 and 8) feature women who agree to degrade themselves (according to them) for money. In dialogue 5, the courtesan Leaena admits to a liaison with a wealthy lesbian.[22] She admits to the affair not of her own initia-

---

22. For the sexual vocabulary in the dialogue, see Cameron 1998: 142–49. For an attempt to distill the comic and the philosophical in the portrayal of lesbianism, see Gilhuly 2006: 276–77, 286–87, 289. Within *Dialogues of the Courtesans*, this dialogue comes closest to making

tive but in reply to the question of her interlocutor, the courtesan Clonarion. She explicitly says that she is ashamed of the liaison, which she calls "somewhat unusual" (ἀλλόκοτον), and describes the seduction and the foreplay only at Clonarion's prodding. Even then, she tries to present herself as innocent and naive, saying that she had absolutely no idea of what was going on when one of the lesbians kissed and bit her; she refuses to answer Clonarion's question about what she did in bed with the two women, saying that "it's shameful" (αἰσχρὰ γάρ). Although Lucian generally avoids describing the sexual act itself, even in heterosexual encounters,[23] he does not call it shameful or shocking. Whether Leaena's innocence and shock are real or pretended, the dialogue makes it clear that she knew what she was getting into and entered the association for remuneration. She tells her interlocutor, "So I gave in, Clonarion, after she'd begged a lot and had given me a very expensive necklace and dresses of fine linen" (παρέσχον, ὦ Κλωνάριον, ἱκετευούσης πολλὰ καὶ ὅρμον τινά μοι δούσης τῶν πολυτελῶν καὶ ὀθόνας τῶν λεπτῶν).

In dialogue 8, an aging courtesan with twenty years of experience behind her and satirically named Ampelis, "Young Vine," confesses to allowing herself to be abused for money. The conversation arises from the complaint of the eighteen-year-old courtesan Chrysis, "Goldie," that her client hit her when he thought—incorrectly—that she was selling her services to a wealthier customer. Ampelis tries to convince her that if a man is not jealous, does not get angry, and does not hit the courtesan, he does not really love her. When the young Chrysis expresses reluctance to get beaten up and says that even though her lover hits her, he does not give her a bean, Ampelis relates a personal experience to convince her of the value of driving her man to violent jealousy. As Ampelis tells it, while she was with a well-paying client, she closed her door on an erratic customer who saw her only at intervals, demonstrated little passion, and paid her sparingly. After a while, his wish to outdo his rival enflamed his passions. He waited outside her door, and when it opened, he wept, hit her, tore her dress, threatened to kill her, and, in the end, gave her a talent to buy her services for eight months.

---

explicit references to the sexual act, and these are carefully restricted. Nonetheless, some scholars believe that this collection of dialogues may offend some modern readers; see Jenkins 2005: 387–93.

23. Cf. Selene's words to Aphrodite about her sneaking to be with Endymion when he is asleep: "Then I creep down quietly on tip-toe, so as not to waken him and give him a fright, and then—but you know; there is no need to tell you what happens next" (*Dialogues of the Gods* 232, trans. Macleod).

As Lucian depicts them, the courtesans who are emotionally involved with their customers suffer from their misplaced trust and affections. But the more hard-boiled courtesans who look out for their financial interest suffer from the dilemmas they face and the sacrifices they must make—in dignity, integrity, pleasure, and safety—to secure their living.

The Ideal Courtesan

To complete this survey of the courtesans in Lucian's dialogues, a few words are in order about the courtesan Tryphena of dialogue 11, who falls between the two types already discussed. Tryphena is the ideal courtesan. She is caring and accommodating but has the social intelligence and ability to put her ego aside, enabling her to get what she wants. The dialogue opens with her solicitously asking her client, who is in bed with her but has placed his coat between them, why he is so despondent and not enjoying her company even though he paid for it. She makes him feel comfortable, conveys that she likes him and would like to enjoy their time together, and gets him to open up and to confess that he loves another courtesan, who had rejected him. She fights for him by convincing him that her rival is really old and ugly. There is a brief hitch when she learns that he had hired her services only to get back at the other courtesan. Her first reaction is to get up and leave—that is, to stand on her dignity in face of the insult, much as Philinna had done when her lover humiliated her. However, Tryphena quickly overcomes her pique when the client declares that he is no longer interested in the other courtesan and proposes that they hug and kiss and make love. Her warmth, perspicacity, and ability to put aside her ego, while preserving her self, make her stand out above the other courtesans Lucian depicts.

Lucian's Attitudes toward Courtesans

Like other writings of the Second Sophistic, *Dialogues of the Courtesans* is a derivative work that builds on earlier Greek sources. The situations depicted and even many of the courtesans' names can be found in New Comedy and other works dating back to the Hellenistic period. What makes these dialogues special, perhaps even unique, is their attempt to present the lives and conduct of the courtesans from the courtesans' own perspective. That the dialogues sound the voices of the courtesans themselves enables and, to some extent, inclines Lucian to employ understanding and sympathy when presenting conduct that can easily be criticized. Lucian's projection of the courtesans' voices does not refute Gilhuly's contention that the dialogues are infused with male subjectivity.[24] Having been written by a man, how could they be otherwise? But it befits the generally sympathetic picture that the dialogues paint of these courtesans.

With the exception of Tryphena, whose blend of savvy and good-heartedness is as commendable as it is rare (certainly in the world of *Dialogues of the Courtesans*, but outside it as well), all the courtesans have their shortcomings, and some have more than others. Yet they are satirized for follies, not sins, and their depiction is more favorable than that found in other works, including Lucian's own. None of the courtesans in these dialogues drives her lover to suicide, as did the courtesan Myrtium in Lucian's *Dialogues of the Dead* (443) and the courtesan from in his *Voyage to the Underworld* (6.9). None is lascivious or driven by lust, as Apollodorus' Neaera was said to have been.[25] None speaks in obscenities, as do *hetaerae* in Athenaeus' *Deipnosophistae*.[26] Unlike courtesans in Menander's plays, the courtesans in *Dialogues of the Courtesans* are not blamed for being greedy or overcharging; they are depicted as poor women—sometimes desperately poor—doing what they must to keep body and soul together. Even where a courtesan calculatingly chooses a wealthier patron over a poorer one, the rebuke is directed not at her but at the patron who expects to get a great deal for very little.[27]

In *Toxaris: On Friendship* (13.14, 13.18), Lucian terms a wife's infidelity and deception as "courtesan-like" behavior. In *Dialogues of the Courtesans*, he shows the pressures that are behind his courtesans' manipulations, deceits, and resort to multiple partners. In *De Domo* (7.11) and *True Histories* (2.46.3), Lucian criticizes the deceptive adornments that courtesans use to lure their customers. In *Dialogues of the Courtesans*, the vain efforts of his older courtesans to make themselves look younger elicit more pity than scorn and highlight that these women are about to lose their livelihoods. In his *True Histories*

24. Gilhuly 2007.
25. Miner 2003.
26. McClure 2003b.
27. For the image of the greedy *hetaera* in Greek comedy, see discussion in Henry 1985: 30, 34–38, 47–48, 109–13. Traill (2008: 95) claims, "The gold-digging *meretrix avara*, 'greedy prostitute,' so familiar from Roman comedy and the letters [*sic*] of Lucian and Alciphron is rare in Menander but attested." This claim does not apply to the *Dialogues of the Courtesans*.

(2.18.6), *Dialogues of the Dead* (25.10), *Timon* (12.5), *De Domo* (7.11), and *Double Indictment* (31.5), Lucian blames courtesans for harm that men suffer at their hands. In *Dialogues of the Courtesans*, he places the responsibility on the men. Where they squander their money on *hetaerae*, it is the men's doing, not the fault of the *hetaerae*. Where men fall prey to jealousy, it is their lust and possessiveness that are to blame, not the ploys of the *hetaerae*.

Athenaeus on Courtesans

According to Gilhuly,[28] "there is evidence of a growing negative moral tinge" to the *hetaera*'s profession during the Second Sophistic. Lucian's *Dialogues of the Courtesans* may be viewed as a corrective or defense. So may the portrait of the courtesan that emerges from book 13 of Athenaeus' *Deipnosophistae*, a collection of excerpts and anecdotes that are presented as the conversation of twenty-three men who met at symposia in Rome on a number of occasions. Most of book 13 deals with women.[29] Athenaeus, born c. 170–230 CE, wrote in Greek while living in Rome. Although it is likely that the *Deipnosophistae* was composed after *Dialogues of the Courtesans*, it provides us with a perspective from which to appreciate Lucian's unique accomplishment.[30]

Book 13 brings together the negative and positive views of courtesans in Greek writings and, we may assume, in Athenaeus' own day and place. It begins with the negative view, expounded by the philosopher Cynicus, that, because of her rapacity and conniving, the courtesan is a "calamity" and "mighty pest" to the man who keeps her (*Deipn.* 567d).[31] Courtesans are wealthy, Cynicus continues, because they set "traps . . . to catch a man's substance" (*Deipn.* 567–68) and because "to make their gains and plunder their neighbors, they count all other means as trivial, but stitch plots against all" (*Deipn.* 568a). There are statements berating the young men who frequent brothels (569a), but the focus of the opprobrium is mainly on the courtesans

---

28. Gilhuly 2006: 278 with n. 14.
29. For the structure of the work as a whole, see Wilkins 2000: 23–37. For book 13 in particular, see Henry 1992: 261–65; Hawley 1993. For analysis of both Athenaeus' discussion of women in other parts of his work and their interchangeability there with food, see Henry 1992: 255–65.
30. "There is a sense in which the work of Athenaeus stands very close to that of Lucian," says Anderson (2000: 2183–84).
31. Cf. the description of Helen in Aesch. *Ag.* 716–36, where she is compared to an innocent lion cub that is kept at home and that grows and endangers the residents of the house.

themselves. The criticism is epitomized by Epicrates' portrait of the courtesan Laïs (in his play Ἀντιλαΐς, "Against Laïs"), who is described as both
drunk and lazy and caring only for what she may eat and drink all day
(*Deipn.* 570b). The portrait goes on to present Laïs and other courtesans as
predators, comparing them to eagles who, when young, "snatch up . . . and
carry off . . . the sheep and hares" but, when old, lose their power to hunt.
Thus Laïs, the portrait concludes scornfully, was savage and hard to get
when she was a "fresh young chick" but will humbly take any comer for a
low fee now that she is older (*Deipn.* 570c–d). None of these aspersions is
sounded in *Dialogues of the Courtesans*, other than to refute them.

Moreover, these negative portrayals are less frequent than positive portrayals in Athenaeus' compilation. Myrtilus, who delivers most of the positive views, distinguishes between so-called αὐλητρίδες (flute girls) who ply
their trade for money and those who are "able to preserve a friendship without trickery" (φιλίαν ἄδολον, *Deipn.* 571a–e), whom he refers to as ἑταῖραι
(real companions/courtesans). A few paragraphs later, continuing with his
praises, he quotes the comic poet Ephippus' description of how courtesans
use their kisses, attentiveness, and flattery to lift the spirits of downcast clients (*Deipn.* 571f). Other banqueters praise specific courtesans: a courtesan of
refined table manners (*Deipn.* 572a) and courtesans who saved their city from
capture (*Deipn.* 572e–f, 573d) or who served as respected companions to
kings and venerated historical figures, giving them good counsel and bearing
them sons, some of whom became important figures in their own right
(*Deipn.* 573a, 576d–577d).[32] Several sections are devoted to the clever statements of courtesans, whose wit and astuteness stand out against the conceit
and self-absorption of their less perspicacious clients (*Deipn.* 577d–585f).

Scholars differ in their appraisal of Myrtilus' praise of courtesans. Hawley
(1993) suggests that it undercuts the stereotypic view of the *hetaera* as pretty,
witty, and wise. McClure states that Myrtilus delivers what amounts to an encomium of *hetaerae*, which unmasks the hypocrisy of philosophers.[33] Henry
(1992) distinguishes Athenaeus' ultimately favorable depiction from the picture that emerges from Lucian's *Dialogues of the Courtesans*. Writing from a
feminist vantage point, Henry argues that Myrtilus' defense—no less than
Cynicus' critique—provides a "pornographic representation" (266) of women

32. By some authorities, this is true of Themistocles (576d), the general Timotheus (577b), and
the orator Aristophon (577c).
33. McClure 2003b: 265, 290.

whose sole reason for being is to please men. Even their witticisms and clever anecdotes are geared for the amusement of men. Moreover, Henry points out, in all of the considerable talk about courtesans in Athenaeus' work, no mention is made of "the grimmer realities of prostitutes' lives" (265).

In contrast, these grimmer realities stand out in Lucian's work. Whether positive or negative, the anecdotes and statements collected in Athenaeus' work reflect the male perspective—a concern with how the conduct of the courtesans harms or benefits the men who hire or keep them. Cynicus lambastes what courtesans supposedly do to men. Myrtilus praises what they do for men. In contrast, Lucian shows what is done to them.

Works Cited

Anderson, G. 2000. "Athenaeus: The Sophistic Environment." *ANRW* II.34.3: 2173–85.

Baldwin, B. 1961. "Lucian as Social Satirist." *CQ*, n.s., 11.2: 199–208.

Baldwin, B. 1977. "Lucian and Theophrastus." *Mnemosyne* 30: 174–76.

Branham, R. B. 1989. *Unruly Eloquence: Lucian and the Comedy of Traditions.* Cambridge, MA: Harvard University Press.

Braund, D., and Wilkins, J., eds. 2000. *Athenaeus and His World: Reading Greek Culture in the Roman Empire.* Exeter: University of Exeter Press.

Cameron, A. 1998. "Love (and Marriage) between Women." *GRBS* 39: 137–56.

Davidson, J. N. 1997. *Courtesans and Fishcakes: The Consuming Passions of Classical Athens.* New York: St. Martin's.

Faraone, C. A., and McClure, L. K., eds. 2006. *Prostitutes and Courtesans in the Ancient World.* Madison: University of Wisconsin Press.

Gilhuly, K. 2006. "The Phallic Lesbian: Philosophy, Comedy, and Social Inversion in Lucian's *Dialogues of the Courtesans.*" In Faraone and McClure, 274–91.

Gilhuly, K. 2007. "Bronze for Gold: Subjectivity in Lucian's *Dialogues of the Courtesans.*" *AJP* 128: 59–94.

Gulick, C. B. 1950. *Athenaeus VI., The Deipnosophists, Book XIII–XIV to 653b.* Cambridge, MA: Harvard University Press.

Hall, J. 1981. *Lucian's Satire.* New York: Arno.

Hawley, R. 1993. "'Pretty, Witty, and Wise': Courtesans in Athenaeus' *Deipnosophistai* Book 13." *International Journal of Moral and Social Studies* 8.1: 73–89.

Henry, M. M. 1985. *Menander's Courtesans and the Greek Comic Tradition.* Frankfurt am Main: Peter Lang.

Henry, M. M. 1992. "The Edible Woman: Athenaeus' Concept of the Pornographic." In Richlin, 250–68.

Hopkinson, N. 2008. *Lucian: A Selection.* Cambridge: Cambridge University Press.

Jenkins, T. E. 2005. "An American "Classics": Hillman and Cullen's *Mimes of the Courtesans.*" *Arethusa* 38: 387–414.

Jones, C. P. 1986. *Culture and Society in Lucian.* Cambridge, MA: Harvard University Press.

Kurke, L. 1999. *Coins, Bodies, Games, and Gold: The Politics of Meaning in Archaic Greece.* Princeton: Princeton University Press.

Lateiner, D. 2006. "Mothers in Ovid's *Metamorphoses.*" *Helios* 33.2: 189–201.

LeGrand, P. 1907. "Les Dialogues des courtisanes comparés avec la comédie." *REG* 20: 176–231.

Licht, Hans [P. Brandt]. 1925–28. *Sittengeschichte Griechenlands.* Dresden: P. Aretz.

Licht, Hans [P. Brandt]. 1975. *Sexual Life in Ancient Greece.* Trans. J. H. Freese. Ed. L. H. Dawson. Westport, CT: Greenwood. First published 1932.

Macleod, M. D. 1961. *Lucian.* Vol. 7. Cambridge, MA: Harvard University Press.

Macleod, M. 1974. "Lucian's Knowledge of Theophrastus." *Mnemosyne* 27: 75–76.

McClure, L. K. 2003a. *Courtesans at Table: Gender and Greek Literary Culture in Athenaeus.* New York: Routledge.

McClure, L. K. 2003b. "Subversive Laughter: The Sayings of Courtesans in Book 13 of Athenaeus' *Deipnosophistae.*" *AJP* 124: 259–94.

Miner, J. 2003. "Courtesan, Concubine, Whore: Apollodorus' Deliberate Use of Terms for Prostitutes." *AJP* 124: 19–37.

Mras, K. 1916. "Die Personennamen in Lucians Hetärengesprächen." *WS* 38: 308–42.

Olson, S. D. 1992. "Names and Naming in Aristophanic Comedy." *CQ* 42: 304–19.

Petersen, L. H., and Salzman-Mitchell, P., eds. 2012. *Mothering and Motherhood in Ancient Greece and Rome.* Austin: University of Texas Press.

Richlin, A. 1984. "Invective against Women in Roman Satire." *Arethusa* 17: 67–80.

Richlin, A, ed. 1992. *Pornography and Representation in Greece and Rome.* Oxford: Oxford University Press.

Sidwell, K. 2000. "Athenaeus, Lucian, and Fifth-Century Comedy." In Braund and Wilkins, 137–52.

Sidwell, K. 2004. *Lucian, Chattering Courtesans, and Other Sardonic Sketches.* London: Penguin Books.

Strong, A. K. 2012. "Working Girls: Mother-Daughter Bonds among Ancient Prostitutes." In Petersen and Salzman-Mitchell, 121–39.

Swain, S. 1996. *Hellenism and Empire: Language, Classicism, and Power in the Greek World, AD 50–250.* Oxford: Clarendon.

Traill, A. 2008. *Women and the Comic Plot in Menander.* Cambridge: Cambridge University Press.

Wilkins, J. 2000. "Dialogue and Comedy: The Structure of the *Deipnosophistae.*" In Braund and Wilkins, 23–37.

CHAPTER 13

Omnia Movet Amor

Love and Resistance, Art and Movement, in Ovid's Daphne and Apollo Episode (*Metamorphoses* 1.452–567)

Judith P. Hallett

My essay pays tribute to Donald Lateiner as teacher and scholar. It examines an Ovidian narrative from the *Metamorphoses*, the story of Daphne and Apollo in book 1, to argue that Don's writing on various aspects of Ovid's words—the skillful employment of mimetic syntax, the frequent and memorable inclusion of duality and doubling as significant motifs, and the portrayal of mythic artist figures, often as surrogates for Ovid himself—not only enriches reading, thinking, and teaching about this complex, richly rewarding Roman poet but also illuminates this episode and its major themes of love, resistance, and art. Yet it underscores as well the importance of movement as a theme in this episode from this epic poem; it thereby points up the significance and wider applicability of Don's groundbreaking scholarly studies on nonverbal behavior, gesture, and kinesis, especially in Homeric epic and Herodotus.[1]

In this analysis, I will devote my closest attention to the language of the story's opening lines, 452–73. Here Ovid introduces and emphasizes the nar-

---

1. See Lateiner's important work on mimetic syntax (1990), duality and doubling (2013), and mythic artist figures (1984) in the *Metamorphoses*, as well as on affect displays (1992) and nonverbal behavior in Homer (1995), Herodotus (1987), and the *Metamorphoses* (1996); these studies in particular have influenced the discussion to follow.

rative's key concepts—love and resistance, art and movement—through significant word choice, placement, and repetition. In these twenty-two lines, Ovid also avails himself of a literary strategy he deploys later in this same episode and throughout the *Metamorphoses*, that of alluding to earlier Latin poetic texts. Such intertextual "touches" help to characterize Apollo, Daphne, and Cupid, the story's principal figures, as well as to facilitate Ovid's explorations of relationships between artistic creation and human culture in this episode.[2] Ovid's depiction of Cupid here, at the start of this narrative, highlights the love god's role as *primum mobile* in the story's plot and presages Ovid's later emphasis on physical and emotional movement by Daphne and Apollo after Cupid manages to wound them both. At the same time, Ovid accords prominence to the theme of duality and doubling in his representation of Cupid's two arrows, a theme that later resonates in Ovid's portrayals of Cupid's victims.

Love, Art, Resistance, and Movement in Metamorphoses 1.452–73

Ovid introduces *Metamorphoses* 1.452–567, his account of the unsuccessful pursuit of the nymph Daphne by the god Apollo, with five, strategically positioned words: *Primus amor Phoebi Daphne Peneia*, "First love, of Phoebus Apollo, Daphne, daughter of Peneus." This introduction begins with a phrase consisting of a masculine adjective and its noun (*primus amor*, "[the] first love") and concludes with a phrase consisting of a feminine noun and its adjective (*Daphne Peneia*, "Daphne daughter of Peneus"). Both of these phrases are in the nominative case and frame another masculine noun, Apollo's epithet *Phoebi*, a subjective genitive form technically indicating possession. With these five words, Ovid announces *amor*, "love," and its predicate here, Daphne, as his narrative themes. Through the central positioning of *Phoebi* in a "doubly functioning" (*apo koinou*) grammatical role, he identifies both *amor* and Daphne as belonging to Apollo and thus supposedly under Apollo's control.

But the three words occupying the center of that verbal quintet, the nouns

---

2. For intertextuality, see, e.g., Morgan and Harrison 2008, on the ancient novel, another area of research in which Lateiner has made major contributions; for Ovidian intertextuality in particular, see Knox and Casali 2009.

amor Phoebi Daphne, themselves foreshadow the issues and enumerate the major characters, in Ovid's narrative. The story about Phoebus Apollo that Ovid proceeds to narrate prominently features the god who is himself named Amor, Cupid, as Apollo's antagonist. It portrays Amor, moreover, as actually controlling the narrative by punishing Apollo's arrogance with *amor*—for a love object who is repeatedly described as fleeing and resisting him. So, too, Ovid displays his distinctive and masterful use of mimetic syntax by placing Daphne's name at the end of this list, after both Amor and Phoebus. In this way, her name itself enacts, visually and aurally, her efforts at fleeing and resistance.

Ovid utilizes the first twenty-two lines of the Daphne and Apollo episode, 452–73, much as he does the very first line itself, to announce these narrative themes of love and resistance, specifically resistance by fleeing. Throughout the remainder of the episode, he underscores these themes in the most literal way possible, by repeated use of the same or etymologically kindred words for love and fleeing. He employs the noun *amor*, "love," and the related verb *amare*, "to love," thirteen times in the episode. *Amor* itself, moreover, appears three times in lines 452–73: in, as we have seen, the first line of the narrative, 452; at line 461, where Apollo derisively tells Cupid to "be content to stir up some love affair or other" (*amores*); and at 469, where Ovid observes that one of Cupid's arrows, that which pierces Apollo, "creates love" (*facit amorem*). Ovid also uses the verb *fugere*, "to flee," along with nouns, verbs, and adjectives that share the same root, twelve times during the episode: in lines 452–73, we find *fugat*, describing Cupid's arrow that "causes love to flee," in both lines 469 and 471.

At the same time, these twenty-two lines introduce two other important themes in the episode, those of art and movement. It is striking that Ovid does not associate art with Apollo, god of poetry, in the episode's opening lines. Later in the episode, at line 524, Apollo cites, among his assets as a sexual partner, his own *artes* that benefit all but their master, after he mentions his artistic domain with the claim, in a sexual double entendre, that through him "poems harmonize with their sinewy lyre strings" (518: *per me concordant carmina nervis*).[3] As we will observe, Daphne's metamorphosis into

---

3.   For the sexual sense of *nervus* (discussed again in the next section of this essay), see Adams 1982: 21, 38, 222n2, 224; LaFleur 1999: 28, on *Amores* 1.1 (LaFleur does not discuss the word's connotations in his earlier presentation of the Daphne and Apollo episode); Hallett 2012a and 2012b: 21.

a tree and Apollo's reaction to it, in lines 548–67, foreground Apollo's role as control-seeking love artist, through their evocation of Horace's *Odes* 3.30 and through the description in 549 of the bark that covers Daphne as *tenui libro*, a "book," "slender" in the fashion of erotic elegy.[4]

But in these twenty-two opening lines, Ovid represents Cupid alone as engaged in different types of artistic activity, as what Lateiner might call "an Ovidian artist."[5] At 455, in another sexually and literarily charged play on words, he states that Apollo had initially seen Cupid bending his bow with the sinewy part pulled back, *adducto . . . nervo*, using the noun later employed for Apollo's lyre strings. When, in 461, Ovid depicts Apollo as dismissively telling Cupid to be content stirring up *amores* of some sort, he may pun on the meaning of *amores* as "love poems"; at 467, Ovid states that Cupid "took his stance" on the shady summit of Parnassus, a locale ordinarily associated with Apollo himself and poetic inspiration.[6] At 469, moreover, Ovid characterizes Cupid's two weapons as *diversorum operum*, "of different purposes," employing *opus*, a term signifying a work of art, to refer to what his arrows achieve on their two targets.[7]

So, in these twenty-two lines, Ovid portrays Cupid as in motion, putting his arrows in motion, and causing others to move by so doing. Apollo, Ovid says, had first seen Cupid "bending his bow" (and recalling the epic hero Odysseus by so doing). Cupid responds to Apollo's taunt that such "courageous weapons" (456: *fortibus armis*) better befit his own shoulders, by declaring in 463–64 that while Apollo may pierce all things with his bow, his own bow may pierce Apollo. Ovid then describes Cupid's rapid ascent to Parnassus in 466 with a phrase that interweaves an ablative absolute with an ablative of means, *eliso percussis aere pennis*, "the air having been crashed through

4. For *liber* here as both "bark" and "book," see Farrell 1999; for Ovid's own associations between the adjective *tenuis* and elegy, see, e.g., *Amores* 3.1.9 (where the personified figure of elegy is dressed in a *vestis tenuissima*); see also the discussion in Keith 1994.
5. See Lateiner 1984. Cupid's boastful claim in 464–65—*quantoque animalia cedunt / cuncta deo, tanto minor est tua gloria nostra*, "to the same extent that all animals are lower than a god is your glory less than ours"—also contributes to his characterization as an artist figure: it recalls Horace's prophecy of his poetic immortality in *Odes* 3.30, echoed, as we will see, by Apollo's words at the end of the episode. For Ovid's portrayal of major figures in the *Metamorphoses* specifically as surrogates for his narrative *persona*, see Pavlock 2009 (though Pavlock does not deal with this episode).
6. For Ovid's representation of Parnassus as Apollo's "turf," see, e.g., *Metamorphoses* 11.165.
7. For Ovid's own use of *opus* for a work of poetic art, see, e.g., *Amores* 1.1.14, evoked in this episode (where the poet-speaker, like Apollo here, indignantly addresses Cupid), and 1.1.27.

after his feathers had been struck," emphasizing Cupid's speedy movement by placing the two perfect passive participles first. Cupid next figures as the subject of the active verbs *prompsit* in 468 ("he pulled out" two weapons), *fixit* in 463 ("he drove it" in the nymph, Peneius' daughter, with the same verb as the doubly functional *figat*), and *laesit* in 473 ("he wounded" Apollo's innermost feelings).

The following line, *protinus alter amat, fugit altera nomen amantis*, "at once one of the two—a man—loves, the other—a woman—flees the name of a lover," immediately resumes and elaborates the themes of love and resistance, with the chiasmus of the word order stressing the incompatibility of Cupid's two victims. Ovid proceeds to use a series of active verbs and participles to describe Daphne's reactions, all of them physical movements: *coercebat* in 477 ("she forced" her hair); *aversata*, "having turned away from those pursuing her," in 478; *lustrat*, "she roams," in 479.[8] Ovid first depicts Apollo's reactions with verbs of feeling and sensation: *amat*, "he loves," and *cupit*, "he desires," in 490; *cupit* and *sperat*, "he hopes," in 491. He then likens Apollo's passion to grain stalks and hedges set aflame in 492–96 and details Apollo's sensory responses to Daphne's beauty with *spectat*, "he looks at," in 497 and with various forms of the verb *videre*, "to see," in 498, 499, and 500.

Ovid next assigns Apollo a twenty-one-line speech pleading with the fleeing Daphne to stop and appreciate his many assets (504–34), delineating, with several other active verbs, the sources of Daphne's physical appeal as she flees (525–30). The poet then concentrates on Apollo's own physical movements. He expands his description of how Apollo follows Daphne's footsteps (532: *sequitur*) with a six-line simile comparing Apollo to a Gallic dog in pursuit of a rabbit. It concludes with the remark in 539 that the same situation prevailed with the god and the maiden, *deus et virgo*, "the god swift out of hope, the maiden swift out of fear" (*hic spe celer, illa timore*).[9] In 540, Ovid uses the more intensive *insequitur*, "he chases," for Apollo's pursuit,

8. One might read *aversata* as a deponent participle in the middle voice, but as it is a transitive verb form taking a direct object (*petentes*, those who pursue her), Ovid clearly uses it in an active sense.
9. In describing Apollo's pursuit of Daphne at 530–42, Ovid uses, in the third-person singular, both *sequor* and *insequor*, two of the same verbs that feature in his earlier description of Apollo's words of entreaty to Daphne at 504–24. Significantly, many of the verbs Apollo employs in his entreaty are not action verbs but, rather, forms of the verb "to be." Apollo thereby underscores the static nature of who he is and what he has to offer, an identity contrasting to that of the "kinetic" Daphne, which Ovid uses multiple active verbs to represent.

which eventuates in the details of how Daphne transformed into a laurel tree. Verbs of action and motion (the perfect active participle *complexus*, "having embraced," in 555 and *[oscula] dat*, "gives kisses," in 556) combine with verbs of feeling (*amat* and *sentit* in 553–54) in Ovid's description of Apollo's response to the tree that was once Daphne. Strikingly, in 567, the final line of the narrative, Ovid attributes this formerly kinetic form of vegetation with physically active movement, observing that when she nodded (*adnuit*), her leafy top appeared to have shaken its boughs (*agitasse*).

Intertextualities in the Characterizations of Apollo, Daphne, and Cupid: Apollo as Horatian Artist

In *Metamorphoses* 1.456, the fifth line of the Daphne and Apollo narrative, shortly before he has Apollo tell Cupid to be content with stirring up *amores*, Ovid pointedly echoes the opening poem of his own *Amores*. By rebuking Cupid with the words *"Quid" que "tibi, lascive puer, cum fortibus armis?"* Apollo recalls the question voiced by the poet-speaker at *Amores* 1.1.5, *Quis tibi, saeve puer, dedit hoc in carmina iuris?* "What gives you, savage boy, this legal power over poems?" Three lines earlier, moreover, Ovid uses the adjective *saevus* for Cupid's *ira* against Apollo, thereby recalling the *Amores* passage as well.

By evoking his own *Amores* 1.1 at the start of the Daphne and Apollo episode, Ovid also signals to his readers that Apollo will be no match for Cupid. After the poet-speaker rebukes Amor in *Amores* 1.1, he is wounded by Cupid's arrows, which render him helplessly amorous and reduce him to writing love poems in elegiac couplets rather than military epic in dactylic hexameters. Ovid also identifies Apollo, god of poetry, with himself, a mere love poet under Cupid's control, by recalling lines 25–26 of *Amores* 1.1. There Ovid offers the lamentations "That boy had unerring arrows [*certas . . . sagittas*]" and "Love reigns in an empty heart [*in vacuo pectore*]." Ovid's Apollo asserts in Metamorphoses 1.519–20 that "indeed our arrow is unerring, however, one arrow is more unerring than ours [*certa quidem nostra est, nostra tamen una sagitta certior*], [Cupid's arrow] which has created wounds in an empty heart [*in vacuo . . . pectore*]."

Nevertheless, Ovid's introductory words about Cupid, as I have noted, represent Cupid as an artist, too, and a far more successful one than Apollo.

Furthermore, at the end of the Daphne and Apollo episode, Ovid recalls and "bookends" his allusions to his own *Amores* 1.1 by engaging intertextually with another, earlier work of Roman poetry, Horace's *Odes* 3.30, in which Horace proudly describes his poetry as a means to immortality, a *monumentum aere perennius*, "a monument more enduring than bronze." For example, *Odes* 3.30 ends with Horace's request to the Muse Melpomene to "gladly surround [*cinge*] his head with the laurel from Apollo's shrine at Delphi [*Delphica lauro*]." In *Metamorphoses* 1.549, Ovid employs the same verb, *cingere*, to describe, with a vividly pictorial interlocking of key words, the literal surrounding of Daphne's tender, heart-beating chest by thin bark (*mollia cinguntur tenui praecordia libro*) and hence the creation of "Delphic laurel."

In these evocations, Ovid identifies Apollo with one of his own literary contemporaries as well as with himself. But just as Ovid portrays himself as literarily unequal to Cupid in *Amores* 1.1 and diminishes Apollo's artistic stature in identifying Apollo with himself, so he subtly criticizes both Apollo and Horace through these evocations. Indeed, by initially referring to Apollo with the adjective *superbus* in *Metamorphoses* 1.454, Ovid recalls Horace's comment to Melpomene in the final two lines of *Odes* 3.30, *sume superbiam / quaesitam meritis*, "Accept the proud honor won by your merit." In recalling Horace's *Odes* 3.30 later in the narrative, Ovid emphasizes Apollo's *superbia*, his excessive, arrogant pride, evinced in Apollo's insistence on outdoing Horace himself as a prophetic poet.

In lines 6–14 of *Odes* 3.30, Horace intones a vatic prediction, with five verbs in the future tense about the immortality that his poetry will achieve for him. Apollo's words to the transformed Daphne at *Metamorphoses* 1.557–65 similarly serve a prophetic function, but with seven such verbs. As noted above, at *Odes* 3.30.5–16, Horace tersely orders Melpomene to encircle his hair, *comam*, with laurel, *lauro*, specifically Delphic laurel (*Delphica*), as the reward for his literary achievement. At *Metamorphoses* 1.557–65, Ovid has Apollo lecture the transformed Daphne about how she will serve him in future. He calls Horace to mind by proclaiming, *semper habebunt te coma, te citharae, te nostrae, laure, pharetrae*, "Our hair will always have you, our lyres will always have you, our quivers will have you, laurel"—also awarding *coma*, "hair," pride of place, but employing many more words and an anaphoric tricolon crescendo.[10]

---

10. As Donald Lateiner has pointed out to me, the repeated *te . . . te . . . te*, voiced as part of a

Then, too, Horace predicts, *dicar . . . dum Capitolium scandet cum tacita virgine pontifex*, "I will be recited . . . as long as the chief Roman priest will climb the Capitoline Hill accompanied by a silent maiden, a Vestal Virgin." At *Metamorphoses* 1.559–60, Ovid's Apollo tells Daphne, *tu ducibus Latiis aderis, cum laeta triumphum vos canet et visent longas Capitolia pompas*, "you will be present for the Latin leaders when a happy voice will sing a triumph and the Capitoline Hills will see long processions." He thereby envisions not merely a single occasion of Roman religious solemnity, with the Capitoline Hill as its subject, as does Horace, but multiple and magnificent celebrations of Roman military might witnessed by the pluralized Capitoline Hill itself. Significantly, too, Horace's phrase *virgine tacita*—used for the Vestal who, he proclaims, will accompany the chief Roman priest when his own poetry is read in the future—aptly applies to the silenced former maiden Daphne herself.

While narrating the tale of Daphne and Apollo, Ovid takes the opportunity to reflect on the power of art—specifically of literature, his own artistic domain—and, in this context, to problematize the relationship between culture, as represented by art, and nature. Ovid's use of a word that means both "bark" and "book" to describe what encloses the transformed Daphne both recognizes Daphne's narrated experience as art and validates his own narration as such. In her transformed identity as a laurel tree, Daphne is also forced to serve not only Apollo but also the emperor Augustus, both in their roles as protectors of culture: Apollo tells Daphne that she will stand before the doors of Augustus' palace as a most faithful guardian. Yet Ovid's narrative repeatedly associates Daphne with nature, characterizing her as rejecting artifice and as beautified by the act of fleeing, her mode of physical resistance to Apollo.

At the same time, however, Ovid portrays Daphne as resisting "the call of nature" in refusing to wed, as well as in denying the sexual appeal of her physical beauty. Still, even though Daphne resists and rejects sexual activity, Apollo, compelled by Cupid's arrow to love and lust, cannot. Ovid's evocation of *Amores* 1.1 in his portrayal of both Apollo and Cupid warrants further notice because, as we have seen, *nervus*, the noun that he employs for the

---

prophecy, is also hymnic phrasing, suggestive of prayers of appeal to the Greco-Roman gods. But Apollo's words here represent the de facto opposite of a hymn to a divinity, since they are addressed by a divinity to a human, after his prayer-like entreaties to her have failed. Again, we encounter Ovid's use of an inversion motif, much like his portrayal of Cupid as taking his stand on Apollo's own Mount Parnassus.

string of Cupid's bow and the strings of Apollo's lyre, figures in an elaborate sexual double entendre at *Amores* 1.17–18. There Ovid describes the rising and falling of the elegiac couplet itself with several sexually charged words, including not only *nervus*, "sinewy part," but also *surgere*, "rise up": he thereby defines this meter as operating in the manner of a male sexual organ, alternatively turgid and detumescent.[11]

In the final couplet of *Amores* 1.1, Ovid accepts Cupid's elegiac meter, along with the sexual rhythms it personifies, as necessary to his amatory and poetic success. With the verb *cingere* and an address to the Muse, he recalls Horace's climactic words in *Odes* 3.30, proclaiming, "Muse, be encircled with Venus' myrtle from the seashore on your golden tresses, to be set to rhythm in eleven feet." Ovid's Apollo resists and taunts Cupid and Cupid's *amores* (loves and love poems) as inferior and unmanly. But even in the *Metamorphoses*, a text composed exclusively in virile dactylic hexameters, Cupid prevails.

Duality and Doubling in the Representation of Cupid's Impact

Finally, in this narrative as in so many other Ovidian texts, Ovid plays with the notion of duality and doubling, in the form of the number two itself as well as through the echoing and mirroring effects of repetition. At *Metamorphoses* 1.468–69, Ovid describes Cupid as pulling from his quiver and then shooting *duo tela / diversorum operum*, "two weapons of different purposes." In describing these two different purposes in 469–71, Ovid echoes his words about the first in his words about the second: *fugat hoc, facit illud amorem: / quod facit, auratum est et cuspide fulget acuta, / quod fugat, obtusum est et habet sub harundine plumbum*, "this arrow puts love to flight, that arrow creates it: that which creates love is golden and gleams with a sharp point, that which puts love to flight is blunt and has lead beneath its shaft." Not only does each line begin with the relative pronoun *quod*, followed by the third-person singular active verb previously employed to denote its action (*facit* and *fugat*). Each line also contains a neuter descriptive adjective (*auratum* and *obtusum*), the verb form *est*, and the conjunction *et*. Both of these lines feature elision of the adjective with the following word *est*, with a metrical caesura at that point. In

---

11. For Ovid's sexually charged description of the elegiac meter, see Hallett 2012a: 261 and 2012b: 221–22.

this way, they create the rhythmic effect achieved by the first half of an elegiac pentameter line, reminding the reader that the episode centers on Cupid's realm of *amores*, love and love poems.[12]

Verbal effects of doubling and mirroring figure in Ovid's descriptions of Cupid's two victims, too. In two successive lines relating the backstory of Daphne's relationship with her father, 481–82, the poet writes, *Saepe pater dixit, "Generum mihi, filia, debes"; saepe pater dixit, "Debes mihi, nata nepotes,* "Often her father said, 'Daughter, you owe me a son-in-law.' Often her father said, 'Female child, you owe me grandchildren.'" The two lines are by no means identical. Ovid employs the noun *filia* in the first and the noun *nata* in the second, places the repeated verb *debes* in different positions within the hexameter line, and uses two different metrical patterns. Yet both lines begin with the same phrase (*saepe pater dixit*), include the pronoun *mihi* as well as the verb form *debes*, and address Daphne by a term of kinship immediately after the word *mihi*.

At lines 492–96, moreover, Ovid integrates doubling into the simile that describes Apollo's passion, likening it to both dry grain stalks and a hedge set afire. Doubling and duality loom large in many later episodes in the *Metamorphoses*, most notably that of Narcissus and Echo in the third book and Baucis and Philemon in the eighth; they also figure in his other elegiac poetry, from the earlier *Amores* to the later *Tristia*. Ovid's decision to include this motif here in the poem's first "love story" thus links the tale of Daphne and Apollo to other narratives within and beyond this epic work.

Conclusion

Reading Ovid's Daphne and Apollo narrative through a "Lateinerian lens" yields numerous insights into this episode, one of major and influential moment in and beyond the *Metamorphoses* itself. Other concerns of Lateiner's abundant, original, and provocative published scholarship, among them those related to gender and feminism and to poetic representations of animals and plants, could just as easily have been adopted in the questions posed of this text and of Ovid's style and message. While Daphne's father

---

12. For Ovid's integration of elegiac elements into the epic *Metamorphoses*, see Pavlock 2009, especially 14–37; for other elegiac and programmatic aspects of the Daphne and Apollo episode, see Harrison 2002: 88.

may not have been able to make good on his demand that she "owed" him grandchildren and a son-in-law, I am pleased to provide, unbidden, a token offering, which I hope will attest to what so many of us owe Donald Lateiner and his work.

Works Cited

Adams, J. N. 1982. *The Latin Sexual Vocabulary*. London: Duckworth.

Farrell, J. 1999. "The Ovidian Corpus: Poetic Body and Poetic Text." In P. Hardie, A. Barchiesi, and S. Hinds, eds., *Ovidian Transformations*, 127–41. Cambridge: Cambridge Philosophical Society.

Hallett. J. P. 2012a. "Authorial Identity in Latin Love Elegy: Literary Fictions and Erotic Failings." In B. K. Gold, ed., *A Companion to Roman Love Elegy*, 268–84. Chichester: Wiley-Blackwell.

Hallett. J. P. 2012b. "Anxiety and Influence: Ovid's *Amores* 3.7 and Encolpius' Impotence in *Satyricon* 126ff." In M. P. F. Pinheiro, M. B. Skinner, and F. I. Zeitlin, eds., *Narrating Desire: Eros, Sex, and Gender in the Ancient Novel*, 211–22. Berlin; Boston: De Gruyter.

Hardie, P. 2002. *Ovid's Poetics of Illusion*. Cambridge: Cambridge University Press.

Harrison, S. 2002. "Ovid and Genre: Evolutions of an Elegist." In P. Hardie, ed., *The Cambridge Companion to Ovid*, 79–94. Cambridge: Cambridge University Press.

Keith, A. 1994. "*Corpus Eroticum*: Elegiac Poetics and Elegiac *Puellae* in Ovid's *Amores*." *CW* 88.1: 27–40.

Knox, P. E., and Casali, S. 2009. "Ovidian Intertextuality." In P. E. Knox, ed., *A Companion to Ovid*, 341–54. Chichester: Wiley-Blackwell.

LaFleur, R. A. 1999. *Love and Transformation: An Ovid Reader*. 2nd ed. Glenview, IL: Scot, Foresman.

Lateiner, D. G. 1984. "Mythic and Non-Mythic Artists in Ovid's *Metamorphoses*." *Ramus* 13: 1–30.

Lateiner, D. 1987. "Nonverbal Communication in the Histories of Herodotus." *Arethusa* 20: 83–119, 143–45.

Lateiner, D. 1990. "Mimetic Syntax: Metaphor from Word Order, especially in Ovid's Poetry." *AJP* 11: 204–37.

Lateiner, D. 1992. "Affect Displays in the Epic Poetry of Homer, Vergil, and Ovid." In F. Poyatos, ed., *Advances in Nonverbal Communication: Sociocultural, Clinical, and Esthetic Perspectives*, 255–69. Amsterdam: John Benjamins.

Lateiner, D. 1995. *Sardonic Smile: Nonverbal Behavior in Homeric Epic*. Ann Arbor: University of Michigan Press.

Lateiner, D. 1996. "Nonverbal Behaviors in Ovid's Poetry, Primarily *Metam.* 14." *CJ* 91.3: 225–53.

Lateiner, D. 2013. "Poetic Doubling Effects in Ovid's 'Ceyx and Alcyone.'" In B. Gold, D. Lateiner, and J. Perkins, eds., *Roman Literature, Gender, and Reception: Domina Illustris*. London: Routledge.

Morgan, J. R., and Harrison, S. 2008. "Intertextuality." In T. Whitmarsh, ed., *The Cambridge Companion to the Greek and Roman Novel*, 218–36. Cambridge: Cambridge University Press.

Pavlock, B. 2009. *The Image of the Poet in Ovid's Metamorphoses*. Madison: University of Wisconsin Press.

CHAPTER 14

Verbal Behavior in the *Iliad*

Eliot Wirshbo

The title of this essay is a wink at Don Lateiner's *Sardonic Smile: Nonverbal Behavior in Homeric Epic*. That egregious work opened up an entirely new way of seeing Homer. The present, exiguous offering begins from the hypothesis that the repetitions found in the *Iliad*, vestiges of generations of traditional poets, not only are due to a drive to achieve thrift in expression[1] but also reveal an underlying attitude toward human endeavor. Differently put, the formulas are not merely a functional response to the exigencies of the oral performance insofar as they supply a relief from thinking and a chance to plan the lines ahead; tellingly, they offer a glimpse into their creators' (and audiences') way of viewing the world.

The outlook that I would posit as behind the adoption of formulas is a leveling one that reduces all endeavor to a sameness at the very moment when we might be more inclined to seek and "celebrate" difference. A clue to this attitude can be found in an extra-Homeric scene that will help to establish the approach followed in this essay, the encounter of Solon and Croesus in book 1 of Herodotus.

I

Three words in the Herodotus passage strike the reader as reminiscent of Homer: at *Iliad* 1.32.6, Solon avers that a prosperous man is better able to

---

1. See Parry 1971: the formula "made the process of versification easier" (14); "convenience of versification alone determines the choice of" a particular verbal element (22); formula patterns are "systems which . . . show the utility of the repeated expressions in Homer" (312).

avert *ate* than a poorer man, which recalls to the Homerist the *ate* that lays low Agamemnon and Achilles (and perhaps Paris).[2] In the same passage, various forms of *olbos* and *ploutos* are reminiscent of the *Iliad*, specifically Achilles' poignant reference to the fate of his father at 24.536 (and also of Priam's state at 543), where we are told that Peleus, despite great *olbos* and *ploutos*, was not destined to remain free of evils.[3]

Of course, Solon's particular words to Croesus are meant to draw out the ultimate implication behind his general vision of human life, which itself has a quasi-mathematical neatness: in the long run, all the many and varied days of a person's life tend to average out to about the same. A series of good days or years or decades is meaningless in itself, because a kind of law of reversion to the mean dictates that the peaks and valleys of a person's life will even out over time. The mighty are likely to fall, the helpless may be raised up, and all mortals will end up not very different from one another, so that, taking the long view, the apparent distinction between a blessedly prosperous Croesus and an unknown Tellus is meaningless. Everything balances out when no one escapes death; the seemingly unexceptional person may actually be better off than the outwardly fortunate one, in that he cannot, in his mean existence, be subject to the overwhelming loss that awaits the temporarily happy one.

Behind the apparent variety of human life, there is thus a basic, grinding sameness, whose effect is to level off the heights of accomplishment attained by a Croesus—or an Achilles—and to render these standouts equal to the average warrior or subject in the end. Solon's wisdom is to see the similarities (similes?) beneath the surface differences. As a wise man, he peers through the temporary advantages of worldly blessedness and recognizes that what appear to be the great achievements of the greatest individuals are, in the long view, simply ephemeral fruits ripe to be ground down along with the futile efforts of the ordinary populace. Ironically, it is these latter people who possess greater potential for distinction, since they begin from a position of minimal expectations yet may rise to admired heights by dint of modest achievement. Thus all human distinctiveness is temporary and misleading; the higher truth is that human striving for excellence is futile. The stark, outward asymmetry between high and low only obscures the hidden reality,

---

2.   Whether *ates* or *arches* is used of Paris at *Il.* 3.100, 6.356, and/or 24.28 is not important here. If anything, the point of this essay would render such an issue quaint and unanswerable.

3.   For a more detailed summary of this passage in Herodotus, see H.-P. Stahl's contribution in this volume.

which is that, taken all in all, there is a pervasive sameness in human life despite appearances. It is a form of wisdom that we might expect from the wise old men and women of folklore: do not exult in triumph or wallow in misery, for one never knows where one will end up.[4]

The glory that a Homeric hero seeks is a perfect concomitant to this Solonic attitude, for he aims only for a moment-to-moment distinctiveness, bound by the knowledge that one of two dueling warriors will take *kudos* while the other yields it.[5] The field of battle is thus the perfect arena for Solon's insight to play itself out: as Alvin Gouldner had it, the Homeric warrior is engaged in a zero-sum game, where victory and defeat perfectly complement each other, with neither party distinguishing himself for long.[6] The symmetry that informs human life dictates that each hero eventually succumbs to another, that differences be reduced to sameness and that distinctions be leveled.[7]

Of course, there is a way to transcend the inevitable decline that awaits all, and that is to withdraw from the race when at the top, which is what Tellus and Cleobis and Biton unintentionally do. Achilles has opted for precisely this alternative: to bypass the unavoidable decline from the zenith of achievement by choosing to have his life terminated while he is still in possession of enviable powers. But his sense that all the signs of superiority do not cleave to him, that the same middling existence that dogs everyone else has affixed itself to him too, is the cause of Achilles' righteous indignation.[8] The special dispensation purportedly established by his earlier choice to die young is not operative, to the consternation of an Achilles who believed that he had secured unending asymmetry for himself while alive. But the significance of this fragile balance between distinction and ordinariness is something that will better emerge after further consideration of the attitude behind the oral style.

---

4. Kirk (1990: 219) offers a very good discussion on the balance between heroic and homey in a scene like that between Hector and Andromache in book 6, which seems the stylistic counterpart to the oscillation to which Solon adverts.
5. The either-or aspect of the winning of *kudos* is expressed at, e.g., *Il.*8.141, 15.491, and 15.595. Sarpedon's famous culminating line at 12.328 amounts to the same idea, though it specifically mentions *eukhos* rather than *kudos*.
6. Gouldner 1965:49–51.
7. A somewhat philosophical Achilles expounds on this very subject to Lycaon at *Il.* 21.106–13. For other falls from acmes in Herodotus, see Lateiner 1982.
8. At *Il.* 9.318–20, Achilles laments that there is no meaningful distinction between shirker and hard fighter. At 9.410–16, he mentions the two alternatives placed before him.

II

It seems a modest proposition that, on any number of random dates over a period of centuries, innumerable bards were faced with a decision to, say, describe a battle scene with a simile. Which simile a particular poet picked on a particular occasion must have been dictated by some combination of personal choice, familiarity with tradition, and the perceived receptivity of the audience at the moment of delivery. It is even possible that a perfectly appropriate simile, one whose pertinence to its location might elicit the modern-day appraisal that it is "artistic" or "authentic," will have been selected.

Sometimes, however, a choice of simile may seem inexplicable, and some interpretive "English" may be needed to account for what the text yields. At *Iliad* 6.506–11 and 15.263–68, for example, we have two occurrences of an identical simile, used first to describe Paris making his way from his tête-à-tête with Helen and then to describe Hector as he revives from an encounter with Ajax, with each instance employing a horse-freed-from-its-stable vignette. Which one is original or more appropriate? I am in agreement with those who believe that we cannot hope to answer this question,[9] but I think that we may provisionally substitute a different query, the sort that a reader innocent of two hundred years of scholarship might ask—namely, why would a bard decide, "I can just use that horse simile here, the one (by me or another) that described a sort of parallel occurrence"? There is room to speculate usefully about the occupational attitude toward words of the bard or, better, of the innumerable bards who recited the *Iliad* through the years with the aid of the aforementioned wisdom of Solon, a wisdom or worldview that seems to be reflected again and again in the diction of the poem and in the architecture of numerous passages. The important Solonic principle behind the *Iliad*'s composition can best be illuminated in the examination of the slightly puzzling descriptions, the ones that require special pleading to mitigate their oddity.

Glaucus' philosophical reflection on human life (*Il.* 6.145–49) provides a good illustration of Solon's principle, for his inquiry (basically) "Why ask what family a human being belongs to?" movingly introduces a version of

---

9. Janko 1992: 256. Kirk (1990: 220, on *Il.* 6.447–79, where Hector repeats Agamemnon's words at 4.163–65) finds, "Repeated language can take on different colouring according to context, without awkwardness or loss of impact. To decide which of these two contexts is 'original,' and declare the other to be derivative in some sense, is obviously wrong in principle."

the sage's counsel to Croesus.[10] In Diomedes' cautious query about his identity, Glaucus finds an occasion to reflect on the transience of mortal life. This rumination will prove to be ironic, in that Glaucus' life will be saved by the very fact that the "leaves" put forth in human families are not, as he implies, untraceable in their millions but can be found to be connected to other, significant "leaves" that, though dead, prove life-saving. Yet his stoic stance on human life remains, and that position is decidedly Solonic: attempts at supersession are futile, because the distinctions between one stock of leaflike excrescences and another are obliterated by time, and trying to claim some mark of uniqueness for oneself is as misguided, we might say, as Croesus' doomed sense of his own importance.

This attitude can be found in what Homer says, too.[11] At *Iliad* 19.301–2, the female slaves in the Greek camp are moved by Briseïs' lament over Patroclus and join in the groaning. Yet while they are ostensibly crying for Achilles' slain companion, they are, the poet says, bewailing their own woes. This seems to be a variant note struck on Glaucus' humans-as-leaves motif, for the description is essentially a simile saying that the woes of another remind a person of his or her own, thus suggesting that there is a shared woefulness pervading human life.

The poet who produces this covert simile is adopting the Solonic perspective expressed in Herodotus, saying that the sorrow elicited by the death of Patroclus is reminiscent of the slave women's own sorrows.[12] Just as the envi-

---

10. Edwards (1991: 314) suggests that Glaucus (as well as Aeneas in his similar statement at *Il.* 20.213–14) means to imply the answer, "since it [i.e., his family] is so famous."

11. That the feelings of a character may not jibe with what the bard or bards thought is not a trivial objection to this parallel between the sentiments of poet and fictional creation. Griffin (1986) avers that there is a gulf between what the poet allows himself to say and what his characters are permitted to utter. Yet Griffin does acknowledge that the characters are made to say things that the poet simply felt unable to pass along in his own narrative, being constrained by certain traditions of bardic propriety (46). It is in the emotional, personal expressiveness newly afforded to characters in their speeches, according to Griffin, that the Homeric poet broke through the limitations of traditional epic, which had formerly been dispassionately focused on telling stories and had eschewed a humanitarian, subjective point of view (49–50). See also Hainsworth 1993: on *Il.* 11.670–762, for how there may be a congruence between characters' and narrator's voices: "Nestor tells his tale generally in the same manner as the narrator of the *Iliad*. Like the poet he knows what the gods did . . . , and unlike speakers in the *Iliad* he avoids subjective language . . ." Cf. Athena's description of Olympus to Ares as "where the seat of the immortals is," an entirely superfluous comment from one god to another, appropriate only to the poet or a mortal (5.360); cf. also Hector's reference to himself as *dio* at 7.75, a type of epithet not normally bestowed by a character upon himself.

12. This reminiscence occurs however uniquely constituted that mild warrior is; on this matter, cf. Griffin 1986: 44.

able *olbos* of a Peleus or a Croesus may be a mere cover for the disaster that the long view perceives as awaiting those seemingly fortunate men, the outwardly sincere regret of the slave women in book 19 for their beloved Patroclus may in fact conceal what is really under the surface of their lamentation——rueful sorrow for themselves. The loss of Achilles' nonpareil *therapon* is not really different from the other losses one feels; in fact, despite the uniqueness of the loss, a certain sense of similarity/simile is evoked within the observer, so that the sadness for another triggers a personal sadness for one's own lot.

A bit later, we are afforded another glimpse of this attitude, which may be represented by the admonition "Say anything you want, but remember that words only imperfectly capture the surface of things; these things are themselves fleeting and can only be tentatively rendered; their momentary significance must recede in importance before the greater truth that underlies all human activity and that will ultimately reassert itself." At *Iliad* 20.248–49, Aeneas characterizes words (or perhaps the tales that people tell) as meaningless, revealing an insight into speech that it is tempting to attribute to a bard reciting the *Iliad*. For what is the point of all this retailing of one's lineage, Aeneas claims, Glaucus-like, when mortals' tongues can twist in any direction?

This reflection means more than "talk is cheap," because Aeneas is going beyond the specific situation in which he is involved and referring generally to the ability of words to be twisted so as to say anything, to fabricate meaning whimsically. His words here seem more like an insight from a bard who has come to see that he can manufacture vignettes out of a flexible storehouse of verbal materials and can thus describe greatly differing people and situations in the same way.[13] Those vignettes keep the story going, but it is pointless to inquire into their truth, beauty, or appropriateness when one expression tends simply to beget another (*Il.* 20.250). Anything can be uttered, but that utterance contains no truth uniquely appropriate to a specific situation. This position with respect to the substitutability of words must have been observed by a number of bards throughout the entire creative and rhapsodic periods. Any commentator who has remarked that a particular simile was better employed in one place than another has passed Aeneas' sentence on

---

13. MacLeod (2001: 299) cites Hesiod and the proem to the Catalog of Ships in *Iliad* 2 as evidence for the bardic recognition "that singers can lie." Griffin (1986) might add that the poet recognizes that he has the power to express emotions never before expressed in heroic verse, though only by assigning those expressions to others.

the text, for the passage where the allegedly inferior employment occurs is thereby adjudged an example of a bard's mere manipulation of words, of simply using the tongue to produce one epos after another.

III

The wisdom of the Herodotean Solon sheds light on the outlook of the *Iliad* in another way: it presents pithily the thesis that the manifold discrepancies between one human life and another are merely the surface concealments of an underlying sameness. Outward differences mask a sort of sub rosa symmetry. When things get out of whack, a divine force is brought to bear to create likeness out of unevenness, and we can describe that force as "grudging" or one of "(re)distribution,"[14] for it both abhors gross deviations from the middling norm of human existence and jiggles humans' fortunes so as to level them out. This tendency to impose a normative balance is a basic principle of Homeric composition. It is found in the frequent recourse to chiasmic constructions on the level of the single line, in the tendency to compose speeches in the symmetrical arrangement known as ring composition, and in the architecture of the poem as a whole, with its large-scale balance between books 1 and 24, 2 and 23, and so forth.

This affinity for the balanced gets Homer into trouble at times, for he can rarely think through his large-scale diptychs so as to present them clearly. In other words, the impulse to express story elements in balanced terms (which embodies Solon's insight that all things tend to even out) often ends in muddles that seem to be beyond the bard's capacity to imagine fully. Examples of this habit include the reversal of roles entered into by Trojans and Greeks, so that the besieged become the attackers and the invaders become the defensive players;[15] the purportedly illustrative story of Meleager, which ends in

---

14. Herodotus uses the words *to phthoneron* (1.32.1) and *nemesis* (1.34.1). What descends on Croesus is not so much righteous indignation—cf. Apollo's words to Croesus at 1.91.1—as a rebalancing of a situation that has become disproportionate. This sense of an imbalance is also found in the *Iliad*, when, for instance, Poseidon feels *nemesis* to be treated unfairly by Zeus, with whom he should be on an even basis (15.208–11), or when Zeus, as if to motivate the entirely unmerited death of Hector, accuses Hector of acting out of proportion (17.205), implying that a righting of a wrong must come. Hector has only done what Zeus has prompted him to do.

15. Hainsworth's headnote to book 12 (1993: 313–16) covers the various ineptitudes exhibited in this particular impulse to portray a battlefield turnabout. Hainsworth later asserts (345,

unintelligible confusion over which army is the attacking one and which the defensive;[16] and the story of *ate* and the *litai*, which confuses cause and effect.[17] But it is perhaps more convincing to test on smaller cases the claim that Homer is so influenced by the principle of symmetry that he often slips into regrettable descriptions. (The principle of Aeneas enunciated above holds: the story advances no matter which way the tongue twists.)

At *Iliad* 22.93–96, Hector is described in a simile that evokes its seeming counterpart at 3.33–37. In each, a deadly snake awaits a man approaching on a mountain. In each, the snake is a formidable lurker who frightens or is on the verge of frightening the advancing man. Each simile intensifies its scene by momentarily holding off a fateful duel about to be fought between two main characters, yet the second simile, which recalls the earlier one just as the stallion simile featuring Hector recalled the one featuring Paris, is entirely inappropriate,[18] for no sooner is Hector described as unyielding—as having unquenchable might, just like that coiled, poisonous snake with a baleful look in its eye—than he is made to contemplate flight. The simile simply does not jibe with the description of Hector that follows, which shows him to be near-frantic with self-recriminations and wishful thinking.

A comparison potentially suited to an important duel was summoned up from the bard's simile hoard despite the fact that it was to be associated with an action that was out of keeping with its actual context. The logic of balanced patterns—Paris and Hector as contrastive brothers, as participants in

---

on lines 258–60) that "the substantial foundations and superstructure described in these verses are more appropriate to permanent town-walls than to an improvised fieldwork," which well expresses the difficulty a plausibility-seeking reader faces. Discussing an earlier passage, Kirk (1990: 288) claims that "realistic criteria cannot . . . be invoked" to explain what is going on at the building of the Achaean wall.

16. Hainsworth (1993: on 9.552) sets out the "lack of clarity," which he attributes to "the desire to make parallel the situations of Meleagros and Akhilleus."

17. The *ate* that drove Agamemnon to an act of, well, *ate* (in itself an example of a sort of thinking that closely links cause and effect, as if the motivation of an action and the result of that action are to be identically named) was followed by his having recourse to the *litai* in the form of the embassy to make things right (Hainsworth 1993: 127). If Achilles fails to accept the *litai*, Phoenix implies, he will be plunged into *ate*, because the ignored *litai* will go to Zeus and beg him to see to it that *ate* afflict the stubborn Achilles. There is thus a loop that makes both *ate* and *litai* consequences of reckless acts brought on by *ate*. Hainsworth (on 9.511) well captures the Homeric circular, "frontsy-backsy" quality by saying that Phoenix "makes what is usually said as an explanation of what has happened into a prediction of what will happen."

18. Scott (2009: 72), however, calls it "an appropriately warlike simile." Fränkel (1921: 69) withholds judgment but quotes Leaf to the effect that the simile does not accurately portray a snake's behavior.

duels, as duelists in matchups that are uneven; a tableau of a snake frightening a man who intrudes on its territory, with the man jumping back in terror
at the sight of the deadly snake poised to strike—overrode the logic of the
situation. The simile's placement in book 22 betrays a sense in the poet that
the ingredients for a man-recoils-from-snake simile have a certain (tangential) appropriateness, but the elements of the later scene that have been altered from book 3 (omitting, of course, the impossible question of priority of
composition) render the scenario puzzling as soon as the narrative resumes.
The impulse to balance Paris versus Menelaus with Hector versus Achilles
has overcome the mechanics of the scene and produced a simile for which
only great critical flexibility can account.[19]

IV

The entire passage surrounding the encounter of Paris and Menelaus (*Il.*
3.21ff.) is a rich field for tracing the bardic love of antithesis in a variety of
forms. There is balance between (a) the seizing of the limbs of the startled
man in the simile by trembling and (b) the grabbing of his cheeks by paleness
(34–35); between Hector's wish that Paris had been (a) unborn and (b) unwed
(40); between the acknowledgments that Paris was (a) of fine form but (b) of
no might (45); and between the characterizations of him as (a) a joy to enemies and (b) a disgrace to himself (50–51). Paris responds with his own symmetrical phraseology—which seems to me simply another expression by a
character of the bardic/Solonic sense that things in the world are balanced–
–in his statements that Hector has offered a criticism that is (a) appropriate
and (b) not inappropriate (59); that (a) the gods give gifts and that (b) a person who wants them cannot simply take them (66); that Paris himself is ready
to (a) fight and (b) do battle (67); and that there should be a division along
(unsurprisingly) symmetrical lines: (a) Trojans here and (b) Greeks there (68),
with (a) Paris and (b) Menelaus set in the middle (69), so that the one who (a)
wins and (b) is stronger (71) will get (a) Helen and (b) all her possessions,
with the results that (a) the Trojans will inhabit Troy and (b) the Greeks will
return to their homes (74–75). Whether we call this parallelism, antithesis, or

---

19. Richardson (1993: 117) daintily covers the inconcinnity by saying that "internally [Hector]
is in a turmoil of uncertainty."

symmetry, it is really one species of the larger tendency to see things in counterbalancing units.[20] More than a neat, convenient way to express the details of a speech, it is a way of conceiving of the world, of organizing experience.

A bit later, Paris avers that his defeat by Menelaus is not a serious mark against him, for he will beat his counterpart next time (3.439–40). Later still, at 6.339, he turns this claim into a generalization worthy of Solon or Homer: victory alternates between men. This sentiment ought not to be dismissed as the typical self-deception of a character who shirks responsibility (Kirk 1990: 204 ad loc.), for it is consistent with the views of others about how the world works.[21] Paris' assertion expresses Homer's own way of thinking, which is that words, speeches, and whole stories reflect a world whose underlying nature is in balance, with predictable adjustments whenever that balance shifts.[22] This can also be seen in verbal framing, as at 3.164, where Priam declares that, to his mind, not Helen but the gods are responsible for the war, or at 3.143, where the two handmaids, in a common configuration that I have always thought of as "framing the lady," accompany Helen to the walls of Troy.

Zeus himself, whose fondness for granting and withdrawing favors supports Paris' assertion that victory alternates between opponents (cf. his tendency to mix up goods and evils in the bestowals he makes from the contraposed jars on the floor of his house at 24.527–33), also can speak in this balanced way. At the beginning of book 8, when he addresses the assembled divinities, (a) he spoke, and (b) they listened (4). His words are (a) to all the gods and (b) to all the goddesses (5). He places a prohibition on (a) every female and (b) every male (7–8). He causes the very order of letters to rebalance when he warns (10–11) against any effort to go and help either mortal side (*ethelonta/elthont'*), as if there is an underlying connection between going and helping.[23] The following lines feature the fancied journey of any violator of

20. Cf. Fränkel 1973: 54: "Qualities could be conceived only if opposites were conceived at the same time" (though Fränkel is here explaining the nature of the gods).
21. Cf. Nestor at 8.141–43, e.g., on how Zeus gives glory to one side and then another.
22. As examples for the way that characters reveal the thinking or, at least, the phraseology of Homer, we have Athena (cited in n. 10) using a descriptive term oddly out of place for a god; Achilles uttering poignant similes typical of the narrator five times (cf. Griffin 1986: 53); Nestor reflecting Homer's often-stated view of the superiority of earlier ages (1.260–61); Poseidon at 13.101–4 uttering a simile of a type normally found in the narrative; and Priam doing likewise with a simile at 3.197–98 that has been called "closely parallel to the *poet's* frequent use of animal similes outside the speeches" (Lloyd 1987: 190; emphasis original).
23. Kirk (1990: ad loc.) says that "the jingle . . . may have seemed attractive"; in that adjective lies a whole *Weltanschauung*.

Zeus' prohibition not (a) up to Olympus but (b) down to Tartarus, a balance between distances up and down, another call to all gods and goddesses, a phrase featuring earth and sea, and a final mention of gods and men (12–27).

V

Gravitating toward balance in details ranging from brief phrases to the worldly fortunes of great characters (like Peleus, Achilles, and Priam) is to be found everywhere in Homer's ways of setting up scenes and creating parallels where none need to exist to tell the story or even adorn it; these reflect the leveling, balancing, symmetry-seeking mind at work.[24] We learn only at *Iliad* 22.147–52 that the Scamander has twin springs, one hot and one cold, a detail whose only reason for inclusion seems to be its appeal to the aesthetics of symmetry.[25] When, at the start of book 11, Zeus begins to execute his agreement to glorify Hector and cause destruction among the Greeks, he surprisingly acts first to cause success for the Greeks. One can account for this by attributing perversity to the father of gods and men,[26] but it seems simpler, amid so many other examples of a strange oscillation hither and thither in the presentation of details, to attribute the god's action to a tendency in the bard to picture decisive events as both one way and the other, because any extreme suggests the opposite extreme. Defeat implies victory, and since Solonic wisdom knows that a life that is thriving implies the cessation of thriving and perhaps death, victory suggests defeat as soon as it is announced. As in the often uncanny similes, whose "secret . . . lies in . . . the juxtaposition of sameness and difference,"[27] we are forced to experience both sides of significant actions, much as Solon warns that loss is an inevitable counterpart of success.

---

24. G. E. R. Lloyd (1987: 90–91) treats of this mode of thought, but via a different *methodos*. He says that "polar expressions" are used "to achieve a certain emphasis," "to express a general notion," and "to express an alternative." Whereas the emphasis of Lloyd's interest is in tracing a style of *thinking*, the emphasis of my aim here is to explore a *style* of thinking, motivated by a sense that a clearer understanding of that style will illuminate the workings of the poem. To recognize that Milton's *Paradise Lost*, for example, is shot through with oxymora offers the critic a suggestive stylistic parallel to the opposition of God and Satan; to recognize that the lines of Ovid's *Metamorphoses* contain numerous metamorphic *polyptota* adds a fitting structural grace note to that work on altered forms.

25. For a symbolic interpretation of the two opposed springs, see Duban 1980: 13.

26. Hainsworth (1993: on 11.3) notes that "as usual the will of Zeus is accomplished by a devious route; catastrophe will be preceded by victory."

27. Fränkel 1997: 105.

In *Iliad* 12, Pirithous and Polypoetes are depicted as inside, outside, and again inside the Achaean wall,[28] whose penetration by Trojan forces will have dire consequences. Homer gives no indication of any advance or retreat on the part of these two defenders. It is as if such a significant moment is conceived from both the inside and the outside, in a manner reminiscent of the way that the early Italians thought of a gate as *mana*-filled because it led both into and out of an enclosure. It seems as if simply the dichotomous, inner-outer nature of the significant activity described—defend and attack, repel and advance—leads to the characteristic lapse on the part of a bard whose outlook tends to see the inside and the outside as not so diametrically opposed as we do. In a variant on this mode of conceiving of things, a case involving two strands of detail that go in confusing directions, the two Aiantes are hard for the bard to keep track of, so that we find "the lesser Ajax" sometimes referring to Ajax Oïleus, sometimes to Teucer, as if the distinction were not vital.[29]

As mentioned, having it both ways sometimes gets the narrative into trouble. Did Hector quail before Achilles during the earlier part of the war, or was he a formidable match even for the doughty Myrmidon? At 15.722, Hector implies that he was champing at the bit to fight; at 7.113–14, Agamemnon warns Menelaus that even Achilles feared to face Hector. Yet Achilles himself claims, not surprisingly, that Hector would not come out to face him (9.351–55). Special pleading can account for each varying mention of such a battlefield matchup, but the incompatibility of all the testimonies taken together urges us toward a position somewhat like the one recommended for tragedy by Easterling, who suggests that the inconsistent statements uttered by characters be taken merely as advancing the drama; incompatible utterances create a desirable complexity and do not require careful weighing to determine our responses.[30] Still, this impulse by the bard to have it both ways when strongly dichotomous alternatives are offered seems a stylistic trait so strong as to possess explanatory power as an organizing principle for the entire poem.[31]

---

28. Hainsworth 1993: on 12.127–53.
29. Janko 1992: on 13.46 and 13.177–78.
30. Easterling 1977: 126.
31. Whitman (1958: 249–84) felt that patterns of Geometric art offered a visual concomitant to the large-scale, repeating structures of the *Iliad*. It seems to me that post-Geometric pottery, produced over the large span of time in which the reciters of Homer were flourishing, contains a regular feature suggestive of the same sort of small-scale symmetries that we

VI

All the previously mentioned instances (some of them old analytic chestnuts) of a sort of reciprocity that seems to inform the organization of the *Iliad* on various levels—word choice, scene depiction, plot development—point to a different understanding of what we have before us when we read the poem. Saying that the poem is about things evening out, about how an extreme action will have an extreme consequence,[32] reduces the meaning of the poem to a more intelligible level and relieves us from relying on the eschatological claims often made for it. To claim that when Priam comes to ransom Hector at the climax of the poem, he and Achilles "experience the limiting finitude of the heroic consciousness" (Redfield 1975: 216) or "share a sublime vision of the human condition" (Schein 1984: 159) removes the experience of the poem to a realm that our critical imaginations may wish to visit but that the action itself never inhabits.

The *Iliad* deals with a person who goes too far and then gets his comeuppance. That comeuppance is predictable, though its form is unexpected, because it comes via a tangential vulnerability (Patroclus) within the otherwise-unassailable protagonist, much as Croesus' vulnerability is through his son. What Achilles discovers is that an equal fate (*ise moira*, 9.318) really awaits us all, despite his conviction that he is special and has secured for himself a unique end. This conviction leads him to make a request that attracts the attention of that grudging force in the universe that seeks to keep things in balance.[33] The fulfillment of this wish of his throws things out of equipoise

---

find everywhere in the *Iliad*. Again and again, we see on vases the names of figures—often, opposed fighters—written from left to right for one character and from right to left for a nearby one. Sometimes, in scenes of battle, the name of one warrior may be included from top to bottom facing left, while the name of the other fighter is presented from top to bottom facing right, with the letters facing upward on one side and downward on the other. The choice to write names in this fashion is akin to the contraposed animals and decorative objects we see everywhere on ceramic art (indeed, in Near Eastern art millennia before the Greeks). A name written one way—whether by artist or special "captioneer"—elicits a name written in an opposed way. Such an artistic choice must be grouped with the attitude that seems to be almost a physical law in Homer: every significant action, statement, tableau, or fate has a counterbalancing one, whether in the life of a real or fictional character or in the mind of the poet. For numerous instances of this phenomenon, see Friis Johansen 1997: esp. figs. 13, 15, 18, 25, 35, and 79. For the view that early Greek pottery exhibits a different, tripartite organization pertinent to the *Iliad*, see Andreae and Flashar 1977.

32. Significant in this regard is the term *exaision aren* (rendered "disproportionate demand" in Edwards 1991: 6), which I would suggest is as central to Achilles' downfall as Croesus' arrogance is to his. Janko (1992: on 15.498–99) discusses the importance of this term.

33. Cf. Hdt. 1.32.1: *to theion pan . . . phthoneron*. I do not believe that Zeus' "plan" is anything

and requires a terrible, unpredictable *nemesis* to put things and people back into their places. To see the *Iliad* in terms set out by Herodotus' Solon is to account more plausibly for features that ultimately reveal an ethos familiar from bits of folk wisdom we all recognize—watch what you wish for, and be humble, for there is a paradoxical pattern to life that sometimes rears up and bites you if you are not careful.[34] This attitude pervades the very style of the *Iliad*, which is ultimately a reductive style in that it sees actions as part of unchanging patterns of human behavior. The clearest indication of this outlook is in the diction of the poem, the repetitiveness of which blatantly announces the unwavering pattern of human life.

Thus, in a way, the lesson that is finally brought home to Achilles is about sameness, the same sameness that, to judge from the way little attempt is made by the oral style to see uniqueness in human events, the bard must ascribe to life's patterns. The bard knows (or the bards who recited various forms of the *Iliad* over centuries know) that a plume may nod down from the helmet of a loving father as well as from that of a questionable leader and that variants on a fire simile may be used with impunity in utterly different situations. This flexibility represents an important truth, one that Achilles, in his obsession with his own uniqueness, fails to recognize. What Achilles finally succumbs to in the climactic epitome of similes in the scene with Priam—where Achilles is, in effect, compared to Hector, Peleus, Priam, and Patroclus and where Priam is likened to Peleus, Patroclus, and Achilles (and Hector?)—is the bardic insight that the same descriptions apply to different people. The sharp distinctions that, like Croesus, Achilles would have operative in the world are illusory. The Achaean learns the lesson that Homer understands

---

but a stopgap response to an uncomfortable *do ut des* predicament or has any more of a connection to Achilles' fate than an extemporizing strongman's would to keep the action moving. At the beginning of book 2, Zeus is not the picture of an omniscient god whose course of action is clear. The *noema* of Zeus—presented as though it, rather than Achilles' extravagant prayer, had dictated the course of action (17.409)—has its own muddled features consistent with the type of wayward symmetries traced here. He speaks solemnly about saving Hector's life and then withdraws his comment, claiming that he has not spoken with *thymoi prophroni* (22.183–84). He seconds Hector until the Trojan's success can whimsically be viewed as another example of immoderate behavior deserving of divine begrudging and (re)distribution. He scolds him (17.204–6) for despoiling the "mild" companion of Achilles who himself had killed so many Trojans and allies. Truly is the tongue *strepte* and the *mythoi pantoioi* (20.248–49).

34. Cf. Boedeker's contribution in this volume, on Herodotus' murdered messengers and the patterns of fate encountered by their murderers' descendants.

from his career as an oral poet: there is just not that much importance in one's words, because everyone is the same and because anything can be said.[35]

Works Cited

Andreae, B., and Flashar, H. 1977. "Strukturäquivalenzen zwischen den homerischen Epen und der frühgriechischen Vasenkunst." *Poetica* 9.2: 217–65.

Duban, J. M. 1980. "Distortion as a Poetic Device in the 'Pursuit of Hektor' and Related Events." *Aevum* 54.1: 3–22.

Easterling, P. J. 1977. "Character in Sophocles." *G&R* 24.2: 121–29.

Edwards, M. W. 1991. *The Iliad: A Commentary*. Vol. 5, *Books 17–20*. Cambridge: Cambridge University Press.

Fränkel, H. 1921. *Die homerische Gleichnisse*. Göttingen: Vanderhoeck und Ruprecht.

Fränkel, H. 1975. *Early Greek Poetry and Philosophy*. Trans. M. Hadas and J. Willis. New York: Harcourt Brace Jovanovich.

Fränkel, H. 1997. "Essence and Nature of the Homeric Similes." In G. M. Wright and P. V. Jones, eds., *Homer: German Scholarship in Translation*, 103–23. Oxford: Clarendon. First published in 1921.

Friis Johansen, K. 1997. *The Iliad in Early Greek Art*. Copenhagen: Munksgaard.

Gouldner, A. 1965. *The Hellenic World: A Sociological Analysis*. New York: Harper and Row.

Griffin, J. 1986. "Homeric Words and Speakers." *JHS* 106: 36–57.

Hainsworth, B. 1993. *The Iliad: A Commentary*. Vol. 3, *Books 9–12*. Cambridge: Cambridge University Press.

Janko, R. 1992. *The Iliad: A Commentary*. Vol. 4, *Books 13–16*. Cambridge: Cambridge University Press.

Kirk, G. S. 1985. *The Iliad: A Commentary*. Vol. 1, *Books 1–4*. Cambridge: Cambridge University Press.

Kirk, G. S. 1990. *The Iliad: A Commentary*. Vol. 2, *Books 5–8*. Cambridge: Cambridge University Press.

Lloyd, G. E. R. 1987. *Polarity and Analogy: Two Types of Argumentation in Early Greek Thought*. Bristol: Bristol Classical Press.

MacLeod, C. W. 2001. "Homer on Poetry and the Poetry of Homer." In D. L. Cairns, ed., *Oxford Readings in Homer's Iliad*, 294–310. Oxford: Oxford University Press.

---

35. A primitive version of this essay was discussed by several colleagues at the University of California, San Diego, in November 1982. To the nonpareil Don Lateiner, I should like to pose this question: when I greeted your early inquiry into nonverbal behavior with a dismissive shrug (as memorialized in the acknowledgments to *Sardonic Smile*), was I playing Solon to your self-absorbed Croesus, or was I the clueless Croesus to your penetrating Solon? Homer could see it either way.

Parry, A. 1971. *The Making of Homeric Verse: The Collected Papers of Milman Parry*. Oxford: Clarendon.

Redfield, J. 1975. *Nature and Culture in the Iliad: The Tragedy of Hector*. Chicago: University of Chicago Press.

Richardson, N. 1993. *The Iliad: A Commentary*. Vol. 6, *Books 21–24*. Cambridge: Cambridge University Press.

Schein, S. 1984. *The Mortal Hero: An Introduction to Homer's Iliad*. Berkeley: University of California Press.

Scott, W. C. 2009. *The Artistry of the Homeric Simile*. Lebanon, NH: University Press of New England.

Whitman, C. H. 1958. *Homer and the Heroic Tradition*. Cambridge, MA: Harvard University Press.

CHAPTER 15

Shipwreck Narratives in Homer's *Odyssey* and Coetzee's *Foe*

James V. Morrison

This essay explores shipwreck stories found in Homer's *Odyssey* and J. M. Coetzee's novel *Foe* (1986). In the *Odyssey*, shipwrecks are central to the epic's plot, reducing Odysseus to the most desperate circumstances. A storm destroys his ship; he reaches shore, alone and desperate; he then meets a female benefactor who is a threat in some ways. These misadventures endanger his life, his return, his marriage, and the fate of his kingdom. Of particular interest is how the poet varies each shipwreck scenario in narrative terms. We encounter first- and third-person narratives, distinct audiences, and a different status for each shipwreck story: actual, recollected, fictional—and figurative (23.233–41).

There are, of course, other extremely influential shipwreck narratives after Homer, especially Shakespeare's *The Tempest* (1611) and Defoe's *Robinson Crusoe* (1719). These narratives continue to resonate down to the present day. Works by Stanford (1992) and Hall (2008) make evident how far Homer's shadow extends. As Homer, Shakespeare, and Defoe are "rewritten" by later authors, each successor illuminates different facets of the original work. For example, Walcott's *Omeros* (1990) highlights the paradoxical nature of the sea as bringing pain and suffering yet also serving as a healer; Césaire's *A Tempest* (1968) focuses on the power struggle between Prospero and Caliban.

A very common feature of shipwreck narratives is that the survivor takes on the role of storyteller (cf. Crusoe's chronicle in Defoe's 1719 novel). This essay will make use of Coetzee's novel *Foe* (1986), a rewriting of Defoe's novel, as a means of exploring shipwreck tales and the degree to which the storyteller controls the narrative. This juxtaposition of ancient epic and modern novel will help us reconsider Odysseus' ability as narrator of both invented and apparently autobiographical disasters at sea. My goal is to combine two interests of Donald Lateiner (Homer and shipwrecks) and to add the perspective from Coetzee's modern work to highlight the shipwreck survivor's need to control the narrative of his or her life, if not the events themselves.[1]

Shipwreck Narratives in Homer's Odyssey

Of Odysseus' numerous arrivals by sea—some by choice, others forced by wind or storm—only two are by shipwreck. The first takes place near the end of Odysseus' voyage from Calypso's island to Scherie, the island of the Phaeacians. Here Homer presents the longest description of a storm and wreck, expanded by the inclusion of seven speeches and four similes.[2] He presents the forces of nature: clouds gather, the sea becomes rough, land and sea are hidden by clouds, and the sky blackens like night (5.291–96). The traveler's reaction follows: remembering Calypso's ill-omened prediction, Odysseus foresees his own death (5.305–12). When storms arise at sea, the traveler frequently reacts by expressing fear and despair. Damage to the vessel is then described: a great wave comes; Odysseus falls from his craft and loses his steering oar; the sail is torn; and the ship's tackle falls into the sea. Homer here introduces the first simile, comparing the wave driving the ship to wind driving thistle stalks (5.327–32).[3] Next, the sea goddess Leucothea advises Odysseus to take off his clothes, tie an immortal veil around his chest, and swim for shore (5.333–50). Later, a second goddess, Athena, helps by "tying down" the winds (5.382). Odysseus ends up floating for two days, expecting to die (5.388–89); finally, on the third day, calm returns, and he sights land and considers how to make his way safely ashore. Homer's description thus indicates the possible features of the shipwreck episode: forces of nature; the traveler's reaction; a wave hitting the ship; people being thrown into the wa-

---

1. In exploring shipwrecks, Lateiner's "Heavy Weather in Petronius" (under revision) contrasts the novelistic feature of lovers clinging to one another on stormy seas with epic's "lonely heroes"; Lateiner is also working on a forthcoming monograph on the Ceyx and Alcyone shipwreck story found in Ovid's *Metamorphoses*. Lateiner's work on Homer ranges broadly in subject matter from prayers, teeth, laughter, and sneezing to nonverbal behavior more generally.
2. See de Jong 2001: 594–95, app. D, "'Storm' Scenes in the *Odyssey*."
3. Other similes include comparisons with chaff in the wind (5.368–70), an ailing father (5.391–99), and an octopus torn from its undersea den (5.430–33).

ter; divine aid—as well as Poseidon's anger; a decision to abandon ship; then a period of floating, swimming, or paddling on the sea. Homer displays great skill in his extensive elaboration of this exciting sequence.

Odysseus is then confronted by the island's rough breakers and cliffs (5.419–22). A wave drives him onto a rock, nearly killing him (5.435–37). Next, Odysseus beseeches a river god to pity him; his supplication is granted (5.441–53). Finally, Odysseus makes it to shore and collapses (5.453–57). Despite his exhaustion, Odysseus revives and, following Leucothea's instructions, unties the scarf and hurls it back into the sea. He then kisses the earth (5.458–64). In discussing this episode and what follows, scholars have noted Odysseus' emergence from the sea as a "rebirth," the presumed *theoxeny* (for both Nausicaa and Odysseus), Odysseus' inordinate reluctance to reveal his name to the Phaeacians, the potential for romance with Nausicaa, and the problematic Phaeacians, who are both hospitable and threatening.[4] The singer Homer has executed a tour de force, exhibiting his skill in detailing this scene with speeches and evocative imagery.

This first shipwreck story, presented in the third person by the singer, highlights Odysseus' autonomy. The gods play a dominant role, yet Homer also presents Odysseus' decisions regarding Leucothea's advice, how to approach the island, and, later, where to spend his first night on the island. Beyond this, Homer emphasizes Odysseus' courage and perseverance (see 5.430–35). Yet while Odysseus makes independent decisions, he is also subject to forces beyond his powers to resist.

This episode sets the stage for Odysseus to play a new role: that of storyteller, first in his appearance to Nausicaa, then to her parents (6.169–74, 7.248–55, 7.264–86), and finally during the long night of tales in books 9–12. Odysseus gains sympathy with these audiences by recounting his misadventures at sea. The shipwreck survivor Odysseus becomes a singer of tales.

The second shipwreck is told to the Phaeacians by Odysseus himself in book 12. Odysseus recounts how he and his men had been kept by contrary winds on the island of Thrinacia, where the herds of the sun god Helios graze. After a month of near starvation, Eurylochus convinces the men to feast on Helios' cattle (as Odysseus naps). Once Odysseus' men have slaughtered the cattle, Zeus promises Helios he will destroy their ship.

Once the men sail off and reach the point where "no land is in sight,"

---

4. See Newton 1984 on rebirth imagery; Kearns 1982 on *theoxeny*; Scodel 1999b: 81 on the problem of Odysseus' "truly remarkable" evasiveness among the Phaeacians; Rose 1969 on the "unfriendly Phaeacians."

Zeus sends a dark cloud over the boat, and a mist sets in (12.403–6). Winds knock down the mast, the helmsman spills overboard, and Zeus splits their ship with a lightning bolt (12.407–19). Zeus' action is fast and efficient: there are no speeches and only two short similes. Odysseus' men have been punished for breaking the oath they took not to eat Helios' cattle.

Contrasting Odysseus' story with the shipwreck narrative in book 5, we appreciate how little detail is presented in book 12, through only twenty-two lines of verse. The longest section concerns the aftermath in which Odysseus constructs a makeshift raft by lashing together the ship's keel and mast (12.420–25). The wind drives him back to the tidal whirlpool Charybdis. When she sucks down the sea (and his raft), he hangs suspended over the vortex from the branch of a fig tree, "like a bat," waiting all day until Charybdis spits out his keel and mast (12.426–46). Then carried by a current, he reaches Calypso's island (12.447–50). This is the final tale told to the Phaeacians.

This second shipwreck story, including a vivid remembrance of the smell of sulphur (12.417), is told by Odysseus as a first-person narrative. Unlike the shipwreck narrative in book 5, we find only short similes, no speeches, and no divine aid. Not only is the narrative more abbreviated; it also serves to emphasize Odysseus' endurance and survival skills, this time without the help of the gods. When his men are dead and the ship lies in splinters, Odysseus does not give up. He grabs the mast and keel and fashions a raft. When Charybdis sucks down his puny craft, he hangs on for what seems like an eternity until his raft is belched forth. It is another nine days to Calypso's island.[5]

While the singer Odysseus does not elaborate as Homer does in book 5, this section gains in pathos by introducing the survivor as the storyteller. Indeed, in ancient literature, first-person narration becomes a conventional feature of shipwreck tales.[6] Homer structures his narrative in such a way that Odysseus has taken control of the story itself. This is highlighted by his near omniscience; he even knows what Zeus says to Helios (note 12.389–90).

Let us turn to the "Cretan tales" and the motif of shipwreck once Odys-

---

5. Odysseus' tenacious will to survive is emphasized by the brief bat simile (12.433) and when Odysseus clings to the underside of the big ram in Polyphemus' cave (9.420–30). Such resiliency is a requisite trait for shipwreck survivors.
6. Thimmes (1992: 61) observes, "This technique allows the author to omnisciently detail the physical elements of the voyage/storm/shipwreck, while permitting a speaking character to personally testify to the danger of the situation." See Robbins 1975; MacDonald 1999: 88–89. First-person narration also occurs in the nearly four-thousand-year-old Egyptian "Tale of the Shipwrecked Sailor," which can be found in Parkinson 1997: 89–101.

seus arrives in Ithaca. After proving himself to be a good host and a loyal servant, Eumaeus asks his guest who he is, where he comes from, and how he reached Ithaca (14.185–90). Instead of the truth, Odysseus fashions an entirely fictional "biography." Of great interest are the echoes and adaptations of his own personal history.

Odysseus tells Eumaeus that he is Aithon from Crete, a bastard son of a rich man. According to his story, he ventured to Troy and was later kidnapped and sold into slavery, only to be rescued, in a sense, by shipwreck. After ten years at Troy, seven years in Egypt, and a year in Phoenicia, he headed toward Libya but was enslaved. This sea voyage, however, met with a storm and wreck, washing him ashore as sole survivor in Thesprotia, in northwest Greece near Ithaca (14.293–315). Received kindly by a king, he was soon robbed by sailors, escaping only when they landed on Ithaca (14.316–59).

Once again, Odysseus takes over as the first-person narrator of a set of adventures including a shipwreck. He includes wonderfully compelling details that promote verisimilitude: his father was Castor, son of Hylax; he led nine overseas raids before Troy; they feasted for six days before journeying to Egypt; when he escapes in Ithaca, he describes how he wades in water up to his chest, with a cloak over his head, before swimming along the shore to freedom.[7] Such vivid—and plausible—detail adds a feel of realism to what we know to be a patently false yarn. Eumaeus says he believes it, except for the part about Odysseus' imminent return from Dodona (14.321–33).

Most important, it is difficult not to notice the echoes of Odysseus' own life in the tale he tells of the Cretan wanderer.[8] In the Egyptian episode when his men start a raid against orders, we think of Odysseus' men in Thrace recklessly attacking the Cicones (14.257–72; cf. 9.43–61). He also speaks of seven years in Egypt and one in Phoenicia (mirroring his time with Calypso and Circe).[9] Odysseus next recounts how a lightning bolt split the ship during the storm off Crete and left the Cretan wanderer as the only survivor. He recounts this episode in language almost identical to that he used to tell the Phaeacians of the actual shipwreck after his crew leaves Thrinacia. Once more, he hangs onto a mast for dear life and floats for nine days (cf. esp. 14.301–4 with 12.403–6, 14.305–9 with 12.415–19). Even his encounter in Thesprotia parallels Nausicaa's rescue of him on Scherie (after his other ship-

---

7.   For a discussion of verisimilitude in Greek epic, see Scodel 1999a: 1–83.
8.   See de Jong 2001: 353–54 on fact, fiction, and "allomorph."
9.   See Scodel 2002: 63–64.

wreck). In Odysseus' Cretan tale, though, it is the king's son—not a daughter—who gives him clothes and leads him to his royal father for escort home (14.317–34; cf. 6.137–320, 7.142–334).

Odysseus' first-person narrative in book 14 differs from the one in book 12 in two significant ways. First, he repeatedly refers to Zeus (eight times) and "god" or "the gods" (five times). We might understand this in terms of what Scodel calls "an implicit competition in pathetic storytelling . . . in which the winner is entitled to the most pity."[10] Odysseus presents himself as living a wretched life subject to the will of the gods (only once does Zeus help him, at 14.310). Obviously his immediate goal is to gain Eumaeus' sympathy.

Second, Odysseus' story in book 14 is complicated by its falsehood, some of which incorporates or adapts various events from Odysseus' own experience. Another way to put this is to say that Odysseus now displays further mastery—and manipulation—as a singer of shipwreck stories. Odysseus once again proves his skill at storytelling (as he did in Scherie), but here Homer suggests how a storyteller may construct an effective yet fictional tale based partly on "real-life" experience. We appreciate not only Homer's artistry found in the first fourteen books—the realistic detail and artful design—but also Odysseus' skill. In a sense, Odysseus is doing what the singer Homer has been doing. Scodel argues that Odysseus' fictions in book 14 "reveal how the poet works when his freedom to invent is greatest and when he is least likely to rely on an audience's familiarity with the stories."[11]

Odysseus had previously invented a shipwreck in book 9. When Polyphemus asked Odysseus where his boat was (9.279–80), Odysseus responded,

> Poseidon the earthshaker smashed my ship:
> he dashed it against the rocks at the far end of your island,
> driving it against a cliff, as the wind carried us in from the sea.
> But these men and I escaped sudden death.

(9.283–86)

In this instance, the shipwreck motif is manipulated by Odysseus to deceive Polyphemus and keep him from destroying their seaworthy vessel. This might be seen as an instance of Odysseus acting as an "apprentice" storyteller of ship-

---

10. Scodel 2002: 82.
11. Scodel 2002: 62–63.

wrecks: his first attempt is brief yet critical for survival. By book 14, Odysseus is more experienced and professional in his storytelling abilities.

The invented shipwreck tale in book 14 may be seen as an instance of Odysseus taking control. In his two actual shipwrecks (in books 5 and 12), Odysseus was subject to the force of wind, waves, and the gods' hostility; he was dependent on the generosity of Calypso and Nausicaa. This lack of control contrasts with Odysseus' authority over the stories he tells, a point I will return to shortly.

The final appearance of shipwrecks in the *Odyssey* occurs in book 22. When all of Penelope's doubts about Odysseus' identity have vanished, she rushes to throw her arms around her husband. Penelope and Odysseus raise a cry of lament, and as Odysseus holds his wife in his arms, Homer introduces a simile.

> As when land joyfully appears to swimmers
> whose well-built ship Poseidon shattered
> on the sea, driven by wind and heavy waves.
> Only a few escape the gray sea, swimming
> toward land. Much brine is caked on their skin,
> and joyfully they step onto land, fleeing disaster.
> So then did her husband joyfully appear to her looking at him,
> and she never let go of his neck with her white arms.
>
> (23.233–41)

The particulars of this simile—a shipwreck sent by Poseidon, swimming for one's life, sea salt clogging pores, finally emerging gratefully onto dry land—come close to recapitulating Odysseus' adventures. Yet when Homer begins the simile, it is not clear whether Odysseus or Penelope is the subject of the comparison—they are simply left in an embrace. Only as the simile concludes do we realize that it is Penelope who looks at her husband with the same joy that a shipwrecked survivor experiences upon reaching dry land. The point is that Penelope, who has never been shipwrecked, has undergone adventures and endured suffering equal to that of her husband. Both Penelope and Odysseus are survivors of comparable trials; these two belong together.

In this climactic scene, Homer uses the shipwreck experience as a means not only to recapitulate the wanderings of Odysseus but also to link such heroism to the figure of Penelope.[12] The previous two shipwreck stories (in books 12 and 14) were told by Odysseus; in a sense, Homer has now reclaimed the shipwreck episode as his own, reminding his audience that the singer is in full control of the narrative.[13] These treatments of shipwreck reveal Homer's skill in presenting this motif with various narrators (the singer or Odysseus) and actual, invented, or figurative shipwrecks.

Shipwreck Survivors and Narrative Competition in Coetzee's Foe

An extremely common feature of shipwreck narratives is that the survivor takes on the role of storyteller: Odysseus tells the Phaeacians (and many others) of his adventures; Defoe's Crusoe writes a chronicle; many critics have seen Shakespeare's Prospero as both playwright and director of the events on his island. A relatively recent work, Coetzee's Foe (1986), introduces two important innovations: the first is to have a woman, Susan Barton, washed up on an island where Cruso (spelled with no e) and Friday have previously been stranded—it is unusual to encounter a female castaway. The second innovation is that Coetzee uses the Crusoe tale as a means of exploring the nature of storytelling, truth, and the ownership of tales. Within the novel, there is a contest not only about who tells the story but about what sorts of shipwreck stories should be told.

Before the novel begins, Susan Barton has traveled from England to Brazil to seek her abducted daughter. She gives up hope after two years and is returning to England when her ship suffers a mutiny. She is set adrift in a rowboat, reaching an island where Cruso and Friday were wrecked some years before. Cruso's only project is to build extensive walled terraces, though he has no seeds to plant. Friday is a Negro slave who fishes, plays the flute, and is unable to speak because his tongue has been cut out; according to Cruso, slave traders did this (23).[14]

Susan spends many months on the island; a ship, the Hobart, then arrives. Cruso and Friday must be forcibly brought aboard. After Cruso dies during

---

12. On "sex-reversal" in similes, see Foley 1978; Winkler 1990; Gainsford 2003: 55 and n. 39.
13. Odysseus goes on to tell Penelope of his adventures, including the shipwreck after leaving the island of Helios (esp. 23.330–33). This is more of a shared report: Homer gives Odysseus' account in the third person. Surely this is not the last time Odysseus will tell his story.
14. Susan wonders whether Cruso might have cut out Friday's tongue for the sin of cannibalism (95).

the voyage, Susan and the mute Friday arrive in England. The final two-thirds of the novel takes place there, as Susan attempts to have the "story of the island" told with the help of Mr. Daniel Foe, a character based on the actual novelist of the original Robinson Crusoe novel.

Coetzee's novel is preoccupied with the struggle over who will tell the story of Susan, Cruso, and the island. Indeed, the work itself begins with quotation marks—the first three-quarters of Coetzee's novel consists of a memoir and letters written by Susan Barton to Mr. Foe. At first, Susan insists she has "no art"' certainly she is no "born storyteller" (40, 81).[15] Indeed, she has a commonsense view of stories.

> All I can say is what I saw, I wrote. I saw no cannibals; and if they came after nightfall and fled before dawn, they left no footprint behind. (54; cf. 47)

Because Susan believes she lacks the necessary skill, she beseeches Foe to write the story (51–52). She fears that if this story is not told, she and Friday will be forever obscure (81); if Foe writes down their story, however, he may liberate Susan and return Friday to Africa (63).

Yet Susan comes to ruminate on how the story should be told. It is extremely important that the tale of the island be told truthfully.[16] She tells the captain of the *Hobart,*

> I would rather be the author of my own story than have lies told about me. . . . If I cannot come forward, as author, and swear to the truth of my tale, what will be the worth of it? I might as well have dreamed it in a snug bed in Chichester. (40)

Susan also stresses the importance of including "particulars" in stories. Specific detail makes each story distinctive, as she tells Cruso on the island.

> All shipwrecks become the same shipwreck, all castaways the same castaway, sunburnt, lonely, clad in the skins of the beasts he has slain. The truth that makes your story yours alone, that sets you apart from the old mariner by the fireside spinning yarns of sea-monsters and mermaids, resides in *a thousand*

---

15. Susan also states, "I will say in plain terms what can be said and leave unsaid what cannot" (120); initially, she thinks that her memoir of the island is "dull and vacant and without life" (126).
16. According to Susan, a fixed record is necessary because memory alone is fallible (17). She is convinced that from age, isolation, and memory, Cruso "no longer knew for sure what was truth, what fancy" (12).

touches which today may seem of no importance, such as: When you made your needle (the needle you store in your belt), by what means did you pierce the eye? When you sewed your hat, what did you use for thread? *Touches like these will one day persuade your countrymen that it is all true, every word,* there was indeed once an island in the middle of the ocean where the wind blew and the gulls cried from the cliffs and a man named Cruso paced about in his apeskin clothes, scanning the horizon for a sail. (18; my italics)

Including "a thousand touches" is the way to make a story one's own and to persuade readers that what is told is true.[17] Recall that extensive detail served to persuade audiences of the veracity of Odysseus' shipwreck narratives (both true and false stories).[18] Susan soon acquires an awareness of the devices a writer employs—episodes, digression, similes, and figures of speech—and demonstrates her own potential as an effective author.

Susan and Foe then compete to see who will tell the shipwreck tale. During this contest, the quotation marks that have begun and closed each paragraph from the beginning of the novel disappear for the final forty pages of *Foe*, and the narrator from "outside" the story tells of Susan's and Foe's actions and words. Foe believes that the story of the island is part of a larger story that begins in London and includes Susan's quest for her daughter, her daughter's search for Susan, the shipwreck, and each woman's return to England. Foe's approach is to impose a fivefold division on the narrative that contains features such as novelty, reversal, and reunion (117). But Susan maintains the integrity of her own version.

The story I desire to be known by is the story of the island. You call it an episode, but I call it a story in its own right. It commences with my being cast away there and concludes with the death of Crusoe and the return of Friday and myself to England, full of new hope. (120–21)

Susan bases her repudiation of Foe's suggestions on the criterion of truth and her own vision.

---

17. Corcoran (1996: 259) discusses Susan's theory of fiction: "her belief that attention to detail matters . . . [which] become[s] an authentication of experience and a guarantee of its substantiality." Susan regrets that she has not brought back proof from the island, such as a feather or "a thimbleful of sand"—all she has are her apeskin sandals (51).
18. Homer uses Alcinous to remind us of Odysseus' skill in book 11, when Alcinous praises his guest Odysseus as a talented and convincing teller of tales (11.363–69).

Once you proposed to supply a middle by inventing cannibals and pirates. These I would not accept because they were not the truth. Now you propose to reduce the island to an episode in the story of a woman in search of a lost daughter. This too I reject. (121)

The characters grapple with the philosophical issue of chance and design in life—and in literature. In Coetzee's *Foe*, Susan believes, at first, in a world of luck (30; cf. 20). Yet her thoughts about chance and design evolve. As she explains, her story comes to be presented not in random fashion but from conscious decisions.

My life did not begin in the waves . . . [My life before the island] makes up a story I do not choose to tell . . . *I choose rather to tell of the island, of myself and Cruso and Friday and what we three did there: for I am a free woman who asserts her freedom by telling her story according to her own desire.* (131; my italics)

Susan's identity as a "free woman" derives in part from her autonomy as a storyteller. While her own life may not have followed a path she desired, she insists on control over *her story.*

An essential feature of shipwrecks is lack of control, yet the story you tell is your own—it becomes a way of regaining control. In Coetzee's *Foe*, the shipwreck survivor's role as storyteller becomes the central issue. Like Odysseus, the character of Susan demonstrates a psychological truth about those who have experienced shipwrecks and their aftermath. She refuses to cede authority over the story of her life, a story that defines who she is.[19] We find a different sort of dynamic in the *Odyssey*; Homer constructs different scenarios with first- or third-person narratives and actual, recalled, invented, and figurative shipwrecks. Yet the overall arc suggests Odysseus' desire to control the story of what happens to him. The "ownership" of these shipwreck tales is first demonstrated by Homer, then subsumed by the figure of the storyteller Odysseus, and ultimately reclaimed by the singer.

---

19. For two other fascinating aspects of Coetzee's work that I do not explore here, see Morrison 2014: 172–77. First, while Susan and Foe contend with one another over how to tell the story, there is another story—Friday's tale—that is "the heart of the story" and yet remains untold. Second, in many ways, there is a contest "outside" the novel between Coetzee and Defoe.

Listening to Shipwreck Tales

The story of Odysseus is a tale of great suffering. At the time of shipwreck, Odysseus expects to die and never knows—even if he survives—whether he will see his wife and family again. Yet we are drawn to such tales. Why? As Odysseus and Eumaeus tell each other the tales of their lives (in Odysseus' case, a fictional one), Eumaeus ponders the odd experience of finding delight in hearing sad stories.

> Let us two drink and eat in the tent
> and delight [*terpometha*] in the painful sorrow of each other,
> remembering. For a man who suffers much and wanders much
> delights [*terpetai*] afterward even in his own past sorrows. (15.398–401)

Writers and philosophers have long wondered why we enjoy reading sad stories or watching tragedy on the stage.[20] Homer has no answer, but he recognizes that—with distance—there is a pleasure in remembering even the hardest parts of our lives.

In fact, this is what happens when we read the *Odyssey* or Coetzee's *Foe*. As readers, we learn about Odysseus' many troubles—his mother dies while he is away, his wife is beset by aggressive suitors, and so on. Yet, in the right circumstances, we enjoy this and want to hear more. Why are we fascinated by shipwrecks and such near-death experiences? Why, many years later, do we "delight in past sorrows"? Is it because it is not happening to us—is it merely the vicarious thrill of hearing what happened to some other unlucky soul? Perhaps there is a tinge of envy for the experience of these marvelous adventures. But perhaps we envy more a storyteller who has such fascinating stories to tell about his or her own life. It is not only the adventure that inspires an audience; it is the ability to control the story of what has happened to you.

Works Cited

Corcoran, P. 1996. "*Foe*: Metafiction and the Discourse of Power." In L. Spaas and B. Stimpson, eds., *Robinson Crusoe: Myths and Metamorphoses*, 256–66. London: Palgrave Macmillan.

---

20. Note the four instances of *terpomai*, "to delight," at 15.391, 393, 399, and 401.

de Jong, I. D. F. 2001. *A Narratological Commentary on the Odyssey.* Cambridge: Cambridge University Press.

Foley, H. 1978. "'Reverse Similes' and Sex Roles in the *Odyssey.*" *Arethusa* 11: 7–26.

Gainsford, P. 2003. "Formal Analysis of Recognition Scenes in the *Odyssey.*" *JHS* 123: 41–59.

Hall, E. 2008. *The Returns of Ulysses: A Cultural History of Homer's Odyssey.* Baltimore: Johns Hopkins University Press.

Kearns, E. 1982. "The Return of Odysseus: A Homeric Theoxeny." *CQ* 32: 2–8.

MacDonald, D. R. 1999. "The Shipwrecks of Odysseus and Paul." *New Testament Studies* 45: 88–107.

Morrison, J. V. 2014. *Shipwrecked: Disaster and Transformation in Homer, Shakespeare, Defoe, and the Modern World.* Ann Arbor: University of Michigan Press.

Newton, R. M. 1984. "The Rebirth of Odysseus." *GRBS* 25: 5–20.

Parkinson, R. B., trans. 1997. *The Tale of Sinuhe, and Other Ancient Egyptian Poems, 1940–1640 BC.* Oxford: Clarendon.

Robbins, V. K. 1975. "The We-Passages in Acts and Ancient Sea Voyages." *Biblical Research* 20: 5–18.

Rose, G. P. 1969. "The Unfriendly Phaeacians." *TAPA* 100: 387–406.

Scodel, R. 1999a. *Credible Impossibilities. Conventions and Strategies of Verisimilitude in Homer and Greek Tragedy.* Stuttgart: Teubner.

Scodel, R. 1999b. "Odysseus' Evasiveness and the Audience of the *Odyssey.*" In E. A. Mackay, ed., *Signs of Orality: The Oral Tradition and Its Influence in the Greek and Roman World,* 79–93. Leiden: Brill.

Scodel, R. 2002. *Listening to Homer: Tradition, Narrative, and Audience.* Ann Arbor: University of Michigan Press.

Stanford, W. B. 1955/1992. The Ulysses Theme. A Study in the Adaptability of a Traditional Hero. Dallas: Spring Publications.

Thimmes, P. L. 1992. *Studies in the Biblical Sea-Storm Type-Scene: Convention and Invention.* San Francisco: Mellen University Press.

Winkler, J. J. 1990. *The Constraints of Desire: The Anthropology of Sex and Gender in Ancient Greece.* New York: Routledge.

CHAPTER 16

Phrontisterion 2.0

Aristophanes' *Clouds* and
Plato's Critique of Pedagogies
in the *Symposium*

Bruce Heiden

As all readers of Plato's *Symposium* know, the character "Aristophanes" represents the canonical author of Athenian dramatic poetry. Moreover, several of Aristophanes' plays are relevant to the dialogue. Like the *Symposium*, Aristophanes' *Clouds* spotlights the wise man "Socrates"; and in the *Symposium*, Alcibiades quotes (approximately) a verse from *Clouds* describing Socrates (362, at 221b). Plato's *Symposium* and Aristophanes' *Thesmophoriazusae* also have a common character in "Agathon." *Lysistrata* and the *Symposium* share the theme of eros and its benefits. *Birds* shares the theme of cosmic origins with the speech of "Aristophanes" in the *Symposium*.

Additionally, at the moment in the *Symposium* that amounts to the entrance of "Aristophanes," Plato provides his character with a bit of business such as Aristophanes staged in his own plays. After the speech of Pausanias, "Aristophanes" is struck by a sudden attack of hiccups that forces him to defer his turn at speaking (185c–e). On the stage, Aristophanes' characters sometimes complain of uncontrollable internal spasms that signify disgust.[1]

---

1. Rettig 1876: 161. Differences between hiccups, vomiting, and choking should not be belabored. According to Aristodemus, the witness who (as reported by "Apollodorus") reported the party at the home of Agathon, the apparent cause of "Aristophanes'" hiccups was overeating (πλησμονῆς, 185c). To an onlooker, then, "Aristophanes" seemed possibly about to hurl.

In *Clouds*, the Better Speech says the Worse Speech makes him feel like puking (906–7); later, the Better Speech says that the sight of an unfit boy dancing at the Panathenaea almost makes him choke (988–89). The Worse Speech says, in turn, that he felt like he was "choking in his guts" (πνιγόμην τὰ σπλάγχνα, 1036) while listening to the Better Speech and waiting for a chance to reply. The hiccupping that strikes "Aristophanes" in the *Symposium* apparently gestures toward Aristophanes' works and suggests that the speech preceding it could be thought of as provoking revulsion.[2]

This possibility is supported by the brief exchange that follows the speech of Eryximachus, the doctor. "Aristophanes" has succeeded in stopping the gagging by implementing Eryximachus' suggestions, and he makes a medical observation of his own (189a), which Eryximachus recognizes as some kind of a joke at the expense of medical science (γελωτοποιεῖς, 189a). But Eryximachus does not think the joke is funny, and he warns "Aristophanes" not to fool around in making his speech. The comic poet replies that in cracking jokes, he would be bringing the benefit of his Muse (189b), which is a general reference to Aristophanes' plays. But "Aristophanes" says he is more concerned about making a fool of himself (καταγέλαστα). Eryximachus replies that "Aristophanes" is being falsely modest in order to mock others but escape the consequences ("You think you can score a hit and flee," 189b). This stealthy mockery is what I have proposed as the effect of the hiccups.

But whom has "Aristophanes" hit, why, and with what? Arieti has suggested that Pausanias, whose conclusion immediately precedes the onset of hiccups, resembles the Better Speech in *Clouds*, because both make claims to moral virtue that are falsified by their sexual lust for boys' bodies.[3] This is true. But the resemblance between Pausanias and the Better Speech is only one strand in a network of relationships between *Clouds* and the *Symposium*. Through "Aristophanes'" gesture toward the Phrontisterion, the *Symposium* cues attention to an earlier critique of pedagogies that the dialogue systematically adapts and deepens. Plato's upgraded Phrontisterion, including the pivotal speech on eros that it ascribes to "Aristophanes," effectively acknowledges a debt that philosophy owes to the poet of *Clouds*. A concise review of *Clouds* will help make clear the critique of pedagogies on which Plato draws.

---

2. Commentary on this passage often emphasizes the change in order of speakers; the most recent contribution is O'Mahoney 2011.

3. Arieti 1991: 114.

The Phrontisterion in Aristophanes' Clouds

In Aristophanes' *Clouds*, the Athenian farmer Strepsiades has gone into debt by indulging his son's horse-racing hobby. Intending to defraud his creditors and get away with it, Strepsiades conceives the idea of sending his son to the Phrontisterion, because he has heard that its inhabitants are "smart souls" (ψυχῶν σοφῶν, 94), who,

> if one pays them money, teach
> how to prevail by speaking both justice and injustice. (98–99)[4]

Strepsiades wants his son to learn the "unjust speech" and defeat the creditors' legitimate lawsuits (116–18). He has a confused idea that the Phrontisterion is home to various sorts of scientific knowledge and applied skills, including rhetoric, but this knowledge interests him solely because it is useful for performing injustice. He is eventually proved more right in this belief than he ever imagined, for he becomes his own son's victim.

Clouds states explicitly and emphatically that Strepsiades is an *erastes* and that his plan to subvert justice is a form of eros. Observing Strepsiades' abuse of his creditors (1303–6), the Cloud Chorus reflects that he is crazed with passion (ἐρασθείς) and exemplifies "desire for bad deeds" (τὸ πραγμάτων ἐρᾶν φλαύρων). At the climactic moment when Strepsiades blames the Cloud Chorus for misleading him, they explain that they did it to teach him a lesson, because he is "a lover of base business" (πονηρῶν ὄντ᾽ ἐραστὴν πραγμάτων, 1459). *Clouds* is a forerunner of the *Symposium*, because, like Plato's dialogue, Aristophanes' comedy is a meditation on eros, justice, and scientific expertise. It shows the Athenians a city that sorely needs someone to teach its citizens justice and to correct their eros.

Such a teacher is not to be found in the Phrontisterion. The central figure of the Phrontisterion is "Socrates," a natural scientist who investigates the anatomy of microscopic creatures and, above all, atmospheric phenomena—he is a *meteorosophistes* (360). "Socrates" is also a scientist of speech whose expertise includes the rhythms and proper inflection of words. His rhetorical expertise is a caricature of teachings associated with the sophists Protagoras and Prodicus.[5]

---

4.   All translations in this essay are mine.
5.   Dover 1968: 179.

The Phrontisterion also includes the Better and Worse Speeches, the feature that attracted Strepsiades. These Speeches represent alternative pedagogies, but their critical common feature is that they are both *speeches* that partner in debate and exercise an art of persuasion adaptable to the defense of either pedagogy. Their agon parodies Prodicus' *Choice of Heracles*, a famous sophistic performance in which the youthful hero must choose his life path by weighing the competing appeals of two figures, one representing the life of virtuous self-discipline, the other the life of pleasant self-indulgence.[6]

The Phrontisterion's Better Speech is a caricature of the traditional gentleman's pedagogy that inculcated manly virtues through drills in gymnastics, musical performance, and memorization of poetry. The "justice" of this pedagogy is fundamentally *sophrosune* (962), or moderation of one's physical appetites and pleasures. The fundamental incentive to moderation is shame (fear of disapproval). The properly educated boy avoids what appears ugly (αἰσχϱόν, 1020) and imitates what appears seemly (καλόν, 1021). But the Better Speech's own self-description reveals that the adults who were supposedly the role models of modesty were obsessively attracted to young boys and could hardly control themselves unless the boys helped them out by maintaining their modesty (973–80). The traditional *paideia* makes boys more desirable and cultivates the erotic temptation of forbidden fruit.

The Worse Speech, in contrast, caricatures a modern schooling that rejects the traditional gentleman's *paideia* on the ground that moderation amounts to nothing more than denial of the natural desire for sexual pleasure (1071–74). The modern schooling bases all conduct in nature. Nature is the body, its desires are compulsory (ἀνάγκας, 1075), and moderating their satisfaction achieves nothing good (1062). The Worse Speech rejects any grounds for shame and denies that justice even exists (902). It claims that the modern schooling's many adherents are very intelligent but that their superior intellect consists only of skill at speaking persuasively about nature and the body. The Worse Speech takes the scientific investigations of the Phrontisterion, which were supposed to be secret (140), and develops them into a rhetorical pedagogy that is potentially available to anybody.

In the Phrontisterion, Strepsiades' son Pheidippides learns both the Better and Worse Speeches and deploys elements of both in his defense of father beating. Pheidippides claims that father beating is a form of justice (1405). In

---

6.   This is the version narrated by Socrates at Xen. *Mem.* 2.1.21–34. On Prodicus and the agon, see Papageorgiou 2004.

fact, according to Pheidippides, striking one's father is beneficial for the father (1411) and virtually amounts to a form of education corresponding to the beating of children by their elders, that is, to the pedagogy of the Better Speech (1411). Channeling the Worse Speech, he also claims that striking one's father is natural because animals of other species do it (1427–29).

The final teacher in the Phrontisterion is a team of visiting faculty, the Cloud Chorus, who are divinities that "Socrates" and other experts worship. The Clouds do not teach the experts, but their support makes expertise possible (317–18, 331–34). Above all, they enable experts to impress and humiliate nonexperts and thus to reduce them to deference. As weather phenomena of unstable shape, the Clouds represent the deceptiveness of appearances to the unschooled eye. But the Clouds also deceive the experts, who are not their sole or primary beneficiaries. The Clouds wish good for the city and explain that they bring it blessings (577). Their weather disturbances are signs that advise the Athenians to avoid bad policies or leaders, like Cleon (580–86). The Clouds therefore act as a sort of Socratic *daimonion* for the whole city. Later, in the second parabasis, they explain how they reward justice (δικαίων, 1116) and punish impiety (1121), and they appeal to the city to act justly toward the Clouds themselves, the Moon, and the poet of *Clouds*. They deceive lovers of wickedness like Strepsiades in order to teach them an ethical lesson (1458–61). Thus the Clouds are teachers, but unlike the other teachers of the Phrontisterion, they are ethical teachers. In effect, the Clouds are more philosophical than "Socrates." Apparently, they are figurative surrogates of the poet, since it was Aristophanes who, in *Knights* (581), warned the Athenians about the Paphlagonian, that is, Cleon. These figures and themes from *Clouds* are revisited in the first four speakers of the *Symposium*.

Phaedrus: Recent Graduate of the Phrontisterion

In Plato's *Symposium*, the agenda is set by Eryximachus, who is a doctor and lends his authority as an expert on the body to support the symposiasts' disinclination to drink heavily again after the previous day's sousing. Like "Socrates" in the Phrontisterion, Eryximachus is a natural scientist. He is also the *erastes* of Phaedrus, who says that he always obeys Eryximachus, especially regarding medicine (περὶ ἰατρικῆς, 176d). Like Pheidippides in *Clouds* (1467, 1431), Phaedrus is a pupil devoted to his teacher. Since Phaedrus is

Eryximachus' *paidika*, he surrenders his body to the doctor's physical pleasures as well as to his therapeutic treatments; the difficulty of distinguishing
the two is inherent in the doctor's authority and appeal.

Eryximachus introduces the evening's pastime by recalling Phaedrus'
complaint that poets have composed songs praising other gods but not Eros
(*Symp.* 177a). This resembles a point the Clouds make about themselves: that
although they benefit the city, they alone receive no sacrifices and libations
from the clever (σοφώτατοι) citizens of the audience (*Clouds* 575—78). Phaedrus says Eros is neglected by poets and professors (σοφιστὰς, *Symp.* 177b),
such as the "excellent" Prodicus, who Phaedrus remarks wrote in praise of
Heracles but not of Eros. Evidently, Phaedrus knows and admires Prodicus'
Choice of Heracles, the model for the agon between the Better and Worse
Speeches in *Clouds*. Phaedrus has also read a learned monograph about salt.
In short, Phaedrus is a young man who has been through the comprehensive
modern curriculum combining traditional, scientific, and rhetorical school-
ing, the same curriculum that Aristophanes caricatured in *Clouds*.

Phaedrus' speech reveals his devotion to the traditional *paideia*, in his
praise of Eros for its power to encourage "seemly deeds" (καλὰ ἔργα, 178c)
and discourage the shameful. Men so educated love honor (φιλοτιμούμενοι,
178c) and avoid unmanliness (ἀνανδρίαν, 178d), and an army comprised of
such men would be victorious in battle, even though outnumbered. Thus
they are like the victors at Marathon, the most distinguished alumni of the
Better Speech (*Clouds* 986). Phaedrus also shows respect for age in praising
Eros as the eldest of gods (*Symp.* 178a–c), and he draws liberally upon poets
for authority.

While the Better Speech in *Clouds* disingenuously disavows the erotic
feelings associated with the traditional *paideia*, Phaedrus, in contrast, endeavors to show that Eros is compatible with the gentleman's *paideia*, in fact in-
strumentally indispensable to it, and should be praised precisely for that reason. This maneuver improves on the Better Speech's transparently
hypocritical defense of modesty. Phaedrus represents Eros purely as a stimu-
lus to honor. He views Eros from the standpoint of a well-behaved *eromenos*
who scrupulously observes the Better Speech's injunction against any display that might acknowledge the body's eroticism or provoke desire in others. From Phaedrus' speech, one would never guess that lovers were attracted
to one another by physical desire. Rather than avoiding the shameful, Phaedrus' version of the traditional *paideia* improves its concealment.

Phaedrus' regard for authoritative wisdom combines the modern and traditional schools without recognizing any conflict. In quoting poetry, he draws indiscriminately on Hesiod, Homer, Acusilaus (a genealogist who claimed to correct Hesiod's facts), and the metaphysician Parmenides. He also ridicules Aeschylus (Αἰσχύλος δὲ φλυαρεῖ, 180a), in tones reminiscent of Pheidippides in *Clouds* (1366–67). In praising how Eros inspires shame, Phaedrus says that a lover would be more pained to be observed doing something shameful by his beloved than by anyone else, specifically including his father (ὑπὸ πατρός, *Symp.* 178d). This recalls Pheidippides' disrespect for his father Strepsiades and his reverence for his teachers (*Clouds* 1467).

Pausanias: Professor in the School of Eros

Pausanias' speech in Plato's *Symposium* complements Phaedrus' by accepting its praise of eros as *paideia* from the perspective of the pupil-*eromenos* and adding the perspective of the teacher-*erastes*. By depicting all eros as pedagogical and praiseworthy, Phaedrus implicitly reconciled the alternatives of virtuous abstention and vicious indulgence in Prodicus' *Choice of Heracles* and the debate of the Better and Worse Speeches. Pausanias reinstates the distinction between praiseworthy and blameworthy, but he redescribes it as a choice between two kinds of erotic indulgence, the praiseworthy corresponding to the Better Speech, the blameworthy to the Worse. But just as the Better and Worse Speeches are both speeches and teach persuasion rather than either self-discipline or scientific knowledge, Pausanias' pedagogical eros teaches seduction and aims at carnal pleasure, just like the vulgar appetite that Pausanias purports to disdain.

Pausanias begins by acknowledging that Phaedrus' praise of Eros would be fine if Eros were a single thing, but that since it is not a single thing the "more correct" procedure would be to begin by defining the subject precisely. Pausanias is clearly a product of Prodicus' teaching of correct diction, like "Socrates" in the Phrontisterion.

Pausanias infers that there must be two Erotes corresponding to the two Aphrodites of myth, of whom the elder, known as the Heavenly Aphrodite, is the offspring of only one parent, Uranus, while the younger, known as the Common Aphrodite, is the daughter of Zeus and Dione. The characteristics of the Common Aphrodite, her corresponding Common Eros, and the man who might be called the "Common Erastes," associate them all with the Worse Speech. The Common Aphrodite is the younger Aphrodite and therefore the less revered and more modern. She is also natural, because she was conceived in the natural way, through sexual union of male and female. Pausanias' Common Eros is simply the body's appetite for pleasure in copulation with other bodies. As a body's impulse to please itself, the Common Eros cares little about the bodies it uses, and it takes satisfaction in bodies of either gender. Moreover since resistance or modesty would interfere with its pleasure, the Common Eros prefers bodies with dull brains and easy morals (181b). This kind of Eros is therefore considered shameful and should be forbidden by law (181e–182a). The Common Erastes cannot be trusted to keep his word or his promises (183e). This is a version of the Worse Speech's shameless and indiscriminate hedonism.

In contrast, the Heavenly Eros is a version of the Better Speech's schooling in modesty. It derives from the Heavenly Aphrodite, who is older (πρεσβυτέρα, 180d) and therefore revered and is not born from a mother (ἀμήτωρ, 180d), that is, not of physically natural birth. The Heavenly Eros is seemly (καλόν), and seemliness is why it is praiseworthy. It is also educational: the Heavenly Erastes makes the *paidika* wise and good (σοφόν τε καὶ ἀγαθόν, 184d), while the *paidika* needs education (παίδευσιν, 184e) and other wisdom (σοφίαν, 184e). The *erastes* and the *paidika* are both law-abiding (νόμον ἔχων ἑκάτερος, 184d), and both act with justice (δικαίως, 184d).

The Heavenly Eros seems honorable because what attracts it is not body but mind (181c, 183e). Nevertheless, the Heavenly Erastes is also attracted to his pupil's body and seeks satisfaction in sexual union with him. He curiously identifies the presence of a boy's intellect by observing his incipiently thickening beard (τῷ γενειάσκειν, 181d). This concrete token of the maturing body is only a bit less intimately graphic than the "image of youth" (εἴδωλον . . . τῆς ἥβης, *Clouds* 976) that the Better Speech says modest boys must avoid impressing in the sand lest the sight excite their lovers; even more directly comparable would be the fluffy pubic hair whose appearance enthralls the Better Speech (τοῖς αἰδοίοισι . . . χνοῦς . . . ἐπήνθει, 978).

Like Pheidippides' argument in *Clouds* for the justice of beating parents for their own improvement, Pausanias' speech in the *Symposium* argues for the justice, lawfulness, and admirability of a personal practice normally condemned by fathers (183c). This requires interpreting existing custom in a novel way: two unrelated customs, neither of which legitimates boys' consensual submission to seducers, are combined (184c–e), and a new *nomos* prohibiting the (Common) molestation of younger boys is recommended (181e; this is to protect the reputation of the Heavenly Erastai, who discriminatingly pursue slightly older boys). Pausanias incorporates the Worse Speech by praising society for making Eros an exception to the usual standards of decency: most people praise *erastai* for doing things that would otherwise bring reproach (183b). The exemption even includes violation of one's oath (183b). In the Phrontisterion, the Better Speech concedes that with respect to eros, the Worse Speech prevails with the majority; in the *Symposium*, Pausanias goes even further and asserts that in the case of Eros suspension of decency is a fine thing.

Eryximachus: Nature's Expert

When Pausanias finishes speaking "Aristophanes" is next in order of seating, but he is overtaken by hiccups and cedes his place to Eryximachus. I have suggested that "Aristophanes'" gagging would remind readers of moments in Aristophanes' plays, especially *Clouds*, where references to stomach spasms function as gestures of disgust. Since "Aristophanes" turns to Eryximachus for treatment, the gagging interlude also reemphasizes that the next speaker is a doctor and an expert on the natural cosmos. As I have noted, Eryximachus is like the Phrontisterion's "Socrates," who investigates physical phenomena and worships the Clouds, divine patronesses of *sophistai* and *iatrotekhnai* (*Clouds* 332). Plato's "Aristophanes" correctly anticipates that the doctor will regard his gagging as a purely physical phenomenon that provides an opportunity for displaying his scientific learning and medical skill. Eryximachus sees no ethical implications.

When "Aristophanes" appeals to Eryximachus to stop the gagging or, if he cannot do that, to take "Aristophanes'" turn (*Symp.* 185d), Eryximachus' answer is predictably short on humility: he promises to fulfill both alternatives—to cure the gagging but to take "Aristophanes'" turn anyway—as if this were a double service ("I'll do both," 185d). Rather than stop "Aristophanes'" gagging, however, Eryximachus proposes a series of measures: (a) holding the breath for a long time; (b) if that does not work, gargling with water; (c) if neither works, inducing a sneeze by tickling the nostril; and (d) if the tickling does not work the first time, repeating it. The confidence and concreteness of Eryximachus' prescriptions are belied by the acknowledged possibility that every one of his measures may fail. Meanwhile, the comic poet, who seems to think that the doctor's long-windedness is delaying the treatment, urges him to get started with his encomium (185e), that is, to shut up about cures for hiccups. On this note, Eryximachus begins.

Eryximachus takes over Pausanias' distinction between good Eros and bad, but he abandons the identification of bad eros with the body and good eros with the mind. For Eryximachus, all eros is bodily, because all existence is matter, and human eros is simply one manifestation of a balance of material opposites that applies to everything in the cosmos. The distinction between bad and good is therefore between sick and healthy. The sick body is excessive in consuming what it enjoys, while the healthy body consumes moderately, in accordance with nature.

Eryximachus regards nature as necessity, and he thus aligns with the principle of the Worse Speech that physical desires must be indulged. Neither Eryximachus nor the Worse Speech subjects nature to an ethical principle. Nevertheless, in a procedure that reverses Pausanias', Eryximachus reintroduces the para-ethical principle of decorous moderation by redescribing it as an effect of a healthy physical regimen administered by an expert. Eryximachus neither advocates nor excuses injustice, but having adopted nature as guiding principle, he has no means of preventing injustice and no grounds for condemning it. Like "Socrates" in the *Clouds*, Eryximachus proclaims a knowledge that obscures the ethical dimension of human conduct. The scientist's power over nature is very limited: Eryximachus can do nothing to forestall the destructive effects of weather (188a–b). Unhealthy human behavior — insolence toward the gods, parents, and the law — requires intervention and treatment by the mantic art, which differs from natural science (188b–d). Recall that the Clouds explained that their weather phenomena *were* omens.

When Eryximachus finishes, he asks "Aristophanes" to take his turn in praising Eros, since he notes that the hiccups have stopped. "Aristophanes" affirms that they have, but he adds that they did not stop until he induced sneezing, that is, that breath holding and water gargling did not succeed. This leads "Aristophanes" to his own medical observation, namely, that the proper ordering of the body (τὸ κόσμιον, 189a) has a desire (ἐπιθυμεῖ) for noises and itches (189a). As I noted earlier, Eryximachus recognizes that this comment is some kind of a joke, but he does not find it either meaningful or funny. He warns "Aristophanes" to be serious, threatens to prevent him from mocking (189a), admonishes him to put his mind to the task, and suggests that if "Aristophanes" gives a proper speech, Eryximachus might let him off for the joking he has already done. Eryximachus is clearly playing the role of a stern schoolmaster—the Better Speech with a scientific curriculum—to "Aristophanes'" naughty schoolboy.

"Aristophanes": Wisdom's Inspiration

In Aristophanes' *Clouds*, an ethical alternative to the teaching of the Phrontiste-rion is presented by the Cloud Chorus, who are closely associated with the author. In the *Symposium*, the conversation and speech of "Aristophanes" pres-ent a clear break from the three figures who precede him. "Aristophanes'" posi-tion begins to emerge in his facetious medical observation about sneezing and "the arrangement of the body." Eryximachus has just concluded his speech by ascribing cooperative relationships among men and between men and gods to the mantic art, not the medical art. Since Eryximachus, who confesses that mantic art is needed, offers no explanation of how it might work, it is relevant to point out that sneezes were popularly and traditionally thought of as omens.[7] Obviously, they are not considered omens by Eryximachus, who regards them as reflexes that may be controlled and directed to serve physical objectives (in this case, suppressing the gag reflex). "Aristophanes'" joke mimics the natural-ist perspective, but whereas Eryximachus discusses nature as an object of in-vestigation that a scientific expert like himself can explain and control, "Aristo-phanes" states that what he has experienced is not readily understood and that it induces wonder (ὥστε με θαυμάζειν, 189a). By this phrase alone, Plato sig-nals at once that the comic poet of the Phrontisterion should be thought of as a kind of philosopher (cf. Pl. *Tht.* 155d). "Aristophanes'" insight into humanity and its order suggests that the decorum of the body is not a static harmony imposed on passive material by an expert technician but a desire (ἐπιθυμεῖ). Contrary to what natural scientists assume, nature appears to be animated, and its indecorous urges—which would include erotic longings and orgasms—might contribute to its proper order. Therefore, they should be freely enjoyed, even stimulated, rather than inhibited or concealed, as the three previous speakers have all attempted to do. "Aristophanes'" joke is therefore a preview

7.   Lateiner 2005.

of his unique tribute to Eros. And although sneezing plays no role in "Aristophanes'" discourse, it does turn out that Eros makes the soul into a kind of oracle (192c–d).

As "Aristophanes" begins, he distinguishes himself from the three previous speakers by insisting that humans do not perceive the power of Eros at all (παντάπασι, 189c), whereas the previous speakers all agreed that the benefits of Eros were known widely if not universally. "Aristophanes" says that if mortals understood Eros, they would honor the god Eros with the greatest offerings and cults, while the god has none at present (189c). This should recall a claim the Clouds make for themselves:

> O most clever audience, give us your attention please.
> You have wronged us, and we are accusing you face to face.
> For we, more than all the gods, bring benefit to your city,
> but to us alone you never make sacrifices or libations,
> although we always look out for you. (*Clouds* 575—79)

It would appear that Plato's "Aristophanes" represents an adaptation of the Cloud Chorus, who, I already noted, are teachers of ethical wisdom. The point of "Aristophanes'" speech at the symposium is not just to praise Eros but to provide a teaching that disciples (the other symposiasts) will, in turn, teach others (*Symp.* 189d). "Aristophanes" begins like a scientist, with a discourse about human nature (τὴν ἀνθρωπίνην φύσιν, 189d), and his frequent use of illustrative analogies suggests the speech mannerisms of "Socrates" in *Clouds* (e.g., 385) and real Greek scientific writers.[8] But unlike scientists and the Worse Speech, "Aristophanes" denies that the present condition of humans is natural or necessary, since humans only began to feel eros when the gods modified them by splitting them and making other elective adjustments.

"Aristophanes" emphasizes that erotic desire is not actually a body's physical desire for pleasure in coupling with other bodies (τῶν ἀφροδισίων συνουσία, *Symp.* 192c) but a longing of the soul (ψυχή, 192c) for something it cannot express, much less gaze on or embrace. Lovers wish for a union that outlasts even death (192e). This applies to all lovers, including those like adulterers (τῶν μοιχῶν, 191d), whose transient pleasures were cited by the Worse Speech as typical of nature and necessity (*Clouds*, 1075–76).

---

8.   Nieddu 2007: 251—56.

Thus "Aristophanes" reverses the significance of nature, which is not the permanent condition of humans but a state that humans have left behind, possibly forever. Eros is characteristic of humankind's postnatural state. In their natural state, when humans did not reproduce sexually or feel sexual desire, they were arrogant, violent, and attempted to overthrow the gods (*Symp.* 190b); by nature, humans were unjust (τὴν ἀδικίαν, 193a), like Strepsiades. But this state of injustice, although natural, was not necessary: the gods modified it. Their purpose in doing so was ethical, to limit the ability of humans to do injustice. But Eros also had unforeseen effects that contributed to its ethical purpose. It made mortal happiness depend on the gods, thus giving mortals reason to please the gods with piety (193a). Since the divided condition of mortals was imposed on the human race collectively, the hope for its alleviation depends on humans' collective piety and gives each mortal an interest in promoting the piety of the others (193c). Eros thus establishes a relationship that binds all mortals together and that binds the human race and the gods.

The implication that Eros exists to limit injustice — that its very purpose is ethical — adds to Plato's characterization of "Aristophanes" as a kind of philosopher.[9] The clinching moment of this characterization is "Aristophanes'" quotation of Hephaestus' imaginary speech to the embracing lovers (192d). Hephaestus' queries constitute a kind of *elenkhos* that produces aporia in its interlocutors (ἀποροῦντας, 192d).

In the course of the *Symposium*, the speech of "Aristophanes" therefore enjoys the privileged position of being the first to adumbrate the type of pedagogy that opposes both traditional discipline and natural science by attending reverently to the desires of the soul: philosophy. The comic poet receives this distinction because the actual plays of Aristophanes — above all, *Clouds* — exposed the ethical barrenness of existing paradigms of knowledge and, through the Cloud Chorus, pointed to the Muses as the source of an alternative pedagogy. In the *Symposium*, Plato adapts and modifies the Phrontisterion's critical caricature of modern learning, highlighting and extending its implicit pedagogical trajectory. What we might refer to as "Phrontisterion 2.0" also generously suggests that even these deficient pedagogies manifest, if only unintentionally, an inchoate aspiration to the ethical wisdom of philosophy. The comic poet Aristophanes is not the last word in philosophy, but

---

9.   Cf. Nieddu 2007: 247−48.

then, in the *Symposium*, neither is Socrates, who repetitively transmits Diotima's speeches although he himself may not fully understand their teaching (210a). It is no wonder that, as the *Symposium* concludes, Socrates bores "Aristophanes" to sleep with his theoretical argument that the poet who commanded the expertise (τέχνη, 223d) of composing tragedy could also compose comedy. In *Clouds*, Aristophanes himself did both in a single play, only he did it through inspired ethical wisdom rather than rhetorical expertise: the same poet composed tragedy, comedy, and philosophy. In the *Symposium*, Plato's adaptation of the Phrontisterion acknowledges Aristophanes as a forerunner and inspiration in the passionate pursuit of wisdom.

Works Cited

Arieti, J. A. 1991. *Interpreting Plato: The Dialogues as Drama*. Savage, MD: Rowman and Littlefield.

Dover, K. ed. 1968. *Aristophanes, Clouds*. Oxford: Clarendon.

Lateiner, D. 2005. "Telemakhos's One Sneeze and Penelope's Two Laughs (*Odyssey* 17.541–50, 18.158–68)." In R. J. Rabel, ed., *Approaches to Homer: Ancient and Modern*, 91–104. Swansea: Classical Press of Wales.

Nieddu, G. F. 2007. "Aristofane a Simposio: Buffoneria o Comicità 'Urbana'?" *Lexis* 25: 241–65.

O'Mahoney, P. 2011. "On the 'Hiccupping Episode' in Plato's *Symposium*." *CW* 104: 143–59.

Papageorgiou, N. 2004. "Prodicus and the *Agon* of the *Logoi* in Aristophanes' *Clouds*." *QUCC*, n.s., 78: 61–69.

Rettig, G. F. 1876. *Platonis Symposium*. Halle: Verlag der Buchhandlung des Waisenhauses.

CHAPTER 17

Hephaestus' Winged Shoes
and the Birth of Athena

Daniel B. Levine

Two Questions

On four sixth-century Attic black-figure vases portraying the birth of Athena, the god Hephaestus wears winged shoes as he leaves the scene. Since this type of footwear is not typically associated with the god of the forge, one might wonder why Hephaestus is so attired on these vases. Wings imply speed; perhaps they show his haste. If so, why do the wings appear only in these sixth-century examples? Another question arises when we note several literary sources relating that Hermes struck Zeus' head with an ax to facilitate Athena's birth. Since no extant representations depict Hermes in this role, we may justifiably ask where this notion arose, especially considering that one of our ancient sources specifically states that Hermes was so depicted in archaic art. In short, we face two questions about early depictions of the birth of Athena: (1) why do some Athenian artists depict Hephaestus wearing winged shoes in some of the earliest scenes, and (2) what is the source of the literary tradition that Hermes acted as midwife for Athena's birth?

In response, this essay suggests that (1) we can explain Hephaestus' footwear by considering the possibility that traditional depictions of Perseus fleeing from the Gorgons influenced these early painters of Birth of Athena scenes and (2) claims that Hermes wielded the ax might have arisen from viewers mistaking a painted Hephaestus for Hermes, partially due to the fact that Hephaestus wears winged shoes, which were later Hermes' consistent attribute.

Iconography: Hephaestus and the Birth of Athena

According to the most common myth of Athena's birth, Zeus impregnated the goddess Metis, swallowed her, and allowed the embryonic Athena to gestate in his body. When it was time for Athena to be born, Zeus summoned Hephaestus and asked him to strike his head with his ax. Hephaestus did so, and the goddess sprang forth, fully formed and armed. Beginning in the second quarter of the sixth century BCE, this myth took physical form in numerous vase paintings of Athena's birth, many of which portray Hephaestus as the weapon-wielding "midwife." This is his main role in the story, and he was probably so depicted in the east pediment of the Parthenon.[1]

Sixth-century black-figure vase painters often depict a seated Zeus flanked by the Eileithyiae (birth goddesses) and several other figures, while an armored Athena emerges from his head. When Hephaestus appears in these scenes, he generally is shown holding an ax and departing, having done his part to bring forth his sister. Examples include an Athenian amphora from Etruria (ca. 575–525) showing a seated Zeus giving birth to Athena. Behind him stand Apollo, Hera, and Poseidon; Hephaestus runs away to the left behind them, holding his ax in his right hand and looking back as he hastily departs.[2] A scene by the Antimenes Painter (ca. 550–500) portrays Hermes on the left, wearing winged shoes and watching the birth, while Hephaestus, barefoot and holding a double ax, departs on the right.[3]

Red-figure examples differ in some ways from the sixth-century scenes.[4]

---

1. For literary sources and a discussion of red-figure depictions of Birth of Athena scenes, see Arafat 1990: 32–39. Some stories relate that Hephaestus was Hera's parthenogenetically produced offspring, born after Athena—in response to Zeus' self-production of Athena (Hes. *Theog.* 927–33). In this regard, Fineberg (2009: 276) remarks, "Mythic genealogies often defy temporal logic."

2. Group E, from Vulci, British Museum B147, Beazley 310304, ABV 135.44, cf. Schefold 1992, Fig. 6 A. Interestingly, Hephaestus' raised running left leg overlaps the lotus/palmette design beneath the handle, making it look as though both his thigh and ankle have wings, hastening his departure. It is difficult to know if this is intentional or a happy coincidence.

3. Athenian black-figure neck amphora, Vulci, ca. 550–500, British Museum B 244, Beazley 320085, *ABV* 271.74; cf. Burow 1989, pl. 32, no. 32 (A, B). On the ax as Hephaestus' attribute in scenes of Hephaestus' return to Olympus after exile, see Fineberg 2009: 293n29.

4. As Arafat (2001) notes, in the archaic Birth of Athena scenes, "Zeus is generally much more

In a fragment from an early fifth-century red-figure krater (ca. 500–450), the Syleus Painter shows Hephaestus (name inscribed) standing immediately beside the goddess as she emerges from Zeus' head. Hephaestus faces the action with upraised hand and does not seem inclined to run away, as in earlier depictions.[5] In a fifth-century red-figure Athenian hydria (ca. 475–425), a young beardless (and barefoot) Hephaestus runs away from the birth scene, holding his ax in his left hand.[6] Hephaestus is not present in every sixth- and fifth-century Birth of Athena scene; but when he does appear, his role is mainly to depart with his ax.[7]

Hephaestus' Winged Shoes at the Birth of Athena

Four Attic black-figure vase paintings of Athena's birth from ca. 570–525 show Hephaestus departing with his ax as the goddess emerges from Zeus' head. These scenes generally conform to the iconography previously described, except that the smith god wears winged boots on the following vases, a feature that does not occur in such scenes after 525.

Figure 1. Tyrrhenian amphora, Kyllenios Painter, Cerveteri, ca. 575–525.[8]

agitated than in the Classical period" (38–39), which "is one of the many signs of a changing attitude towards the gods in the Classical period; as, for example, Hephaistos becomes less deformed in scenes of his Return, so Zeus becomes more stately in his appearances on vases" (35).

5. Red-figure krater fragment, Locri, ca. 500–450, Reggio Calabria Museo Nazionale 4379, Beazley 202504.
6. Painter of Tarquinia 707, ca. 475–425, Beazley 214704; cf. Mannack 2001, pl. 2.
7. Some vases showing the birth of Athena without Hephaestus include the following: Athenian black-figure cup A, Painter of Louvre F 28, ca. 575–525, Beazley 302576; Athenian black-figure amphora B, side A, Group E, ca. 575–525, Louvre F 32, Beazley 310303; Athenian black-figure amphora B, Group E, Etruria, ca. 575–525, Boston Museum of Fine Arts 00.330, Beazley 310305 (in this scene, Hephaestus is absent, but Hermes appears in winged shoes); Athenian black-figure amphora B, Princeton Painter, ca. 550–500, Beazley 320417 (with neither Hermes nor Hephaestus; cf. Shapiro 1989a: pl. 14C–D); black-figure amphora B, Psiax, ca. 550–500, Rome, Museo Nazionale Etrusco di Villa Giulia 64217, Beazley 340531 (displaying two Birth of Athena scenes without Hephaestus: one scene with Poseidon and one with Hermes); Athenian black-figure neck amphora, Omaha Painter, ca. 600–550, Louvre E 861, Beazley 350214 (showing neither Hermes nor Hephaestus; instead, we see the Eileithyiae, Hera, Dionysus, Poseidon, and other goddesses). Another Birth of Athena scene shows Hermes with winged shoes but with no other divinities aside from the Eileithyiae: Athenian black-figure amphora B, Group E, ca. 575–525, Richmond, Virginia Museum of Fine Arts 60.23, Beazley 350434. Hermes (with winged shoes) is the lone god with the Eileithyiae in an Athenian black-figure Birth of Athena scene on a neck amphora by the Three Line Group (Nola, ca. 530, Berlin, Antikensammlung F 1862, Beazley 351035).
8. Berlin-Charlottenburg F 1704, Beazley 310014, *ABV* 96.14; cf. Boardman 2001: 50, fig. 59.

Figure names are inscribed, identifying both Hermes ("I am Hermes Kyllenios") and Hephaestus ("Hephaistos" is inscribed between the legs). Zeus sits on a throne with his thunderbolt, helped by the Eileithyiae in giving birth to Athena from his head. To the left, Hephaestus appears anxious to leave quickly, wearing winged boots and running between Dionysus (on the left) and Hermes (on the right). His head is turned back toward Zeus, and his right hand is raised, possibly in surprise. He holds his ax in his left hand, leaning it on his left shoulder. Hermes, without shoes, holds a *kerykeion*. Hephaestus' left booted foot overlaps Hermes' bare right foot, emphasizing the contrast between their feet. This is the only example among the four vases where both Hermes and Hephaestus appear.

Figure 2. Tripod pyxis, C Painter, ca. 575–525.[9] Zeus, seated on a throne, holds a staff while giving birth to Athena from his head; the Eileithyiae flank him. Hephaestus (on the left), wearing winged boots, raises his right hand, possibly in surprise, and looks back as he departs. He holds his ax in his left hand. Hermes does not appear, but Poseidon appears on the left of the scene, also departing and looking back, holding a trident.

Figure 3. Little-master lip cup, Phrynos Painter, ca. 575–525.[10] Zeus, sitting on a throne and holding a thunderbolt, gives birth to Athena from his head. Hephaestus leaves to the right, holding his ax in his left hand, looking back, and raising his right arm, possibly in surprise. He wears winged shoes, one of which overlaps with Zeus' bare left foot. No other figures appear on this side of the vase.

Figure 4. Amphora, Group E, ca. 575–525.[11] Zeus sits on a throne holding a thunderbolt, as Athena springs from his head. Eileithyiae flank them. To the left, Hephaestus wears winged boots, with feet pointing away as he looks back at the birth scene. He holds his ax over his right shoulder.

Birth of Athena vase scenes commenced in Athens in the sixth century amid renewed attention to the city's goddess on the Acropolis and with possible Corinthian connections,[12] perhaps with the encouragement of Pisistra-

---

9. Athens, Paris Louvre CA 616, Beazley 300499, *ABV* 58.122.

10. Athens, London BM B 424, Beazley 301068, *ABV* 168.

11. Basel, Antikenmuseum und Sammlung Ludwig BS 496, Beazley 213, *Metis* 5 (1990): 1–2, 68, fig. 7.

12. Shapiro 1989b: 33. It is notable that the earliest ceramic depiction of the birth of Athena is a pinax fragment of Corinthian clay, Acropolis 2578 (= *LIMC* 2 [1984]: 986, Athena 343), a dedication on the Athenian Acropolis, possibly by a Corinthian artist. Claudia Wagner (2001: 100) discusses the "peculiar idiosyncrasies" of this "singular piece in Corinthian vase painting" and presents several possible explanations. Discussing the inscription and

tus.[13] Brommer and Schefold have written of Hephaestus in myth and art, including in Birth of Athena scenes, but have not discussed the meaning of Hephaestus' winged shoes.[14]

In some scenes where he has struck Zeus' head, Hephaestus appears anxious to leave quickly, alarmed at the unexpected and strange sight of Athena's emergence, fully armored. Winged shoes naturally contribute to this haste; they help quicken the pace of the god who is naturally "slow" and "lame" (*Odyssey* 8.329–32). In general, gods and heroes in Greek art wear winged shoes as "symbols of nimbleness of their flight or the rapidity of their course."[15] In Hephaestus' case, such a depiction is logical, since he was summoned quickly to be the "midwife" for Athena's birth, becomes frightened at the outcome, and consequently runs away. He himself is a slow mover and is therefore the opposite of Hermes, who is the swiftest of the Olympians. It is almost as though these vase painters imply that Hephaestus flees as swiftly as Hermes or Perseus, for both of whom the winged shoe is an attribute.

Winged Shoes in Greek Art: The Priority of Perseus

Archaic Greek tradition associated wings with creativity.

> [i]mages of craftsmen, sometimes winged or wearing winged footwear, contribute to a popular tradition of demon-artists with magic powers, including wings, a common attribute of gods and heroes in Greek art. (Morris 1992, pp. 191–92)

In fact, a seventh-century relief pithos from Tenos containing one of the earliest plastic depictions of Athena's birth portrays all its figures with shoul-

---

its use as a dedication, Wachter (2001: 33) notes, "In fact, the discrepancy between the style and the alphabet suggests that it was produced for this purpose [dedication], either by a Corinthian working in Athens (and using Corinthian clay), or—which seems the more likely explanation to me—by a Corinthian in Corinth working for export to Athens."

13. Cf. Shapiro 1989a: 43. Shear (1978: 2–3) points out the striking chronological coincidence between Pisistratus and the "significant aggrandizement" of Athena's cult in Athens after 566/5.

14. Shapiro 1989a; Schefold 1992; Brommer 1961, 1978. While he does not comment on the winged shoes, Brommer (1978: 16, 152) does assert that Hephaestus is associated with boots—in that he wears them in some scenes (especially those when he is returning to Olympus)—and that, in myth (Hyginus *Fab.* 166), he created shoes for the gods, including a sandal of adamant that held Hera fast.

15. Gialouris 1953: 293.

der wings: Zeus, Athena, the two attendants, and a winged figure watching from above—a tableau which Morris calls "the most fantastic scene of crafts-manship in early Greek art."[16] Thus, Hephaestus' black-figure winged shoes might hearken back to an earlier tradition linking wings with art, including the Iliadic description of Achilles' Hephaestus-produced armor, which liter-ally allows the hero to fly (*Il.* 19.386).

Nicolaos Gialouris' study of πτερόεντα πέδιλα (winged sandals) shows that the earliest and most numerous scenes of characters in winged shoes (from the seventh and sixth centuries) are those of Perseus and the Gorgons:[17] Perseus in winged shoes on a metope of the Temple of Apollo at Thermon (ca. 625),[18] the wing-shoed Gorgon on a terra-cotta relief plaque from Syracuse (ca. 620),[19] and Perseus in winged shoes on an Attic black-figure louterion from Aegina by the Nessos Painter (ca. 615–600). To these, I add a proto-Attic Eleusis neck amphora portraying Perseus' feet inside white painted boots with petite wings (ca. 670);[20] a Cycladic relief amphora (ca. 660) showing Per-seus wearing winged shoes and decapitating Medusa;[21] and the Gorgon Painter's name vase (ca. 600–550), an early Attic black-figure dinos that in-cludes Perseus, Hermes, and the three Gorgons wearing identical winged shoes.[22] It thus seems clear that tradition gave winged shoes to Perseus and the Gorgons prior to Hermes.[23]

---

16. Morris 1992, p. 16; Figs. 13, 14a–e.
17. Gialouris 1953: 316, 319–20.
18. Athens, National Archaeological Museum 13401. See Woodward 1937: 27 and fig. 1a.
19. Payne 1971: 81, fig. 23E; Woodward 1937: 30, fig. 2. The early Thermon and Syracusan ex-amples hint that Attic winged shoes were based on Corinthian models.
20. Polyphemus Painter, Archaeological Museum of Eleusis 2630, Mylonas 1957: pl. 10. Mylo-nas notes, "[Perseus] is represented as taking a long stride and his winged *endromides* are indicated by a narrow ribbon of white painted around his boots and ending on top in a feather-like shape" (123). Although he includes Mylonas' picture of Perseus in winged shoes (ill. 149), Carpenter (1991: 256) does not include this scene in his list of winged boots as attributes of Perseus.
21. Louvre CA 795. This Cycladic relief amphora found in Boeotia also suggests that Perseus' winged boots were of extra-Attic origin.
22. Black-figure dinos, Athens, ca. 600-550, Louvre E 874, Beazley 300055.
23. Gialouris (1953) divides winged-shoe representations into "Ionian" and "Attic" types. He shows that after winged sandals on Perseus, Gorgons, and Hermes, artists later created winged *endromides* (traveling boots) of the "Ionic" type for "demons," Nike, nymphs, Har-pies, Boreads, and Paris (298–302). In the "Attic" type, winged shoes are found on Perseus, Gorgons, Hermes, Atalanta, Icarus, "demons," Ares, Eris, and Dionysus (302–8). In an "Attico-Ionian" style of winged boot, Gialouris catalogs Gorgons, Hermes, Apollo, Per-seus, and Boreas (308–11). Winged shoes are rare in Greek art of the fourth century BCE (311). Gialouris' catalog is not exhaustive; he does not include any of the four vases in which Hephaestus wears πτερόεντα πέδιλα, perhaps because their impressionistic gen-eral form, without incised detail, does not allow them to fit into one of his three styles. He

In Attic black-figure pottery, early examples of Hermes' winged shoes appear roughly a generation before the Birth of Athena scenes commence. Some early examples include an oinochoe from Vari by the Gorgon Painter (ca. 600–590)[24] and the Gorgon Painter's name vase (cited above). Works by the Gorgon Painter's contemporaries, the KX Painter and Sophilos, do not show Hermes with winged shoes, with the exception of Sophilos' Erskine dinos (ca. 600–550), where the tops of Hermes' winged shoes appear above the chariot in which he rides with Apollo.[25] He appears with winged shoes in a Judgment of Paris scene (ca. 575–525)[26] and on an Attic cup showing Hermes accompanying Perseus and Athena (ca. 575–525);[27] his winged shoes continue to appear throughout the history of black- and red-figure vase painting, though Hermes also often appears barefoot.[28]

Gialouris notes that neither Homer nor Hesiod mentions winged shoes — for any divinity — nor does the *Homeric Hymn to Hermes*.[29] The earliest literary

---

observes that none of Greece's Near Eastern neighbors represented figures wearing winged shoes before the sixth century; it is exclusively an ancient Greek creation: "les dieux ou génies chaussés de chaussures ailées sont une création purement grecque" (314–15). On Perseus' winged shoes, their religious and symbolic connotations and relation to Hermes, see Cursaru 2013.

24. Attica (Vari), ca. 600–590, Athens National Museum 19159, Beazley 300326, LIMC Hermes 230. This figure is mistakenly identified as Perseus in Kaltsas 2007, p. 198.

25. Athens, British Museum BM 1971.11–1.1, Beazley 350099.

26. Black figure hydria, close to the Painter of London B 76, Athens, ca. 575–525, Basel, Market, Munzen und Medaillen Auktionen 51 (1975) 118, Beazley 82, LIMC Hermes 454c; see also column amphora, Lydos and his group, Athens, ca. 575–525, Paris, Louvre C 10633, Beazley 310279, LIMC Hermes 455c; and black-figure neck amphora: Judgment of Paris, Antimenes, ca. 550–500, Florence Mus. Arch. 3856, Beazley 320192, LIMC Hermes 456c.

27. C Painter, Athens, ca. 575–525, London, BM B380, Beazley 300468, ABV 5, 9, LIMC Hermes 488a. Siebert 1990, p. 327: "Hermes, caduceus at an angle, left arm bent at the elbow, with large strides follows Perseus, who is placed at the front of the fugitives." Brijder 1983 attributes this cup to his Cassandra Painter.

28. Siebert (1990: 383–84) has collected, by subject, all the instances in which Hermes appears in wingless shoes, barefoot, and with and without winged shoes. He attempts to explain Hermes' frequent barefootedness: "The winged shoes, which he wears as boots or sandals, form part of the normal equipment of Hermes, and so one can well ask why, more often than one might think, he gives them up for wingless footwear or to go barefoot. In the series of Italiot vases his bare feet are part and parcel of his body's nudity. Otherwise it does not seem that the customs of the workshop or the time period can help to explain the choice of the painters. Certain subjects and contexts are more determinant here." Siebert discusses the lack of shoes in intimate scenes and in cultic scenes, where swiftness is not necessary, and in the combat scenes where Hermes is a fighter and does not use magical means to win. He does not, however, discuss the assemblies and company of the gods in this regard, though these are the most frequent scenes in which Hermes appears (and with which the present analysis is most concerned). On the many meanings of Hermes' (unwinged) footwear in Homeric epic, see Cursaru 2012.

29. Gialouris 1953: 316.

reference to winged shoes is, in fact, to Perseus' πτερόεντα πέδιλα that appear on a shield that Hephaestus creates, coinciding chronologically with the earliest pictorial representations of Perseus in this footwear (from the seventh and sixth centuries).[30] Why might artists have painted Hephaestus wearing the winged boots that had been traditionally associated with Perseus and the Gorgons and that were just becoming part of Hermes' iconography? Since depictions of Perseus in winged shoes predate or, as in the case of the C Painter, are contemporary with similar shoes for Hermes, it is likely that at least a generation of artists was accustomed to portraying the slayer of the Gorgon in his traditional footwear. When there was an impetus for portraying a similar myth, it is likely that they adapted the pattern they had used until that time.

The Perseus myth and that of the birth of Athena are structurally similar. I suggest that the following narrative parallels between the stories influenced the artists to give "Perseus' shoes" to Hephaestus in the four vases previously cited. In their respective myths, both Perseus and Hephaestus, armed with sharp weapons (sword, ax) are compelled to approach characters of great power (Medusa, Zeus), each of whom displays images of their destructive capability (snake hair, thunderbolt). Each approaching character strikes at the head of the dangerous figure, and the result of the blow is the birth of a new and unusual character from the head (Pegasus, Athena). The weapon wielder then flees. Similar stories may give artists the opportunity to produce similar images.

I propose that when Attic artists were called on to depict the myth of Athena's birth in the second quarter of the sixth century, they added wings to Hephaestus' shoes because they were working in a tradition that depicted Perseus in a similar role. The earliest representations of Perseus with winged shoes depict that hero fleeing after he has struck Medusa (Eleusis amphora,

---

30. Ps.-Hes. *Scutum* 216–17, of Perseus: τὼς γάρ μιν παλάμαις τεῦξεν κλυτὸς Ἀμφιγυήεις, / χρύσεον· ἀμφὶ δὲ ποσσὶν ἔχεν πτερόεντα πέδιλα (Thus did the renowned Lame One fashion him [Perseus] with his hands, / golden; and he had winged shoes about his feet). Cf. Most 2006: lviii: "The *Shield* is generally dated to sometime between the end of the 7th and the first half of the 6th century BC." The scholiast to Apollonius of Rhodes' *Argonautica* 4.1515 cites the second book of the Athenian Pherecydes' ΙΣΤΟΡΙΩΝ (ca. first half of the fifth century) regarding Perseus' winged shoes, borrowed from and returned to the nymphs: τὰς Νύμφας, αἳ ἔχουσι τὴν Ἄιδος κυνέην καὶ τὰ πέδιλα τὰ ὑπόπτερα καὶ τὴν κίβισιν . . . ἱστορεῖ Φερεκύδης ἐν τῇ δευτέρᾳ (the Nymphs, who held Hades' helmet and the winged sandals and the sack . . . Pherecydes tells the story in the second book) (*FGRHist* I, 11; Jacoby 1947; Gialouris 1953: 316–17).

Thermon metope, and Aeginetan krater fragment). In the Birth of Athena scenes in which Hephaestus wears winged shoes, the god also flees after having struck Zeus. Although there are no exact parallels of pose, the structural parallels between the stories make it likely, I think, that black-figure Attic artists in the mid-sixth century BCE were influenced by the "hit-and-run" tradition of the Perseus/Medusa myth when portraying Hephaestus in the Birth of Athena scenes and so assigned winged shoes to Hephaestus. Thus artistic tradition transfers Perseus' πτερόεντα πέδιλα to Hephaestus for a short time in midcentury, before they become Hermes' reliable identifying attribute beginning in the fifth century.[31]

Hermes as Ax Wielder at the Birth of Athena

Several literary variants of the myth represent Hermes wielding the ax at Athena's birth. The first-century BCE Epicurean Philodemus—making the point, in his *On Piety* (*Peri Eusebeias*), that the Greeks assumed that their gods were flesh and blood—writes that Hephaestus struck Zeus' head at the birth of Athena. But the same author also provides some variants, including one in which Hermes wielded the ax.

τὴν κεφ(αλὴ)ν ὑ(π)ὸ Ἡφαίστου (δ)ιαιρεῖται, κατὰ (δὲ τ)ὸν Εὔμολπ(ον) . . .
ὑπὸ Παλαμάο[ι](ν)ος· ἔνιοι δ᾽ ὑφ᾽ Ἑρμοῦς παραδεδώκασι(ν). καὶ τῶν
ἀρχαίων τινὲς δημιουργῶν τοῦτον παρεσ(τῶ)τα τῷ Διὶ πο(οῦσι) πέλεκυν
ἔχον(τα), καθάπερ ἐν τῷ τῆ(ς) Χαλκιοίκου. Καὶ τὸν [ο]μηρὸν[32] (δ)ὲ κατὰ
πολλοὺς (διη)ρέθη ἵ(ν᾽ ἐ)ν αὐτῷ τρέφοι τὸν Διόνυσον· καὶ τὸ κεφάλαιον
σαρκίνους (ὑ)ποτί(θ)ενται το(ὺς / θεούς.

[[Zeus] has his head split open by Hephaestus, but according to Eumolpus . . . by Palamaon. And some pass on a tradition [that the head was split open] by

---

31. Hephaestus also appears with winged shoes on an hydria attributed to Lysippides, Athens, ca. 550–500, London BM 302, Beazley 30222, *ABV* 261.40, where the gods Hermes and Hephaestus (both in winged shoes) frame a banquet scene. Beazley (1986: 78) calls this "a unique representation, and not easily explained" and sees Hephaestus as "overcome by the festal splendour" of Dionysus' party, to which he has arrived late. Robertson (1950: 25n9) interprets the scene as "surely the party at which Dionysos made Hephaistos drunk in order to get him back to Olympos." Hedreen (1992: 19–22) analyzes this scene at some length, detailing the elements that tie it to Naxos and Hephaestus' return to Olympus. None of these works discusses Hephaestus' shoes.
32. For the corrected reading (μηρὸν rather than ὅμηρον), see Bücheler 1865: 520–21.

Hermes. *And some archaic artists depict him [Hermes] standing beside Zeus holding an axe,* for example, as in the image in the Bronze House [in Sparta]; and according to many people he was cut open in respect to his thigh in order that he might nourish Dionysus in it. And the main point is that they assume that the gods are made of flesh and blood.] (*Peri Eusebeias* 59)[33]

Philodemus' statement reflects the observations of others who attest to traditions that Hermes or someone else wielded an ax to bring about Athena's birth. Euripides names Prometheus as helping at the birth of Athena, but not specifically as an ax wielder (*Ion* 455). Apollodorus (*Bibliotheca* 1.3.6) follows Euripides, saying that Prometheus "or, as others say, Hephaestus" (ἢ καθάπερ ἄλλοι λέγουσιν Ἡφαίστου) split Zeus' head. Two scholiasts to Pindar's *Olympian* 7.66 mention Prometheus, Palamaon, and Hermes in this role and also relate another version in which the goddess was born from a cloud and brought to light by a blow from Zeus.[34]

Such sources have influenced at least one modern scholar to accept that Hermes played such a role in the artistic program of the sixth-century "Bronze House" of Athena at Sparta. No fragments of this temple have come to light, however, and although Pausanias does say that the "birth of Athena" appeared on this temple, he does not mention Hermes.[35] It is possible, of

---

33. Text from Gomperz 1866: 31.
34. Euripides *Ion* 455: ἐμὰν Ἀθάναν, ἱκετεύω, Προμηθεῖ Τιτᾶνι λοχευθεῖσαν κατ' ἀκροτάτας κορυφᾶς Διός . . . (I beg you, my Athena, brought to birth from the peak of Zeus' head by Prometheus the Titan . . .). Lee (1997: 209–10) suggests that the tradition of Prometheus as Zeus' midwife could have arisen from "Ion's mention of 'prudence' (προμηθίας) in 448, and more generally to stress the foresight of the gods and the role of wisdom in their birth." This is more reasonable than Wilamowitz's unfounded speculation (1926: 107) that Prometheus' role as Athena's midwife came from "an older Attic saga." Cf. scholiast to Pindar *Olympian* 7.66a: "In the works of Mousaius, Palamaon is said to have struck the head of Zeus, when he bore Athena. And some say Prometheus; and Sosibius [third century] says it was Hermes; and Aristocles says that the goddess was hidden in a cloud, and that Zeus, having struck the cloud brought the goddess to light"; 7.66b: "Some say that Palamaon struck Zeus' head when Athena was born; and others say Hermes, and others Prometheus; and Aristocles locates the birth of Athena in Crete. For he says that the goddess was hidden in a cloud, and that Zeus, having struck the cloud brought her to light." A scholiast to Plato's *Timaeus* 23e preserves a version in which Hephaestus makes a sexual request—namely, that Zeus promise to allow him τῇ γεννωμένῃ συνελθεῖν εἰς εὐνήν—a condition of his help in Athena's birth.
    Little is known of Palamaon: he is mentioned as the father of Daedalus (Pausanias 9.3.2) and of Pallas (Philodemus *Peri Eusebias* 33a; Gomperz 1866: 6); his name implies that he was "skillful with his hands" (παλάμη; cf. Hes. *Theog.* 933: ἐκ πάντων παλάμῃσι κεκασμένον Οὐρανιώνων). His name might have been an early epithet for Hephaestus (perhaps reflected in Ps.-Hes. *Scutum* 219: παλάμαις); he might even have been his doppelgänger: see *RE* 18 (1949): 2499–2500, s.v. "Palamaon" (Willi Göber).
35. Delcourt 1957: 140: "Hermès et Prométhée alternent avec Hephaistos comme accoucheurs

course, that there was a local Spartan version of the story and that there were other epichoric variants. In an Attic context (our focus here), Hephaestus' presence at Athena's birth strengthens the connection between these two craftsmen's divinities, whose worship coalesced in the fifth-century temple of Hephaestus and Athena on the Agora hill.

Interestingly, in iconographic representations of Athena's birth, it is the exclusive job of Hephaestus to strike Zeus' head to release his daughter—no other character in Greek art ever wields an ax in this scene.[36] How do we explain the literary tradition that Hermes fulfilled his brother's obligation in scenes that, according to Philodemus, "some archaic artists" created (especially since we cannot know precisely what he means by ἀρχαίων)? It is possible that iconographic representations of Hermes in this role have been lost or not yet discovered. A new discovery could validate this variant on the traditional Birth of Athena scenes. To rationalize the appearance of the other gods in this role, Norman O. Brown suggests that Hermes, Hephaestus, and Prometheus, as variations of the "culture-hero type of god," would each be appropriate to help bring about the appearance of the goddess of crafts and daughter of Metis.[37] This theory can help to account for the literary traditions but does not explain why Hephaestus is the only one in Greek art (aside from the traditional Eileithyiae) depicted as Zeus' "midwife."

I suggest that ancient notions that Hermes held an ax in archaic representations of Athena's birth arose from mistaken observations of sixth-century black-figure vase paintings, some of which portray Hephaestus wearing the winged boots that later became associated primarily with Hermes. Post-archaic ancient observers might have mistaken painted depictions of a wing-shoed Hephaestus for Hermes in such scenes, because winged footgear came

---

de Zeus . . . La présence d'Hermès à côté de Zeus dans un monument aussi ancien que le Temple de Bronze de Sparte (milieu du VIe s.) indique un tradition vénérable." See also Cook 1940: 661n6: "The allusion is very possibly to the work of Gitiadas (Pausanias 3.17.2)." Pausanias' account of the subjects of the "Bronze House" at Sparta simply includes "the birth of Athena" as a subject, without giving any specifics. He does, however, mention that the bronze carries a representation of nymphs giving winged shoes to Perseus: "On the bronze are wrought in relief many of the labours of Heracles and many of the voluntary exploits he successfully carried out, besides the rape of the daughters of Leucippus and other achievements of the sons of Tyndareus. There is also Hephaestus releasing his mother from the fetters. The legend about this I have already related in my history of Attica. There are also represented nymphs bestowing upon Perseus, who is starting on his enterprise against Medusa in Libya, a cap and the shoes by which he was to be carried through the air. There are also wrought the birth of Athena, Amphitrite, and Poseidon, the largest figures, and those which I thought the best worth seeing" (3.17.3, trans. Jones 1918).

36. Shapiro 1989b: 39.
37. Brown 1952: 130–43, esp. 137–39.

to be a central attribute of Hermes from the middle of the sixth century.[38] These postarchaic viewers, accustomed to identifying Hermes by his winged shoes, could easily have mistakenly observed Hephaestus so shod as Hermes. Furthermore, since Hermes, in his winged shoes, is sometimes present in artistic representations of the birth of Athena, the mistake could be reinforced.[39] Finally, confusion could have arisen due to the fact that Hermes sometimes appears in the same pose as the fleeing Hephaestus: departing, looking back, holding a long shaft in one hand and raising his other arm.[40] It is easy to imagine, therefore, that a viewer of later antiquity, seeing an obvious Birth of Athena scene on a vase, might identify as Hermes a bearded figure with winged shoes who carries what seems to be a herald's wand—not looking closely enough to distinguish between Hephaestus' ax and Hermes' caduceus.

Both Hermes and Hephaestus appear in sixth-century vase painting in poses of fleeing and looking back, often with the same gestures, including a raised hand (see Hephaestus in figs. 1–3). Such similar poses could have led to a careless observer's mistake. It is a characteristic of Hephaestus in such scenes to flee and look back, even when he is not wearing the winged shoes, as in a mid-sixth-century Attic amphora (from Vulci) that shows the birth of Athena: Hephaestus (with inscribed name) flees, holding a slender shaft, presumably his ax, the top of which seems not to have been painted (ca. 575–525).[41]

---

38. Siebert 1990: 383.
39. Some examples of Hermes with winged shoes at the birth of Athena in black-figure vase painting include a hydria by the Antimenes Painter (ca. 550–500,Würzburg 309, Beazley 320038, *ABV* 268.28 [= *LIMC* Hermes 684/Athena 371]), an amphora by the Swing Painter (ca. 575–525, Geneva Musée d'Art et d'Histoire MF 155, Beazley 5696, *Para.* 130.18, *CVA* 2, pl. 49.1–3 [= *LIMC* Eileithyia 35b/Hermes 687), a fragment of a black-figure vase by the Painter of Vatican 342, from Locri (ca. 525–475, Reggio Calabria Museo Nazionale 4018, Beazley 351352, *Para* 187.4 [= *LIMC* Athena 366]; and an amphora by the Affecter (ca. 550–500, Florence, Museo Archeologico 92167, Beazley 301363 [= *LIMC* Eileithyia 50]; see Shapiro 1989b).
40. For an explication of how "later viewers" in antiquity could mistake figures in Greek art due to their own contemporary iconographic experience, see Gais 1978; Gais points out that observers of art see what they expect to see. The so-called river gods at the corners of the east pediment of Olympia's fifth-century Zeus temple and the west pediment of the Parthenon were wrongly identified as such by viewers of Pausanias' time, who were used to seeing reclining figures as river gods in Hellenistic and Roman depictions and did not know that rivers were not depicted in this way in the classical period.
41. See above, note 2. Attic black-figure amphora, Group E, Vulci, ca. 560–540, London, BM B 147, Beazley 310304, *ABV* 135, 44. Cf. Lenormant and de Witte 1844–61, Plate LXV-a. One of our four depictions of winged-shoe Hephaestus at the Birth of Athena (Fig. 4) is also the product of Group E, showing that even in the same workshop the god may appear with or without winged shoes.

Hermes (in winged boots) often shares the pose of the fleeing Hephaestus, departing as he looks back and raises one arm,[42] while holding the shaft of his *kerykeion* with the other. An amphora by the Affecter, with a seated Zeus about to give birth to Athena, shows Hermes in this pose on both sides (ca. 550–500).[43] Elsewhere in sixth-century black-figure scenes, Hermes often adopts this pose in the presence of other gods, including on an oinochoe by the Amasis Painter that shows him with Athena (ca. 575–525; fig. 5);[44] on the François vase, which shows him with Thetis (ca. 570);[45] on a cup by the C Painter that shows him with Athena and Perseus (ca. 575–525);[46] and on an amphora attributed to the Affecter that shows him with Dionysus (ca. 530).[47] That Hermes appears in these scenes with other gods (several of whom are seated), in the same or similar pose that Hephaestus assumes when he departs from the Birth of Athena scenes, and holding the shaft of his *kerykeion* may perhaps explain how later viewers might have confused the two in some Birth of Athena scenes, especially when Hephaestus, with his axe, flees while wearing winged shoes and makes the same gesture with his arm.

Conclusion

This essay suggests that we should consider some sixth-century depictions

---

42. According to Siebert, Hermes displays the raised hand gesture 120 times, 91 of which are on black-figure vase paintings. He makes this gesture most often in the company of gods and divine assemblies (49 times) and in depictions of the labors of Heracles (34 times) and the ransom of Hector (5 of 8 cataloged representations; Siebert 1990: 382).
43. Florence, Museo Archeologico 92167, Beazley 301363, Shapiro 1989b: pl. II, figs. 3–4. On the subject of this vase as the birth of Athena, see Shapiro 1989b: 36–37; Mommsen 1975: 65–66; Cook 1940: 665–66.
44. Athens, ca. 540–530, Paris, Louvre F 30, Beazley 310456, *ABV* 152.29 (= *LIMC* Hermes 553).
45. Volute crater, Chiusi, Ergotimos and Kleitias, Athens, ca. 570, Florence, Museo Archeologico 4209, Beazley 300000, *ABV* 76.1 (= *LIMC* Hermes 572).
46. On this vase (Beazley 300468), see above, n. 26.
47. Amphora B, Affecter, Athens, ca. 530, Boston Museum of Fine Arts 01.8053, Beazley 301365, *ABV* 246.72 (= *LIMC* Hermes 658b). Another representation of Hermes (without shoes) in the same pose in Attic black-figure art includes an amphora by the Amasis Painter that shows him with Apollo (ca. 550–500, Basel, Antikensammlung Ludwig 20, Beazley 350465, *Para* 65 [= *LIMC* Hermes 709]). The Affecter favored this pose of Hermes with raised hand in his depictions, including those with a seated Zeus: Attic black-figure amphora, Vulci, ca. 550–500, London BM B 149, Beazley 301348, *ABV* 245.60 (= *LIMC* Hermes 721); Attic black-figure amphora, Vulci, ca. 550–500, Vatican Museum Greg. Etr. 338, Beazley 301312, *ABV* 241.24 (= *LIMC* Hermes 723e); Attic black-figure amphora with seated Hera, ca. 550–500,Tarquinia National Museum 625, Beazley 301358, *ABV* 245.65 (= *LIMC* Hermes 729a); Attic black-figure amphora with Ares, Orvieto, ca. 550–500, New York Metropolitan Museum 07.286.75, Beazley 301339, *ABV* 244.51 (= *LIMC* Hermes 765a).

of Hephaestus in winged shoes at the birth of Athena in relation to Perseus and Hermes, the mythic figures who more commonly wore such footwear. Hephaestus' iconographic similarity to Perseus probably stems from the latter's act of striking Medusa and fleeing the scene of the blow, which structurally resembles Hephaestus' action of striking and fleeing from Zeus' unusual parturition. Later viewers who knew winged shoes as Hermes' attribute may have misunderstood the figure of Hephaestus in the scenes in which that god wears such shoes, and they may have concluded that Hermes (rather than Hephaestus) had struck Zeus' head to cause Athena's birth. Similar poses of the two gods in sixth-century art could have led to further confusion between them.

In his 1978 study of Hephaestus in Greek art, Frank Brommer minimized the relationship between Hermes and Hephaestus, saying that aside from the fact that both were members of the Olympian family, Hermes and Hephaestus were not close.[48] This observation remains true. The alternate literary tradition that Hermes took the task of "midwife" at Athena's birth was based on misunderstood evidence from archaic artists and has led to an assumption that such scenes actually existed. However, in the absence of positive evidence, we can conclude that ancient literary references to Hermes wielding the ax in archaic representations of the birth do not represent an artistic reality. It is more likely that such claims are based on later observations of archaic vases on which Hephaestus wears the winged shoes that were so closely associated with Hermes. The smith god, often characterized by his fleeing stance after Athena's birth, resembles some poses of Hermes in other contexts, making haste in winged shoes, carrying a staff, and looking back with an upraised arm. The πτερόεντα πέδιλα that Hephaestus seems to have inherited from Perseus may have caused some ancient observers to confuse him with Hermes and may have given rise to a literary version of the Birth of Athena scenes that the artistic tradition did not share: that Hermes struck Zeus' head to help with his sister's birth.[49]

---

48. Brommer 1978: 122: "Hermes seems, apart from the fact that also he belongs to the twelve Gods, not to stand in any closer relationship with Hephaistos. . . . From Zeus Hermes received a scepter manufactured by Hephaistos."

49. I am grateful to the following people for their support and encouragement on this project: Dimitris Agrafiotis, Barbara Barletta, Nancy Bookidis, Bob Bridges, Christina Clark, Sylvian Fachard, Nancy Felson, Stephen Fineberg, Edith Foster, Andrea Guzzetti, Bill Hutton, Nigel Kennell, Theo Kopetonsky, Don Lateiner, Gerald Lalonde, Nikolaos Manias, Floyd McCoy, John Oakley, Kirk Ormand, David Romano, Efi Sakellarakis, H. Alan Shapiro, and John Younger. I warmly thank Judith R. Levine for her beautiful line drawings and much more.

Fig. 1. Tyrrhenian amphora, Kyllenios Painter, Athens, ca. 575–525. Berlin-Charlottenburg F 1704. Beazley 310014, ABV 96.14; cf. Boardman 2001: 50, fig. 59. (Line drawing by Judith Levine.)

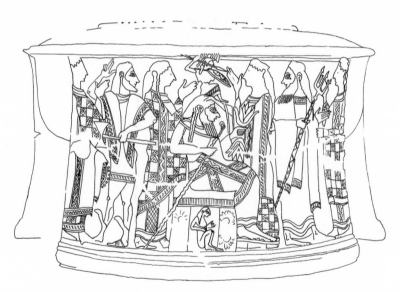

Fig. 2. Tripod pyxis, C Painter, ca. 575–525. Paris Louvre CA 616. Beazley 300499, ABV 58.122. (Line drawing by Judith Levine.)

Fig. 3. Lip cup, Phrynos, Athens, ca. 575–525. London BM B 424. Beazley 301068, ABV 168. (Line drawing by Judith Levine.)

Fig. 4. Amphora, Group E, Athens, ca. 575–525. Basel, Antikenmuseum und Sammlung Ludwig BS496. Beazley 213, Metis 5 (1990): 1–2, 68, fig. 7. (Line drawing by Judith Levine.)

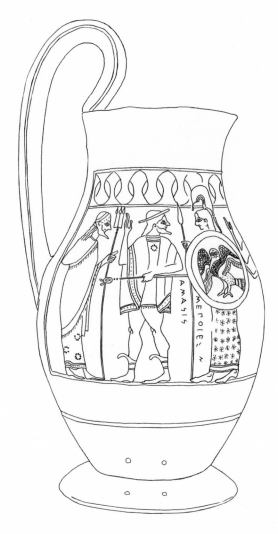

Fig. 5. Oinochoe, Amasis Painter, Athens, ca. 575–525. Louvre F 30. Beazley 310456, ABV 152.29 (= LIMC Hermes 553). (Line drawing by Judith Levine.)

Works Cited

Arafat, K. W. 1990. *Classical Zeus: A Study in Art and Literature.* Oxford: Clarendon.

Beazley, J. 1986. *The Development of Attic Black-Figure.* Berkeley: University of California Press.

Boardman, J. 2001. *The History of Greek Vases: Potters, Painters and Pictures.* London: Thames and Hudson.

Brijder, H. A. G. 1983. *Siana Cups I and Komast Cups.* Amsterdam: Allard Pierson Museum.

Brommer, F. 1961. "Die Geburt der Athena." *Jahrbuch des Römisch-Germanischen Zentralmuseums Mainz* 8: 66–83.

Brommer, F. 1978. *Hephaistos: der Schmiedegott in der antiken Kunst.* Mainz: von Zabern.

Brown, N. O. 1952. "The Birth of Athena." *TAPA* 83: 130–43.

Bücheler, F. 1865. "Philodemos ΠΕΡΙ ΕΥΣΕΒΕΙΑΣ." *Neue Jahrbücher für Philologie und Pädagogik* 91: 513–41.

Burow, J. 1989. *Der Antimenesmaler.* Kerameus 7. Mainz: von Zabern.

Carpenter, T. 1991. *Art and Myth in Ancient Greece.* London: Thames and Hudson.

Cook, A. B. 1940. *Zeus.* Vol. 3, *A Study in Ancient Religion.* Cambridge: Cambridge University Press.

Cursaru, G. 2012. "Les sandales d' Hermès." Pt. 1, "Les Sandales d'Hermès, I: Les ΚΑΛΑ ΠΕΔΙΛΑ Homériques d' Hermès." *RFIC* 140: 20–61.

Cursaru, G. 2013. "Les sandales ailées (πτερόεντα πέδιλα) de Persée." *Gaia* 16: 95–112.

Delcourt, M. 1957. *Héphaistos ou la Légende du Magicien.* Paris: Les Belles Lettres.

Fineberg, S. 2009. "Hephaestus on Foot in the Ceramicus." *TAPA* 139: 275–324.

Gais, R. M. 1978. "Some Problems of River-God Iconography." *AJA* 82: 355–70.

Gialouris, N. 1953. "ΠΤΕΡΟΝΕΝΤΑ ΠΕΔΙΛΑ." *BCH* 77: 293–321.

Gomperz, T. 1866. *Herkulanische Studien Zweites Heft, Philodem Über Frömmigkeit.* Leipzig: B. G. Teubner.

Hedreen, G. 1992. *Silens in Attic Black-Figure Vase-Painting: Myth and Performance.* Ann Arbor: University of Michigan Press.

Henrichs, A. 1975. "Philodems 'De Pietate' als mythographische Quelle." *Cronache ercolanesi* 5: 5–38.

Jacoby, F. 1947. "The First Athenian Prose Writer." *Mnemosyne* 13: 13–64.

Jones, W. H. S. 1918. *Pausanias, Description of Greece.* London: W. Heinemann.

Kaltsas, N. 2007. *The National Archaeological Museum.* Athens: Olkos.

Lee, K. H. 1997. *Euripides, Ion.* Warminster: Aris and Phillips.

Lenormant, C., and de Witte, J. 1844–61. *Élite des monuments céramographiques: Matériaux pour l'histoire des religions et des moeurs de l'antiquité 1.* Paris: Leleux.

Mannack, T. 2001. *The Late Mannerists in Athenian Vase-Painting.* Oxford: Oxford University Press.

Mommsen, H. 1975. *Der Affecter*. Mainz: von Zabern.

Morris, S. P. 1992. *Daidalos and the Origins of Greek Art*. Princeton: Princeton University Press.

Most, G. 2006. *Hesiod, Theogony, Works and Days, Testimonia*. Cambridge, MA: Harvard University Press.

Mylonas, G. 1957. *Ο Πρωτοαττικός Αμφορεύς της Ελευσίνος*. Athens: Archaeological Society at Athens.

Papastamos, D. 1970. *Melische Amphoren*. Münster: Aschendorff.

Payne, H. 1971. *Necrocorinthia: A Study of Corinthian Art in the Archaic Period*. College Park, MA: McGrath.

Pfuhl, E. 1923. *Malerei und Zeichnung Der Griechen*. Vol. 3. Munich: F. Bruckmann.

Robertson, M. 1950. "The Origins of the Berlin Painter." *JHS* 70: 23–34.

Schefold, K. 1992. *Gods and Heroes in Late Archaic Greek Art*. Trans. A. Griffiths. Cambridge: Cambridge University Press.

Shapiro, H. A. 1989a. *Art and Cult under the Tyrants in Athens*. Mainz: von Zabern.

Shapiro, H. A. 1989b. "Poseidon and the Tuna." *AC* 58: 32–43.

Shear, T. L., Jr. 1978. "Tyrants and Buildings in Archaic Athens." In W. A. P. Childs, ed., *Athens Comes of Age: From Solon to Salamis*, 1–19. Princeton: Archaeological Institute of America.

Siebert, G. 1990. "Hermes." In *Lexicon Iconographicum Mythologiae Classicae*, V.1: 285–387. Zürich: Artemis.

Wachter, R. 2001. *Non-Attic Greek Vase Inscriptions*. Oxford: Oxford University Press.

Wagner, Claudia. 2001. "The Worship of Athena on the Athenian Acropolis." In S. Deacy and A. Villing, eds., *Athena in the Classical World*, 95–104. Leiden: Brill.

Wilamowitz-Moellendorff, U. von. 1926. *Euripides, Ion*. Berlin: Weidmann.

Woodward, J. M. 1937. *Perseus: A Study in Greek Art and Legend*. Cambridge: Cambridge University Press.

CHAPTER 18

From Papyrus to Peppercorns

The Tradition of Significant Objects in the Alexander Romance

Brad L. Cook

However many extraordinary deeds were done and whatever far lands were reached by Alexander the Great, the legendary Alexander always outperformed and outtraveled his historical self. But when the legendary Alexander's world turned modern, as marked in 1467 by Vasco da Lucena's revival of the historical Alexander at the expense of the Romance,[1] the glory of the Alexander Romance was quickly eclipsed, and the Romance has lain in a sort of scholarly never-studied land over the centuries. Today, with cultural studies and the literature of the whole world within our ken, the once-upon-a-time almost global popularity of the Alexander Romance calls for particular study.[2] In this environment, instead of labeling the flexibility of the Romance to move through languages, cultures, and time as a characteristic of an unstable, subliterary text, lacking a defining narrative, we should study the Alexander Romance as an "open," adaptable text. David Konstan has opened a new vista on the Romance by writing of the "cunning of the open text," examining how the openness of the text reveals the ingenuity of Alexander.[3] My goal is to show how the text's openness calls forth the ingenuity of the

---

1. See the prefatory remarks in his French version of Quintus Curtius' Life of Alexander; the preface is printed in Bossuat 1946: 210–15, esp. 213 (for the preface and selected passages in modernized French, see Collet 1995: 565–68); cf. McKendrick 1996: 16–17.
2. On the many languages and versions of the Romance, see Zuwiyya 2011; Stoneman 2008; Ross 1988; Cary 1956.
3. Konstan 1998, followed by Hägg 2012: 99.

context, by which I mean the writers or redactors of different versions, languages, and eras. To reveal the ways in which these different redactors capitalized on the text's openness as they adjusted, altered, and enhanced the Romance, I will focus on their use of "significant" objects. By examining such objects—which serve as "communicative social artifacts," as Don Lateiner has shown for other texts[4]—I will put on display the ingenuity of the redactors of the Alexander Romance and how they took advantage of the adaptability of this open text to overcome multilingual, transcultural, era-bridging challenges worthy of Alexander, historical or legendary.

Three examples of the use of significant objects illustrate well the different methods employed by redactors as they adjusted, translated, and enhanced the Alexander Romance through the ages and from one language and culture to another. The three examples appear during the accounts of (1) Alexander's conception, when the Egyptian Nectanebus sends a dream to Philip to persuade him that Olympias has been made pregnant by the god Ammon (rather than the disguised Nectanebus); (2) the siege of Tyre, when a dream comes to Alexander foretelling the defeat of Tyre; and (3) a prebattle exchange of letters between Darius and Alexander. I will here examine these episodes in the Greek redactions from the fourth to the seventeenth century,[5] then turn to the fourth-century Latin version of Julius Valerius, the tenth-century Latin version by the archpriest Leo, and the three so-called J1, J2, and J3 (or "I" for "Interpolation") redactions that developed from Leo's version; of the many other ancient and medieval versions, only a few can be briefly considered here.[6] These three episodes employ the following significant objects in the earliest Greek version: (1) Egyptian papyrus and a signet ring engraved with a lion, the sun, and a spear; (2) a ball of cheese; and (3) a whip, a ball, and a box of gold—all of which will be variously retained, adjusted, and supplemented.

The first example appears, significantly, when Alexander is engendered. His father in the Romance is not Philip or even Zeus but Nectanebus, who was, in real life, the last pharaoh of Egypt, driven from power in 342 by the

4.   Lateiner 1995: 17.
5.   Scholars speak of five or more Greek recensions, some extant in one manuscript: α (3rd cent. CE), β (5th cent.), λ (8th cent.), ε (8th/9th cent.), and γ (9th cent.). There are also the metrical Byzantine version (1388), the late Byzantine prose version (15th cent.), the *Rimada* (1529), and the *Phyllada* (17th cent.). See the editions in the TLG. See Hägg 2012: 119–34 for a detailed summary of recension α.
6.   See Hägg 2012: 399–401 for bibliography; Ross 1988. Cf. Stoneman 2008: 230–54; Zuwiyya 2011.

Persians. In the Alexander Romance, this fantastic Nectanebus is not merely a royal refugee but a magician, who uses his powers to seduce Olympias into thinking that the god Ammon desires to have a child by her. After working his magic on Olympias, he realizes that Philip also needs to be persuaded that a god has visited his wife, so he sends a hawk to Philip with a dream. In the dream, Philip sees "Ammon" lie with Olympias then rise and say, "In your womb, you carry my child."

1.8.2. Ὑπενόησε δὲ καὶ τὴν φύσιν αὐτῆς Νειλώᾳ βίβλῳ καταρράπτειν αὐτὸν καὶ σφραγίζειν δακτυλίῳ χρυσῷ ἐν λίθῳ γλυφὴν ἔχοντι κεφαλὴν λέοντος, ἡλίου κράτος καὶ δοράτιον·... 3. Ταῦτα ἰδὼν ἀνίσταται καὶ μεταπεμψάμενος ὀνειροπόλον διηγεῖται τὸν χρησμόν. ὁ δέ φησι· Βασιλεῦ καθὼς ἐθεάσω γέγονεν ἔγκυος Ὀλυμπιάς, πλὴν ὑπὸ θεοῦ. τὸ γὰρ σφραγίζειν τινὰ τὴν φύσιν αὐτῆς πίστεως γέμει 4. οὐδεὶς γὰρ κενὸν ἀγγεῖον σφραγίζει, ἀλλὰ μεστόν. ἐπειδὴ δὲ βίβλῳ καταρραφεῖσα ἦν ἡ φύσις, Αἰγυπτία ἐστὶν ἡ σπορά· οὐδαμοῦ γὰρ βίβλος γεννᾶται εἰ μὴ ἐν Αἰγύπτῳ· πλὴν οὐ ταπεινή, ἀλλὰ λαμπρὰ ἡ τύχη καὶ ἔνδοξος καὶ ἐπίσημος διὰ τὸν χρυσοῦν δακτύλιον. 5. τί γὰρ χρυσοῦ ἐνδοξότερον, δι' οὗ καὶ θεοὶ προσκυνοῦνται; ὁ δὲ ἥλιος ὁ τῆς γλυφῆς, κεφαλὴ λέοντος καὶ δοράτιον λόγον ἔχει τοιοῦτον· ὁ γὰρ γεννώμενος μέχρι τῆς ἀνατολῆς φθάσει ὥσπερ λέων, δορυαλώτους τὰς πόλεις ποιούμενος.

[1.8.2. And he [Philip] thought that [the god] stitched up her "nature" [vulva] with Nilotic papyrus and sealed it with a gold ring that had a stone engraved with the head of a lion, the force [rays] of the sun, and a spear.... 3. Having seen these things, he arose, and having sent for a dream interpreter, he explains the oracle. And he says, "King, just as you saw, Olympias has become pregnant, and that by a god. For the act of someone sealing her 'nature' marks a guarantee, for no one seals an empty vessel, but a full one. And since her 'nature' was sewed up with papyrus, the seed is Egyptian, for papyrus grows nowhere except in Egypt. Moreover, this is no foul fortune but glorious and honorable and noteworthy, because of the gold ring. 5. For what is more honorable than gold, with which even gods are worshiped? And the sun in the engraving, the head of the lion, and the spear have the following significance: the one begotten will go to the east like a lion, taking the cities captive by the spear."] (rec. α, 1.8.2–5)[7]

---

7. Translations throughout this essay are the author's.

Nectanebus is ingenious. What he has said and done in the dream are not false, and the significant objects help disguise the truth itself: Olympias has been impregnated by an Egyptian who is regal, just not divine, and Alexander will, in fact, do what the seal stone prefigures. The verification of the begetter's identify is in the sewing up with "Nilotic" papyrus,[8] which also serves to safeguard what the "god" has sown. Difficulties with some details, however, will soon appear in Greek redactions, and even more difficulties arise when the papyrus moves into other cultures.

The inventive application of the papyrus seems a bit unusual, and this will complicate the scene's transmission. People in the eastern Mediterranean were certainly not becoming ignorant of the Nile River, but "Nilotic" is soon dropped, perhaps as redundant.[9] The ninth-century recension γ, instead of having Philip observe Nectanebus doing the stitching, has him performing the stitching himself. Is the redactor having Philip play the role of an Amphitryon, at least in dream form, or is this a mistake? Something like a mistake has happened with "her nature," the grammatical object of the stitching, in that it is lacking at this point in the manuscripts, thus the accusative form of "papyrus" (βιβλίον in rec. γ) becomes the object of the stitching. When the dream interpreter speaks, "her nature" does appear, but now as the thing that is sealed, and the interpreter explains awkwardly that "with regard to your stitching up the papyrus," it grows only in Egypt, so the offspring will be Egyptian. The fourteenth-century Byzantine metrical version manages to merge recension γ with the older versions so that Philip (1) stitches up the papyrus (βιβλίον), (2) seals "my wife's nature," (3) and stitches up "that [ταύτην] one," namely, her "nature," φύσις (lines 385–87). The interpreter there speaks only of the first two actions (lines 395–401). Though the magical, or perhaps practical,[10] function of the papyrus as seed keeper has been completely lost, the otherwise pointless handling of the papyrus at least served as a paternity clue like some DNA marker, pointing to Egypt.[11]

---

8. The solitary manuscript of recension α reads ἵλωα; a single recension β manuscript preserves νειλῶα (others have εἰλωά, ἐνίλωα).
9. The dream is absent from recension ε, the Byzantine prose version, the *Rimada*, and the *Phyllada*.
10. This wholly unsafe suturing sounds oddly like the modern use of temporary ligaturing known as cervical cerclage, used to prevent premature movement (cf., perhaps, Ovid *Met.* 9.299–300); but papyrus, though employed in other ways, especially as ash, in ancient medicine, was not used for suturing at all (I thank Larry Bliquez for his expert knowledge on the tools, materials, and practices of ancient physicians).
11. Papyrus was in use as paper in Byzantium, though very rarely, down to the eleventh century; see the twelfth-century Eustathius' note on *Od.* 21.391 for its recent disuse.

The papyrus' role in Latin is initially retained, though simplified. Julius Valerius has Philip say to the interpreter: *tum mulieris virginal biblo contegere . . . visebatur* (Then he [a certain god] was seen to cover his wife's maidenly part with papyrus). The interpreter explains that the seed must be Egyptian (1.8). The papyrus will not, however, appear in the descendants of Leo's Latin version (and, thus, not in Europe's many vernacular versions of the Romance). Leo retains the stitching, as evidenced in the oldest manuscript, dated c. 1000, some fifty years after Leo's trip to Constantinople, where he acquired a Greek version of the Romance: *apparuit ei* [Philip] . . . *quasi videret celata membra illius consuere atque signare aureo anulo* ("It appeared to him . . . as if he saw him [Ammon/Nectanebus] sew up her hidden parts and seal them with a gold ring," 1.8 Pfister). In the three Latin recensions J1–3, the sewing occurs, but the above-quoted *celata membra* (hidden parts) become *os vulve illius* (the opening of her vulva). The papyrus and any mention of Egypt is completely gone, but the closing of the previously vague or euphemistic "nature" and "hidden parts" is replaced now with anatomically explicit language that has become an action to be described but not decoded or read. This part of the dream has lost its significant object and Egyptian message; the stitching has become merely preparatory to the subsequent sealing, whereas the stitching originally served as a unique telltale of Alexander's special paternity.

The second significant object used by Nectanebus, the ring with its seal stone, will retain its function and message intact, though some slight variation will arise. The act of sealing is explained by the interpreter as like the act of a merchant sealing a vessel to show that it is full, the specific imagery of the seal encoding the vessel's contents. Of the three original elements of the seal, the lion's head stays unchanged. The ἡλίου κράτος (force of the sun) will be translated in different ways but will be some visible piece of the sun. The weapon portrayed will remain a δοράτιον (little spear) through nearly all the Greek versions but becomes a sword elsewhere. The message conveyed by the three symbols is always the same: to foretell the strength, direction, and method of Alexander's future. In Latin, Julius Valerius transfers all the details precisely. Leo's translation starts with all three elements: *caput leonis, claritatem solis, gladium* ("head of a lion, brightness of the sun, a sword," 1.8 Pfister). But the poor interpreter, at least in the earliest manuscript, skips the sun and transfers its meaning to the lion: *caput namque leonis atque gladius talem intellectum habet, quia ille, qui nasci debet, pertinget usque ad orientem pugnando atque per gladium capiendo civitates* ("for the head of the lion and sword bear such a meaning, that the one who is going to be born will go all the way to the East, fighting and conquering countries with the sword," 1.8 Pfister).[12] The later Latin versions and their vernacular descendants all corrected this slip and restored the sun to the seer's reading. This first use of significant objects, the papyrus and gold seal ring, has had a mixed fate. The papyrus was constrained by cultural usage: where or when papyrus was not used, its message was lost. The seal ring, with its emblematic lion, sun, and weapon, was culturally common; thus it was retained and bore its significance successfully across time and languages.

Unlike the seal ring, the second use of a significant object starts out so linguistically embedded that it will be compelled to go through significant alteration to function in other languages. The context is historical: the siege of Tyre. Alexander's lightning-like speed has been slowed by the difficulty of the siege, but he receives a dream foretelling success.

7. ὁρᾷ δὲ κατὰ τοὺς ὕπνους ἕνα <τῶν> τοῦ Διονύσου προπόλων Σάτυρον ἐπιδιδόντα αὐτῷ τυρόν, αὐτὸν δὲ λαβόντα τοῖς ποσὶν αὐτὸν συμπατεῖν. 8. ἀναστὰς δὲ διηγήσατό τινι ὀνειροπόλῳ· ὁ δὲ εἶπε· "Βασιλεῦ Ἀλέξανδρε, σοὶ Τύρος γίνεται ὑποχείριος διὰ τό σε τυρὸν τοῖς ποσὶ καταπεπατηκέναι."

[And he sees in his dream one of the attendants of Dionysus, a satyr [saturos], giving him a cheese [turos], and he takes it and treads on it with his feet. 8. And after rising, he recounted it to a certain dream interpreter, and he said, "King Alexander, Tyre [Turos] is subject to you since you [se] have trod down the cheese [turos] with your feet."] (rec. α, 1.35.7–8)

The presence of a satyr in the story is at least as old as Plutarch's *Alexander* and may be much earlier. In Plutarch, the satyr's action differs greatly: he runs away from Alexander, who then pursues and catches him, which foretells—so the seer explains, through a cleaving form of etymological foresight—that "his [*sa-*] will be Tyre [-*tyros*]" (σὰ γενήσεται Τύρος, Plut., *Alex.* 24.8–9). There is no cheese in Plutarch's version. It could be said that the cheese is redundant: the *turos* in *saturos* has taken the play-on-words role. Earlier, however, with Nectanebus' hawk-sent dream, the Greek version showed a penchant for complexity of messaging. So the wordplay with *sa-*

---

12. The twelfth-century Paris manuscript has the same slip (Schnell 1989: 132).

turos here is clever. But perhaps the great king Alexander chasing a satyr was deemed undignified, so that later tellers of the tale built on the wordplay and introduced a cheese (a ball of mizithra or a semi-aged kefalaki?), which can be crushed underfoot, like the walls and people of Tyre. The verbally encoded oracle (*sa-turos*) is thus supplemented with a gestural treatment of a second encoded element (*turos*), and the gesture of stomping and the ruining of the cheese are far more grimly appropriate than a game of tag.

This creativity of the Romance in introducing significant stomping will be carried into other languages, but the thing stomped will need to be reinvented.[13] Julius Valerius gives one version of how the cheese changes in Latin: *in somnio Saturum conspicatur assem sibi Tyrum porrigentem eumque proiectum sese pedibus protrivisse. quod interpretibus haud difficile in enodando fuit: Tyrum enim proteri mox pedibus haberi principis respondere* ("in a dream, he sees a satyr holding out to him a Tyrian coin, and he sees that he himself, after throwing it down, trampled it with his feet. This was hardly difficult for the interpreters to explain: they answered that Tyre was soon going to be trampled under the king's feet," 1.35 Rosellini). The object here, *as Tyrus* (Tyrian coin), works. The satyr is not explained, yet he can be viewed, without complications, as a divine messenger, but the coin is a creative replacement for the cheese. Whereas the Greek "cheese" had embodied Tyre verbally, the Tyrian coin equates to the city synecdochically, whatever the redactor may have thought appeared on a Tyrian coin of the day.[14] This cleverness of the *as Tyrus* is overlooked by the latest edition of Valerius, which prints (in the body of the text) τυροῦ[m] (*sic*) in place of the manuscripts' *Tyrum*, an emendation originally made by Angelo Mai in 1817.[15] But the early seventh-century Syriac version supports the creative alteration of the cheese to a coin: "Dionysus was standing and holding a Tyrian daric in his hand, and he gave it to Alexander," and the interpreter explains, "The daric which Dionysus gave thee represents the country that is going to be delivered over to thee" (Budge 1889: 44–45).

In the Syriac version, however, Alexander does not trample on the coin. As Dionysus hands the coin to Alexander, a cluster of grapes from a garland around the god's head falls to the ground; Alexander steps on them, and

---

13. The fifth-century Armenian version transliterates "Saturos," keeps the cheese, and mystifies the message.
14. Consider British Museum 1906.0713.1, a mid-fourth-century Tyrian double sheckel.
15. Mai 1817: 52: "Igitur *assem* τυροῦ intelligas *casei orbem* aut *segmentum*" (Therefore you should understand 'a coin of *turos*' as a ball or piece of cheese).

wine flows forth. Of this, the interpreter explains that the people of Tyre will fall and pour forth their blood like wine. Whereas Julius Valerius kept one object (newly changed to a coin) with two actions (handing over and crushing), the Syrian version added a second object, connecting the transfer of authority to the coin and connecting the crushing to the grapes. When a distinctive feature, such as this coin, is found in two or more non-Greek versions, it is common to postulate a lost Greek parent. For instance, a hypothetical recension δ* is thought to stand behind the Syriac version and Leo's Latin version. But in Leo's Latin descendants, there is no coin (or satyr or Dionysus), only a single grape, *uva*. In a dream, Alexander sees a grape in his hand, throws it down, treads on it, and sees wine come forth (1.35 Pfister and J1–3). We have, then, a mysterious sequence: coin (Julius Valerius), coin and grape (Syriac), grape (Leo). Only one thing is clear: they all lack cheese. If some lost Greek version was the first to change the cheese to a coin, perhaps there was a concern that the etymological wit was less than clear, but at least the message of a divine transfer of authority over the city, whether etymologically or numismatically, was embodied in the significant object. Likewise, the introduction of Dionysus may have been due to some fuzziness about what satyrs are, and, of course, Dionysus is a god, while satyrs are mere sidekicks. That Dionysus is then supplemented by grapes as well is to be expected, but the transference of the crushing from coin to grape is quite creative, bringing with it the ominously flowing wine. If all these adjustments were not made in a Greek version, they were, at the least, carried out by someone who fully understood the original Greek cheese, its symbolical handing over and crushing. In all the versions, from the complex Syrian to the (overly) simplified Latin version of Leo's descendants, a significant object or two serve both to enhance the narrative and also to reveal the varying creativity of the translating redactors.

The third use of significant objects displays an adjustment similar to the cheese/coin/grape but adds additional, local flavor. Leading up to each of the battles between Alexander and the Persian king Darius III, the historical and legendary traditions both report a series of ambassadorial and epistolary exchanges between the two rulers. In one set of these exchanges in the Romance, the messages are sent in a verbal form as well as a nonverbal one. Darius initiates the exchange with a threatening letter that is accompanied by three objects: σκῦτος καὶ σφαῖρα καὶ κιβωτός χρυσίου ("a whip and a ball and a chest of gold," rec. α, 1.36.1,). Darius does not leave the objects voiceless, however: the accompanying letter speaks for the objects, explaining that Darius intends the whip to be used on Alexander himself, since he is still a child and "needs to be taught a lesson"; the ball is for Alexander to play nicely with his chums; the chest of gold is to help Alexander pay his way home. Alexander retorts with a reinterpretation of the objects.

σὺ μὲν ἐμοὶ ταῦτα ἔπεμψας χλευαζόμενος, ἐγὼ δὲ αὐτὰ ὡς ἀγαθὰ σημεῖα ἀπεδεξάμην. καὶ τὸ μὲν σκῦτος ἔλαβον, ἵνα ταῖς ἐμαῖς λόγχαις καὶ ὅπλοις δείρω τοὺς βαρβάρους καὶ ταῖς ἐμαῖς χερσὶν εἰς δουλείαν ὑποτάξω. τῇ δὲ σφαίρᾳ ἐσήμανάς μοι, ὡς τοῦ κόσμου περικρατήσω· σφαιροειδὴς γὰρ καὶ στρογγύλος ὑπάρχων ὁ κόσμος. τὴν δὲ κιβωτὸν τοῦ χρυσίου μέγα μοι σημεῖον ἔπεμψας, σεαυτῷ δὲ ὑποταγὴν ἐμήνυσας· ἡττηθεὶς γὰρ ὑπ' ἐμοῦ φόρους μοι χορηγήσεις.

[You sent these things as a mockery, but I received them as good omens. The whip I took that I may thrash your barbarians with my spears and arms and with my hands subject you into servitude. You signified to me with the ball that I will control the world, as it is round and shaped like a ball. And you sent the chest of gold as a great omen for me, but you revealed subjugation for yourself, for you will be defeated by me and bring me tribute.] (rec. α, 1.38.7)

Darius has made an error similar to that of his ancestor Darius the Great, the recipient of the famous, letterless, fully nonverbal Scythian assemblage of a bird, a mouse, a frog, and five arrows (Her. 4.131).[16] Darius III has also failed to manage the message, and, as sender, his presumption is all the greater, as is evident from his reaction to Alexander's retort. Darius writes to his satraps, boasting how he will whip Alexander and send him packing with a rattle and knucklebones (κρόταλα καὶ ἀστράγαλοι, rec. α, 1.39.4). He attempts to carry on and fashion his communication still with objects, but they are now only words, soon to be manifestly empty. Alexander, in comparison, will quickly back up his countermessaging of the objects with arms.

This exchange of letters and objects between Alexander and Darius is kept unchanged in most of the subsequent Greek versions. But the late Byzantine prose version has combined the whip and the ball into a spinning top

16. Moderns may call to mind how the dauphin plays Darius to Henry V's Alexander: he sneeringly sends him some tennis balls, and Henry repurposes the significant objects as wittily as Alexander or more so (Shakespeare, *Henry V*, 1.2.259–69).

and its whip, γουργουρίστρια ξύλινη καὶ βίτζα, and has added mustard seeds, σιναπόσπορον (§34, mss. E, F, and V and the *Phyllada*).[17] Darius explains that the top and its whip are for him to play with and that the two bags of mustard seed are sent so he may learn how immense the Persian army is. Alexander chewed some mustard seed, spat them out, and wrote to Darius,

8. Καὶ νὰ ἡξεύρῃς ἀπὸ τώρα αὐτοκράτοραν τοῦ κόσμου ὁλουνοῦ μὲ ἐποίησες· τέτοια σημάδια ἔδειξες εἰς ἐμένα. 9. Ὡσὰν τὸ γύρισμα τοῦ ξύλου ὁποῦ γυρίζει ἐμπρός μου, οὕτως θέλω γυρίσει καὶ τὸν κόσμον ὅλον θέλω ἐπάρει. Καὶ εἰς ἐσένα θέλω κινήσει νὰ ἔλθω. Καὶ τὸν σιναπόσπορον ἐμάσησα καὶ ἔπτυσά τον, οὕτως καὶ τὰ φουσάτα σου μὲ τὸν θεὸν τὰ θέλω τζακίσει καὶ καταπατήσειν.

[And you should realize as of now that you have made me ruler of the whole world: such signs you sent to me. 9. Just as the spinning of the wooden top that spins before me, so I will spin and I will lay hold of the whole world; and I will set forth to come to you. And I chewed the mustard seed and spat it out; so too your armies, by God, I will crush and trample upon.] (ms. E, 34.8–9)

Alexander also gives the messenger a bushel of peppercorns, πιπέρι, stating that his strength is like that of the peppercorns. The combining of the original whip and ball into a paired top and driving whip is creative and effective, but the juxtaposing of the similarly lachrymatory mustard seeds and peppercorns does not make sense.[18] When did these develop-

---

17. The *Phyllada*'s βέργα, if translated as "stick" rather than "switch," could turn the top into the hoop used in trundling (κρικηλασία).

18. The mustard seed here is probably brown mustard seed (*Brassica juncea*), which is much more pungent than white mustard seed (*Sinapis alba*) but not quite as hot as black mustard (*Brassica nigra*). When first crushed and mixed with water, as in Darius' mouth, any mustard seed is much more pungent than the prepared mustard taken for granted these days, though even the Chinese hot mustard and "hot" Dijon-style mustard available in grocery stores, both using brown mustard seed, are something more than most yellow hot dog mustards. (Modern science informs us that white mustard seed's pungency comes from sinalbin, while sinigrin is the key element in brown and black mustard seed.) Pliny the Elder speaks of three types of mustard seed and describes *sinapi*, most likely brown mustard, as "most sharp in flavor and fire-like" (*acerrimum sapore igneique effectus, NH* 19.170–71); he reports Pythagoras' praise of mustard's power "since no other spice penetrates into the nose and brain more" (*quoniam non aliud magis in nares et cerebrum penetret, NH* 20.236); most relevant for the comparison above, he comments that long pepper, which was much more expensive than black or white pepper, "was most easily adulterated with Alexandrian [brown] mustard" (*piper longum facillime adulteratur Alexandrino sinapi, NH* 12.28).

ments take place, and are they due to linguistic complications or intentional cultural adjustments?

The original three objects—the self-flagellating whip, the amusing ball, and the per diem gold—are kept by Julius Valerius and the fifth-century Armenian version. The first seeds appear in the seventh-century Syriac version. That version follows the Greek text very closely, but just at the point when Darius boasts of how many troops he has—"not even one counting the grains of sand would count so high" (rec. α, 36.4)—the Syriac version has a new, fourth object: "I have sent thee ten measures of sesame seed, that thou mayest know that I have myriads of troops even as these grains of sesame" (Budge 1889: 46). Alexander, in turn, sends a "bushel of mustard seed," which results in the expected chewing and spitting (Budge 1889: 50). Leo's Latin version and its descendants have different seeds but a similar opposition: mild *sementis papaveris* (poppy seed) versus pungent *piper* (peppercorn). As with the dream at Tyre and the shift from cheese to grape(s), if something like a hypothetical recension δ* is behind the grape(s) shared by the Syriac and Leo's Latin version, is some such Greek version also the inventor of the use of seeds and spices? There is a hypothetical fourteenth-century Greek recension ζ* that has poppy seeds and peppercorns, as evidenced by its fourteenth-century Serbian offspring, which has *maka* and *pipri*, transliterations of Greek μήκων/μάκων (poppy seed) and πίπερι (Mod. πιπέρι, "pepper").[19] So perhaps some earlier Greek version introduced seeds and spices, but the Syriac version creatively adjusted the poppy seeds and peppercorns to the culinary parallel of sesame and mustard seeds. Both poppy and sesame seeds were common seeds, though sesame had a greater and more varied role in the kitchen; mustard seeds were far more common and local to Syria and all of Eurasia, whereas pepper, long or black, was imported and expensive. Perhaps the adjustment was a matter of taste; either way, the new pairing successfully transferred the powerful message of poppy versus pepper. How the late Greek version lost the original, contrasting message and ended up with the similarly pungent mustard seeds and peppercorns remains a mystery.

Can some earlier Greek source, reconstructed or extant, also reveal the origin of the whipped top of the fifteenth-century Greek version? The Syrian version has the whip and ball of the earliest Greek version. By the time Leo acquired his Greek version, however, a reinvented toy had appeared: a ball

---

19. Christians 1991; see Moennig's 2009 summary and bibliography.

and polo stick, *zocani quod factum est de virgis, que curvantur a capite* ("a *zocani*, which is made from sticks that are curved at the head," J1).[20] A ninth- or tenth-century handbook on dreams by "Achmet" states that "if someone sees himself on a horse with the king or noblemen driving the ball or playing with a *tzukani* [ἐλαύνει τὴν σφαῖραν ἤτοι τζυκανίζει]," he is playing polo.[21] The word *čowgān*, like polo, came west from Persia and, through some lost Greek recension, ended up in Latin as *zocani*. Perhaps an internationalist Greek of the ninth or tenth century changed the original insulting gift of a self-punishing whip and childish ball to a paired ball and stick that invites Alexander to learn to engage the Great King in sport, in the game of kings.

The whipped top, then, does not descend from some sixth-, ninth-, or fourteenth-century lost Greek recension that leaves footprints in other versions. Whipped tops are very ancient—consider the top whipped by Hermes on the kylix attributed to Douris[22]—and are common to many cultures. The top and whip of the fifteenth-century Greek version looks like a creative innovation, parallel to the polo stick and ball, yet more dramatic. When Alexander reinterprets the polo stick, he says that the kings of the world will bend down before him just as the head of the stick bends down. Given a whipped top, Alexander turns it to represent how he will spin across the face of the earth and zoom into Darius' very presence. Wherever the whipped top started, in whichever language and culture,[23] it is distinctly Greek in the late Byzantine version.[24] "Spinning" or "speedy top" would capture the creative and effective Greek meaning(s) of this newly enhanced toy and of Alexander's intended significance.

Pursuit of these significant objects in other versions of the Alexander Romance reveals further creative adjustments and additions to the objects and their significance. I offer two twelfth-century examples from distant parts of Eurasia. In Nizami's *Iskandarnamah*, Iskandar (i.e., Alexander) strews Dara's sesame seeds on the ground and watches the birds swoop in to devour them:

---

20. J2 and J3 read similarly (though the mss. read *zoca*); the Bamberg ms. simply has *virga curvata*.
21. Drexl 1925: §154.
22. Baltimore, Johns Hopkins University B9, Beazley 205298.
23. Due to some transliterated Serbian words, the fifteenth-century Greek version is said to be derived from the Serbian version (Moennig 2009: 250 and bibliography), but the Serbian text in Christians 1991: 96–99 has *strougla*, a sort of rattle, and *kolo drebeno*, "wooden ring."
24. The γουργουρ- root in the various words used in the manuscripts may derive from the ancient and modern γυρ- root meaning "turn" or "circle," though I would lean toward a derivation from γρηγορ- (quick), through metathesis and vowel alteration. See Thumb 1912: §§6.3, 31.1. Cf. fourteenth- or fifteenth-century Γούργουρας/ος for Γρηγοράς/ος and adverbial γουργόν/ά for γρήγορα.

such will be the fate of Dara's armies. But Iskandar sends no spicy response; the birds are his mustard seed. In the contemporaneous French Romance, Alexander, in a right chivalrous gesture, sends Darius back his *gant* (gauntlet), full of pepper, and explains, *Ausi com li lyons prent et ocist l'atoivre, / Qui est haus et creüs comme <g>rains de genoivre, /Vos conquerrons en champ et vostre gent atoivre;* ("Just as the lion seizes and kills the cattle, | Mighty and powerful like a juniper berry, | We shall conquer you and your noble entourage in battle," 2:116, 2525–27). Here, we have new gestures and added flavors (cf., perhaps, Pliny *NH* 12.7.29). When the original significant objects move into other cultures and are suddenly found to be less than clear or even silent, they mutate and adjust to the new language and culture, and from these mutations and enhancements, we can see the "openness" of the Alexander Romance in action.

These few examples of significant objects display, as has been said of Herodotus' broader array of nonverbal communication, "an aspect of literary method that conveys the cultural context and personal psychology of his participants great and small" (Lateiner 1987: 107). In the earliest cultural context of the Alexander Romance, in the eastern Mediterranean of the Hellenistic world, things like papyrus and a seal ring, cheese, a whip, a ball, and a box of gold all made sense and carried inaudible meanings that were heard and understood by the participants. As the cultural context changed, the meaning of the objects and the function of that meaning in the narrative was retained. The objects themselves, however, were adjusted, supplemented, or reshaped, to varying degrees and in varying ways. By studying that process, we can examine the psychology not of the participants but of the redactors of the Romance as they grappled with the semantic and semiotic challenges of conveying Alexander and his legendary deeds to new audiences across languages, cultures, and millennia.

Works Cited

Bossuat, R. 1946. "Vasque de Lucène, traducteur de Quinte-Curce (1468)." *Bibliothèque d'humanisme et renaissance* 8: 197–245.
Budge, E. A. W. 1889. *The History of Alexander the Great, Being the Syriac Version.* Cambridge: Cambridge University Press.
Cary, G. 1956. *The Medieval Alexander.* Cambridge: Cambridge University Press.
Christians, D. 1991. *Die serbische Alexandreis.* Cologne: Böhlau.
Collet, O., ed. 1995. "Extraits de *Faits du Grand Alexandre* de Vasque de Lucène." In D. Régnier-Bohler, ed., *Splendeurs de la cour de Bourgogne*, 565–627. Paris: Laffont.

Drexl, F., ed. 1925. *Achmetis Oneirocriticon*. Leipzig: Teubner.

Hägg, T. 2012. *The Art of Biography in Antiquity*. Cambridge: Cambridge University Press.

Konstan, D. 1998. "The Alexander Romance: The Cunning of the Open Text." *Lexis: Poetica, retorica e communicazione nella tradizione classica* 16: 123–38.

Kroll, W., ed. 1926. *Historia Alexandri Magni*. Berlin: Weidmann.

Lateiner, D. 1989. *The Historical Method of Herodotus*. Toronto: University of Toronto Press.

Lateiner, D. 1995. *Sardonic Smile: Nonverbal Behavior in Homeric Epic*. Ann Arbor: University of Michigan Press.

Mai, A. 1817. *Itinerarium Alexandri, item Iulii Valerii de rebus gestis eiusdem Alexandri libri tres*. Milan.

McKendrick, S. 1996. *The History of Alexander the Great: An Illuminated Manuscript of Vasco da Lucena's French Translation of the Ancient Text by Quintus Curtius Rufus*. Los Angeles: J. Paul Getty Museum.

Moennig, U., ed. 2009. "Alexanderroman." In *Kindlers Literatur-Lexikon*, 1.246–50. 3rd ed. Stuttgart: Metzler.

Pfister, F., ed. 1913. *Der Alexanderroman des Archipresbyters Leo*. Heidelberg: Carl Winter.

Rosellini, M., ed. 2004. *Iulius Valerius, Res gestae Alexandri Macedonis translatae ex Aesopo graeco*. Corr. ed. Munich: K. G. Saur.

Ross, D. 1988. *Alexander Historiatus: A Guide to the Medieval Illustrated Alexander Literature*. 2nd ed. Frankfurt: Athenäum.

Schnell, R. 1989. *Liber Alexandri Magni*. Munich: Artemis.

Stoneman, R. 2008. *Alexander the Great: A Life in Legend*. New Haven: Yale University Press.

Thumb, A. 1912. *Handbook of the Modern Greek Vernacular*. Trans. S. Angus. Edinburgh: T&T Clark.

Zuwiyya, Z. D., ed. 2011. *A Companion to Alexander Literature in the Middle Ages*. Leiden: Brill.

Bibliography of Donald Lateiner to 2014

1972

Review of H. C. Cannon, trans., *Ovid's Heroides* (New York, 1971). *ACR* 2: 177.

1973

Review of R. Wind and H. J. Dell, trans., *Pseudo-Xenophon: The Old Oligarch* (Macungie, PA, 1972). *ACR* 3: 206.

1975

"The Speech of Teutiaplus." *GRBS* 16: 175–84.

1976

"Tissaphernes and the Phoenician Fleet." *TAPA* 106: 267–90.

1977

"Heralds and Corpses in Thucydides." *CW* 71: 97–106.
"No Laughing Matter: A Literary Tactic in Herodotus." *TAPA* 107: 173–82.
"Obscenity in Catullus." *Ramus* 6: 15–32. Reprinted in J. Gaiser, ed., *Oxford Readings in Catullus* (Oxford: Oxford University Press, 2007), 261–81, and ed. Lawrence J. Trudeau. *Classical and Medieval Literature Criticism*, vol. 141 (Detroit, MI: Gale, 2012).
"Pathos in Thucydides." *Antichthon* 11: 42–51.

1978

"Ovid's Homage to Callimachus and Alexandrian Poetic Theory." *Hermes* 106: 188–96.
"Wilamowitz' Second Century." *CW* 71: 455–57.

1980

"A Note on ΔΙΚΑΣ ΔΙΔΟΝΑΙ in Herodotus." *CQ* 30: 30–32.

1981

"An Analysis of Lysias' Political Defense Speeches." *RSA* 11: 147–60.

1982

"The Failure of the Ionian Revolt." *Historia* 31: 129–60.
"The Man Who Does Not Meddle in Politics: A Topos in Lysias." *CW* 76: 1–12. Translated in D. Spatharas and L. Tzallela, eds., *Peitho: Dekatria meletemata gia ten archaia rhetorike* (Athens: Smilê, 2003), 384–402.
"A Note on the Perils of Prosperity in Herodotus." *RM* 125: 97–101.
Review of F. L. T. Tasolambros, *In Defense of Thucydides* (Athens, 1979). *CP* 77: 264–68.

1983

Review of M. Gagarin, *Drakon and Early Athenian Homicide Law* (New Haven, 1981). *AJP* 104: 404–9.
Review of J. F. Kindstrand, *The Stylistic Evaluation of Aeschines in Antiquity* (Uppsala, 1982). *CW* 77: 59.
Selected Papers of Lionel Pearson. Coedited with S. Stephens. Chico, CA: Scholars Press.

1984

"The Epigraph to Joyce's *Portrait.*" *CML* 4: 77–84.
"Herodotean Historiographical Patterning: 'The Constitutional Debate.'" *QS* 20: 257–84.
"Mythic and Non-mythic Artists in Ovid's *Metamorphoses.*" *Ramus* 13: 1–30.
Review of N. Goldman and L. Szymanski, *English Grammar for Students of Latin* (Ann Arbor, 1983). *Stentor* 2.2: 19–20.
Review of G. F. Plowden, *Pope on Classic Ground* (Athens, OH, 1983). *CML* 4: 167–71.

1985

"Limit, Propriety, and Transgression in the *Histories* of Herodotus." In M. Jamison, ed., *The Greek Historians: Literature and History; Papers Presented to A. E. Raubitschek*, 87–100. Saratoga, CA: Anma Libri.

"Nicias' Inadequate Encouragement (Thuc. 7.69.2)." *CP* 80: 201–13.

"Polarità: Il principio della differenza complementare in Erodoto." *QS* 22: 79–103.

Review of V. J. Hunter, *Past and Process in Herodotus and Thucydides* (Princeton, 1982). *CP* 80: 69–74.

1986

"The Empirical Element in the Methods of the Early Greek Medical Writers and Herodotus: A Shared Epistemological Response." *Antichthon* 20: 1–20.

Review of M. Lang, *Herodotean Narrative and Discourse* (Cambridge, MA, 1984). *CW* 79: 289.

1987

"Nonverbal Communication in the *Histories* of Herodotus." *Arethusa* 20: 83–119, 143–45.

Review of M. Ostwald, *Autonomia: Its Genesis and Early History* (Oxford, 1982). *AncPhil* 6: 195–99.

1988

"Petronius and Other Classics in Meredith's *The Egoist*." *Petronian Society Newsletter* 18: 4.

Review of S. Portch, *Literature's Silent Language: Nonverbal Communication* (New York, 1985). *Style* 22.4: 664–70.

1989

The Historical Method of Herodotus. Phoenix Supplementary Volumes 23. Toronto: University of Toronto Press. Corrected paperback ed., 1991.

Review of S. Forde, *The Ambition to Rule: Alcibiades and the Politics of Imperialism in Thucydides* (Ithaca, 1989). *CHOICE* 27-0105.

Review of R. Sealey, *The Athenian Republic: Democracy or the Rule of Law?* (University Park, PA, 1987). *CW* 82: 311–12.

"Teeth in Homer." *LCM* 14: 18–23.

1990

"Deceptions and Delusions in Herodotus." *CA* 9.2: 230–46. Reprinted in J. Krstovic, ed., *Classical and Medieval Literature Criticism*, vol. 17 (New York: Gale, 1996).

"Mimetic Syntax: Metaphor from Word Order, especially in Ovid's Poetry." *AJP* 111: 204–37.

Review of D. Fehling, *Herodotus and His 'Sources': Citation, Invention, and Narrative Art*, trans. J. G. Howie (Leeds, 1989). *CW* 84: 75–76.

Review of R. Martin, *The Language of Heroes* (Ithaca, 1993). *CHOICE* 28-0192.

Review of A. Melville, trans., *Ovid, The Love Poems* (Oxford, 2008). *CHOICE* 28-2036.

Review of A. Parry, *The Language of Achilles and Other Papers* (Oxford, 1989). *CHOICE* 28-0193.

Review of B. Reardon, ed., *The Collected Ancient Greek Novels* (Berkeley, 1989). *CHOICE* 27.3-3779.

Review of R. K. Sinclair, *Democracy and Participation in Athens* (Cambridge, 1991). *CJ* 85: 359–60.

Review of J. Solodow, *The World of Ovid's Metamorphoses* (Chapel Hill, 1988). *CP* 85: 232–35.

1991

Review of T. Cole, *The Origins of Rhetoric in Ancient Greece* (Baltimore, 1991). *CHOICE* 28-6164.

Review of K. Dowden, *Death and the Maiden: Girls' Initiation Rites in Greek Mythology* (London, 1989). *CW* 85: 140–41.

Review of J. A. S. Evans, *Herodotus: Explorer of the Past* (Princeton, 1991). *BMCR* 02.05.08.

Review of J. Ferguson, *Among the Gods: An Archaeological Exploration of Ancient Greek Religion* (London, 1989). *CW* 84: 322–23.

Review of J. A. Hanson, trans., *Apuleius, The Metamorphoses* (Cambridge, MA, 1989). *CW* 84: 473.

Review of A. Mandelbaum, trans., *The Odyssey of Homer* (New York, 1991). *CHOICE* 28-4417.

Review of B. Reardon, *The Form of Greek Romance* (Princeton, 1991). *CHOICE* 29-1428.

Review of C. Starr, *The Birth of Athenian Democracy* (Oxford, 1990). *BMCR* 02.01.17.

Review of D. Whitehead, *Aineias the Tactician: How to Survive under Siege* (Oxford, 1990). *BMCR* 2.6: 400–404.

1992

"Affect Displays in the Epic Poetry of Homer, Vergil, and Ovid." In F. Poyatos, ed., *Advances in Non-verbal Communication: Sociocultural, Clinical, Esthetic, and Literary Perspectives*, 255–69. Amsterdam: Benjamins.

"Heroic Proxemics: Movers and Shakers in the *Odyssey*." *TAPA* 122: 133–63.

Anchor Bible Dictionary, vol. 3, s.v. "Historiography, Graeco-Roman." Garden City, NY: Anchor Bible.

Review of D. Arnould, *Le rire et les larmes dans la littérature grecque d'Homère à Platon* (Paris, 1990). *AJP* 113: 448–52.

Review of M. Bettini, *Anthropology and Roman Culture* (Baltimore, 1991). *Vergilius* 38: 171–76.

Review of J. Bremmer, ed., *From Sappho to de Sade: Moments in the History of Sexuality* (London, 1989). *CW* 86: 73–74.

Review of B. MacQueen, *Myth, Rhetoric, and Fiction: A Reading of Longus's Daphnis and Chloe* (Lincoln, NE, 1990). *CW* 85: 711.

Review of C. J. Swearingen, *Rhetoric and Irony: Western Literacy and Western Lies* (Oxford, 1991). *CHOICE* 29-4321.

1993

"Elizabeth Hazelton Haight." *CO* 70: 97–98.

"Gilbert Highet to E. H. Haight, a Letter from Post-war Germany." *QS* 38: 131–41.

"The Perception of Deception and Gullibility in Specialists of the Supernatural (Primarily) in Athenian Literature." In R. M. Rosen and J. Farrell, eds., *Nomodeiktes: Greek Studies in Honor of Martin Ostwald*, 179–95. Ann Arbor: University of Michigan Press.

Review of J. Gould, *Give and Take in Herodotus* (Oxford, 1991). *CW* 86: 249–50.

Review of C. Edwards, *The Politics of Immorality in Ancient Rome* (Cambridge, 1993). *CHOICE* 31-826.

Review of S. Reece, *The Stranger's Welcome: Oral Theory and the Aesthetics of the Homeric Hospitality Scene* (Ann Arbor, 1993). *CHOICE* 31-0196.

Review of H. Versnel, *Inconsistencies in Greek and Roman Religion*, vol. 2, *Transition and Reversal in Myth and Ritual* (Leiden, 1993). *BMCR* 04.06.10.

"The Suitors' Take: Manners and Power in Ithaka." *Colby Quarterly* 29.3: 173–96.

1994

Biographical Dictionary of North American Classicists, s.vv. "E. H. Haight," "D. N. Robinson," "William G. Williams," and "Richard Parsons." Westport, CT: Greenwood.

Review of G. Anderson, *The Second Sophistic: A Cultural Phenomenon in the Roman Empire* (New York, 1993). *BMCR* 94.10.06.

Review of N. Austin, *Helen of Troy and Her Shameless Phantom* (Ithaca, 1994). *CHOICE* 32.3-1351.

Review of E. Badian, *From Plataea to Potidaea: Studies in the History and Historiography of the Pentecontaetia* (Baltimore, 1993). *CW* 88: 219–20.

Review of N. Felson-Rubin, *Regarding Penelope: From Character to Poetics* (Princeton, 1994). *CO* 72: 37.

Review of J. Gager, *Curse Tablets and Binding Spells from the Ancient World* (New York, 1992), and C. Faraone, *Talismans and Trojan Horses* (Oxford, 1992). *JECS* 2.3: 340–44.

Review of D. Konstan, *Sexual Symmetry: Love in the Ancient Novel and Related Genres* (Princeton, 1994). *CHOICE* 32-4754.

Review of H. Parry, *Thelxis: Magic and Imagination in Greek Myth and Poetry* (Lanham, MD, 1992). *CW* 88: 134–35.

1995

Review of R. Ancona, *Time and the Erotic in Horace's Odes* (Durham, NC, 1994). *CHOICE* 33.6-0741.

Review of D. Rayor and W. Batstone, eds., *Latin Lyric and Elegiac Poetry* (New York, 1994). *CHOICE* 32-6064.

Sardonic Smile: Nonverbal Behavior in Homeric Epic. Ann Arbor: University of Michigan Press. Corrected paperback ed., 1998.

1996

"Elizabeth Hazelton Haight, a Biography." *CW* 90: 153–66.

"Nonverbal Behaviors in Ovid's Poetry, primarily *Metam.* 14." *CJ* 91: 225–53.

The Oxford Classical Dictionary, 3rd ed., s.vv. "Gestures," "Aristagoras," "Histiaeus," and "Ionian Revolt." Oxford: Oxford University Press.

Review of A. Cameron, *Callimachus and His Critics* (Princeton, 1995). *CHOICE* 33.6-3145.

Review of A. Sharrock, *Seduction and Repetition in Ovid's Ars Amatoria II* (Oxford, 1994). *CW* 89: 507–8.

Review of N. Shumate, *Crisis and Conversion in Apuleius' Metamorphoses* (Ann Arbor, 1996). *CHOICE* 34.4-2008.

Review of S. Stephens and J. J. Winkler, eds., *Ancient Greek Novels: The Fragments* (Princeton, 1995). *Arachne* 3.1: 99–103.

Review of G. D. Williams, *Banished Voices: Readings in Ovid's Exile Poetry* (Cambridge, 1994). *CW* 90: 452–53.

1997

"Homeric Prayer." *Arethusa* 30: 241–72.

Review of K. Cooper, *The Virgin and the Bride: Idealized Womanhood in Late Antiquity* (Cambridge, MA, 1996). *CHOICE* 34-4300.

Review of D. Lyons, *Gender and Immortality: Heroines in Ancient Greek Myth and Cult* (Princeton, 1997). *CHOICE* 35-0107.

Review of N. Thompson, *Herodotus and the Origin of the Political Community: Arion's Leap* (New Haven, 1996). *Historian* 59.4: 938–39.

1998

"Blushes in the Ancient Novels." *Helios* 25.2: 163–89.

"In Pursuit of Missing Persons." Review of Paul Zanker, *The Mask of Socrates* (Berkeley, 1995). *Semiotica* 121: 241–61.

Review of W. Anderson, ed., *Ovid's Metamorphoses Books 1–5* (Norman, 1997). *CW* 91: 431.

Review of S. Pulleyn, *Prayer in Greek Religion* (Oxford, 1998). *AHB* 12: 140–41.

Review of G. S. Shrimpton, *History and Memory in Ancient Greece* (Montreal, 1997). *AHR* 103.4: 1227–28.

Review of D. R. Slavitt, trans., *Broken Columns: The Achilleid of Publius Papinius Statius and The Rape of Proserpine of Claudius Claudianus*, with an afterword by David Konstan (Philadelphia, 1997). *CHOICE* 35-5488.

"Thucydides and Commentaries." Review of S. Hornblower, *Commentary on Thucydides*, vol. 2 (Oxford: Clarendon Press, 1996). *Histos* 2: 279–301.

1999

Review of P. G. Bahn, ed., *The Cambridge Illustrated History of Archaeology* (Cambridge, 1999). *Historian* 61.2: 484–85.

Review of S. I. Johnston, *The Restless Dead: Encounters between the Living and the Dead in Ancient Greece* (Berkeley, 1999). *CHOICE* 37-1376.

Review of J. Marincola, *Authority and Tradition in Ancient Historiography* (Cambridge, 1997). *AJP* 120: 303–7.

Review of W. Thalmann, *The Swineherd and the Bow: Representations of Class in the Odyssey* (Ithaca, 1998). *CW* 93: 219–20.

2000

"Abduction Marriage in Heliodorus' *Aethiopica*." *GRBS* 38: 409–39.

"Marriage and the Return of Spouses in Apuleius' *Metamorphoses*." *CJ* 95: 313–32.

Review of B. Ankarloo and S. Clark, eds., *Witchcraft and Magic in Europe*, vol. 2, *Ancient Greece and Rome* (Philadelphia, 1999). *BMCR* 2000.10.24.

Review of C. Cox, *Household Interests: Property, Marriage Strategies, and Family Dynamics in Ancient Athens* (Princeton, 1998). *AHR* 105.3: 979–80.

Review of R. Hooper, trans., *The Priapus Poems: Erotic Epigrams from Ancient Rome* (Urbana, 1999). *CHOICE* 38-3767.

Review of N. Lowe, *The Classical Plot and the Invention of Western Narrative* (Cambridge, 2000). *BMCR* 2000.11.28.

Review of J. Romm, *Herodotus* (New Haven, 1998). *Historian* 62.3: 695–96.

2001

"Hesiod's Concept of Hope (*Elpis*)." *HopeWatch* 10: 1–2, 4.

"Humiliation and Immobility in Apuleius' *Metamorphoses*." *TAPA* 131: 217–55.

Review of G. S. Aldrete, *Gestures and Acclamations in Ancient Rome* (Baltimore, 1999). *CW* 94: 201–3.

Review of J. Dee, *Epitheta Hominum apud Homerum* (Hildesheim, 2000). *BMCR* 01.01.14.

Review of M. Depew and D. Obbink, eds., *Matrices of Genre: Authors, Canons, and Society* (Cambridge, MA, 2000). *CHOICE* 38.9-4887.

Review of S. Montiglio, *Silence in the Land of Logos* (Princeton, 2010). *Phoenix* 55.1–2: 168–71.

"Sixth-Century Greece: Sparta and Athens." In B. Vivante, ed., *Events That Changed Ancient Greece*, 64–76. Westport, CT: Greenwood.

2002

"Just Like Us? Hand and Face in Ancient and Modern Naples." Review of Andrea de Jorio, *Gesture in Naples and Gesture in Classical Antiquity* (Bloomington, 2002), a translation of *La mimica degli antichi investigata nel gestire napoletano*. *IJCT* 8: 234–44.

"Pouring Bloody Drops (*Iliad* 16.459): The Grief of Zeus." *Colby Quarterly* 38.1: 42–61.

Review of M.-L. Desclos, ed., *Le rire des Grecs: Anthropologie du rire en Grèce ancienne* (Grenoble, 2000). *BMCR* 2002.07.17.

Review of M. Edwards, *Sound, Sense, and Rhythm: Listening to Greek and Latin Poetry* (Princeton, 2002). *CHOICE* 39.7-6257.

"The Style of Herodotus: A Case Study (7.229)." *CW* 95: 363–71.

2003

"Is Teaching Classics Inherently Colonialist? A Response." *CW* 96: 427–33.

Review of M. Alden, *Homer beside Himself: Para-narratives in the Iliad* (Oxford, 2001). *CR* 53.1: 3–5.

Review of C. Dougherty, *The Raft of Odysseus: The Ethnographic Imagination of Homer's Odyssey* (Oxford, 2001). *AHR* 108.2: 556–57.

Review of B. Graziosi, *Inventing Homer: The Early Reception of Homer* (Cambridge, 2002). *CHOICE* 40-2625.

Review of T. Harrison, *Divinity and History: The Religion of Herodotus* (Oxford, 2002), and R. Thomas, *Herodotus in Context* (Cambridge, 2002). *CP* 97: 371–82.

Review of R. Omitowoju, *Rape and the Politics of Consent in Classical Athens* (Cambridge, 2002). *BMCR* 2003.03.31.

Review of S. Tougher, ed., *Eunuchs in Antiquity and Beyond* (London, 2002). *BMCR* 2003.10.12.

Review of D. Wilson, *Ransom, Revenge, and Heroic Identity in the Iliad* (Cambridge, 2002). *Hermathena* 173.4: 187–92.

"Tlepolemus the Spectral Spouse." In M. Zimmerman, S. Panayotakis, and W. Keulen, eds., *The Ancient Novel and Beyond*, 219–38. Leiden: Brill.

"When Romans Climb Socially: Snobbery, Snafus, and Snide Remarks." Review of Brian Krostenko, *Cicero, Catullus, and the Language of Social Performance* (Chicago, 2001). *Semiotica* 144: 359–75.

2004

"Continuity between Ancient Roman and Medieval British Gestures." Review of C. H. Dodwell, *Anglo-Saxon Gestures and the Roman Stage* (Cambridge, 2000). *IJCT* 10: 454–64.

The Histories of Herodotus. Trans. G. C. Macaulay. Revised translation with introduction, annotations, bibliographies, notes, and *Nachleben*. New York: Barnes and Noble. Corrected hardback ed., 2005.

"Homeric Insults: Dis-honor in Homeric Discourse." Thirty-fifth Annual Gail A. Burnett Lecture, California State University, San Diego.

"The *Iliad*: An Unpredictable Classic." In R. Fowler, ed., *The Cambridge Companion to Homer*, 11–30. Cambridge: Cambridge University Press.

Review of G. Anderson, *Fairytale in the Ancient World* (London, 2000). *Scholia*, n.s., 13: 140–44, http://www.casa-kvsa.org.za/ScholiaUpdate/2004/04-33and.htm.

Review of V. Bers, trans., *Demosthenes, Speeches 50–59* (Austin, 2003). *BMCR* 2004.01.06.

Review of J. Dee, *Homer: Repertorium Homericae Poiesis Hexametricum* (Hildesheim, 2004). *BMCR* 2004.11.24.

Review of G. A. Kortekaas, *The Story of Apollonius King of Tyre: A Study of Its Greek Origin and an Edition of the Two Oldest Latin Recensions* (Leiden, 2004). *CHOICE* 42-2047.

Review of J.-D. Le Roy, *The Ruins of the Most Beautiful Monuments of Greece*, trans. D. Britt (Los Angeles, 2004). *BMCR* 2004.09.28.

2005

"The Pitiers and the Pitied in Herodotus and Thucydides." In R. Sternberg, ed., *Pity and Power in Ancient Athens*, 67–97. Cambridge: Cambridge University Press.

"Proxemic and Chronemic in Homeric Epic: Time and Space in Heroic Social Interaction." *CW* 98: 413–21.

Review of H. D. Cameron, *Thucydides Book I: A Students' Grammatical Commentary* (Ann Arbor, 2003). *NECJ* 32.3: 250–52.

Review of N. Spivey and M. Squire, *Panorama of the Classical World* (London, 2004). *BMCR* 2005.05.38.

Review of H. van Tress, *Poetic Memory: Allusion in the Poetry of Callimachus and the Metamorphoses of Ovid* (Leiden, 2004). *CHOICE* 42.10-5711.

Review of M. Zimmerman et al., eds., *Apuleius Madaurensis, Metamorphoses Book IV 28–35, V, and VI 1–24: The Tale of Cupid and Psyche*, Groningen Commentaries on Apuleius (Groningen, 2004). *BMCR* 2005.08.24.

"Signifying Names and Other Ominous Accidental Utterances in Classical Historiography." *GRBS* 45: 35–57.

"Telemakhos' One Sneeze and Penelope's Two Laughs." In R. Rabel, ed., *Approaches to Homer, Ancient and Modern*, 91–104. Swansea: Classical Press of Wales.

"Turn Your Thumb." Review of A. Corbeill, *Nature Embodied: Gesture in Ancient Rome* (Princeton, 2004). *IJCT* 12: 103–8.

2006

"Comments on Commentaries." Review of L. Scott, *Historical Commentary on Herodotus Book 6* (Leiden, 2005). *Exemplaria Classica* 10: 292–316.

"Mothers in Ovid's *Metamorphoses*." *Helios* 33.2: 189–201.

Review of M. Beagon, *The Elder Pliny on the Human Animal: Natural History Book 7* (Oxford, 2005). *BMCR* 2006.01.53.

Review of D. Hawhee, *Bodily Arts: Rhetoric and Athletics in Ancient Greece* (Austin, 2004). *CW* 99: 468–69.

Thucydides, Peloponnesian War. Trans. Richard Crawley. New York: Barnes and Noble.

2007

"Contest (*AGON*) in Thucydides." In J. Marincola, ed., *The Blackwell Companion to Greek and Roman Historiography*, 336–41. Oxford: Oxford University Press.

"Oracles, Religion, and Politics in Herodotus' Histories." Appendix P in R. Strassler, ed., *The Landmark Herodotus: The Histories*, 810–15. New York: Anchor Books.

Review of P. Bing and J. S. Bruss, eds., *Brill's Companion to Hellenistic Epigram* (Leiden, 2007). *CHOICE* 45-1306.

Review of A. M. Bowie, *Herodotus, Histories Book VIII* (Cambridge, 2007). *BMCR* 2008.07.34.

Review of P. Cartledge, *Thermopylae: The Battle That Changed the World* (Woodstock, 2006). *MiWSR* 2007.01.01.

Review of A. Dalby, *Discovering Homer: Inside the Origins of Epic* (New York, 2007). *Historian* 69.4: 819–20.

Review of G. A. A. Kortekaas, *Commentary on the Historia Apollonii Regis Tyri* (Leiden, 2007). *BMCR* 2007.06.44.

Review of R. Rosen, *Making Mockery: The Poetics of Ancient Satire* (Oxford, 2007). *CHOICE* 45-1307.

2008

"Ancient Italic Postures and Posturing." Review of J. R. Clarke, *Looking at Laughter: Humor, Power, and Transgression in Roman Visual Culture* (Berkeley, 2007), and M. B. Roller, *Dining Posture in Ancient Rome: Bodies, Values, and Status* (Princeton, 2006). *IJCT* 15: 618–34.

Review of D. Asheri et al., *A Commentary on Herodotus Books I–IV*, ed. O. Murray and A. Moreno (Oxford, 2007). *CHOICE* 45-3621.

Review of R. Waterfield, *Xenophon's Retreat: Greece, Persia, and the End of the Golden Age* (Cambridge, MA, 2006). *MiWSR* 2008.10.03.

2009

"Feminist Mentoring: Stumbling Towards Welcome Assistance." *Cloelia* 39.1: 10–13.

"Greek and Roman Kissing: Occasions, Protocols, Methods, and Mistakes." *Amphora* 8.1: 17–18.

Review of S. Hornblower, *A Commentary on Thucydides III* (Oxford, 2005). *CHOICE* 46-6034.

Review of E. Irwin and E. Greenwood, eds., *Reading Herodotus: A Study of the Logoi in Book 5 of Herodotus' Histories* (Cambridge, 2007). *CR* 59.1: 45–49.

Review of R. Scodel, *Epic Facework: Self-presentation and Social Interaction in Homer* (Swansea, 2008). *CHOICE* 46-6035.

Review of M. Winkler, *The Roman Salute: Cinema, History, Ideology* (Columbus, 2009). *CHOICE* 46-6705.

"Tears in Apuleius' *Metamorphoses*." In T. Fögen, ed., *Tears and Crying in Graeco-Roman Antiquity*, 277–96. Berlin: De Gruyter.

"Tears and Crying in Hellenistic Historiography: Dacryology from Herodotus to Polybius." In T. Fögen, ed., *Tears in the Graeco-Roman World*, 105–34. Berlin: De Gruyter.

"Transsexuals and Transvestites in Ovid's *Metamorphoses*." In T. Fögen and M. Lee, eds., *Bodies and Boundaries in Graeco-Roman Antiquity*, 125–54. Berlin: De Gruyter.

2010

The Homer Encyclopedia, s.vv. "Bathing," "Body Language," "Feasting," "Ivory," "Laughter," "Oaths," "Youth," "Old Age," "Olives," "Omens," "Prayer," "Trees," "Utensils," and "Weeping." Hoboken, NJ: Wiley-Blackwell.

Review of M. Gagarin, ed., *Oxford Encyclopedia of Ancient Greece and Rome* (Oxford, 2010). *CHOICE* 47-4795.

Review of W. A. Johnson, *Readers and Reading Culture in the High Roman Empire* (Oxford, 2010). *CHOICE* 48-0715.

Review of C. Teixeira et al., *The Satyricon of Petronius: Genre, Wandering, and Style*, translated from the Portuguese by Martin Earl (Coimbra, 2008). *BMCR* 2010.04.34.

Review of T. Whitmarsh, *The Cambridge Companion to the Greek and Roman Novel* (Cambridge, 2008). *AHB* 24: 143–51.

2011

"Herodotus: The "Father of History" or the "Father of Lies"?" *ETHOS* 13: 8.

Review of C. Alexander, *The War That Killed Achilles* (London, 2010). *Historian* 13.2: 370–71.

Review of J. E. Lendon, *Song of Wrath: The Peloponnesian War Begins* (New York, 2010). *CHOICE* 48-5250.

Review of T. Whitmarsh, *Narrative and Identity in the Ancient Greek Novel: Returning Romance* (Cambridge, 2011). *CHOICE* 49-1311.

2012

Encyclopedia of Ancient History, s.vv. "Contemporary History," "Erga," "Historia," and "Horography." Hoboken, NJ: Wiley-Blackwell.

"Gendered Spaces in the *Aithiopika* and *Apollonius King of Tyre*." In M. Futre Pinheiro, M. Skinner, and F. Zeitlin, eds., *Narrating Desire: Eros, Sex, and Gender in the Ancient Novel* , 49–76. Berlin: De Gruyter.

"Herodotos the Pathographer: Persian and Hellenic Displays of Grief." *SCI* 31: 133–50.

"Oaths in Herodotus' and Thucydides' *Histories*." In E. Foster and D. Lateiner, eds., *Thucydides and Herodotus: Connections, Divergences, and Reception*, 154–84. Oxford: Oxford University Press.

Review of L. Calder, *Cruelty and Sentimentality: Greek Attitudes to Animals, 600–300 BC* (Oxford, 2011). *BMCR* 2012.02.37.

Review of J. Grethlein, *The Greeks and Their Past: Poetry, Oratory, and History in the Fifth Century BCE* (Cambridge, 2010). *Historian* 73.4: 871–72.

Review of J. Grethlein and C. Krebs, eds., *Time and Narrative in Ancient Historiography: The "Plupast" from Herodotus to Appian* (Cambridge, 2012). *BMCR* 2012.11.43.

Review of M. Jones, *Playing the Man: Performing Masculinities in the Ancient Greek Novel* (Oxford, 2012). *CHOICE* 50-1908.

Review of A. Kershaw, *The Envoy: The Epic Rescue of the Last Jews of Europe in the Desperate Closing Months of World War II* (Cambridge, MA, 2010). *MiWSR* 2012.024.

Review of S. Montiglio, *Love and Providence in the Ancient Greek Novel* (Oxford, 2012). *CHOICE* 50-2818.

Review of D. Munteanu, *Emotion, Genre, and Gender in Classical Antiquity* (London, 2011). *BMCR* 2012.01.04.

Review of L. H. Peterson and P. Salzman-Mitchell, eds., *Mothering and Motherhood in Ancient Greece and Rome* (Austin, 2012). *CHOICE* 50-0588.

Review of G. Schmeling, *A Commentary on the Satyrica of Petronius* (Oxford, 2011). *CHOICE* 49-6117.

Review of D. Steiner, ed., *Homer, Odyssey Books XVII–XVIII* (Cambridge, 2010). *CJ–Online,* 2011.12.03.

Thucydides and Herodotus: Connections, Divergences, and Reception. Coedited with E. Foster. Oxford: Oxford University Press.

2013

"Gendered and Gendering Insults in the Latin Novels." *Eugesta* 3: 303–51.

The Greek Tragedy Encyclopedia, s.vv. "Blush and Pallor," "Chronemics," "Gestures and Body Language," "Greeting and Departure Protocols," "Kiss," "Laughter," "Leakage," "Phonation," "Proxemics," "Silence," "Smiles," and "Weeping." Hoboken, NJ: Wiley-Blackwell.

"Homer's Social-Psychological Spaces and Places." In M. Skempis and I. Ziogas, eds., *Geography, Topography, Landscape*, 63–94. Berlin: De Gruyter.

"Introduction to a Force of Nature: Judith P. Hallett." In D. Lateiner, B. Gold, and J. Perkins, eds., *Roman Literature, Gender, and Reception: Domina Illustris; Essays in Honor of Judith Peller Hallett*, 1–9. New York: Routledge.

"Poetic Doubling Effects in Ovid's 'Ceyx and Alcyone, *Met.* xi.'" In D. Lateiner, B. Gold, and J. Perkins, eds., *Roman Literature, Gender, and Reception: Domina Illustris; Essays in Honor of Judith Peller Hallett*, 53–73. New York: Routledge.

Review of E. Baragwanath and M. de Bakker, *Myth, Truth, and Narrative in Herodotus* (Oxford, 2012). *Ancient Narrative* 11: 5.

Review of D. Hamel, *Reading Herodotus: A Guided Tour through the Wild Boars, Dancing Suitors, and Crazy Tyrants of the History* (Baltimore, 2012). *CHOICE* 50: 2510.

Review of J. Karski, *Story of a Secret State: My Report to the World* (London, 2011), *MiWSR* 2013.072.

Review of J. Mynott, trans., *The War of the Peloponnesians and the Athenians* (Cambridge, 2013). *AHB* 3: 87–89.

Review of T. O'Sullivan, *Walking in Roman Culture* (Cambridge, 2011). *CW* 106: 526–28.

Roman Literature, Gender, and Reception: Domina Illustris; Essays in Honor of Judith Peller Hallett. Coedited with B. Gold and J. Perkins. New York: Routledge.

The Virgil Encyclopedia, s.vv. "Blush," "Kiss," "Laughter," "Smell," "Smiles," "Taste," "Touch," and "Weeping." Hoboken, NJ: Wiley-Blackwell.

2014

"Emotional Displays in the Dramas of Aiskhylos and the Histories of Herodotos." In S. Constantinidis, ed., *The Tragedies of Aeschylus: The Cultural Divide and the Trauma of Adaptation.*

"Insults and Humiliation in Fifth-Century Historiography and Comedy." *Histos* Supplements 2.

"Nonverbal Expression of the Emotion of Disgust in Early Greek Texts: Epic, Tragedy, and Comedy." In D. Cairns and D. Nelis, eds., *Ancient Emotions.*

"Obscenity in Herodotus." In D. Dutsch and A. Suter, eds., *Ancient Obscenities: Forms, Functions, and Receptions.* Ann Arbor: University of Michigan Press.

Raubitschek, Antony Erich. *An Autobiography of Antony Erich Raubitschek.* Edited with Introduction and Notes by Donald Lateiner. *Histos* Supplements 1. http://research.ncl.ac.uk/histos/documents/So1LateinerRaubitschekAutobiography.pdf.

Review of L. Fulkerson, *No Regrets: Remorse in Classical Antiquity* (Oxford, 2013). *CJ–Online,* 2014.09.03.

Review of S. Harding, *The Last Battle: When U.S. and German Soldiers Joined Forces in the Waning Hours of World War II in Europe* (Boston, 2013). *MiWSR* 2014.024.

Review of E. Sanders et al., *Eros in Ancient Greece* (Oxford, 2013). *Mnemosyne* 67: 1–6.

Review of J. Skinner, *The Invention of Greek Ethnography: From Homer to Herodotus* (Oxford, 2012). *Historian* 76.2: 427–428.

Review of C. Vout, *Sex on Show: Seeing the Erotic in Ancient Greece and Rome* (Berkeley, 2013). *CHOICE* 51-5402.

"*Scortum, scorteus, scortatus* in Petronius' *Satyrica* and Apuleius' *Metamorphoses*." EuGeStA Lexicon, 15 May 2014 http://eugesta.recherche.univ-lille3.fr/spip.php?article102.

"*Virgo, uirginitas, uirginalis, uirgineus, uirguncula* in Petronius' *Satyrica* and Apuleius' *Metamorphoses*." EuGeStA Lexicon, 15 May 2014 http://eugesta.recherche.univ-lille3.fr/spip.php ?article103.

Contributors

Deborah Boedeker is a professor emerita of classics at Brown University. From 1992 to 2000, she directed Harvard's Center for Hellenic Studies together with Kurt Raaflaub. Her scholarship has focused on early Greek poetry and historiography, particularly their interaction with religious and mythological traditions. Boedeker's authored and edited or coedited volumes include *Aphrodite's Entry into Greek Epic*; *Descent from Heaven: Images of Dew in Greek Poetry and Religion*; *Herodotus and the Invention of History*; *Democracy, Empire, and the Arts in Fifth-Century Athens*; and *The New Simonides: Contexts of Praise and Desire*. Her recently completed and current projects feature Sappho, Euripides, Hipponax, and Herodotus.

Christina A. Clark is an associate professor of classical and Near Eastern studies at Creighton University. She has research interests in the representation of nonverbal behaviors in ancient literature and art, gender, and narratology. As a junior fellow at the Center for Hellenic Studies, Clark, inspired by Donald Lateiner's *Sardonic Smile*, began studying the ways in which Greek lyric poets used nonverbal behavior, and she has gone on to publish articles on Sappho, Alcman, Bacchylides, Catullus, Lucretius, Vergil, and now Lucan. She is currently working on a book studying nonverbal behavior in early Greek and Roman poetry.

Brad L. Cook currently teaches classics at the University of Mississippi, after teaching at other places, including Ohio Wesleyan University, where he met the honoree of this volume and began to learn how to be a teacher-scholar.

Cook's published articles examine the lives, texts, and traditions of and about Demosthenes, Philip II, Alexander the Great, and Cicero, from antiquity to the Renaissance.

Carolyn Dewald is a professor of history and classics at Bard College. She has written a number of articles on Greek historiography, the introduction and notes to the Oxford World's Classics translation of Herodotus translated by R. Waterfield (1998), and *Thucydides' War Narrative: A Structural Study* (2006). She coedited (with John Marincola) the *Cambridge Companion to Herodotus* (2006) and is currently coediting (with Rosaria Munson) the volume on book 1 of Herodotus' *Histories* in the Cambridge Greek and Latin Classics series.

Ellen Finkelpearl is a professor of classics at Scripps College in Claremont, California. She is the author of *Metamorphosis of Language in Apuleius*, *A Survey of Scholarship on Apuleius' Metamorphoses* (with Carl Schlam), and *An Apuleius Reader*, and she is coeditor of *Apuleius and Africa*. She has also written on the representation of animals in antiquity and the modern world.

Edith Foster is a Senior Research Associate at Case Western University and a Fellow at the Institute for Advanced Studies at the University of Strasbourg. In addition to articles and book reviews, she is the author of *Thucydides, Pericles, and Periclean Imperialism* (Cambridge University Press, 2010), coeditor (with Donald Lateiner) of *Thucydides and Herodotus* (Oxford University Press, 2012), and coeditor (with Sara Forsdyke and Ryan Balot) of the forthcoming *Oxford Handbook of Thucydides*. Foster received her bachelor's and master's degrees from the University of Toronto, and her PhD in classics from the University of Chicago. She is presently working on a commentary on book four of Thucydides for the Cambridge Greek and Latin Classics series and a monograph on the battle narratives in Herodotus, Thucydides, and Xenophon.

Carolin Hahnemann is a professor of classics at Kenyon College in central Ohio, about forty miles from Ohio Wesleyan University, which has been home to Don Lateiner for more than thirty years. Under his friendly influence, she has continued to be interested in the textual evidence for ancient gestures, a fascination she first developed in graduate school at Brown University. Her research focus, however, lies in Greek tragedy, especially the fragmentary plays of Aeschylus and Sophocles.

Judith P. Hallett, a professor of classics and Distinguished Scholar-Teacher at the University of Maryland, College Park, has published widely in the areas of Latin language and literature; ancient Greco-Roman women, sexuality, and the family; and classical education and the reception of classical literary works in twentieth-century America. Her books include *Fathers and Daughters in Roman Society: Women and the Elite Family* (Princeton University Press, 1984); *Compromising Traditions: the Personal Voice in Classical Scholarship*, with Thomas van Nortwick (Routledge, 1997); *Roman Sexualities*, with Marilyn Skinner (Princeton University Press, 1997); and *British Classics outside England: The Academy and Beyond*, with Christopher Stray (Baylor University Press, 2008). Among other publications she has edited are a special double issue of *Classical World* (1996–97) on outstanding North American women classicists and a special issue of *Helios* (2006) on Roman mothers, to which Donald Lateiner contributed an important essay. In 2013, Routledge published *Roman Literature, Gender and Reception: Domina Illustris*, edited by Donald Lateiner, Barbara Gold, and Judith Perkins, a volume of nineteen essays collectively honoring Hallett and her work.

Bruce Heiden is a professor of classics at Ohio State University. He is the author of *Tragic Rhetoric: An Interpretation of Sophocles' Trachiniae* (Lang, 1989) and *Homer's Cosmic Fabrication: Choice and Design in the Iliad* (Oxford University Press, 2008), as well as many articles on ancient Greek and Latin literature. His translations of poetry from Greek, Latin, and French have appeared in *The Greek Poets: Homer to the Present* (Norton, 2010), *Hudson Review*, *Southwest Review*, and other publications.

Rachel Kitzinger is the Matthew Vassar Professor of Greek and Latin Language and Literature at Vassar College. She is the author of *The Choruses of Sophocles' Antigone and Philoctetes: A Dance of Words* (2008), as well as articles on Sophoclean tragedy. She is also the cotranslator (with Eamon Grennan) of *Oedipus at Colonus* (2005), the coeditor (with Michael Grant) of *Civilization of the Ancient Mediterranean* (1988), and a director of productions of Greek tragedy in Greek and in English.

Daniel B. Levine has taught classical studies at the University of Arkansas since 1980. Beginning with articles on laughter in the *Odyssey*, his publications have dealt with Greek poetry and a wide variety of other classical subjects, including reception studies. He has thrice directed summer sessions for the American School of Classical Studies at Athens and often travels to Greece with students from his own institution. He received an *ovatio* from the Classical Association of the Middle West and South (1996) and the Excellence in the Teaching of the Classics award from the American Philological Association (1992).

Judith Levine earned her degree in high fashion design from Les Écoles de la Chambre Syndicale de la Couture Parisienne and has worked in film and still photography in France as a stylist and costume designer. She has also been a partner in Bag Ladies, a company producing one-of-a-kind wearable art. Currently, she works as a photo stylist specializing in package photography and, in her spare time, completes interior design and special graphics projects for private clients and nongovernmental organizations. Fond of the American School of Classical Studies at Athens, she has enjoyed working over the years to help her husband, Daniel Levine, with his research and with bringing the classics into modern lives. She is particularly proud of her service as a member of a team of parents who successfully lobbied their local school board to hire art teachers for all area elementary schools, for, as we all know, art is a discipline and not merely "recess with crayons."

John Marincola is the Leon Golden Professor of Classics at Florida State University. He was Donald Lateiner's student at the University of Pennsylvania from 1977 to 1979. His books include *Authority and Tradition in Ancient Historiography* (1997), *Greek Historians* (2001), and, with M. A. Flower, *Herodotus, Histories Book IX* (2002). He is currently at work on monographs on Plutarch and the Persian Wars and on Hellenistic historiography.

Michael McOsker is a graduate student at the University of Michigan. His interests are in papyrology, Greek poetry, and Hellenistic philosophy, especially Epicureanism. Don Lateiner was his undergraduate professor, adviser, and mentor. McOsker's dissertation is on Philodemus of Gadara's poetry and poetics, and he has spent a year and half in Italy editing the papyri of Demetrius Laco's *On Poems.*

James V. Morrison, the Stodghill Professor of Classical Studies, has taught at Centre College in Danville, Kentucky, since 1993. He offers courses in Greek and Latin language and literature, ancient history, comedy and satire, and the freshman humanities sequence. His books include *Homeric Misdirection: False Predictions in the Iliad* (1992), *A Companion to Homer's Odyssey* (2003), *Reading Thucydides* (2006), and *Shipwrecked: Disaster and Transformation in Homer, Shakespeare, Defoe, and the Modern World* (2014). His next project will be an exploration of ancient and modern comedy and satire.

Rosaria Vignolo Munson is the J. Archer and Helen C. Turner Professor of Classics at Swarthmore College. She is the author of *Telling Wonders: Ethnographic and Political Discourse in the Work of Herodotus* (2001), *Black Doves Speak: Herodotus and the Language of Barbarians* (2005), and several articles on Herodotus. She has edited the volume on Herodotus in the Oxford Readings in Classical Studies series (2013) and is currently coediting a commentary on book 1 of Herodotus' *Histories* for the Cambridge Greek and Latin Classics series.

Hanna M. Roisman is the Arnold Bernhard Professor in Arts and Humanities at Colby College, Maine. She was a junior fellow at the Center for Hellenic Studies at Harvard University. She specializes in early Greek epic, Greek and Roman tragedy, and classics and film. In addition to articles and book chapters, Roisman has published *Loyalty in Early Greek Epic and Tragedy* (1984), *Nothing Is as It Seems: The Tragedy of the Implicit in Euripides' Hippolytus* (1999), *Sophocles, Philoctetes* (2005), and *Sophocles, Electra* (2008). She is the editor of the *Encyclopedia of Greek Tragedy* (2013) and coauthor of *The Odyssey Re-formed* (1996), *Euripides, Alcestis* (2003), and *Euripides, Electra* (2010).

Jeffrey Rusten teaches Greek literature at Cornell University, where he is also a member of the graduate program in theater. He has translated Theophrastus' *Characters* and Philostratus' *Heroicus* (Loeb Classical Library) and supplied translations (alongside Jeffrey Henderson, David Konstan, Ralph Rosen, and Niall Slater) for *The Birth of Comedy: Fragments of Ancient Greek Drama, 500–250 B.C.* (Johns Hopkins University Press). He has written commentaries on Thucydides' book 2 (Cambridge University Press) and Sophocles' *Oidipous Tyrannos* (Bryn Mawr Commentaries), edited the Oxford Readings in Classical Studies volume on *Thucydides* (Oxford University Press), and coedited essays on Thucydides by Mabel Lang and Jacqueline de Romilly. Rusten also spent a year as Whitehead Visiting Professor at the American School of Classical Studies at Athens. His research specialties are Thucydides, ancient historiography, Athenian and later comedy, and tragedy and the Athenian tragic theater.

Hans-Peter Stahl is a professor emeritus at the University of Pittsburgh. His publications, which include books and many articles, span over five decades. To mention his books only, his work began with analysis of Plato in *Interpretationen zu Platons Hypothesis-Verfahren: Menon, Phaidon, Staat* (1956). It subsequently extended to historiography in *Thukydides: Die Stellung des Menschen im geschichtlichen Prozeß* (1966), possibly his most famous book, which attained enduring importance and was translated by the author himself in 2003 as *Thucydides: Man's Place in History*. His other books include *Propertius: "Love" and "War"; Individual and State under Augustus* (1985) and *Vergil's Aeneid: Augustan Epic and Political Context* (1998). Stahl is presently engaged in a large-scale study of the *Aeneid*.

Daniel P. Tompkins (BA Dartmouth College, PhD Yale University) taught in the Department of Greek and Roman Classics at Temple University, retiring in 2010. He also taught at Wesleyan University and Swarthmore and Dartmouth Colleges. He has written on Moses Finley, Thucydides, Homer, the ancient city, Wallace Stevens, just war theory, and various topics in higher education. His current projects include the intellectual development of M. I. Finley and language and politics in the speeches in Thucydides.

Eliot Wirshbo did his graduate work at the University of Pennsylvania, where Don Lateiner was known to the graduate students for his acuity and indefatigability. Since 1982, Wirshbo has been a lecturer at the University of California, San Diego, where he teaches Latin and Greek. He has published articles in a variety of journals and is presently living the good life in California, where he enjoys teaching, cop videos, and unwholesome food.

Index

significant object, 282, 284–86, 288, 289n16, 292–93

simile, 143n2, 144, 144n5, 173, 184, 211, 216, 220, 222–24, 226, 226n18, 227, 228n22, 229, 232, 236, 236n3, 238, 238n5, 241, 242n12, 244

Socrates, 136, 248, 250, 251n6, 252, 254, 256, 257, 259, 261

Solon, 75–76, 76n3, 77, 79, 82, 83, 83n6, 99, 132, 219–21, 221n4, 222–23, 225, 227–29, 232

Sophocles, 87–88, 93, 93n18, 94n20, 95, 97, 98–99, 101, 169

Sparta, 28n3, 44, 54n45, 63, 64, 75, 79, 105, 105n9, 107–10, 113, 125, 128, 271, 272n35

Spartans, 35, 36n23, 43, 43n6, 44, 45, 52, 53, 54, 62, 66, 66n11, 67, 67n15, 68, 68n16, 69–70, 70n19, 70n21, 71, 78–81, 90, 103–8, 108n16, 110n26, 111–12, 272

speeches, 38, 60n3, 61, 62n7, 66n14, 72, 84n7, 116, 116n1, 117, 117n3, 118, 118n7, 119n9, 120, 122–24, 128, 223n11, 225, 228, 228n22, 236–38, 251, 253, 254, 261; deliberative, 116; display, 116, 123

spinning top, 289

stage direction, 163

stasis, 33n19, 34, 38, 51, 52, 52n37, 122, 122n13, 123

stepmother (wicked), 168–70

Stoics, 144n4, 148n15, 151n26, 155, 155n46, 173, 174, 174n5, 183, 186, 186n41, 186n43

storyteller, 86, 235, 237–38, 240, 242–43, 245–46

sufferings, 28, 29, 38, 38n28, 42, 47, 132, 133

superstition, 134, 134n15, 184

supplication, 162n8, 163n12, 164n19, 165, 165n23, 165n24, 237

Syracuse, 33n19, 38, 45, 72, 116, 116n1, 117, 117n3, 117n5, 118, 124–25, 267

Susan Barton, 242, 242n14, 243, 243n15, 243n16, 244, 244n17, 245, 245n19

sword, 106, 153, 160–61, 166, 166n29, 167, 167n31, 167n33, 168–69, 169n39, 170, 285–86

Talthybius, 109, 111; cults of, 105, 105n9, 110; wrath of, 105, 107, 108, 109, 111

tears, 128, 130–32, 145, 173, 176, 176n15, 177n15

Tecmessa, 93–94, 94n21, 94n22, 94n23, 95

Tellus, 220–21

terateia, 134, 134n16, 135–36

Thales of Miletus, 46

Theseus, 163, 167–69, 169n39, 170, 170n43

Thucydides, 27, 27n1, 28–31, 31n11, 32–33, 36, 36n24, 37–38, 38n27, 38n29, 41, 41n1, 42–43, 43n5, 44, 44n9, 45–46, 46n15, 46n16, 46n17, 47, 47n19, 48–50, 50n29, 51, 51n30, 52, 52n37, 52n38, 53, 53n41, 53n43, 53n45, 54–56, 60, 60n3, 61–62, 62n6, 63–66, 66n12, 66n13, 67, 67n15, 68, 68n16, 69–70, 70n20, 71, 71n23, 72, 74, 74n2, 76, 78, 78n5, 80–84, 84n8, 91n12, 100n36, 103, 104n4, 107n14, 111–13, 113n41, 117, 117n3, 118–20, 120n11, 121–22, 124–25, 127

Timaeus of Tauromenium, 127, 133, 134n14, 137; his use of dreams and prodigies, 134

timor, 148, 211

tokens of recognition, 167, 169

tragedy, 52n36, 87, 93n18, 95n24, 98, 124, 128, 129, 161, 163, 166, 166n30, 170, 230, 246, 261

tragic history, 129, 129n3

translation, 27, 30, 33, 35, 285

trepidus, 146, 146n11

trilogy, 169, 170, 170n43

truth, in history, 128, 134–35, 137

Tyre, 282, 286–88, 291

Vasco da Lucena, 281

vase painting, 168, 263, 265n12, 273; archaic, 262, 263n4, 266, 271, 272, 275; Attic, 262, 264, 267, 268, 273, 273n40, 274n47; Black Figure, 168, 272, 273n39, 274n42, 262, 264, 267, 268, 274n47

verisimilitude, 144, 153, 153n38, 239, 239n7

virtus, 143–44, 144n4, 148n15, 149–50, 150n22, 152, 154, 155

voltus/vultus, 145, 147, 151, 152

Vulteius, 149–51

vulva, 283, 285

war, 28–29, 29n4, 29n5, 30–31, 31n10, 31n11, 32, 32n12, 33, 33n16, 34, 34n21, 35, 35n22, 36–38, 41–43, 44n10, 45, 46, 48, 50–51, 51n33, 52–53, 54n45, 55–56, 62, 66, 68, 69, 77–78, 79, 80, 84n8, 100,